The Book of the Caill

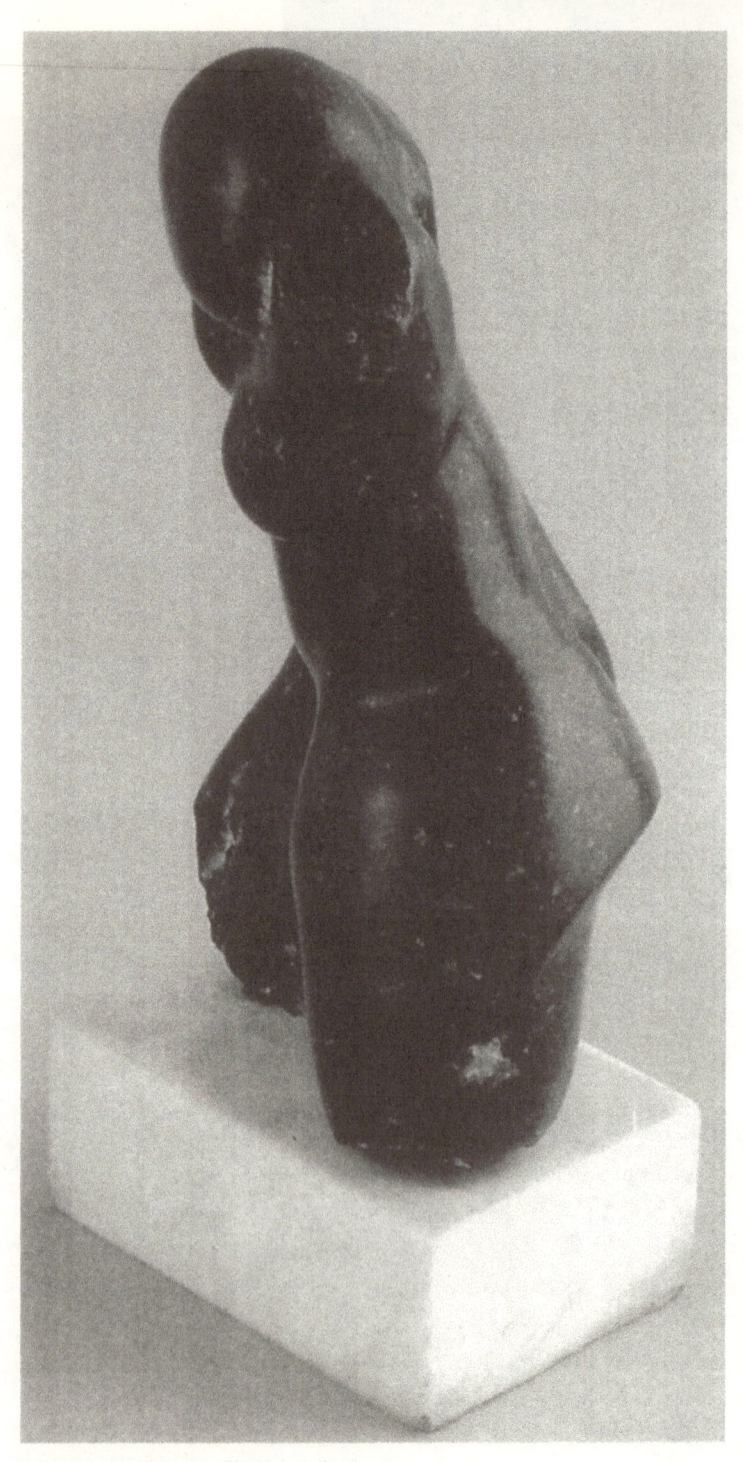

Landscape figure (Bob Mulcahy)

THE BOOK OF THE CAILLEACH
Stories of the Wise-Woman Healer

Gearóid Ó Crualaoich

CORK UNIVERSITY PRESS

First published in 2003 by
Cork University Press
Youngline Industrial Estate
Pouladuff Road, Togher
Cork
Ireland

© Gearóid Ó Crualaoich, 2003

Reprinted 2006, 2007, 2015, 2017, 2019, 2021 and 2022

All rights reserved. No part of this book may be reprinted or reproduced by any electronic, mechanical or other means, now known or hereafter invented, including photocopying and recording or otherwise, without either the prior written permission of the Publishers, or a licence permitting restricted copying in Ireland issued by the Irish Copyright Licensing Agency Ltd, The Irish Writers' Centre, 25 Denzille Lane, Dublin 2.

British Library Cataloguing in Publication data
A CIP catalogue record for this book is available from the British Library

ISBN 978-1-85918-412-7

A CIP record for this publication is available from the Library of Congress

Library of Congress Cataloging-in-Publication Data

O'Crulaoich, Gearoid, 1940-
   The book of the Cailleach : stories of the wise-woman healer /
   By Gearoid O'Crulaoich.
     p. cm.
   Includes bibliographical references and index.
   ISBN 1-85918-372-7 (alk. paper)
   1. Tales—Ireland. 2. Women healers—Ireland—Folklore. 3. Oral tradition—Ireland. 4. Folk literature, Irish. I. Title.
   GR153.5.O324 200
   I398.2'09417'02—dc22

                                                                  2003016244

Typeset by Redbarn Publishing, Skeagh, Skibbereen, Co. Cork
Printed and bound by
CPI Group (UK) Ltd, Croydon, CR0 4YY

www.corkunivesitypress.com

Do Gay agus Sorcha an leabhar seo

Contents

Foreword	xi
Acknowledgements	xiv
List of Illustrations	xvii

Part One: Tradition and Theory

A perspective on Irish oral tradition	3
Oral narrative as literature	12
The representation of the feminine	25
Historical displacement of the autonomous female	38
Retention/Reinterpretation of the autonomous female	52

Part Two: Stories of the Cailleach and the Wise-Woman

Introduction	81
Stories of the Cailleach	100

Intimations of a female-centred cosmos   100

1.	The Cailleach Bhéarrthach and the cold of May-day Monday	100
2.	Cailleach Bhéarra's shower of stones	104
3.	The Cailleach Bhéarach and the walker	106
4.	The mark left by Cailleach Bhéarra	109
5.	Cailleach Bhéara (Dún Chaoin)	111

Victories of a male-centred social order   113

6.	The Cailleach Bheurr and Loch Bà–I	113
7.	The Cailleach Bheurr and Loch Bà–II	115
8.	The Cailleach of Gleann na mBiorach and the black bull	120
9.	The Cailleach Bhéarach and Donnchadh Mór Mac Mánais	132

Displacement of the feminine in a male-centred symbolic order   144

10.	The Cailleach Bhéarthach (Carna: Áird Thoir)	144
11.	The Cailleach Bhéarra and Saint Caitiairn	146

12.	Meelick Round Tower	148
13.	'Don't believe a woman's words'	150
14.	Ana Ní Áine	150

Retention of the feminine in a vernacular accommodation   163
15.	The Cailleach Bhéarthach (Carna: Cill Chiaráin)	163
16.	The Cailleach Bhéarach (Ballycastle)	167

STORIES OF THE WISE-WOMAN   174

Accommodating female knowledge and power   174
17.	The woman who used to see the fairies	174
18.	Máire Ní Mhurchú and the carters	175
19.	Incident recounted of a healing woman from Baile Bhoithín–I	178
20.	Máire Ní Mhurchú and the priest	181

Ordinary troubles remedied through resort to wise-woman   183
21.	The stolen colt and the wise-woman	183
22.	Máire Ní Chearbhaill and the heifer	185
23.	Incident recounted of a healing woman from Baile Bhoithín–II	187
24.	Incident recounted of a healing woman from Baile Bhoithín–III	189

Wise-woman reveals deeper significance of life events   192
25.	Máire Ní Mhurchú and my own mother	192
26.	Máire Ní Mhurchú and the miner	195
27.	Saint Fanahan's Well and Máire Liam	199
28.	The girl who was struck dumb	201
29.	Carn Tighearna	204
30.	Máire Ní Chearbhaill and the blow from the red-haired woman	208

Wise-woman is able to remedy extraordinary affliction   210
31.	Máire Ní Mhurchú and the woman who was 'swept'	210
32.	Máire Ní Mhurchú and the young man who was 'swept'–I	215
33.	Máire Ní Mhurchú and the young man who was 'swept'–II	220
34.	Seán 'Ac Séamais	224

Part Three: *Scéalta i dtaobh Cailleach Bhéarra agus i dtaobh na Mná Feasa*

Preface	233
Scéalta I dtaobh Cailleach Bhéarra	235
Comharthaí soirt ar an mbaineannacht a bheith i gcroí lár na cruinne	235
1. An Chailleach Béarrthach agus fuacht Luan Lae Bhealtaine	235
2. Cioth cloch na Caillighe Béarra	237
3. An Chailleach Bhéarthach agus an coisí	237
4. Rian na Cailli Béaraighe	239
5. Cailleach Bhéara (Dún Chaoin)	239
Bua na fíreannachta sa tsaol sóisialta	240
6. A' Chailleach Bheurr agus Loch Bà–I	240
7. A' Chailleach Bheurr agus Loch Bà–II	241
8. Cailleach Ghleann-na-mBiorach agus an tarbh dubh	244
9. An Chailleach Bhéarach agus Donnchadh Mór Mac Mánais	247
Díspeagadh na baineannachta laistigh den réimse siombalach fireannach	254
10. An Chailleach Bhéarthach (Carna: Áird Thoir)	254
11. An Chailleach Bhéarra agus Naomh Caitiairn	254
12. Meelick round tower	255
13. 'Ná creid briathra mná'	255
14. Ana Ní Áine	256
Buanú na baineannachta i gcomhoiriúntas an choitinn	258
15. An Chailleach Bhéarthach (Carna: Cill Chiaráin)	258
16. An Chailleach Bhéarach (Baile an Chaisleáin)	260
Scéalta I dtaobh na Mná Feasa	264
Ag glacadh le fios agus le cumas na mná	264
17. An bhean a chíodh na 'fairies'	264
18. Máire Ní Mhurchú agus na carréaraithe	264
19. Eachtruighthe ar bhean leighis a bhí i mBaile Bhoithín–I	265
20. Máire Ní Mhurchú agus an sagart	266

An cruachás á riaradh trí dhul i muinín na mná feasa 266
21. *An bramach a goideadh agus an bhean feasa* 266
22. *Máire Ní Chearbhaill and the heifer* 267
23. *Eachtruighthe ar bhean leighis a bhí i mBaile Bhoithín–II* 267
24. *Eachtraithe ar bhean leighis a bhí i mBaile Bhoithín–III* 268

Léiríonn an bhean feasa an bhrí cheart atá le cúrsaí an tsaoil 268
25. *Máire Ní Mhurchú agus mo mháthair féin* 268
26. *Máire Ní Mhurchú agus an maidhnéir* 270
27. *Saint Fanahan's Well and* Máire Liam 271
28. *An cailín ar baineadh a hurlabhra dhi* 272
29. *Carn Tighearna* 272
30. *Máire Ní Chearbhaill and the blow from the red-haired woman* 273

É ar chumas na mná feasa fóirithint ar an bhfuadach sí 274
31. *Máire Ní Mhurchú agus an bhean a fuadaíodh* 274
32. *Máire Ní Mhurchú agus an buachaill a fuadaíodh–I* 276
33. *Máire Ní Mhurchú agus an buachaill a fuadaíodh–II* 277
34. *Sean 'ac Séamais* 278

Notes and References 281
Bibliography 288
Manuscript Sources 293
Index 295

Foreword

This book aims to provide a variety of general and academic readers with access to a selection of some thirty stories from Irish folklore. The stories are presented in a setting that holds that such traditional legends can work for their hearers and, now, for their readers too, in ways that combine art and instruction. The readers of this book are thus invited to engage imaginatively with these stories of the *cailleach* (supernatural old female) and the *bean feasa* (wise-woman) – female figures of folk legend who are imbued with a sense of the mysterious – and to ponder, with the author in his commentaries on the stories, the significance of what they represent.

That they do represent something valuable is witnessed by their retention and transmission as stories over the generations though not, of course, in an unchanging way. The discipline of folklore – *Béaloideas* or Folkloristics, as it is variously called – has had to learn and is still learning, how to study the process whereby stories are continuously transformed, in performance and transmission, in ways that reflect the changing historical and socio-political circumstances of their narration, and yet continue to maintain and to articulate, under the surface, a considerable degree of insight into the deeper realities of human life and culture. This insight, when combined with special qualities of expression, with verbal and histrionic excellence on the part of the narrator, turns the traditional narrative, on occasion, into something that has qualities we associate with great literature.

Even without any claims to their being akin to great literature, traditional legends such as those dealt with here, speak to us of the fundamental workings of the individual mind and heart as these have been observed and represented in the shared, communal wisdom of common culture. The question of their ability to function as literature, in some respects, is discussed in Part One. Also discussed is the very pertinent question of whether women and the feminine, so clearly designated a secondary role in so much of traditional culture, high and low, are represented in these stories in any way that gives genuine voice to the feminine. It is my contention that such traditional legends as are discussed here give genuine expression – in different ways and to varying degrees – not only to the female gender, in social terms, but also to feminine aspects of the human psyche and to the feminine side of a gendered conception of landscape, social environment and cosmos that finds imaginative expression in many human traditions. One might venture to suggest that the representation of, or at least the aspiration towards, harmonious male/female relationship in each of these spheres – the individual, the social and the environmental/cosmic – lies at the heart of the cultural self-knowledge that these legends externalize .

The emphasis of the book, overall, is on the stories themselves as they emerge from their primary existence as oral narrative to connect with our imaginations. One wishes to impose as little shackling constraint as possible on the free flow of the imaginative process whereby these stories proceed from the traditional culture of an earlier Ireland to the attention of a contemporary audience and readership. I have been content to let the stories speak for themselves, to the extent of not imposing any extra level of standardization on the Irish texts beyond what their original transcribers thought fit for the purposes of recording them. Neither have I tried to analyze in a comprehensively detailed way what the stories 'mean'. My concerns have been to provide adequate access to the stories and to respond to them in a way that, hopefully, points the reader in a similar direction to that of their original audiences by examining the significance of characters, motifs, symbols and so on. The reader is thus encouraged to see with something of a native eye that which the stories represented to the native ear.

If it is important to emphasize the stories as dynamic creations of imagination, one would also want to emphasize in equal measure, both the traditional frameworks of significance and interpretation that operated in the Ireland in which these stories circulated, and the validity of individual interpretations and applications of the stories' significance then and now, over and above what might have found overt representation in a public domain. I venture to suggest that such private, individual application of the significance of legends such as are presented in this book, operated as a kind of therapy in the pre-modern world. In this light they are to be regarded not only as cultural heritage but also as a potentially therapeutic creative resource. As such they have a capacity, in our own times, to play a part in enlarging and enriching the imaginative lives of their readers. It can be further argued that such a role continues, in a sense, an artistic role they have always played and relates them to some degree with the insights of contemporary theory across a range of disciplines. In particular, the legends of resort to the wise-woman present human circumstances that can appear similar to some of the circumstances in which resort is had, in contemporary culture, to psychotherapy. Such an understanding of the psychic significance of traditional legends of the *cailleach* and *bean feasa* is not, however, in any way a requisite for recognizing their worth as folklore and as potential literature. Part One attempts to strengthen that sense of worth by drawing attention to the ways in which the figures and symbols of these legends have developed within a cultural discourse of story and verse stretching back, in Ireland, over a millennium and a half. In the face of that tradition and in the sure knowledge that the reader's imagination when engaged by these stories, will soon leave my own interpretative explorations here far behind, it is with a sense of humility as much as a sense of authorship that I bring this Foreword to a close.

Gearóid Ó Crualaoich
(February 2003)

ACKNOWLEDGEMENTS

For financial assistance with the publication costs of this book I am very grateful to: University College, Cork, Arts Faculty Publication Fund; The National University of Ireland Publications Scheme.

I am personally and professionally indebted to many people and institutions for help and encouragement provided while this work has been in preparation. My colleagues in the Department of Béaloideas at UCC, Diarmuid Ó Giolláin, Stiofán Ó Cadhla, Marie-Annick Desplanques and Síle de Cléir (a former colleague) have, unfailingly, facilitated my research and my writing in many different ways. The students of *An Léann Dúchais* and of Folklore, at both undergraduate and postgraduate stages of their own careers, have also contributed insights and criticisms. I am grateful for the opportunity afforded to me by UCC, during several periods of study leave, to benefit from engaging in research and teaching at other institutions. In particular I have benefited from periods at the University of Edinburgh and at Boston College. Joseph Nagy of the University of California, Los Angeles, was an early encourager of my research interests in responding to a paper of mine given at the Celtic Congress of 1983 at Oxford University and I was later enabled, with his help, to spend a fruitful period at UCLA. The late Adele Dalsimer and her colleagues in Irish Studies at Boston College – Kevin O'Neill, Robert Savage and Philip O'Leary, together with William Neenan, SJ, then Academic Vice-President of Boston College – were ever welcoming and supportive of my work. Trips to Boston were always made easier with the help of Irish Studies Secretary Catherine McLaughlin. I thank Tomás Ó Cathasaigh of the Celtic Department at Harvard University for affording me the opportunity to deliver a seminar on an aspect of my work in the course of which, and subsequently, I benefited from the scholarly, generous and heartening encouragement of Elizabeth Gray, also of Harvard, which spurred me on at a crucial stage. I am especially grateful to all at the School of Scottish Studies Archives at the University of Edinburgh and in particular to Margaret MacKay (Director), John McQueen (former Director), to the late Donald Archie MacDonald, to Morag MacLeod, to Emily Lyle as well as to the support staff of the School who facilitated me. I also thank John Shaw, John MacInnes, Gary West and the late Alan Bruford for their friendship and their assistance at the School at various times.

I am grateful to Professor Séamas Ó Catháin, Head of the Department of Irish Folklore, UCD, for permission to reproduce texts from the Archive of the Irish Folklore Commission and from publications issued under the imprint of the Institute of Irish Folklore and the Folklore of Ireland Society, including the Society's journal, *Béaloideas*. The following excerpts from the Irish Folklore Collection (IFC), are published here by kind permission of the Head of Department of Irish Folklore, University College, Dublin: IFC, 4, 262–63; IFC, 11, 103–105; IFC, 17, 12–13; IFC, 22, 305–310; IFC, 30, 131; IFC, 49, 143–44; IFC, 54, 49–51, 72–4; IFC, 74, 14, 22–24, 261–62; IFC, 85, 346–50; IFC, 159, 473–78; IFC, 217, 553–54; IFC, 437, 392, 393; IFC, 612, 245–51, 251–57, 257–62, 262–68; IFC, 623, 117–21, 122–23; IFC, 788, 130–131; IFC, 842, 60–63; IFC, 850, 346–50, 526–29.

For permission to reproduce further copyright material I am grateful to the following: An Clóchomhar (agus an tOllamh Breandán Ó Buachalla); Coiscéim (agus Máirtín Verling); The Thomson Gale Group for permission to quote from *Other People's Myths* by Wendy D. O'Flaherty, © 1988 Macmillan, Library Reference, reprinted by permission of the Gale Group; Comhlucht Oideachais na hÉireann; Cork University Press (Cló Ollscoile Chorcaí); An Cumann le Béaloideas Éireann, le haghaidh an Sgeulaidhe Gaedhalach, 132–36 agus 145–49; Scéalta ón mBlascaod 79–81; *Béaloideas* 56 (1988) 153–78; *Béaloideas* 62/3 (1995) 145–62. An Gúm; Dubhghlas Sealy (and the heirs of the Douglas Hyde estate); Frank Cass Publishers, for permission to use material from the chapter 'The merry Wake' in Donnelly and Miller, *Irish Popular Culture 1650–1850*; National University of Ireland, Maynooth (the Librarian); Oifig an tSoláthair (Government Publications Office); Royal Irish Academy (the Librarian); *An Sagart* (Maigh Nuad) and Donnchadh Ó hAodha; School of Scottish Studies Archives (The University of Edinburgh); The Tavistock Press (and Professor Jean La Fontaine); The Educational Company of Ireland; The O'Brien Press (agus an tOllamh Patricia Lysaght); University of Edinburgh Press (and the late Dr Andrew Duff-Cooper) in respect of the chapter 'Contest in the Cosmology and the Ritual of the Irish "Merry Wake"' in *Contests–Cosmos*, 6 (1990); University of Missouri Press (and Professor John Miles Foley) in respect of material reprinted from *Oral Tradition in Literature* edited by John Miles Foley, by permission of the University of Missouri Press. Copyright © 1986 by the Curators of the University of Missouri.

The Librarian and Library staff of the Boole Library at UCC, especially the staff at Special Collections, have at all times been prompt and helpful to me in my work.

I am grateful to the staff of Cork University Press for advice and support in the preparation of this work for publication.

The arduous task of typing and retyping drafts of every portion of the book was undertaken, since the beginning, by Veronica Fraser of the Department of History, UCC. My debt to her is immense and I thank her for her cheerfulness and for her willing and skilful support over a long time. A reorganization of the final draft, together with attendant emendations, was undertaken at short notice by Maeve McDevitt, Department of Béaloideas, UCC, to whom I am also extremely grateful.

I wish also to express my thanks to three friends for their interest and encouragement. They are Peter O'Connor, Seán O'Keeffe and my dear brother-in-law, the late Matt Kingston.

ILLUSTRATIONS

Frontispiece: 'Landscape figure'. Sculpture by Bob Mulcahy. Reproduced courtesy of the estate of the late artist.
Pg.78: 'Telling Tradition'. Photograph by George Pickow of Mrs Elizabeth ('Bess') Cronin. Reproduced by courtesy of Dr. Dáibhí Ó Cróinín and the librarian of NUI, Galway (The Ritchie–Pickow Collection)

Plate Section:
Plate 1. *Emain Macha*/Navan Fort (Co. Armagh). Photograph by Cambridge University Collection of Air Photographs.
Plate 2. 'Red Woman'. Painting by Katherine Beug. Reproduced by courtesy of the artist.
Plate 3. *Oileán Buí*/Dursey Island (Co. Cork). Photography by Cambridge University Collection of Air Photography.
Plate 4. 'Loch Bà' (Isle of Mull). Photograph by James Westland Photography, Isle of Mull, Scotland.
Plate 5. 'Crows'. Painting by Tadhg Mac Suibhne. Reproduced by courtesy of the artist.
Plate 6. 'Sacred Animal' Painting – by anonymous artist – in author's possession.
Plate 7. '*De Ensomme, To Mennesker*/The Lonely Ones, Two Human Beings. Woodcut by Edvard Munch. Reproduced under licence from DACS, London.
Plate 8. 'The *Cailleach*/Kilcatherine Stone' (Co. Cork). Photograph by John Eagle Photography, Eyeries, Beara.

PART ONE

Tradition and Theory

A Perspective on Irish Oral Tradition

Writing at the beginning of the twentieth century, Wood-Martin[1] makes reference to the propensity of writers on Irish cultural matters to begin with the Flood and take in everything that happened after. The Flood will actually get a mention in this work too but an even more elusive and daunting starting point is proposed: human consciousness or more precisely, how consciousness is the matrix wherein meaning is generated out of the experience of existence, and cultural tradition is established out of the sharing of experience and the collective representation of meaning.

The focus of this book is on certain symbols and particular symbolic processes that appear to characterize Irish cultural tradition over a long period of time. The symbols consist of personifications in female form of the creative power of the human imagination; the processes are the ways in which these personified figures are manifested in the imaginative life and the cultural knowledge which Irish people have participated in and held in common.

Taken as a whole this imaginative life and cultural knowledge can be regarded as constituting a universe of discourse that is both a symbolic product of consciousness in Ireland and a symbolic process whereby Irish experience is represented and communicated within Irish consciousness and Irish culture. The term *coimcne* was used a thousand years ago to mean just such a shared universe of cultural discourse.[2] Its literal meaning is 'mutual wisdom' and it emphasizes both the sharing of cultural knowledge and the central importance of the knowledge shared; such knowledge being necessary for the comprehension of life experience and the proper conduct of social life. Anthropology is one discipline that has set itself the task (among others) of understanding the nature of human culture and of cultural process[3] and it is useful to pick out and consider some theories that have been developed within anthropology in this regard.

Culture as adaptation

Along with all other living creatures, humans live in an adaptive, ecological relationship with their environment. The human environment is made up of several different layers of life experience and human ecology or cultural adaptation is therefore very complex. The three chief layers of life experience and cultural adaptation which it is useful for our purposes to distinguish are the physical, the social and the symbolic.

Human adaptation to the physical environment (that is, to landscape and climate), gives rise to a technological universe of discourse all of its own. This technological universe of discourse is grounded in a detailed knowledge of the resources which the particular environment offers in terms of flora and fauna and also in terms of inert but important resources such as water, minerals, oil and so on. As well as knowledge, the technological universe of discourse comprises 'know-how', or ways to do things with the knowledge of the environment. Much of the knowledge and the 'know-how' is rendered visible and tactile in the form of the artefacts of what is known as material culture, the 'concrete' manifestation of culture and cultural knowledge in the physical domain. Mobile phones, laptop computers and the other items of hardware in today's information age are examples of material culture that give continuous access to another kind of environment again, the virtual environment of the worldwide web, that is the setting, increasingly, for so much of human work.

Technology and material culture serve a very basic function with respect to *sustaining* human life through the provision, at base, of the fundamental necessities of food and shelter. In our own, present-day, cultural world we have developed technology and material culture to a degree that is so far advanced from the provision of only the fundamental necessities that we easily forget that for 99 per cent of the human era relatively simple foraging and hunting technologies were successful in providing humans everywhere with food, shelter and a generally comfortable, if frugal, lifestyle that was accompanied by a world of a symbolic and imaginative order as rich and as complex as our own, or any other world of human culture. Nowadays most Irish people have comparatively little contact with the primary level of physical environment as producers and providers, though we are all, of course, consumers of environment, whether as processed goods or as services or as recreational retreat. Our lifestyle and our cultural life as a whole, however, always start from and continue to be grounded in our physical existence in the 'natural' world.

Another environment to which humans adapt is the environment that consists of other people, the social environment. In the case of human social environmental adaptation the resulting social knowledge is immensely richer and more complex than that to which the social environmental adaptation of other social creatures (ants or apes) gives rise. This is due to the qualitatively profound degree to which human consciousness differs from that of our fellow creatures, in terms of symbolic imagination and symbolic communication. Within family life, economics, politics or the law, cultural knowledge and cultural know-how serve to *regulate* human life with regard to the protection of the weak, the promotion of the strong and the preservation of order and equity, as these are understood, in the face of conflicting interests and social and natural upheaval. This social universe of discourse is made manifest in the organizations and structures of social institutions, from the family to the UN and the World Trade Organisation, but consists essentially of the myriad social transactions in which we are continually engaged, physically and symbolically, in the course of our individual and social production and consumption of 'goods' and 'services' physical and symbolic.

The third layer of life experience and cultural adaptation which it is useful to consider here is that of the symbolic order itself. Human consciousness is able, in imaginative terms, to transcend both the physical and social environments in which it is corporeally and socially located and to range back and forward in time and space, apparently without limit. It is also enabled, by imagination, to reflect on itself and to give symbolic representation to both life experience and to the reflection and the communication of life experience that symbols and imagination make possible. Within the symbolic and imaginative universe of discourse life experience is thus *intensified* and *affirmed* through artistic and ritual performances such as those of storyteller or traditional healer, poet, musician or priest. A major aspect of the symbolic universe of discourse with which the performer and the ritual specialist operate, is the concept of an otherworld, or alternative, order of reality to that commonly or routinely experienced. Concern for such otherworld reality and our human relations with its powers is a universal concern in human culture, and finds expression in artistic as well as religious form.

In summary, we can say that physical artefacts, the operation of social institutions and the representation of symbolic otherworlds make manifest in different ways the characteristically human cultural universe of discourse by which means humans live meaningful lives. Meaning emerges – by extraction or construction, depending on whether we emphasize individual or social life – in a transactional process that is rooted in physical sensation, proceeds via affective sentiment and amounts to cognitive sense.

Culture as knowledge

To write like this is, of course, to risk gross reductionism by means of such quasi-mechanical schematization of the apparently seamless experience of the operation of our unified and unitary human existence, which is at once physical, social and symbolic. Nevertheless, for the purposes of clarifying the perspectives which can be brought to bear on Irish cultural tradition regarded as a universe of discourse, we can allow ourselves to bear distinctions such as these in mind. The materials to be presented and discussed in the course of this work draw largely on the symbolic level of Irish cultural tradition but, as such, they are still associated with cultural knowledge of the social and physical orders. In attempting to understand the functioning of their cultural significance it is necessary to regard them in the context of the full discourse of which they are a part and to allow for their import, throughout it, in cultural terms.

Another reason for not wanting to compartmentalize the universe of cultural discourse is that we need to understand it as containing a dynamic flow of cultural knowledge throughout its extent, and images such as that of a sea or ocean of knowledge can give some sense of the ceaseless surging back and forth of cultural creativity, together with its transmission and transformation of meaning. On that ocean of cultural knowledge the individual, the group or the community form, as it were, provisional and dynamic islands of identity, cultural creativity and meaningfulness. These 'islands' are centres of consciousness and centres at which the flow of cultural knowledge from other island-centres is received and retransmitted outwards again in the continual interactions and transactions of life. In this way all humans are forever busy participants in the cultural work of making meaning out of experience and communicating meaningfully with one another. The Swedish anthropologist Ulf Hannerz has developed a way of understanding the continual creation and transmission of cultural knowledge that is especially relevant to the cultural complexities of today's world with its almost instant global communication, its mass media, its travel and cultural convergence, together with its increasing levels of diversity and multiculturalism.[4] The Hannerz model is also valuable in respect of any attempts to trace the continuities and adaptations that mark creativity and transformation within cultural tradition over time, in that it places the creative reproduction of cultural knowledge at the heart of any process of reception – transmission, whether in space or time and keeps us focused on the creative performances of verbal artists and ritual specialists as the imaginative engines of tradition and renewal within the ocean of human imaginative creativity and communication.

For Hannerz it is useful to distinguish between three interrelated dimensions of culture and cultural process:

1   ideas and modes of thought as entities and processes of mind
2   forms of externalization – verbal and institutional (to which I would add 'material')
3   social distribution or the way the cultural inventories of 1 and 2 are spread differentially over a population.

In the Hannerz view culture is essentially a mental phenomenon, made accessible to the senses by means of the continual process of externalization of meanings.

In making use of the Hannerz model to understand the nature of cultural process we should note that it is necessary to understand the characterization of culture as mental phenomenon in a broad sense, compatible with an idea of culture as knowledge that is not restricted to one side of a body–mind duality. In this regard it is interesting to consider how cultural knowledge is given a conventional bodily location in popular usage that corresponds to another schematic approach to distinguishing different forms of knowing. Folk psychology assigns certain kinds of knowledge to the head. We say 'my head was full of useless information'; 'it's there somewhere at the back of my head'; 'I have it on the tip of my tongue'. This knowledge that is popularly associated with the head is, in effect, the kind of knowledge that can be labelled *cognitive* and that is, generally speaking, capable of being rendered verbally. It can be contrasted with *affective* or emotional knowledge, located by popular convention in the heart or abdomen in phrases such as: 'my heart tells me'; 'I should have listened to my gut'. If cognitive knowledge is verbal culture then affective knowledge involves feelings, values, judgements; the cultural fields of ethics and aesthetics and the cultural determination of what is true (or false), beautiful (or ugly), good (or bad). Then, of course, there is another kind of knowledge again, and again differently located in popular understanding. This is the *operant* knowledge of 'how-to-do', conventionally located in the hands and feet and bodily movements of highly skilled performers – sports heroes, musicians, surgeons – and of ordinary individuals, too, who know how to pull a pint, dig a grave, beat a lambeg drum or just tie their shoe-laces – without necessarily being able to put this knowledge 'into words' in any very clear-cut way.

Transmission of cultural knowledge in myth and ritual
Again, in relation to distinguishing different kinds of cultural knowledge, we must beware of over-doing the rigid classification of life or culture. Verbal, cognitive knowledge – for example a story, a nick-name, a scientific formula – can be spoken or used in ethical and unethical, aesthetic and unaesthetic ways. Similarly operant knowledge, knowledge in action, is subject to consideration of appropriateness, just as values and aesthetic judgements are subject to change in the face of new cognitive knowledge (ideas or theories) or new ways of doing things (inventions). Irish cultural tradition, out of which comes the narrative – and ritual – knowledge and externalizations that are the focus of this work has, like other cultural traditions, always had a dynamic and ever-changing nature. In examining the myths and legends that, as verbal or cognitive cultural knowledge make manifest one phase or

other of the Irish worldview – which like all worldviews is under perpetual reconstruction and transformation and in perpetual transmission by externalization – we work within a universe of discourse where the cognitive knowledge of the legend is coloured and contexted by the other kinds of knowledge with which it shares a creative and dynamic existence in the ocean of cultural discourse. This is equally true of the operant knowledge of funerary or healing rituals and of the knowledge – cognitive, affective and conative – that is associated with the representation of the visions and ideals of political and individual liberation. Tradition, with its symbolic representations of cultural knowledge in verbal and behavioural, narrative and ritual form, is anything but a fixed datum of knowledge, a closed repertoire of cultural items whose meaning is stable and determined once-and-for-all. Rather is it the case that, in re-encountering the stories, the customs and the beliefs of Irish tradition, we invite them to speak to us, within their own *and* our universes of discourse, insofar as these merge in the effort we make to clarify the former and to be as fully conscious as we can of its potential for ourselves and for our cultural knowledge of both ourselves and our heritage of tradition. If we can give our fullest attention to the materials we inherit and confront, then we can anticipate an imaginative and creative contribution, on their part, to our own cultural knowledge.

This contribution is something that will emerge from the symbolic richness of the encounter in terms of both access to the shared inherited meanings which adhere to traditional narratives and symbols and our own capacity to relate these imaginatively to our own experiences and to our own contemporary circumstances. A work like Wendy Doniger O'Flaherty's *Other People's Myths*[5] holds out the prospect of our being able to make such connections between our own lives and the stories contained in any or all mythological traditions: Biblical, Greek, Hindu, Chinese, as well as modern media re-tellings, in artistic forms such as film, novels and television drama. O'Flaherty tries to illustrate the dynamic relationship between lives and stories in the following passages:

> To the extent that myth arises out of reality and has an effect on reality, there can be no particular starting point or end point; it is a cycle. Myth and reality are caught up in a complex folie à deux..."[6]
>
> There are times when we confront an actual experience and respond to it as we would respond to the confrontation of a myth. We recognize the myth in moments of real life because we recognize certain archetypal elements common to myth and life; and, as the banality of myth demonstrates, this happens to

everyone, even to the 'plain man.' Jung remarked that 'myth is not fiction: it consists of facts that are continually repeated and can be observed over and over again. It is something that happens to man, and men have mythical fates just as much as the Greek heroes do...'[7]

The mythical events in our lives include, but are not limited to, those formalized in the rituals called rites of passage: the experience of birth (ours or our childrens'), the sudden transition from childhood to adulthood, falling in love, marriage, death – our experience of the deaths of others and our contemplation of our own deaths. We encounter these primal echoes also in classical occasions of joy – plunging into the ocean, galloping on a young horse, climbing mountains, watching geese fly south, returning home after a long journey, listening to sublime music, watching a summer thunderstorm in the middle of the night. And the same feeling overcomes us in moments of modern tragedy – the phone call in the middle of the night, news of failure or desertion, an accident, the diagnosis of cancer, a prison sentence. The private mythic moment is crowded by ghosts whom we cannot identify consciously, but whose multiplicity we are aware of. We know that what is happening to us has happened to them, because we have heard stories about them, and so they are present with us when those things happen again to us. If there is some piece of sad news that our children have to hear in real life, news of a death or a loss, we try to let them hear it from someone we know and trust – an aunt who was with us when we first learned about death ourselves, or a teacher or a wise friend. This is what great myths are – the stories that people all over the world have come to trust with their darkest and most deeply troubling insights...'[8]

Worth recalling here, also, is the remark of Bronislaw Malinowski[9] that, when it comes to cultural life as a 'going concern' (i.e. lived rather than analyzed), myth is not so much a story told as it is a reality lived. Myths are, in a profound sense, the truth of the world. The present work makes no claim on traditional worlds of myth and symbolism outside the sphere of Irish 'folklore', or Irish ancestral, vernacular culture. In presenting a case for the application of such 'creative mythology' to the mythological legends of Irish tradition, this work confines itself to the field of symbolic meaningfulness represented by the ancestral cosmology which Irish mythological legends articulate. That ancestral Irish cosmology – like all cosmologies – comprises the cultural knowledge, in head, and heart and hand (action and artefact), that comprehends and represents in a broad, general way, how the world and human existence have appeared meaningful to its adherents – the bearers and transmitters of Irish tradition – in narrative and in ritual. In particular, I want to explore how the relation between experience and meaningfulness has, in Irish tradition and Irish ancestral cosmology, at the vernacular level, been established and perpetuated in continual transformation, by acts of creative, narrative performance, that is, by the telling of stories. All stories involve in their telling the agency of their narrators whose conscious performance of specific redactions of items of their narrative repertoires have given rise – in the Irish case – to the existence of the corpus of texts we address below. But stories also always involve agency in another sense; this is the imputed agency, not of their narrators, but of their characters, the *dramatis personae* who feature as the actors in their plots. Such actors are presented to us as personages, as fictional constructs who, more or less, resemble the flesh-and-blood humans of our experience of life even though, in some cases, they are clearly creatures deriving, in whole or in part, from the otherworld.

The traditional personification of cultural knowledge

As personages, the imaginary characters who feature in stories personify agencies that the stories present as the vitalizing elements of their action. In many cases, the agencies personified are human agencies, apparently real people. In other cases, the agencies personified are otherworld forces and powers, given quasi-human form by the creative imaginations of the storytellers and the cosmological traditions on which they draw. In all cases, the figures who feature as characters in the stories – whether as symbolic, narrative personifications of flesh-and-blood humans, of divine, otherworld figures or of the cosmic forces of the landscape and the universe – are presented as either female or male creatures. This reflects and corresponds to the universal gendering of personages within human consciousness into the biologically-derived psychic and social constructs of masculinity and femininity. Such gendering is a classification aspect of the 'theory' that cosmology always constitutes, in respect of the conception of the universe as an ordered whole together with a set of governing, general laws.

Among the characters or personages that feature most prominently in the mythological legends and literature of ancestral Irish tradition, is the figure of the otherworld female. This personage is regarded in traditional cosmology as the personification, in divine female form, of the physical landscape within which human life is lived and also of the cosmic forces at work in that landscape. These forces can range from the power of wind and wave – seen at their most dramatic in fierce winter storms – to the pastoral and nurturing fertility forces of plant and animal life-orders within the landscape. They can also be the geotectonic forces whose workings have left the physical landscape as it presents itself to human consciousness and to human life. In the working of that consciousness and in its many different articulations in literary and in other cultural forms, great diversity exists as to the the functions and the specific cultural connotations of the various female figures who can be taken to personify aspects of experience. Prominent among them in the kind of oral narrative material with which this work is concerned – the legends of folklore – is the otherworld female, the *cailleach* of Irish and Scottish Gaelic tradition, regarded as the shaper who has formed the features of landscape. As such a primal territorial personification, the otherworld female becomes identified in Celtic and Irish cultural history, as a royal sovereignty principle in terms of the political ideology of the ruling dynastic lineages.

In the course of time the figure of the royal mother/spouse goddess undergoes transformation into that of the sovereignty queen and suffers stigmatization and displacement in the course of the development of the specifically patriarchal and Christian cultural world of the later Irish middle ages. This work will suggest that behind or beneath the official and learned cultural order which consigned the *cailleach* figure to the discredited margins, vernacular culture and vernacular cosmology retained a more valued and centred sense of the otherworld female that not only endured but actively informed cultural developments – artistic, political and ritual – in the course of the early modern era. Part Two presents texts and commentaries relating to two important strands of otherworld female tradition in the narrative folklore repertoire of rural Irish communities down into modern times. These suggest that the narration and transmission of such material plays an important role in both a) perpetuating an ambivalent accommodation to a cosmology alternative to that of Christianity, and b) adapting some of the features of that alternative cosmology to the historical circumstances of the communities whose traditional inheritance it is within the hybrid and ever-fluctuating life of culture. The strands of tradition in question are those of the otherworld landscape figure *Cailleach Bhéarra* and the apparently flesh-and-blood wise-woman whose mediation – on behalf of her community and her 'clients' – with the otherworld realm, has a therapeutic function that is intriguingly modern. In this first Part the operation of otherworld female tradition is presented and discussed in relation to the question of the representation of the feminine in literature and to the question of the role of otherworld female tradition in providing serviceable coping mechanisms – of a ritual and psychotherapeutic sort – at times of individual and group affliction. The figure and function of the historical, flesh-and-blood, *bean chaointe* (the keening-woman at the wake), reveals how such a 'real' woman can be a manifestation of mythological meanings and values, invoked in the service of emotional well-being. The figure and function of the narratively prominent *bean feasa* (the wise-woman), is explored here to suggest that the many legends of the resort to the wise-woman and of her prescience, may be regarded as a form of traditional, 'therapy' that exhibits features comparable to the professional psychotherapy practiced today. The remainder of this first Part will look at how some of the narrative materials of Irish tradition concerning the *cailleach* and the *bean feasa* can be interpreted in the light of some aspects of literary and feminist theory to which the Irish folklore material seems relevant, as well as in the light of the history of Irish literature and tradition.

Oral narrative as literature

Some discussion is required regarding the fashion in which texts such as the ones presented in Part Two are approached, in the perspective adopted here, for the purposes of their elucidation and contemporary interpretation in a way that remains, in some sense, faithful to the sensibilities and the worldviews of the local audiences among whom these materials originally circulated in narration. This issue of the *meaning* of folklore texts raises several very substantial questions of both theoretical and practical importance. Some of these apply equally to the interpretation of literary as well as folklore texts and arise from a consideration of the nature of narrative itself, whether in the domains of the individual writer of creative literature or that of the storyteller engaging his or her listeners by means of oral speech. In both cases meaning is being communicated in the 'story' that is told, a meaning that can be many-layered and complex, both in what it represents and in how this representation is embodied in words. Thus the meaning of a text – a text of literature or of folklore – is more than that of the surface plot alone. Beyond, or beneath that surface dimension, other levels of meaningfulness are found. Two main levels on which we can recognize these Irish literary and folkloric stories as operating powerfully are the historic and the mythic. To be able to understand them and what they tell us, we require to be aware of and alert to the way they carry reference to socio-political and cosmological traditions in Ireland on the one hand, and to archetypal patterns of a universal human provenance on the other. We can regard them, in this respect, as being both learned and wise and glimpse something of the role they played in pre-modern society when they formed part of a *coimcne*, a shared universe of Irish cultural discourse and identification.

In seeking to comment on them now so as to elucidate some of the significance they carried for their original audiences and still carry for ourselves as we confront them today in written form, we are facilitated by a recognition that while the search for meaning starts from the text, it necessarily goes beyond the text as well. By 'beyond the text' I mean that in the contexts of past literary and cosmological tradition and in the context of a common human concern to discern meaning in the experiences that life brings, the meaning of a text can be emergent rather than something fixed and unitary. Consequently, the work of interpretation is never finished. Given a basic acquaintance with its traditional significance and functions, re-engagement with the text can lead to new insight and an understanding of the relevance of the text's meaning to our own circumstances and concerns. This involves acts of interpretation, on the contemporary reader's part, of both the past and present significance of the text in question, acts that reveal and attest to the creative nature of interpretation itself. Such an engagement with a traditional text is regarded by folklore scholarship as a valid form of reconceptualization or selective construction. As such it involves the symbolic creation of a connection between aspects of the present and an assigned interpretation of the past and its representation in textual tradition.[1] The commentaries I offer on the traditional texts dealt with in Part Two of this work are contributions aiming to assist a reconceptualization of assigned meaning as this emerges from both the identification of possible traditional significances in the stories they relate and their potential significance in respect of the representation of archetypal aspects of their contemporary readers' lives.

A major part of the traditional significations of the stories represented by the texts dealt with in this book arises from the potential of narration to render present, to the imagination and to the emotions, figures who personify elements of ancestral knowledge. These elements comprise knowledge of a profound kind regarding the human condition and the circumstances of human life in the world, which is conceived of as standing in contingent relationship to an otherworld rendered accessible to experience in the symbolic life of narrative and ritual. In confining our attention largely to how the traditional narrative material dealt with here is able to give access to the presence of otherworld reality, in traditional terms, we raise the question of its ability also to provide access to, and to render present to the contemporary reader's imagination and emotions, an order of reality that is talked about in some contemporary discourse as that of the unconscious and the archetypal.

To the extent that the question of the meaning of the text is a question shared by literary critics and by folklorists, it may be useful to discuss their common concerns in a focus that perceives the written and the spoken as two closely-related modalities for the linguistic realization of states of consciousness that are, in one contemporary view, themselves incipiently narrative.[2]

Much attention is devoted nowadays, in the case of both literary criticism and folklore scholarship, to questions pertaining to the actual meaning and/or the capacity for meaningfulness of verbal communication. How can the latter be considered as meaningful at all, in the first instance, and how can meaning be understood as being constructed in terms of symbolic codes operated by 'authors' and by 'listeners' alike? On the one hand, we can suppose that every narration (oral or written) overlies and conceals other possible voices within cultural discourse whose narratives, if 'heard' would attest to alternative identities and identifications to those represented in the narrative claiming attention. As against this perspective there is the point of view, found in both disciplines, that proper narrative scholarship consists, primarily and well-nigh exclusively, in strictly textual work; the establishment of reliable texts and versions, with little regard to, or interest in, possible evaluation or interpretation outside a textual canon.

I hope that the type of discussion of certain texts from Irish narrative tradition undertaken in this work will be of interest to those for whom theory is a primary concern, while not offending those whose main preoccupation is with textual authenticity and integrity, above all else. In respect of the texts treated hereafter I recognize a multitude of properly textual considerations regarding their status and their transmission, considerations that I leave unresolved in a work that aims at imaginative insight as well as the exact scholarly record.

In his famous lecture to the British Academy more than half a century ago, entitled 'The Gaelic Storyteller', *Séamas Ó Duilearga*[3] had this to say regarding *Seán Ó Conaill,* the elderly small farmer cum fisherman from whom he had collected an impressive repertoire of narrative tradition:

> He had a local reputation as a story-teller in a parish where there were many story-tellers and tradition-bearers. He had never left his native district ... He had never been to school, was illiterate ... and he could neither speak nor understand English ... He was a conscious literary artist. He took a deep pleasure in telling his tales; his language was clear and vigorous and had in it the stuff of literature.[4]

This passage certainly provides us with considerable food for thought: the 'conscious literary artist' who can neither read nor write; the oral storyteller who has 'the stuff of literature' in his narration. Today, perhaps, the terms 'literature' and 'literary artist' would be used less freely in respect of practitioners of oral tradition. A fence of theory has been erected between oral narrative and 'true' literature. Literature must be understood as always comprising handiwork in the field of vision – Jacques Derrida's insistence on the fundamental primacy of black marks on white paper at the heart of the text, as discussed and criticized so succinctly by Mark Abrams[5] – as distinct from the spoken-utterance nature of oral narration in the field of hearing. More importantly, we are to understand that writing (the medium of literature) carries human consciousness with it to new levels that are beyond the range of those dependent on speech and the verbal utterances of oral narrative, to represent and give voice to their thinking and their ideas.

This fundamental division between the community of orality and literate society can be understood as an aspect of the division commonly understood to exist between the condition (and concept) of 'tradition' and the condition (and concept) of 'modernity'. Some literary scholars such as Angela Bourke and Gearóid Denvir, who are themselves thoroughly acquainted with Irish oral traditions, would maintain that it is not permissible to engage critically – within a common, culturally comparative and hermeneutic frame – with the product of 'folklore' tradition and that of modern creative literature, since each sort has such a different nature and creative origin. The hermeneutic stance adopted in this work points to my own reluctance to accept so rigorous a division between oral tradition and written literature.

Students of both disciplines will be conscious of the immense contribution to the study of such questions made by Walter Ong. His work is a kind of quantum leap in our understanding, on all sides, of the relationship of the culture of writing to that of speech. Best known of his own work is, perhaps, *Orality and Literacy: The technologising of the word*.[6] I would wish to draw attention also to an article of his[7] dealing with St Mark's Gospel (the first of the gospels), and how it came to be made from the oral narrative tradition, from the legends, the *seanchas*, of the followers of Jesus of Nazareth, in the first years of Christianity. The article appears in a book edited by John Miles Foley, a leading scholar of the Oral Theory of Composition school of literary scholarship. Ong's article deals in a seminal way with the construction and growth of literary capacity and potential, in the case of Mark's gospel, that arises in and develops from the writing down of oral tradition. Ong succeeds in bringing us extraordinarily close to the heart of literary creativity as it occurs, in this instance, in the rendering literate of the gospel narrative. Here is what Foley has to say about it:

> In probing the pretextual world of orality in which the original *kerygma* ['proclamation'] of Jesus existed . . . Ong offers us a wholly revised view of the Gospel of Mark and of all gospels. No matter what existential force the gospels may have for individuals, one must recognise that placing the text of Mark in the context of its oral antecedents and assessing the extraordinary change in phenomenological import necessarily a part of the narratizing process, must affect profoundly the way in which one reads and interprets the gospels as they survive to us. By making evident the dynamics of both the oral Jesus and his Markan remaking, Ong brings us closer to the identity of Jesus and the experience of his teachings as presence. It is difficult to overestimate this achievement.[8]

What Ong shows us in this article – the process of linguistically rendering the identity of the character Jesus and the fashion in which we are made to perceive verbally his teaching, as if he were himself present to us – goes to the centre-ground of some of the chief issues at the heart of the disciplines of folklore and literary criticism. The verbal achievement and expression of personal identity; the provision and communication of actual life-experience by means of the transformational potential of linguistic composition: these are today understood as being fundamental aspects of the understanding of the phenomenon of 'literature'. One recalls the statement of Séamus Heaney's, at the time of his receipt of the Nobel Prize, in regard to just this kind of transformative potential in the case of poetry, and its being both 'true to the impact of external reality . . . and sensitive to the inner laws of the poet's being'.[9] In the literary poetic both of oral narrative performance and of creative writing, we encounter a verbal capacity that stirs us and moves us out of mere 'creaturely existence' in the mundane, workaday world, bringing us vital, vivid experience and acute flashes of comprehension regarding, humanity and the human condition.

One should not take it that in *Orality and literacy* Ong ruled out the oral as a source of 'literature' in the experiential sense of the term. He certainly mounts a devastating critique of the term 'oral literature', calling it a 'preposterous term' and a 'monstrous concept'. He explains how there is, always, a temporal aberration involved in its usage, since that which is 'literature' cannot ever be located, *per se*, within what he terms 'primary oral culture', the culture or cultural situation where (when?) literacy and writing have not yet developed or been acquired. On the other hand, Ong holds that nothing that is written, including any specific 'literary' text, can depart completely from the oral verbal realm because of the nature of the technology whereby literacy is achieved. However much of cultural life is written and literate, however much human consciousness has been transformed and transposed by writing, to sophisticated, self-reflexive planes:

> in all the wonderful worlds that writing opens, the spoken word still resides and lives. Written texts all have to be related somehow, directly or indirectly, to the world of sounds, the natural habitat of language, to yield their meanings ... Writing can never dispense with orality.[10]

The other side of this situation is that 'primary oral culture' comes to an end as soon as ever it is touched by writing. Notwithstanding that the majority of the Irish population could not, until relatively recently (c. 150 years ago), write or read in any language, Irish culture had, simultaneously, been a literate culture for at least 1500 years. *Seán Ó Conaill*, despite his inability to read or write, despite his never having been at school, participated in a culture that was literate to a degree. He was aware of and recognized that world of literacy. He knew and had dealings with its agencies and its representative agents: the priest, the schoolmaster, the policeman and the folklore collector – Ó Duilearga himself.

The social world from which we derive the whole repertoire of Irish traditional oral narrative is similarly poised on the edge of literacy. Along with being 'traditional' (i.e. orality-oriented), it was, of course, a society that was continually undergoing change and social development as, in respect of the transforming social contexts of traditional storytelling at mid-twentieth century, the work of Clodagh Brennan-Harvey makes clear.[11] In focusing on the least literate aspect of the partly literate cultural discourse of the world of Seán Ó Conaill and his like – on the oral narrative repertoire of the elderly, rural and frequently Irish speaking, population of early twentieth century Ireland, the collectors of Irish Folklore tended to bring with them to the field a text-oriented sense of their enterprise that derived from their own formation in literacy (a number of them were trained schoolteachers). Ó Duilearga appears to have been sensitive to this problem in so much as he characterizes in the following interesting and revealing way the gap that he believed existed, in reality, between the mental disposition of the storytellers and that of the collectors, no matter how dedicated and sympathetic:

> the storytellers themselves ... belong to a different world from their commentators and even the best-equipped collector, no matter how much he knows of the material he is recording, feels at times like a child in an infant school under the tutelage of a benevolent but omniscient master.[12]

I believe that the textual orientation (literacy – rather than orality-focused) prevails in the Irish Folklore Commission collecting enterprise, overall, and is given significant expression in the characterization by Ó Duilearga himself of the *'áirneán'* (the 'storytelling assembly'), the chief, male, oral narrative institution of Irish vernacular cultural tradition. In this account the *áirneán* is presented as a kind of hearthside academy with star narrators featuring as professors of oral literature. Ethnographic accounts of storytelling in a variety of cultural traditions establish for us that the *airneán* – the institutionalized vernacular storytelling of daily life – is generally a less deliberate and a far more occasional and contingent process than one is led to believe from Ó Duilearga's description of the Irish traditional storytelling event. In contrast to this account, we have the presentation by Henry Glassie of County Fermanagh storytelling as a far less 'staged' and formalized kind of narrative performance.[13] Account must, of course, be taken of changed social circumstances, changed language-world and differing narrative repertoires, as between Ó Duilearga's *Cill Riailigh* and Glassie's *Ballymenone*. Nevertheless, one can recognize the distinctively literate bent of Ó Duilearga's perceptions. In his own words:

> The repertoire of many storytellers whom I have known reminds one of the omnibus collections of Irish vellum tradition. Those old tradition-bearers, like the old manuscripts, are libraries in themselves. Questioning them we can turn over page after page in their capacious memories ...[14]

This is the voice of a scholar steeped in knowledge of the literate and literary traditions of European high culture for whom it is 'natural' to think in terms of the text. By contrast, the writings of Glassie and Brennan-Harvey provide a corrective to what is an overly academic perspective. In their accounts it is not from, as it were, an archive of texts that the storyteller narrates in authoritative performance. Rather he (or she) participates in an oral event that is far less controlled or directed by any one performer or any one member of the communicative company present. In this perspective, the *áirneán* would appear to resemble the 'session' of the traditional music fraternity rather than the modern, pre-arranged poetry-reading event. On-the-spot creative performance and creative response comprise the content and sequencing of the event and provide whatever significance and meaningfulness that participants – whether as 'artists' or as 'audience' – derive as a consequence of their participation.

This has implications regarding the possibility of oral narrative tradition having the qualities and the outcomes of 'literature'. In the case of literature we accept that the work has an author, writing, in a sense, behind the text.

Even among post-structuralists, who would dissolve or deconstruct the concept of 'author', there is a recognition of individual texts, written or supplied by individual practitioners. In the case of oral narrative performance, it is, of course, individuals who speak the words of the stories on the individual occasions when they might, for instance, be recorded (in writing or on tape). But the audience, the assembly that is the social context of the narrative performance, has a fundamental role in that performance, a role without which no literature-like oral narration can occur. Every such literature-like performance of oral narrative tradition is the product of a socially associative communication process that is essentially different from the communicative process involved in the production and reception of written literature.

Nevertheless, oral narrative and creative writing both provide examples of occasional, verbal art, when 'literature' results from the specific and separate processes of communication involved. Literature, in this sense, happens when the communicative event or act (comprising narration/listening, writing/reading) succeeds in giving rise to a verbally transcendent 'experience' of the 'reality' of human life in terms of the linguistic mode of interpersonal communication. Listener and storyteller, reader and author, joined in verbal communication, have each individually to 'act' so as to strike the spark of 'literature' from that communicative congress. This 'action' happens in the medium of speech sounds, in air, in non-enduring form, in one instance and, in the other, happens in the visual medium of writing, of physical marks made ('inscribed') by hand and hand operated tools (chisel, quill, pen, brush, keyboard, laser), on some substantial material on which the marks endure. For 'literature' to exist it is not sufficient, however, that speech or writing simply take place or be produced. Listening or reading of a 'literary' sort has to take place also for 'literature' to exist. There is a communal aspect to this, in respect of both kinds of media, that is not simply confined to the social audience present at the speech event that features the delivery of an oral narrative. It is at issue also in the case of the non-social (i.e. private) reading activity of the individual reader at a social and temporal remove from any author. This communal aspect is sometimes represented as the 'native ear' within the scholarship of oral narrative or as the 'interpretative community' within the reception theory school of literary criticism. Oral narrative scholarship also speaks of the viewpoint of the traditional storyteller, something which implies listening and speaking, jointly in the case of traditional narrative. Eye and hand, seeing and writing, must be the corresponding pairing in the case of creative writing. We can note how, in each case, what is happening is identical in terms of cultural communication process: a bodily organ is operating to give external representation to 'knowledge' and another bodily organ is operating to register that representation and derive meaning from it. In both cases what happens is properly understood as an instance of technology, 'the physical manifestation of mental schemata' of meaningfulness.[15] In a sense, Ong's *Orality and Literacy* could properly be said to engage with *The [further] technologizing of the word*, to paraphrase its sub-title. Technologized in spoken or written form, the word (i.e. linguistic communication), has the potential of being 'literature' even though most linguistic communication does not achieve, or aspire to, that cultural status in the estimation and understanding of its practitioners and critical commentators.

That which provides the opportunity for 'literature' to happen, to arise, in verbal performance, consists of excellence of speech or writing (as perceived by listeners or readers) together with an epiphanic revelation of experiential truth regarding the human condition which that verbal excellence encompasses semantically and emotionally. Needless to say, this is always a matter of the greatest subjectivity and individual choice and valuation, but one also in which convention and tradition operates. The work of literary critic and of folklorist alike, includes attempting to identify and elucidate such conventions and such patterns in the case both of oral narrative tradition and of creative writing. The fundamental requirement here – one that is, ultimately, more likely than not to be a personal talent – is the ability to recognize, to identify and to reveal or make manifest, the verbal excellence *and* the creative capacity together, in any instance, of oral narration or of writing.

Such 'literary' excellence and capacity may exist within the cultural frames of meaning of a specific interpretative community as an aspect of what is sometimes called local or indigenous knowledge. It may also exist in wider, more 'universal' or 'globalized' frames of meaning, in the case of narratives or verbal performances that are generally perceived to constitute examples of major artistic achievement. Such major art examples (for example the work of a Homer, a Dante, a Goethe, a Chaucer, a Joyce, a Shakespeare) start out, as it were, from the level and the frames of local knowledge but 'carry through' in terms of verbal excellence and epiphanic creative capacity to wider and more globalized interpretative communities, transcending, in translation and transmission, the boundaries of space, time and language variety. In terms of linguistic excellence and of creative capacity, verbal art affords opportunities to listeners and readers to experience delight and fulfilment in an imaginative, experiential engagement with penetrating shafts of insight into the the truth of representative realizations of human life at its greatest, in the experience of a kind of secular Parousia. In particular, 'literature', whether generated out of written or oral narration, affords the possibility of identification on the part of the listener/reader with characters and with life experiences that are 'true', at depths of consciousness beyond the ordinary and the everyday. Such delight and fulfilment, such symbolic and artistic 'making whole' and, as it were, healing, is produced on the basis of creative imagination operating through spoken tradition, in the case of oral narrative (such as the folklore legends dealt with in this book). It is produced on the basis of creative imagination operating through the scribing author in the case of creative writings (the stories and novels of contemporary fiction). In the one case, 'literature', when it happens, is a phenomenon of the sociality of an actual audience. In the other case, 'literature' when it happens, is a phenomen of individual singularity attaining to the virtual sociality of readership.

The same intensified, accelerated nurturing of imagination and of life experience results from 'literary' verbal art (that is to say 'verbal art being literature') whether in the spoken or written modality. As such, whenever and wherever the spark of literature is struck this happens on a cultural foundation that is shared alike by oral narrative tradition and by creative writing. One can now see clearly, as Ong has incontrovertibly shown, that it is creative writing – because of the cultural implications and consequences that derive from the phenomenon of writing itself, as technology – that has greater and far more powerful potential as an instrument for communicating creatively. This is not, however, to deny to oral narrative its own inherent and characteristic potential, in this respect. The texts of the oral narrative presented in this book and the commentaries offered with them, bear witness, hopefully, to the way that traditional material, frequently seen as outmoded, naïve, parochially-bound, can constitute a rich imaginative resource for our own times and our own circumstances in a world where the local and the global are intermeshing at an increased rate for greater numbers and in ways not previously imagined.

The *cailleach* of this work, and her *bean feasa* transform are personages of mythology and legend about whom a great deal of folklore exists. This folklore takes the form, for the most part, of *seanchas*; a term covering oral, local, popular history and tradition as this is communicated in chat or discussion as well as in more formal narration. But *seanchas* has an original, technical meaning of a normative bent, insofar as it originally signified traditional law; the formulation, in narrative account, of that which is correct, wise, true, according to Irish cultural convention and the shared life experience out of which such convention is constructed. Something of this moral and ethical sense of *seanchas* – of the lore of oral narrative tradition – is conveyed by the legends of the *cailleach* and the *bean feasa,* though the lesson they purport to teach regarding human life and the interpretation of its experience, is not so much didactic as imaginatively suggestive à la verbal art and its 'literary' potential. In the way that these traditional oral narratives operated in the communities where they were given renewed expression and transmission, there was an ambiguous 'operational' belief in their truth, a truth of the kind posited by folklore scholarship for all legend narration.[16] They themselves were told as if they *were* true, with the kind of suspension of disbelief involved that is more frequently associated, in critical commentary, with the dramatic performances of theatrical tradition. The central vehicle of this imaginative perception of truth or credibility at the heart of the oral narrative legend is the verbally creative opportunity it makes possible for its audience of hearers (and for us too), to identify, imaginatively, with the characters featured in the narrative by *experiencing* their *presence*. Where and when such imaginative and symbolic transmutation takes place, 'literature' is happening. Creative writing aims to render such happening, such transmutation of consciousness, through the medium of writing to an 'audience' that is, in social and in technical reality, a readership of individuals without any necessary, communal coparticipation. Folklore scholarship today is increasingly investigating the potential of traditional, oral performance, too, to induce such imaginative identification with and such imaginative perception of the presence of legendary personages. Donald Braid[17] in an article in the *Journal of American Folklore* entitled 'Personal Narrative and Experiential Meaning' discusses, as one example, 'how the process of following a narrative can give rise to affectively engaging states of mind'. We can, surely, recognize how such an issue is of common concern to both folklore and literary criticism.

In at least one instance in the legends presented here – that of the 'autobiography' recounted by the *cailleach* to *Donnchadh Mór* (see p. 136, 247) – the question arises as to whether material of traditional oral provenance and, in this instance, masculine transmission, is delivering an archetypal identification of and an archetypal identification with, feminine consciousness that has the potential to be as dramatically and vividly epiphanic as could be expected of any practitioner of creative writing.

And yet there are fundamental differences between the verbal narrative nature of oral legend materials and the textual nature of materials of creative writing. These differences do not amount to an explanation of how creative writing can better achieve its literary intentions. Indeed, in the discussion by John Miles Foley of these differences it is clear that oral tradition is itself a powerfully rich medium for its practitioners and audiences in ways not immediately obvious to the individual reader of the single transcribed text of a traditional legend. Such a single text is a poor record indeed of the imaginative experience which the original narration afforded to the 'insider'

Donegal
FOLK VILLAGE, GLENCOLUMBKILLE

GLENCOLUMBKILLE, CO. DONEGAL: The glen runs back in between the hills from Glen Bay, in surroundings at once peaceful and strikingly picturesque. On the north side rises the noble cliffs of Glen Head. The coast here displays splendid rock scenery, and there is a beautiful strand. St. Colmcille had his retreat in Glencolumbkille, and there is also a tradition that Bonnie Prince Charlie spent some time in this secluded spot. There are several good brown trout streams in the district.

Photo: G. F. Canaday.

For post office use.

5099563002076
Beautiful Ireland is a registered trade mark
of John Hinde Ltd. All rights reserved.

5 099563 163593

Beautiful IRELAND
A JOHN HINDE POSTCARD

guaranteed irish
DL 079
T00143-0019

audience and this must be kept in mind in all our attempts as readers to interpret and respond to traditional oral legends. However fully recorded and transcribed in writing, we must remember that '*An Chailleach Bhéarach and Donnchadh Mór Mac Mánais*' was/is speech, in the first instance. It retains its nature as verbal language, as speech, even as we confront it as a written text printed on the page. John Miles Foley speaks of what is lost in instances such as this in the shift from oral reality to text and what he has to say is especially relevant to attempts, like my own, to deal (in the case of texts), with what is essentially the record of one version of a kind of serial transmission that retains the legend in question within the narrative repertoire of the interpretative community from which the 'text' ultimately derives. In quoting, from Foley's Introduction to the book containing Ong's Markan Gospel article I do not wish to appear frivolous or without respect in making so bold as to want to substitute *Cailleach Bhéarra* where Jesus is the name occurring in the Foley original:

> To come to grips with the 'difference' in the two modes of discourse (which are, as Ong and others have shown, seldom completely separable), it is necessary to appreciate first what the oral economy provided for and even promoted. In primary oral tradition, there simply is no such thing as an omitted story part, or flawed episode, or misnomer. Since the primary oral performance draws its meaning not only from the present event but equally from the diachronic and pan-geographic tradition of which it is only an instance, the process of generating meaning proceeds via metonymy, *pars pro toto*. One text recalls numerous others by synecdoche, just as one phrase or scene is always embedded conceptually in the word-hoard, in the experience of tradition. Under such conditions the oral reality of [*Cailleach Bhéarra*] conjured for its audience not only its present, discrete story-shape, but all story-shapes that oral tradition had gathered about this central figure. Thus does the primary oral culture create and maintain an economy of expression and interpretation that a chirographic culture can never emulate, for the post-traditional text, by cutting itself off from the generative oral tradition ... foregoes the metonymic power of reference inherent in the oral traditional medium[18]

The audience of the traditional *áirneán*, the customary Irish storytelling assembly, engage with articulations of oral narrative tradition – both in *áirneán* assembly and in less formal communicative settings – in terms of a 'vastly different, connotatively explosive mode' to the mode of writing. As a consequence, it is a hopelessly futile task – for both reader and literary critic – to attempt to ascertain the totality of the meaning of any 'text' of oral narrative tradition encountered in written form. The full significance of individual characters and the 'knotty intricacies of small lives' will be outside their readerly perception while being, historically, encompassed in the listener perception of the traditional interpretative community of oral narrative material in the way that Foley explains. The interpretations and commentary offered in this work, as accompaniment to the textual corpus of oral legends presented here in translation, looks for guidance and direction, in going beyond the literal meaning of the written word, to that larger field of narrative tradition in medieval and early modern Ireland on which these 'texts' and the narrative performances that underlie them, draw for the significance of their symbolism, their plots and their characters. My suggestions as to the creative 'reading' of the texts aims to facilitate for other readers an imaginative engagement with them that remains within the parameters of traditional narrative discourse while also facilitating an imaginative re-engagement with them akin to that of 'literature', in the sense that I understand – and have attempted to explain – what literature can be taken to be. From my perspective, a story like that of *Cailleach Bhéarach and Donnchadh Mór Mac Mánais,* the text of which is available to us here out of the traditional oral repertoire of Galway – via the verbal performance of its oral narrator, via the transcription of his listener, via the editorial hand of its first publisher, via my translation of that published version – is a story that operates both as folklore legend and as creative writing. In either case it is a rich, imaginative resource giving its audience and its readership access to a powerful experiential representation of the deeper meanings of human life.

The Swiss folktale scholar Max Lüthi has written illuminatingly of the *märchen* – the international wonder tale of the 'Cinderella', 'Frog King', 'Rapunzel', 'Magician and his Pupil' type – as encompassing in art-form the picture-of-man (i.e. humankind) that was part of the worldview of the vernacular culture of European peoples in pre-modern times.[19] Legends have a similar claim to be representative of the deepest understandings of the meaning of human experience, even if their transmission as traditional lore was largely outside of the more privileged narrative situations in which the longer tales were frequently performed. As traditional lore, however, legends were known to and could be recounted by almost any member of the interpretative community to which they were such a valuable part of the traditional repertoire. Their narration did not require the heights of excellence in verbal performance that was expected of the best of the storytellers in the case of the *märchen* or the hero-tale. Nevertheless, from their basis in plain speech, legends, such as the ones dealt with in this book can convey their listeners and readers to the highest and deepest level of creative imaginative life. One of the aims of this work is to provide a contemporary readership with access, through translation, to the creative, imaginative potential of these stories.

The representation of the feminine

Having indicated the hermeneutic perspective in which my commentaries on and interpretations of the texts presented in Part Two proceed, I turn now to the issue of the status, as representative female figures, of the *cailleach* and *bean feasa* transformations of the otherworld female of Irish ancestral narrative tradition that these texts present. The basic question to be addressed is whether these female personages of traditional narration and the stories about them that have been orally transmitted can be taken to represent, or give utterance to a consciousness or a cultural knowledge that is in any genuine sense feminine, or whether they represent a male definition and projection of the feminine within an essentially patriarchal cultural discourse in which the female voice is equally essentially mute. We can begin by reviewing the narrative and literary history of their construction and development as traditional Irish cultural knowledge.

The evidence of pre-history and of mythology has been taken to suggest that in the Old European, neolithic era, before the spread across the 'European' world of Indo-European-language cultures, cults of a mother-goddess type prevailed throughout the continent.[1] Ireland, too, was inhabited for thousands of years before the coming of the Celts, our first Indo-European immigrants, by peoples whose ideology can be understood to have encompassed religious and cosmological sensibility in respect of a divine female agency who was conceived of as the origin of the physical universe itself and of the life forms contained in its landscapes. On this western outpost of the Old European world, the incoming, patriarchal, Indo-European cosmology of the Celtic speaking cultures, established here by the technological and political hegemony of relatively small numbers of Celtic speaking settlers, took on a significant characterization from the previously dominant matrifocal ideology. Such accommodation is a universal feature of acculturation when, by conquest or peaceful settlement, an ancestral culture is transformed by contact with new cultural forms that come to replace older expressions of worldview. In the Irish case, the cosmology of the incoming Indo-European (Celtic) ideology already had an element of that archaic identification of the cosmic forces of fertility and reproduction with a divine, sovereign, female, landscape figure that finds its fullest historical expression in the early medieval literature of Wales and Ireland. Celtic cultural accommodation to divine mother-goddess traditions of neolithic Old Europe was intensified in Ireland, where an abiding sense of a supreme, sovereign, female, cosmic agency appears to have operated on the incoming culture to a degree that resulted in a continuing, powerful sensibility to the presence in landscape of such divine, female agency – a sensibility that has remained at the heart of Irish ancestral cosmology and mythological legend.

This does not imply the absence of female figures and functions within the incoming Celtic ideology. Indeed, it is necessary for us to note that Professor Jaan Puhvel[2] speaks of a 'transfunctional goddess' within Indo-European mythology itself who matches, in several aspects, anything that has been claimed for an Old European mother-goddess figure. The Indo-European transfunctional goddess figure is, in Puhvel's words[3] 'a great female soil-based, fertility-oriented deity who seems to transcend the class-conscious male gods and to extend her patronage to the society at large', finding her clear reflection in folklore.

Neither should it be imagined that in pre-Indo-European ideology a single, monolithic mother-goddess figure – or cult – existed throughout Old Europe and in earliest Ireland. Such a conception is the product of modern and contemporary reconstructions that arise out of both Enlightenment humanism and the feminist liberation movement and is without any real basis in history or ethnography. Juliette Wood's opening chapter, 'The Concept of the Goddess',[4] in the book of the same name edited by Billington and Green,[5] offers a clear critique and corrective in respect of attempts by some writers to suggest a single mother-goddess tradition.

We can, however, distinguish between the notion of there not being any single tradition in terms of the history and cultural practice of peoples, and a context in which certain fundamental experiences of human life can repeatedly find common forms of popular cultural expression involving the symbolism of a mother-goddess. In a real sense, the materials of folklore that feature the mother-goddess, the otherworld female, are the products both of diverse ancient tradition and of depth psychology in the case of succeeding generations. Lotte Motz[6] offers a balanced and informed view of these issues that does justice both to historical cultural diversity and to psychodynamic reality in the matter of goddess traditions. Motz tellingly opposes this diverse reality to the simplistic abstractions and preconceptions that mark the cult of the goddess in the modern world.

The archaic and continuing Irish sense of a female presence at the heart of reality, at the centre of consciousness and culture, can be understood as deriving jointly from two different projections of the life of the psyche in all humans. One of these has to do with the individual psychoanalytic orientation of the human infant in respect of the mother from whom it is born and on whom it feeds and depends. The other is the symbolic, collective association of the earth itself with the mother as both womb (site of life and nourishment) and grave (site of death and dissolution). Erich Neumann[7] has posited a universal archetype, manifested in the mother-goddess figure, that combines the two fundamental aspects: an elementary (or nourishing) and a transformative (or creative) aspect. While separated in some cultural traditions into complementary archetypal and mythological figures of the Good Mother and the Terrible Mother, the Celtic and earliest Irish mother-goddess figure combines into a single personage these contradictory aspects. For such a *coincidenta oppositorum* Goddess, Neumann reserves the name *Magna Mater* as Great Mother, and regards her as preserving something of an uroboric phase of the original situation of consciousness prior to its splitting into paired and opposed symbolic correlates of primordial psychic experience: presence/absence of mother, provision/deprivation of sustenance, intimate nurture/destructive control and so on. The early Irish mother-goddess displays all these characteristics in the course of tales in which she features as both fecund mother/fertile spouse and as hostile, destructive female/harbinger of death.

The male pantheon of Celtic deities in Irish tradition – Irish reflexes of the figures of the essentially male, Indo-European pantheon – was, it appears, subject to such significant back-pressure from a pre-existing allegiance to a female divine agency that its members are made to fit into a cosmological conception of a universe whose outer and ultimate layer is the domain of a divine female who permeates the whole with her presence and her power. The relationship of the Irish semi-divine hero figure (representing, in narrative, the male deities of the Celtic cosmological pantheon), with the goddess is a central theme of Irish tradition. The tales that relate that relationship and the transformation to which it is subject, in the course of time and history, bear out an observation of Julia Kristeva's regarding the contrasting nature of what she calls woman's time as opposed to linear, male chronology.[8] In this view woman's time (the temporal of the goddess), is cyclical, associated with reproduction and with cosmic rhythm, with the eternal that underlies history, in comparison to the male hero's accomplishments and progress, a progress of historical succession that attempts to evade its mortality by means of making and leaving a heroic mark in the world.

As discussed penetratingly by Máirín Nic Eoin[9], this contrast between female cosmos and male history is further suggested by the views of other women scholars such as Marie-Louise Sjoestedt and Máire MacNeill, who draw attention to the domination of historical myths by divine and semi-divine male gods, whereas topographical myths, recounting the significance of place and physical landscape present, as a recurring theme, the association of specific locations with the deaths and burials of divine and quasi-divine females who give their names to landscape features and to recurring festivals held at these sites as 'sacred assembly' (*oenach*) locations. In MacNeill's view, all such assemblies – Tailtiu, Carman, Emain Macha etc. – that are named from what she calls 'entombed women' were harvest festivals, celebrating the winning from nature of her produce[10]. Similarly Sjoestedt holds that the female deities under whose invocation such sacred assemblies are held, personify the powers of nature – both productive and destructive – powers that man must overcome in order to have them serve him[11]. This he does by violence and he then proceeds by ritual means – the rituals of the recurrent assemblies – to placate and reconcile them. The medieval tales commented on in the next section of Part One illustrate in graphic ways, the thrust of Kristeva's assertion that in such narrative tradition, woman is left 'outside time, with neither past nor future, neither true nor false, buried underground'[12] so that the political or historical significance of women is, symbolically, buried in the landscape. This applies especially to topographic stories, such as the *Emain Macha* tale. On the other hand, the political significance of women is subverted in mytho-historical and political tales, such as *Echtra mac nEchach Muigmedóin*, through being appropriated from hitherto autonomous female divines who are, in the narrative of historical and political propaganda, turned into cyphers of the legitimacy of male dynastic power.

Thus, on the learned level of medieval Irish literary tradition the figure of the mother-goddess is both buried underground and transformed into that of a territorial sovereignty queen whose autonomy and independent authority is diminished and exploited in the politico-literary propaganda of patrilineal dynasties competing for political hegemony[13]. At the popular 'folk' level, however, the figure of the divine female agency, the mother-goddess of landscape, retains her autonomy and majestic authority in the local lore of place and thereby constitutes a traditional cultural resource contributing richly to the creativity of the popular imagination. All over the Gaelic world in Ireland and Scotland, down to the present age, traditions of the *cailleach*, the supernatural female elder, are to be found attached to natural features of the physical landscape – mountains, lakes, rivers, tumuli, caves whose shape she has moulded and whose location she has fixed – and feature also in the abundant stories of supernatural encounter between humans and the native otherworld within that sacred feminine landscape. In many ways the most prominent of these *cailleacha* is the *Cailleach Bhéarra* or Supernatural Female Elder ('Hag') of Beara, one of the great peninsulas of the south-west Irish coast. Beara is the site of the legendary arrival onto the island of Ireland of the human Gaelic population, the Milesian *Gaeil*, who partially displace the mythological *Tuatha Dé Danann* from their former hegemony and cause them to withdraw from the mundane daylight realm into the subterranean and submarine realms of a sacred landscape in which they remain an immortal presence. *Cailleach Bhéarra*, the hag/mother-goddess of Beara is also known at the learned, literary level as a personification of the territorial sovereignty queen, but it is in her presence in popular tradition that her autonomous creative potential resides. In her person she constitutes, in popular tradition, an overarching female matrix of sovereignty and fertile power that is as vast and as untameable as the wild, wide landscape, and that is yet as nurturing and as intimately fruitful for human beings and for human existence as are the services of the *bean ghlúine* (midwife), the *bean* feasa (wise-woman) and the *bean chaointe* (keening-woman), to name three human female personae whose *cailleach*-inspired (and derived) performance of service to the community was so essential. Proactive, female creativity and power is thus seen, in Irish ancestral culture, to be the major source from which emerges both the general form of the physical universe and the security and well-being of the social order in times of stress.

Cailleach Bhéarra it was, and is, whose power and activities have resulted in the shapes of hills, the courses of lakes and rivers, the locations of islands and the presence in the landscape of numerous other natural features. Thunder storms, tides, wind and wave power, all attest to the energy of her abiding presence in the physical realm. While traditional Irish cosmology has nothing to say of an original moment or agent of creation *ex nihilo* and *ab initio*, it privileges a cosmic, female, geotectonic power that has given shape and form to the world throughout the ages. Nature is renewed eternally in the recounting of the tales of how *Cailleach Bhéarra* impressed herself onto and expresses herself within a landscape made both vital and sacred by association with her divine and sovereign presence.

Cailleach Bhéarra it was, and is – along with other local *cailleacha* – who underwrites and legitimizes the performances and activities of a range of female roles that are filled, on occasion, by flesh-and-blood women whose confidence, authority and actual power in the performance of their services derive not from the indulgence of a largely patriarchal social order, but from an issuing forth into that order of an imperative grounded in the popular sensibility of a primarily female origin and order of being (and well-being) for human existence. Stories of paradigmatic encounters between representative human women and the female otherworld abound and they reinforce, in their retelling, that sensibility to and that confidence in a female creativity that was characteristic of ancestral tradition in Irish culture down to our own era. With the modernization of Ireland – involving language shift, urbanization and industrialization – and with the displacement of ancestral concepts of the native otherworld by the tenets of growing Roman Catholic ecclesiastical orthodoxy, the presence and the power of the creative mother-goddess has been greatly diminished. Within modern Catholic culture the two available archetypal female roles are popularly taken to be those of 'Handmaid of the Lord' and 'Mother of Sorrows', neither of which offers much scope for the exericse of autonomous, female, creative potential. There is, I would argue, undoubtedly a sense in which Irish Catholic devotion to the cult of the Virgin 'Mother of God' owes something of its intensity and loyal endurance to its touching on sensibilities that earlier fed on notions of the 'Mother of the Gods': the female agency who reigned in physical life and whose assistance or hostility was said to account for many of the triumphs and vicissitudes of human existence. Similarly, I would argue that the much vaunted Irish openness to a sense of spiritual transcendence is not unconnected to ancestral, cultural sensibilities regarding an otherworld realm that was imminently close at hand – the realm of the *Sí*[14] – and where it is often a Female Divine who is perceived as reigning in peace and beauty. Indeed the lively susceptibility to interpret life-events in terms of contact with this ancestral otherworld realm is found in popular culture in Ireland and Scotland until relatively recently.

It has been asserted[15] that the authoritative self-assurance of the mythological divine heroine extended to her human counterpart in literature – meaning, largely, medieval literature. One may legitimately ask whether such self-assurance also continued, or could continue today, to have some influence on the status and self-assurance of flesh-and-blood women in society. In pre-modern Ireland it certainly did, as the status and authority of such as the 'wise-woman' and the 'keening-woman' shows, but the creative potential of the *cailleach* archetype should not be regarded as being available to women only. The powerful imaginative resource that *cailleach* legends offer to the contemporary imagination is highly relevant to men and women alike and offers an enrichment of gender relationships that draws deeply on common humanity, while honouring both genders. The original cosmological conception of the mother-goddess/*cailleach*, the repertoire of traditional lore and story associated with her presence and activities in the landscape, and the uses to which today's artists, painters and poets (women and men) are putting her image, can all serve to promote a harmonious relationship between the femine and masculine sides of the individual psyche, between the genders in the social order and between society as a whole and the landscape/environment/cosmos that is envisaged increasingly today as a living and precious entity to be imaginatively venerated and practically honoured in ways similar to those that informed the lives and consciousness of our ancestors. Those ancestors saw, in the image of the *cailleach*, a redemptive icon whose power was based on an adult response to the nature and creative potential for living, of the feminine side of existence and who resisted in narrative and ritual ways the subjugation of the female realm by patriarchal Celts or Christians.

The complex and changing nature of the redemptive icon of the *cailleach* figure in popular narrative tradition in Ireland is something that the texts presented in this work illustrate, in terms both of the texts themselves, as narratives, and of the historical transformations to which the perception and function of the *cailleach* figure has been subject in the narrative traditions of earlier eras. While a discussion of this may be postponed (see p. 71) until the corpus of texts presented here from the early modern era has been commented on and explored in the light of the position this sets forth, some questions of a more general nature regarding representation of the female in the texts of both oral and literary narrative can, however, be adverted to here.

Of central concern to anyone advocating these texts of Irish oral tradition as imaginative resources for a contemporary readership is the basic question of whether the *cailleach* and the *bean feasa* figures which they portray can be anymore than stereotypes of feminity within a patriarchal cultural discourse that, at best, ignores and, at worst, oppresses women and the feminine. Feminist criticism has challenged the claim of the canon of male literature, classic or popular, to embody authentic or representative images of the feminine. The position of the present work is that Irish literary tradition, too, exhibits and exemplifies ways in which the feminine is devalued, displaced and suppressed. However, at the popular, vernacular level of cultural tradition, it would appear that oral narratives, such as the ones gathered here, continued to be performed and transmitted so as to give expression to a sensibility, a worldview, that at least comprehends the complementary nature of the feminine and the masculine in life and its cultural representation. As such, the vernacular, oral narrative traditions of the *cailleach* and the *bean feasa* that our texts exemplify give expression to a less patriarchal cultural discourse than is involved in many ways in the case of either the learned, written literature of the pre-modern era or much of the creative writing tradition of the contemporary world as both of these are interpreted and evaluated within feminist theory.

There has been considerable discussion and debate regarding the portrayal of the feminine in the case of the female characters of the *märchen,* the international wonder tale. While the wonder-tale and the *seanchas*/legend with which this work is concerned, are separate and distinct genres of vernacular oral narrative, it is still useful to look at the wonder-tale and examine the significance for audiences and readers of the heroine in stories of the Cinderella type. Some commentators have emphasized the passive and helpless role that such heroines play in the tales, waiting patiently for emancipation by some Prince Charming male[16]. Others have seen that, even though the individual heroine may be initially presented as powerless and dependent, the manner in which these tales develop emphasizes that, overall, women are often more powerful than men, with real trouble coming from a witch or wicked step-mother figure and real help coming from the figure of a fairy godmother or a wise woman[17]. The more psychoanalytic minded of the commentators have emphasized the mistake of addressing only the surface meaning of the tales and of interpreting their significance only in terms of its plot. The cultural complexity of these *märchen*-type international wonder-tales is not to be underestimated in regard to either the deeper cultural levels of their significance or to the complexity of that significance in terms of the tales' transmission as speech event performances or as the 'oral literature' texts of reading events, when their transmission is taking place in written form. J.E. Heuscher[18] has emphasized the degree to which they are subject to all kinds of modifications of their meaning that depend on the psychological make-up of their narrators and their audiences, as well as on the cultural environment in which their transmission takes place. We can extend this emphasis to their transmission in written form also, where it is the psychological make-up of their *readers* that is a major factor in the interpretation of their significance. Whether as oral stories or as texts of 'oral literature', international wonder-tales of the Cinderella type address the struggles of an individual heroine or hero to win through in life, to attain maturity and enlightenment in the face of the hardships and vicissitudes that life offers[19]. Bruno Bettleheim[20] insists that it is mistaken for critics and commentators to see this struggle in rigidly gendered terms that would assign the achievement of individual success in the winning of maturity and enlightenment to one gender only or exclusively restrict the tales – as models of such achievement – to either men or women. Rather is it the case, Bettleheim would argue, that the tales render symbolically for everyone the possibility of such achievement, of such individual winning through to maturity and success. In this perspective, the division of the characters into male and female identities and roles, at the surface level of plot, is incidental in relation to the deeper psychological significance of the portrayal, in verbal representation and performance, of the human capacity to overcome afflicting circumstances and experiences, in order to achieve enlightenment and happiness.

The question of a feminist coding operating within traditional narrative to express a subversive opposition on the part of women to male domination, is also an important consideration bearing on the kind of material with which this work is concerned. In the essays edited by Joan Radner[21] under the title *Feminist Messages: Coding in Women's Folk Culture*, the focus is on the strategies resorted to and developed by female cultural performers and producers to give expression to knowledge and worldviews different from that of the ruling male order. Specific strategies of such coding are suggested in relation to different cultural forms in a variety of women's cultures. In particular it is suggested that implicit coding strategies in women's vernacular cultural performances make potentially accessible to a female audience messages regarding themselves and their experiences that express ideas and values that are at variance with – perhaps diametrically opposed to – those of the prevailing male ideology. While the political and social ideology of the early modern Ireland from which our texts derive was certainly male oriented, it is the case, however, that the texts in question are the result of male transmission/performance, in almost every case, so that any feminist message which they encompass is not of the same implicitly coded variety with which Joan Radner's book is concerned. Specifically Radner and Lanser[22] refer to Peig Sayers, the Blasket Islands storyteller and her propensity, in narrating the kind of tales that were, in Irish tradition, normally the preserve of the male storyteller, to institute major changes of pace, tone and emphasis so as 'to focus attention on the hard lot of women, their courage and their need to stand by one another in a patriarchal world'. On the other hand, the message that we can attribute to the male transmitters of the legends of the *cailleach* and the *bean feasa* that are found in Part Two, is that essentially feminine conceptions of power and wisdom operate along with and outside of male authority in the patriarchal world and that such conceptions are traditionally resorted to and invoked to contain and make meaningful both occasional experiences of affliction and prevailing physical and sociocultural contexts of human existence. These legends render symbolically as do the *märchen*, in the more psychodyamic reading, the possibility of the achievement of security and wisdom – perhaps, security in wisdom – by the individual man and woman. The *märchen* are of the specialized narrative type whose telling requires the verbal excellence of a gifted narrator; also, they are of international provenance. Our texts, however, are legends; they are accounts of popular lore, of local provenance and not restricted in their telling and transmission to the institutionalized performance of the gifted narrator.

Despite the differences of *genre* and of the contexts in which, as oral narrative, the transmission of *cailleach/bean feasa* stories takes place, these stories, too, whether in spoken or written form, show in their own way how meaningfulness and relief can be achieved in affliction and how ancestral imaginative frameworks regarding the personified operations of cosmic power and cosmic forces can provide archetypal resources for the attainment of meaningfulness in the face of life experience. Men and women alike, whether in the pre-modern communities in which these legends circulated in oral transmission, or in the contemporary world where these legends are encountered in written form, have presented to them, as speech-event or as text, narrative accounts of how human individuals (humanly identical to themselves), were enabled to interpret and to cope with the circumstances and the consequences of their being-in-the-world, and give symbolic verbal articulation and representation to that knowledge. Whether regarded as literature or folklore, the *cailleach* and *bean feasa* stories presented here are powerful and potentially therapeutic expressions of creative imaginative life. They are imaginative products of past Irish vernacular cultural tradition but have the capacity to contribute creatively to the cultural imagination of today's world too, in ways that can be guided and legitimated by reference to the cosmological and historical contexts of their composition. The commentaries that accompany the texts offered in Part Two are a contribution to the prospect of readers engaging with them in a way that illuminates their significance as traditional stories and releases their potential as imaginative cultural resources for application by readers to issues of contemporary cultural and individual life.

Given the continued presence of both the figure and the symbolic functions of the otherworld female in the narratives and rituals of Irish vernacular culture on the brink, so to speak, of the modern and postmodern worlds of contemporary culture and society, we should consider aspects of the Irish *cailleach/bean feasa* traditions in the light of issues relating both to feminist literary criticism and to (chiefly) Jungian psychotherapeutic insight. The question of how genuinely representative of the feminine the female figures of a largely male-dominated literary and oral narrative tradition can be has already been raised. Some brief, further discussion of it is appropriate here since a central assertion of this book is that traditional narratives of Irish folklore, such as the legends presented and commented on in Part Two, are evidence of an allegiance to and an articulation of a conception of the reality of human life, externalized in Irish vernacular culture, that both recognizes and honours the feminine as an essential and creatively powerful and productive aspect of that reality. That the great majority of the texts of these legends are the outcome of male transmission and male verbal performance is, in itself, evidence that the worldview which they externalize is a representation of feminine consciousness not entirely obliterated or devalued by the inscription of male structures of power. Despite the patriarchal nature of the social organization and the society within which legends of the *cailleach* and the *bean feasa* circulated in oral transmission over many generations, there has also been cultural space for the presence and the authority of the otherworld female and the feminine to be rendered and represented after a fashion that has the potential to articulate, in an authentic way, the feminine side of human consciousness. Such articulation, in the form of legend-narration concerning the *cailleach* and the *bean feasa,* is vitally sustained and renewed, in performance, as a source of wisdom and therapy. It is also brought to bear, imaginatively, in the narrative performance of the legends, on the life experience of the individual men and women who constitute these legends' interpretative community of *listeners.* In the understanding of culture and cultural process which this book espouses, contemporary *readers* can engage imaginatively with these stories as 'literature', and so release their creative potential as articulations of the poetics of a worldview in which both the male and female orders of consciousness are recognized as standing in positive and active complementary relationship in the cosmos, the environment, the social world and the individual psyche. Such a comprehension of the significance and function of these legends, in both the pre-modern and modern worlds, depends on certain understandings regarding the nature of cultural knowledge and cultural process as well as of individual personhood in the context of that cultural process of communication and social construction.

As regards cultural knowledge and personal identity, the basic insight required, in terms of the position maintained here, is that meaning and identification emerge from the actions of both narrator and audience, writer and readers, in a process of joint or communal creativity, participation in which affords the opportunity for the private application of the significance of the legend to the circumstances of the individual life of the hearer or reader. Neither the 'text' and its 'subject' – the *cailleach* or the *bean feasa* – nor its recipient listener or reader can be reduced to an already-known, meaning or single identity that is consciously and deliberately given, along the lines of Cartesian conceptions of unified subject, fixed categories of gender or a male-derived determination of the definition and function of the feminine. Rather is it the case that these stories, encountered as 'literature' – whether in the narrative or written mode – promote a sense of the possibility of transcending the boundaries of conventional experience and conventional identity in terms of an imaginative creativity that both renews the vitality of the legend itself as an expression of cultural knowledge, and nurtures and enriches the cultural knowledge and the lives of its listeners and readers as themselves subjects-in-process.

The position outlined here can be seen as suggesting a repositioning of the location from which the feminine can be expected to speak, in terms of oral narrative tradition at least, if not in terms of creative writing too. We are seeing how in the literary texts of learned culture in medieval Irish tradition, the figure and the significance of the otherworld female was displaced and devalued. In the eyes of feminist criticism, today, this would bespeak a corresponding denial and discrimination of the feminine in terms of social oppression in the domestic and civil experience of individual women, and one of the central aims of feminist criticism has been to expose what Elaine Showalter has termed 'the misogyny of literary practice'[23]. An initial impetus of what we might term the Anglo-American school of feminist criticism had been to uncover the 'lost' or 'hidden' canon and dynamic of a female literary tradition. The Continental (largely French-language) school of feminist criticism, on the other hand, looking to the insights of linguistics and psychoanalysis rather than of history and sociology, raised fundamental questions regarding the possibility of the feminine achieving any authentic representation in symbolic verbal or literary form. Accepting the psychic reality, as formulated in the writings of Jacques Lacan, that in the development of the human psyche in infancy, symbolism, language, the sense of self and subjectivity develop in such a way as to surpass the feminine aspect of consciousness and leave only the possibility of expression for the masculine subject, feminist critics such as Julia Kristeva, Luce Irigaray and Hélène Cixous have taken the position that it is futile to seek any authentically feminine writing or literary representation in the past. They wish, instead, to identify and promote alternative channels and modalities for the expression of the feminine – such as poetry, rune, chant, incantation, dream – as proposed, for instance, by Janet Todd[24]. A succinct and penetrating presentation of these complex issues is to be found in the essay entitled '*An Bhean is an Bhaineann: Gnéithe Den Chritic Fheimineach*' [The Female and Femininity: Aspects of Feminist Criticism] by the feminist critic Bríona Nic Dhiarmada.[25] They have been, of course, a staple of the late twentieth-century academic discourse of the Western world, as reflected, for example, in such as the David Lodge edited Reader[26] in modern and post-modern literary theory and cultural criticism or, more specifically in a feminist frame, in the Critical Reader[27] edited by Mary Eagleton and treating of specifically feminist literary theory.

Along with the theoretical impossibility – from a psychoanalytic point of view – of the achievement by the feminine of authentic voice or symbolic representation in language and literature, because of a primordial, psychic suppression/ejection of the feminine, there is the specific historical consideration of the displacement and stigmatization of the figure of autonomous, female, cosmic agency in the political ideology and learned literature of early medieval Ireland. One may speculate as to whether other Western ideological and literary traditions involve a similar turn-against-the-feminine that can be associated with specific stages of cultural change. The spread and adoption of Christianity suggests itself, in this regard, as a significant cultural transformation, given the suspicion of and even hostility to the feminine which many leading Christian thinkers and writers expressed in the early medieval period. Again, an excellent Irish-language survey of this issue, together with a penetrating analysis of its consequences for later, and indeed contemporary Irish literary tradition and practice, is available as a major contribution to the debate in Máirín Nic Eoin's book *B'Ait Leo Bean*.[28]

The figures and the stories of the *cailleach* and the *bean feasa* presented here are not, it should be noted, restricted to some kind of female repertoire of Irish vernacular culture, but circulate and are transmitted onwards, in the verbal performance of male and female narrators alike. As such they constitute, it seems to me, a noteworthy presence in Irish cultural process, present and past, of the feminine – conceived of, honoured, yielded to – as important and powerful. This presence and this power is located, not primarily in texts but in the dynamic and creative discourse of an artistic-like narration and performance whose other essential face is the reception and imaginative interpretation work of an audience (and a readership) who participate equally with the narrator in the discourse.

In suggesting that these legends operated, and can continue to operate, as expressive verbal forms within Irish vernacular culture, in a way that can be seen to exemplify, to an extent, the psychodynamic processes of continual transformation and reconstruction to which 'self' and 'person' are subject in the course of social and symbolic life, I want to emphasize again how wide of the mark is the view of folklore as consisting of cultural materials that are static, unitary, bounded or closed. Rather than being static, outmoded or regressive, these materials of Irish folk tradition can constitute a creative contribution to the life of the imagination today and to the imaginative enrichment of individuals who care to engage with them in creative ways. Encountered in such a fashion, the texts and rituals of Irish folklore that feature the figure and the function of the ancestral Irish otherworld female can bear living witness to – and enable access to – sources of imaginative creativity and vitality that deserve to be known more widely.

Historical displacement of the autonomous female

This section of Part One presents and comments on what we may call literary acts of displacement and demonization in respect of the figure and character of the ancestral, autonomous otherworld female of Irish tradition. These prose tales and one poem are discussed as possible evidence of how, in medieval literature, the figure of the otherworld female is deprived of her autonomous sovereignty.

Emain Macha
The medieval story that tells how *Emain Macha* (Navan Fort) near Armagh, got its name, was published by Whitley Stokes[1] and can be summarized as follows:

> Three Ulster kings, *Dithorba*, *Aed Ruad* and *Cimbaeth*, ruled over Ireland in joint sovereignty. Each of them had the kingship for seven years in turn. The arrangement was secured by the sureties of seven druids, seven poets and seven chieftains i.e. in terms of spells and satire and physical force.
> When each of them had been king three times, *Aed Ruad*, the first of them to die, was drowned in *Eas Ruad* and was buried there in the *Sí*, the otherworld mound. His daughter, *Macha Mongruad* demanded her father's turn of the kingship. *Cimbaeth* and *Dithorba* would not surrender the kingship to a woman but she routed them in battle and ruled for seven years. *Dithorba* then died and left five sons who claimed the kingship. *Macha* routed them in battle and banished them to Connaught. Then she married *Cimbaeth*.
> *Macha* visited *Dithorba*'s sons disguised as a hag. One by one they attempt to lie with her but she ties them up and brings them all back to Ulster. Rather than kill them there, she ordered them to dig a ring-fort, as a capital for Ulster and marked out the extent of the fort with the pin of her golden brooch.
> This happened four hundred and five years before Christ and *Emain Macha* lasted as Ulster's capital until four hundred and fifty years after Christ was born.

This tale, from the twelfth-century compilation of *Dindshenchas Érenn* (the Placelore of Ireland) contained in the Book of Leinster, tells how *Emain*

Macha the mythical capital of Ulster, located in a great bronze-age ringfort to the west of Armagh (*Ard Macha*), got its name. It is one of three such accounts, which attribute the name to events involving three different personifications of the goddess *Macha*, the divine autonomous personification of Ulster territorial sovereignty. In this account of the naming of *Emain Macha* the goddess is portrayed as the only daughter of one of three kings who rule Ireland in a joint-sovereignty arrangement. We can take this triple kingship as representing the human, male ruler side of the *hieros gamos*, the sacred marriage of Indo-European and Celtic myth, whereby the royal ruler has as his divine spouse the goddess personification of his territory. In this case the archaic triple nature of the goddess is reflected in the joint reign of three kings, each of whom is to reign in succession, for three seven-year periods in turn.

The otherworld overtones of this arrangement of kings are reflected in the sureties they have, between them, to enforce the cycle of succession: seven druids with their spells, seven warrior-chieftains with their weapons and seven poets with their satires. Thus is invoked the mystical principal of 'prince's truth' (*fír flatha*), a decree that ensures that both land and society will be fertile and will thrive as long as the proper king rules justly. We are reminded here of Julia Kristeva's assertion[2] of the archaic primacy of a woman's time of cyclical, reproductive, cosmic rhythm lying behind history and contrasting with a male linear chronology of progress and historical succession and mortality. When one of the kings in this tale dies – falling out, as it were, of woman's time and disrupting the cycles of sovereignty arrangement – his only child, a daughter, seeks to replace him. At the level of history, of male royal succession, this is opposed as an impossibility by the other two kings; they 'would not surrender the kingship to a woman'.

This woman, daughter of *Aed Ruad* (Aed the Red) has the name *Macha Mongruad*, (Macha of the Red Hair), and she is, in terms of Irish mythic tradition, to be taken as representing the mother goddess cum sovereignty queen spouse to whom her father, as king, has been mystically united. We are told that he died by drowning in *Eas Ruad* (the Red Falls on the River Erne), associated in another tale cycle with the salmon of knowledge, who lived there, fed by the nuts of the hazel tree of wisdom which grew in that place. The hazel tree with its nuts, the salmon and the colour term *Ruad* (red) all have strong associations with the otherworld, and we can understand that Aed's drowning in *Eas Ruad* marks his absorption into that otherworld from which he is replaced by his daughter as representative of the divine, autonomous, female agency who is the personification of the otherworld realm in native Irish tradition. In claiming the kingship in place of her father, *Macha Mongruad* is here reasserting the otherworld female source of sovereignty and opposing historical male succession on behalf of woman's time.

We can also note the way that *Aed Ruad*'s death symbolically complements rather than disrupts the terms of the mystical principles involved in the original arrangement, whereby the three kings reigned subject to the mystical nature of the sureties between them that guaranteed their sovereignty relationships with each other and with the otherworld female sovereignty principal from whom their legitimacy as royal rulers derived. The sureties with which they were bound are comprised of, on the one hand, the otherworld powers of incantation (the druids) and of satire (the poets), and, on the other, of the martial powers of death-dealing in terms of wounding and burning (the warrior-chieftains). Wounding and burning are two of the three kinds of death-dealing that are found linked in the notion of a ritual triple-death. This triple-death motif is associated, in Celtic and Irish tradition, with the legendary triple-killing of the king at *Samhain* (Hallowe'en) and with the symbolic cyclic renewal thereby of otherworld female sovereignty and male royal rule. *Aed*'s death is by drowning, the third kind of death in the triple-death motif, and just as *Aed* is taken from his kingship into the otherworld, so the reign of the other two kings, *Dithorba* and *Cimbaeth*, is symbolically brought to an end too; *Aed*'s drowning is the symbolic equivalent of the subjection to death by wounding and burning (in the terms of the violation of their sureties) of the other two. *Macha Mongruad* proceeds to give effect, in practice, to the ending of the reign of *Dithorba* and *Cimbaeth*, 'routing them in the fight' when they jointly engage in battle with her, in an attempt to oppose male authority to the autonomous sovereignty figure.

Macha, we are told, 'spent seven years in the kingship' a figure that echoes the cyclical rhythm of woman's time and, at the end of that period, reasserts and renews her female, otherworld sovereignty in the routing, on the battlefield, with much slaughter, of the five sons of *Dithorba*, whom she banishes into the Western wastelands, in exile from the social centre of Ulster power and from symbolic accession to sovereignty. Following on this double reclaiming of sovereignty by the female otherworld agency as an autonomous force we are told that *Macha* 'took *Cimbaeth* to be her husband and to lead her soldiery for her'.

In choosing *Cimbaeth*, *Macha* is here exercising the divine female autonomy of a mother-goddess/sovereignty queen in her primordial, independent role. She is not subject to the political ambition of competing male lineages who, in the development of the sovereignty queen myth, transform the divine female sovereignty principle from that of the chooser to that of the 'chosen', making her a kind of political prize, a reward for the attainment of historical, male, political hegemony. The remainder of the tale reinforces this sense of *Macha Mongruad* as a sovereign, autonomous, female force.

In the later development of the sovereignty queen myth, where the otherworld female is the passive icon of male hegemony, we find many tellings of the classic situation wherein the eponymous ruler-to-be – the founder of the dynasty – is said to encounter the mother goddess in the form of a hideous crone and to have the courage to respond to her invitation. This kiss, or embrace, or act of coition transforms the hag into the beautiful, radiant young sovereignty queen who then confers legitimacy of royal rule on the male and his descendants into the future. In the present tale, the classic trope is subverted and made to vindicate the power and autonomy of the goddess. Having previously routed *Dithorba*'s sons and exiled them to Connaught, she now tricks them, while disguised in repulsive form, into attempting to lie with her on the lines of the classic king-to-be/hag encounter that results in male empowerment. What results here is the defeat, capture and humiliation of all five of the prospective claimants of royal status and their prostration back in Ulster before the forces of *Cimbaeth*, the proper king, chosen by her in autonomous exercise of the primordial sovereignty principle.

In declining to have the sons of *Dithorba* killed, as is the wish of the Ulstermen, *Macha* invokes and reinforces the *fír flatha* principle, of just and generous and unblemished sovereign, royal rule. Having firmly fixed this proper order of things in the political world, *Macha* withdraws into the landscape itself and its dominant feature, the great bronze-age ringfort, which, in this tale is dug and built about her as marker of her enduring presence and sovereignty in the territory of the Ulstermen. We are given an etymology for the name *Emain* which purports to derive from the golden brooch that she wore at her neck the pin of which has been used to trace out for her the site of the great ringfort. In this we get a glimpse of the superhuman scale of the goddess as a gigantic presence dominating the landscape, something that endures in the figure and stories of the *cailleach*/hag-goddess of later, vernacular tradition, in which the autonomous sovereignty of a mother-goddess in the natural world continues to be proclaimed. At the learned and literary level of creative narrative and political propaganda, however, the autonomous figure of a *Macha* is transformed into a more pliant female, subservient to the political ambitions, aspirations, and redefinitions of tradition on the part of leaders and lineages operating in men's time, with its linear chronology of heroic accomplishments, mortality and historic succession. This is itself reflected in the present tale in the concluding passage which gives a calculation of the actual, historic reign of the *Ulaid*, the Ulster dynasties whose political hegemony was narratively derived, as in the present story, from the autonomous, female, otherworld, sovereignty personification whose presence and whose name is manifested in the land itself, in *Emain Macha* which is 'Ulster's chief city forever'.

Echtra mac nEchach Muigmedóin

> The king of Ireland, *Eochaid Muigmedón,* had five sons, *Brian, Ailill, Fiachra, Fergus* and *Niall. Mongfhind* was the mother of *Brian, Ailill, Fiachra* and *Fergus* but *Niall*'s mother was *Cairenn. Mongfhind* hated *Niall.* She had made his mother suffer greatly when she was in child with him. When *Niall* was born *Cairenn* abandoned him and no one else would help him for fear of *Mongfhind* and her magical power. But *Torna,* the poet, rescued the boy and made a prophecy that he would rule Ireland as the great *Niall* of the Nine Hostages and that his descendants would rule Ireland forever.

This eleventh-century tale, occurring in written form in the fourteenth century *Lebor Buide Lecain,* (Yellow Book of Lecan), and also published by Whitley Stokes,[3] illustrates two central aspects of the process whereby the figure of the autonomous, otherworld female is devalued and rejected and is displaced in the learned narrative tradition by the subservient and acquiescent figure of the sovereignty queen as handmaid, as it were, of the powerful male ruler. In this tale, recounting the Adventure of the Sons of *Eochaid Muigmedón,* we have presented to us as a baleful, unjust and evil character, the person of *Mongfhind,* queen and spouse of 'wondrous and noble king over Erin', *Eochaid Muigmedón.* Her status as queen, mother of the four young royals and heirs to the kingship and her name *Mongfhind* (the Fair Haired One, the White/Sacred queen), hint at her identity within native narrative tradition, as a representative of the mother-goddess, joined in the mystical union of the *hiros gamos,* the sacred marriage uniting territory and its eternal sovereignty principle with male, mortal ruler. Here, however, it is the destructive, terrible side of the goddess, inimical to human welfare, that is emphasized from the outset. We can understand this as showing the response of the primordial, divine, female figure to her prescient foreknowledge of the imminent appropriation, in historical, man's time, of hegemony and political prominence by the *Uí Néill* dynasty; the status and authority of the goddess is reduced from that of autonomous chooser of her succession of human spouses (c.f. *Meadhbh*) to being merely a foreteller of their royal reign. In this latter role the divine female is seen pronouncing for the hero and eponymous dynastic founder in grateful return for an embrace deigned to her despite her loathsome and repellent aspect.

If *Mongfhind*, the divine female with luxuriant, flowing, fair hair, is the mother of four sons – aspirants to royal rule within the rhythmic cosmic cycles of women's time which is the context of *Eochaid*'s rule – then the fifth son, *Niall*, is immediately presented in the tale as deriving from and representing another order of things; the secular, historical, male order in which *Eochaid* has had – presumably non-mystical – union with *Cairenn Casdub*, daughter of the king of the Saxons in England. By dramatic contrast to *Mongfhind*, *Cairenn* is named *Cairenn Casdub* (*Cairenn* of the tight black curls), a naming that lacks entirely, within native tradition, the otherworld intimations of the name of the mother of *Niall*'s stepbrothers. The portrayal of *Mongfhind*'s hatred for *Cairenn* and the portrayal of her harsh, inimical treatment of *Cairenn*, even in childbirth, is designed to dislodge *Mongfhind* from her role as sovereign goddess, despite her great *cumachta sí* (otherworld powers). It is not the goddess, here, but *Torna*, the male poet – a calling itself endowed in tradition with substantial otherworld association – who is the agent by whom the greatness-to-come of *Niall* is revealed; this having been revealed to him when he 'took the boy into his bosom'. Since later in the story *Niall* himself will have his royal destiny and that of his descendants revealed to him following on his embracing or 'taking to his bosom' of the loathsome hag, we can see in *Torna*'s embrace of *Cairenn*'s son a foreshadowing of the later encounter in which a *Mongfhind* replacement pronounces and confers sovereignty in perpetuity on the line, not in the woman's time succession of *Mongfhind*'s sons, but on the descendants of *Niall*, the hero-warrior of hostages, of battles, of the shedding of blood. If woman's time and its recurrent, reproductive cycles are, essentially, incalculable (as in Kristeva's view), then the existence in men's time of the historical progress, achievement and mortality of *Niall* and his line is signalled in the pronouncement by the poet *Torna* of the prospective rule of *Niall* for twenty-seven years and the tale's further exact identification of the time, place and agent of *Niall*'s death on a Saturday afternoon, on the sea-shore, at the hands of another *Eochaid*.

Later in the story when *Mongfhind* conspires with her four sons so as to bring about the death of *Niall*, *Torna*'s counsel – reflecting in the narrative, 'the voice of the men of *Erin*, that *Niall* should be king after his father' – saves *Niall* from *Mongfhind*'s enmity. She sends the four sons along with *Niall* to *Sithchenn*, the smith, for new arms and having supplied the arms, the smith tells them to go and hunt and try them. 'So then the sons went and hunted', we are told, but they went astray. There follows a paradigmatic account of the encounter of *Niall* (eponymous leader-to-be) with the sovereignty queen in her political-prize role as an unnamed hag-goddess who is transformed by the hero's embrace, an embrace that wins for him from her (whatever her disposition), the conferring of sovereignty on himself and his descendants. 'Henceforth', the wizard magic Smith pronounces – echoing and confirming the judgement of *Torna* and now the nameless sovereignty figure who has become the mouthpiece of 'the men of *Erin*' (where she has previously in the persons of *Macha Mongruad* and of *Mongfhind* been an autonomous agency choosing her mortal royal spouse) – 'he and his children will always have the domination and kingship of *Erin*'.

Aided Chrimthainn maic Fidaig

Another tale, found also in the Yellow Book of Lecan and again published by Stokes,[4] again features *Mongfhind* as the spouse of *Eochaid Muigmedón* and makes even more dramatically clear the rejection and displacement of the autonomous divine female and her expulsion from the realm of historical human affairs, politics and society. She is shown – from the learned narrative point of view – to belong, henceforth, as a demonized figure, to the murky margins of magic and witchcraft and superstition. The tale may be summarized as follows:

> *Eochaid* ruled Ireland as king. His spouse was *Mongfhind* and she bore him four sons, *Brian* and *Fiachra*, *Ailill* and *Fergus*. Their mother dreamed a prophetic dream of their destiny in which her favourite, *Brian*, was champion. When *Eochaid* died and his kingship was to go, not to *Brian*, but to *Niall*, who was also *Eochaid*'s son, but not hers, *Mongfhind* schemed so that her own brother, *Crimthann* would become king instead. While *Crimthann* was abroad in Scotland, *Mongfhind*'s son took the kingdom. When *Crimthann* returned to do battle with them, *Mongfhind* made a false peace between them and arranged a banquet for the opposing sides at which she planned to poison her brother, *Crimthann*, so that her favourite, *Brian*, could become king. To get her brother to do so, she has to drink the poison, too, and she died on the eve of *Samhain*. This was the death of *Mongfhind* the *bean sí*, the otherworld female. *Samhain* is known to the rabble as *Mongfhind*'s feastday and women and common people make petition to her at *Samhain*-eve.

The tale begins by presenting the royal couple. *Eochaid* is 'a noble, venerable king' who had 'assumed the realm of *Erin*' and his spouse *Mongfhind* is, we are told, 'a spouse befitting him'. This 'befitting' carries, in Irish narrative and cosmological tradition, the sense of the otherworld identity of *Mongfhind* as sovereignty queen, given the *hieros gamos* nature of kingship as a royal office wedded to the divine personification of territory. This sense of otherworld identity is further reflected in *Mongfhind's* having a prophetic dream concerning her four sons, whom she has had with *Eochaid* and on whom, as representative of the autonomous female otherworld agency, she wishes to confer future royal sovereignty. Conversely, *Mongfhind*'s human status is reflected in her consulting of the 'wizard' or druid, *Sithchenn*, regarding the significance of her dream. In his reading of her dream, *Sithchenn* confirms to *Mongfhind* that sovereignty and future kingship will indeed adhere to her children, and in particular, to *Brian*, 'the darling of her children'.

When, however, *Eochaid* died, there was, we are told, 'a huge contest about his heritage' and it is a contest between *five* sons of his, since a fifth son, *Niall* exists. He is not the issue of the union of *Eochaid* with *Mongfhind* but – as is made clear in the other narrative about them (though it is not stated in this one) – of another union that *Eochaid* has had with another spouse, *Cairenn Casdub*, daughter of the king of England. What is being registered here is a challenge out of the male time realm of history and political alliance to the women's time order of succession to kingship, represented by *Mongfhind* and her dream. In response to this challenge, *Mongfhind* attempts to have her son *Brian* – her choice of future king – acquire the hero-warrior qualities necessary to gain kingship of the realm in male-time order. To this end she will send him overseas 'to learn soldiership', buying time for his conversion to the status of political, warrior-royal aspirant by persuading the men of Ireland to confer the kingship temporarily on her brother *Crimthann*. That she is able to do this – using, we are told, the arts of magic, sorcery and witchcraft – is both a confirmation of her otherworld identity as spouse of the king and a repositioning of her in the narrative as an agency inimical to the male world of politics and political, as distinct from mystical, succession. *Brian* goes to *Alba* (Scotland), and becomes 'a leader in every art of valour and prowess', a fitting warrior successor to the kingship within the male time dispensation. One recalls similar overseas apprenticeships in the martial arts served by other famous warrior heroes, *Cúchulainn*, for example, and *Fionn Mac Cumhaill*.

In *Mongfhind*'s plan, *Brian* would assume the kingship from her brother *Crimthann*, on his return from *Alba*, at the end of his seven-year warrior-royal formation. The elapse of seven years is, in itself, an indication that male-time order has now been irrevocably established, even in the person and reign of *Mongfhind*'s own brother, whom we now see travelling, in royal progress, throughout the whole of the territory of Ireland, as if confirming and reinforcing the sense of a male sovereignty, maintained by political alliance and military might, rather than by the writ of any sovereignty goddess.

This patrimony of *Crimthann*, representative figure, now, of the new male-time order of sovereignty and succession, is attacked by *Mongfhind*'s four sons, in manifestation of her opposition to that patrimony's threat to the primordial women's time sovereignty dispensation. We can note the significance of their dividing the re-assumption of primordial sovereignty into three, in reflection of the triple nature of the archaic mother-goddess personification we have already noted in connection with the three kings who share royal rule at the beginning of the *Emain Macha* tale. *Mongfhind*'s four sons are to be understood as a triple projection of her sovereignty personification together with a condensation and intensification of the three into the complementary and unitary fourth son, *Brian*.

When *Crimthann* marshals his warrior armies to do battle with *Mongfhind*'s sons – and thereby to oppose, with violence, the women's time sovereignty principle which *Mongfhind* represents and personifies – she attempts to literally disarm the opposing force by attempting to transpose the confrontation from the battlefield to the banqueting hall, where she proposes to administer poison to *Crimthann*, in a resort to sorcery-like tactics. The drink of sovereignty, an element of the ritual trope whereby the goddess traditionally confers legitimacy of sovereign rule on her chosen spouse/ruler-to-be, is here changed into a cup of poison that, in symbolic reversal, is intended to put an end to the sovereign rule of *Crimthann*, and, through him, the whole of male-time sovereign rule, thereby restoring primordial, sovereignty queen, royal order in the reign of her son *Brian*. This set-piece opposition of the two orders of sovereignty climaxes, at the end of the banquet, in the dramatic mortal balance between the two orders when *Crimthann*, with the cup of poison in his hand, says 'I will not drink unless you drink first.' A change, a transposition of immense mythological and cosmological significance is poised to take effect. *Mongfhind* drinks and 'then drinks *Crimthann*', and the human world is never quite the same again. The primordial sovereignty principle, deriving from autonomous, otherworld, female agency is overthrown violently and its sacred sovereign personification, *Mongfhind*, mother goddess, autonomous sovereignty queen *alter ego* and former quasi-divine royal spouse, is rejected and expelled from the world of human affairs – the world that matters to the purveyors of patriarchal power. This is indeed 'The Death of *Mongfhind* the Banshee' (*bean sí*, otherworld sacred female). We can note that in the original Irish this 'Death' is rendered as '*Aided*', a technical literary term meaning 'Violent Death'. The violence involved here is, on the surface of the story, the violence of the self-administration of the poison, but it is also, surely, the violence of the smashing of the status and power of the autonomous, sovereign female and the violence of her ignominious displacement and degrading – in patriarchal narrative eyes – to the rank of a 'banshee' and a witch.

We are told that it was precisely on the eve of *Samhain*, (1 November, the Christian Hallowe'en), that *Mongfhind* died, and that 'the rabble' regard

1 November as *Mongfhind*'s Feast. This observation by the author/scribe is of very considerable importance since it is direct, contemporary fourteenth-century witness to a continued allegiance in Irish vernacular culture (in folk religion and in folklore) to the figure and significance of *Mongfhind*, a version of the female, divine agency, to whom, we are told, petitions are made, at *Samhain* by women and by the common people. This juxtaposition of categories hints at the displacement of the female which this story encompasses, in an 'aside' which affords us a very rare glimpse of imaginative and ritual aspects of non-official or popular, vernacular worldview in earlier Irish tradition. Marie-Louise Sjoestedt has written of this passage:

> It is an instance of the preservation of one of those ancient conservative cults by the less cultivated classes, while they have fallen into the background of the epic tradition, ousted by the prestige of the great male gods.[3]

It is from the traditions of such a displaced or submerged worldview and lifestyle that mythological legends of the *cailleach* and the wise-woman come to us in the repertoire of oral narrative of later generations of 'the common people' (the 'rabble' of our present tale).

Our present tale describes how *Crimthann* too, expired as an outcome of the momentous events of that *Samhain* banquet involving the two orders of sovereignty: that of the autonomous goddess and that of the subservient-to-patriarchy queen whose conferring of royal legitimacy is, as it were, done to order, the order of a political propaganda that serves the interests of historical male succession. *Crimthann* is immured, along with his parents and his foster mother, in a grave-mound at the Mountain-of-the-Throne, a kind of masculine replica of the immuring of *Macha* in the sacred site that locates the mythical centre of *Ulaid* sovereignty and authority for succeeding generations. The succeeding generations of the *Ulaid* (the Ulstermen, of the *Emain Macha* story), can be understood to have reigned in a sacred, female-centred cosmos for as long as the *Ulaid* prevailed (a span of 855 years in the earlier tale), whereas it is *Niall* and his lineal descendants who constitute the succeeding generations who are in this tale to reign and wield royal power in the aftermath of the breaking of the power and position of the goddess. The remainder of the text – another eleven sections following what has been summarized here – recounts the course of the battles of succession and the territorial campaigns of history waged by the descendants of *Brian* and *Crimthann* who operate in a patriarchal cosmos showing little sign of any awareness of otherworld female agency as the origin of their ruling powers.

In the course of time during which, in prehistoric and early medieval Ireland, the female-centred cosmos (personified in the divine figures of such as *Meadhbh* and *Macha* and *Mongruad*) is transformed into the patriarchal cosmos in which the power of the autonomous goddess is appropriated to the historico-political ends of dynastic propaganda, Christianity becomes established in Ireland as another powerful force transforming and displacing the significance of the figure of the divine female. We have seen how, in the tale of the death of *Crimthann*, *Mongfhind* is demonized into the figure of a witch-hag. A major text illustrating this displacement and devaluing – from the Christian perspective – is the ninth-century poem, 'The Lament of the Old Woman of Beare', described as the greatest poem in Old Irish and the subject of much scholarly debate.

The Lament of the Old Woman of Beare

Put by its author – whose gender we cannot definitely determine – into the mouth of a female, the poem delivers a moving articulation of the transience of human life in metaphors and allusions that are heavy with reference to the displacement and appropriation of the archaic autonomy of female agency. Ostensibly an expression of the resignation and acceptance of God's will by an elderly widow who has withdrawn from the world to end her days in a Christian religious community, the poem also gives powerful expression to an alternative dispensation. This dispensation is that of the pre-Christian, ancestral cosmology wherein the female endures as ever-renewed divine agency of the land, the shore and its life-forms and in the ever-renewed agency of the glorious sovereignty queen, choosing to be joined in mystical union with a succession of mortal male rulers for whom she represents nurture and fertility. The poem thus combines in a highly sophisticated manner, the linguistic and emotional embodiment of the apprehension of individual human mortality with the mythological and symbolic embodiment of an apprehension of the ambivalence of ideological context in which this mortality is to be understood. Along with conveying the poet's and the culture's acknowledgement of the destiny of the soul to progress to the eternal Christian otherworld of heaven, the poem conveys also a co-existing resistance to that destiny, in a palpable emotional allegiance to the reality and the renewals of the cycles in a kind of terrestrial marine eternity whose sovereign godhead is more ancestral otherworld female than Christian deity.

The following passages from the poem and its prose introduction are quoted, as illustration, from the edition and translation by Professor Donncha Ó hAodha:[6]

1
Aithbe damsa bés mara;
sentu fom-dera croan;

toirsi oca ce do-gnéo,
sona do-táet a loan.

2
Is mé Caillech Bérre Buí,
do-meilinn léne mbithnuí;
indíu táthum dom shémi
ná melainn cid athléni.

7
Tocair mo chorp co n-aichri
dochum adba díar aichni;
tan bas mithig la Mac nDé do-té do breith a aithni.

8
Ot é cnámacha cáela
ó do-éctar mo láma –
ba hinmainiu, tan, gnítis:
bítis im ríga ána.

9
Ó do-éctar mo láma
ot é cnámacha cáela,
nidat fiu turcbáil, taccu,
súas tarna maccu cáema.

10
It fáilti na hingena
ó thic dóib co Beltaine;
is deithbiriu damsa brón:
sech am tróg, am sentaine.

22
Aminecán morúar dam
– cech dercoin is erchraide –
iar feis fri condlib sorchaib
bith i ndorchaib derrthaige.

23
Rom-boí denus la ríga
ic ól meda is fína;
indíu ibim medcuisce
itir sentanaib crína.

33
Mo thuile,
is maith con-roíter m'aithne;
ro-sháer Ísu Mac Muire
conám toirsech co aithbe.

34
Céin-mair ailén mara máir,
dos-n-ic tuile íarna tráig;
is mé, ni frescu dom-í
tuile tar éisi aithbi.

35
Is súaill mennatán indíu
ara tabrainnse aithgne;
a n-í ro boí for tuile
atá uile for aithbe.

1 Ebb-tide to me as to the sea; old age causes me to be sallow; although I may grieve thereat, it comes to its food joyfully.

2 I am the Old Woman of Beare, from Dursey; I used to wear a smock that was always new. Today I am become so thin that I would not wear out even a cast-off smock.

7 Bitterly does my body seek to go to a dwelling where it is known; when the Son of God deems it time, let Him come to carry off His deposit.

8 When my arms are seen, all bony and thin! – in fondest fashion they acted, once: they used to be around glorious kings.

9 When my arms are seen, all bony and thin, they are not, I declare, worth raising up over handsome boys.

10 The girls are joyful when they approach Maytime; grief is more fitting for me: I am not only miserable, I am an old woman.

22 Woe is me indeed – every acorn is doomed to decay – to be in the darkness of an oratory after feasting by bright candles!

23 I have had my time with kings, drinking mead and wine; today I drink whey and water among shrivelled old women.

33 My flood has guarded well that which was deposited with me; Jesus, Son of Mary, has redeemed it so that I am not sad up to ebb.

34 Happy the island of the great sea: flood comes to it after ebb; as for me, I expect no flood after ebb to come to me.

35 Today there is scarcely an abode I would recognise; what was in flood is all ebbing.

Máirín Ní Dhonnchadha has recently argued[7] that the author of the lament is an historical female poet, *Digdi,* who for the purposes of poetic composition, identified herself in the poem with the figure of *Cailleach Bhéarra.*

Support for the identification of the authorial old woman of the Lament with the hag-goddess in her sovereignty queen aspect is famously available in the prose introduction found preceding the poem in the earliest extant manuscript copy known.

> *Sentane Berre, Digdi a ainm, di Chorco Dubne di .i. di Uaib maic Iair Conchinn. Is dib dano Brigit ingen Iustain. Is diib dono Liadain ben Chuirithir. Is dib dono Uallach ingen Muineghain. Fo-racaib Finan Cam doib ni biad cin caillig n-amra n-ain dib. Is de ro-boi Caillech Berre forre: coica dalta di a mBérri. Secht n-ais n-aited a ndechaid co deged cech fer ec crine uade, comtar tuatha ꝛ chenela a hui ꝛ a iarmui ꝛ cet mbliadna di fo cailliu iarna shenad do Chuiminiu for a cend. Do-sn-anic-si aes ꝛ lobrae iarom. Is ant is-rabard-sii.*

'The Old Woman of Beare, whose name was Digde, was of the Corcu Duibne, that is to say of the Uí Maic íair Chonchinn. Brigit daughter of Iustán belonged to them also, and Líadain wife of Cuirithir, and Úallach daughter of Muimnechán. Fínán Cam has bequeathed to them that they shall never be without some wonderful glorious nun/old woman among them. This is why she was called the Old Woman/Nun of Beare: she had fifty foster-children in Beare. She passed into seven periods of youth, so that every husband used to pass from her to death of old age, so that her grandchildren and great-grandchildren were peoples and races. And for a hundred years she wore the veil, after Cuimíne had blessed it and placed it on her head. Then age and infirmity came to her, and she said: 'Aithbe damsa bés mara'; etc.

The expression of an ambivalence regarding the otherworld – perceived both as Christian and native, ancestral domain – is a kind of leitmotif of Irish traditional narrative, especially in its oral, vernacular reaches. We will see below how the text of a tale collected from twentieth-century narrative tradition echoes the ambivalence of the ninth-century poem, while conveying, on the part of the later narrator, an eager acceptance of the rightness of the Christian victory in the cosmological contest of allegiance. Despite such narrative victory, in the case of both the ninth- and twentieth-century texts, the very transmission in tradition of their encompassing of opposed but accommodated allegiances is an indication of the degree to which ancestral conceptions of otherworld and otherworld female agency (in the person of the hag-goddess) continued to form part of Irish worldview and part of the imaginative repertoire of that worldview to which Irish vernacular and popular cultural forms are heir. Regularly pronounced as overcome and appropriated, displaced and demonized since the early medieval period, the divine otherworld female is, nevertheless, retained and reinterpreted in Irish cultural consciousness and in Irish expressive tradition in ways that this work attempts to present and illustrate.

Retention/reinterpretation of the autonomous female

Despite the declarations of the dethronement and even extinction of the goddess and goddess-related elements of native tradition implied in learned literature, it is the case that the ancestral culture of medieval and early modern Ireland continued to carry forward in literary and vernacular cultural tradition both the figure and the function (in reduced form) of the sovereignty queen on the one hand and of the non-sovereignty, female landscape figure on the other. Here we look at ways in which the worldview of later centuries carried the presence and the significance of the divine female into the early modern era of the eighteenth century and on into the beginnings of the modern world of the twentieth century.

In particular I want to examine that presence and significance, as it can be found in texts that are productive creative expressions, of the political, the literary and the cosmological domains of the native worldview of these later times. In the course of something close on a millennium – from, say, the ninth and tenth to the nineteenth and twentieth centuries – the forms and functions attaching to the figure of the female divine (as sovereignty principle, fairy queen and personification of landscape/wild nature) have been subject to transformation and reinterpretation in accordance with a process that encompasses the retention and simultaneous adaptation of concepts and their externalization in narrative and ritual behaviour, in accord with changing historical and sociopolitical developments.

Bean Sí/Banshee
First let us consider the case of the cosmological tradition of the supernatural death messanger or 'banshee' (*bean sí*, an otherworld female). The definitive

study of this aspect of Irish tradition is that of Lysaght.[1] In *The Banshee*, Patricia Lysaght demonstrates that the origin of this figure – featuring in both the poetry of seventeenth and eighteenth century elegiac laments for deceased domestic leaders and in the later legends of folklore where the death of a family member or neighbour is foreshadowed – is to be located in the medieval figure of the territorial and dynastic sovereignty queen. At its broadest, this tradition of the female divine personification of the relationship of land and people encompasses the figures of *Fodla*, *Banba* and *Ériu*, each being equated with Ireland and the Irish people as a whole. At the regional and local level, the divine female represents the sovereignty principle in respect of more localized dynastic identity, as for example, in the case of the O'Brien dynasty of Thomond in North Munster (*Aoibheall*) and the O'Keeffe dynasty of East and North Cork (*Clíodna*). In the later folklore texts witnessing to the vernacular conception of the anonymous banshee whose cry foretells the death of family relative or neighbour, the specific identification of named female divine with individual family line is reduced or lost completely. Some survival into latest tradition is attested to in the widespread understanding (that the folklore legends convey) that only the hereditary Gaelic families – those whose name contains the prefix Mac or Ó – are culturally marked out, or privileged, by having the deaths of their members signalled by the reduced and anonymous version of the female divine who is reported to cry their deaths into community consciousness.

Following an exhaustive and masterly study of the materials in archival and literary sources from the nineteenth and twentieth centuries representing the existence in later Irish vernacular tradition of a belief in the supernatural female death-messenger, Lysaght examines older literary texts in order to throw light on the origin of this belief. Her hypothesis is that it may be possible to show a relationship between the death-foreboding females of the earlier literary tradition and the death-messenger figure, the *bean sí*/banshee of the early modern and modern eras. Dealing with two categories of earlier death-foreboding-female texts, Lysaght convincingly demonstrates that the posited relationship can account for the distribution of regional names for the death-messenger in later tradition, for her association with families and for the motifs of hair-combing and shirt-washing that occur regionally in legends concerning human encounters with her. The main characteristics of the vernacular traditions of the supernatural female death-messenger she summarizes as follows.

> There is great variation in the traditions about the being but the core of the belief concerns a solitary, crying female supernatural being who is perceived as an ancestress of the family she attends. One discerns in the traditions about her an older 'aristocratic'

being [. . .] who stands in a special guardian-type position to noble and illustrious personages and families, specifically in the context of death. Alongside the predominantly benign and sympathetic aspect of the death-messenger in the traditional material, one also detects a frightening and aggressive aspect to her behaviour . . .[2]

In the case of the death-messenger form, the frightening and aggressive aspect of this otherworld female figure derives from the character and behaviour of the battle-goddesses known from the early literature. These, named as *Mórrígan, Macha,* and *Nemhain* appear on battle-fields and to warriors about to do battle, often in the form of the raven or hooded crow. Thus the name *Badhbh* (Raven) is frequently reported as that of an apparition appearing near water and engaged in the washing of the martial arms or clothing of the warriors who are about to die in the battle which is imminent.

The ancient figures of the sovereignty queen and the battle-goddess who underlie the figure and functions of the *bean sí* are figures from the learned, literate side of ancestral Irish tradition. We can recognize also the retention and reinterpretation in early modern and modern tradition of an otherworld female figure whose origin in early Irish culture lies outside the lines of development of the sovereignty queen figure who was appropriated into the political propaganda of competing lineages. This non-sovereignty queen figure, intimately associated with the physical landscape and its features, has a wise, nurturing, maternal aspect and a destructive, terrifying, hostile one; the latter allied to the fierceness and wildness of forces and aspects of nature and landscape that can threaten to overwhelm human life. In this duality of potential in respect of the human experience of her presence and of her power, the non-sovereignty queen, otherworld female of the non-learned, vernacular or folk tradition also resembles the otherworld female figures of learned literary tradition in their division into affirmative, life-enhancing personifications of sovereignty and territoriality, on the one hand, and terrifying, doom-laden battle-goddess, on the other. Thus, both the ancient sovereignty and non-sovereignty female otherworld figures can be taken to be the source from which early modern supernatural female figures, dealt with below, were developed.

Aisling/Spéirbhean

Moving now to the imagery of the politico-literary discourse of the *aisling* or vision-poetry of the mainly eighteenth-century, Gaelic, Jacobite tradition, we can see how the ancient figure of the sovereignty queen and the topos of the rightful ruler's spiritual marriage to her as divine consort, finds further renewed and transforming expression. The poetry and the political language in question draw their images from an ancestral cosmology and apply it both to the interpretation of contemporary circumstances and to the expressing of a millenarian expectation of redemption and liberation. The recently published and massively comprehensive study by Professor Breandán Ó Buachalla of the construction and growth of the political ideology of the *aisling* genres,[3] illuminates the transformation and reinterpretive application by eighteenth-century Gaelic poets of the divine female sovereignty concept that is a fundamental symbolic principle of ancestral Irish ideas of cultural identity and political hegemony. Emphasizing the underlying continuity of the enduring conceit on which the complex of motifs, themes and metaphors of the *aisling* genres are based, he demonstrates exhaustively the vitality with which the ancestral notion of the sacred relationship of rightful ruler and divine female personification of territory – ultimately Ireland – is given fresh creative expression in a rich corpus of poetry that incorporates the invention of new appellations for the symbolic female. Where the early medieval literature featured the royal names *Meadhbh*, *Macha* and *Mór Mumhan*, as well as *Banba*, *Fodla* and *Ériu*, we now find a set of far more proletarian female names generated by the *aisling* poets to represent the symbolic female personification of the territory and the divine sovereignty of the land of Ireland.

The most widely known of these – partly due to its subsequent use by later literary figures of the Anglo-Irish revival, chief of whom was W.B. Yeats – is the name *Caitlín Ní Uallacháin*. This name for Ireland and Irish sovereignty is generally attributed to the poetic invention of *Liam Dall Ó hIfearnáin*, born in County Tipperary in 1720 and trained in poetry in County Limerick at one of the last bardic academies to survive into the eighteenth century. Other, similarly commoner names for the divine female bestowed by the *aisling* poets include such as *Síle Ní Ghadhra*, *Nóirín Ní Chuileannáin*, *Siobhán Ní Mheadhra*, *Meidhbhín Ní Shúilleabháin* and *Síle Bhán Ní Shléibhín*.

These proletarian appellations for the divine female sovereignty principle of Ireland and the Irish people at the latter part of the eighteenth century can surely be seen – as Ó Buachalla himself suggests[4] – as constituting a Gaelic Irish parallel to the *Marianne* figure of later French popular political discourse and ritual of the nineteenth century. There is, however, one huge contrast between the *Marianne* figure and that of the *Síle Ní Ghadhra*, *Nóirín Ní Chuileannáin* and *Caitlín Ní Uallacháin* sort. The ideology – political and philosophical – in which the *Marianne* figure personifies and represents France and vernacular French aspirations of liberty, is that of a republican discourse. The Irish poetic discourse, expressing the values of a traditional ideology and the aspirations of political freedom for Ireland and the Irish, is the medieval discourse of hereditary royalty. It proclaims, again and again in these *aisling* poems, the imminent restoration of the deposed Stuart dynasty – to rightful rule of the Gaelic world.

Common to both the *Marianne* and the commoner-named Irish sovereignty personifications, however, is an autonomous, female vitality that is given expression in sexual terms. The bare breasts of the *Marianne* as she is represented in popular iconography in nineteenth-century France – as in the statues of her that were paraded in popular ritual assemblies – represent this personal and sexual, as well as political, liberation. A suggested lascivious quality of the Irish commoner, sovereignty personification is to be found in the combination in her – and in her presence in the consciousness of the poetic imagination – of the prospect of both intoxication and sexual bliss in her company, for her chosen companions. This involves both drinking and carnal pleasures and, in the Irish, ancestral, symbolic tradition, harps back directly to similar associations in the case of the great divine sovereignty queens of the earliest medieval period. *Meadhbh* of *Cruachain*, for instance – quasi-divine personification of the sovereignty of Connacht – was noted for her self-proclaimed sexual capacities and her Celtic name is understood etymologically to mean 'she who intoxicates' (c.f. Greek *methu*, 'wine' and Latin *medus*, 'mead').[5]

In this respect (by which the unrepressed carnality of the autonomous female divine is attested), the eighteenth-century *aisling* personifications of sovereignty revert, in a sense, to the earliest state of their royal, medieval antecedents, before their patriarchal subjugation at the hands of the political propagandists of early medieval Ireland, as referred to earlier. Two poems of the North Cork-born *Seán Clárach Mac Domhnaill* (+ 1754) illustrate these themes of carousing and arousal and extracts are quoted by Ó *Buachalla*.[6] (I re-quote them here and give an approximate translation of my own.)

The first extract is from the poem '*An Aisling do rinneas ar Mhóirín*' (The dream vision I experienced of *Móirín*), previously edited and published by Risteard Ó Foghludha[7] in an anthology of Ó Domhnaill's poetry:

Is é deir an macalla den ghlór chaoin,
'*An bhfuileann tú id chodladh, a Mhóirín?*
   siúil cois na toinne
   agus féach ar do dhuine
Tá ag teacht chughat tar uisce le mórbhuíon . . .

Líontar chughainn puins agus beoir chaoin,
Is bímís dá dtarraingt i gcónaí
   cuirfeam an ainnise ar cairde
   go maidean amáireach
's nár chasa go brách ná go deo arís . . .

Faid mhairfidh sin scilling im póicín
Ní scoirfead le cuideachtain Mhóirín,
   olfaimíd sláinte
   an fhir úd tar sáile–
Tadhg is a gharlaigh i gcóistí . . .'

It's what the echo speaks in a gentle voice,
'Are you asleep, Móirín?
   Walk by the wave's edge
   And regard the one
Who is coming to you across the water with a great host . . .

Let punch and smooth ale be poured for us,
And let us constantly be having it in draughts,
   Let us put misery on hold
   Until tomorrow morning
And may it never again return . . .

For as long as a shilling remains in my pocket,
I'll not depart from the company of Móirín,
   Let us toast the health
   of that Person overseas–
Tadhg [the common man] and his crew [to be mounted] in coaches . . .'

This second extract from an Ó Domhnaill poem, '*Seal do bhíos im mhaighdin shéimh*' (For a time I was a placid virgin) was also published by Ó Foghludha:

   '*Seal do bhíos im mhaighdin shéimh*
   is anois im bhaintrigh chaite, thréith
   tá mo chéile ag treabhadh na dtonn go tréan,
   de bharr na gcnoc 'is in imigéin

   Is é mo rogha é a thoghas dom féin
   is maith an domhan go dtabharfainn é
   d'fhonn é bheith ar bord ar long gan bhaol,
   de bharr na gcnoc is in imigéin

   For a time I was a placid virgin
   And now I am a spent, feeble widow
   My spouse is vigorously ploughing the waves,
   Swept from the hills and far away

   He is my own choice one that I picked for myself
   And all the wealth of the world would I give

So that he might be safe on board ship,
Swept from the hills and far away.

An extract from another poem quoted by Ó Buachalla,[8] from an unpublished Manuscript in Maynooth College, '*Araoir im aisling is mé ag machnamh im intinn*' (Last night in a dream vision while I was pondering in my mind) by *Muiris Ó Gríofa*, emphasizes further the female personification figure's autonomy of sexual selection:

> *Is binn do labhair agus d'aithris le díogras*
> *nach luífeadh feasta le beannaphoc coimhtheach*
> *go sínfeadh seascair i bhfarraid a firfhir,*
> *sé an fíorlaoch aoibhinn álainn óg*

> Sweetly she spoke and recounted with fervour
> That she would not lie, henceforth, with the foreign stag
> But stretch out snugly alongside her true man,
> The young, beautiful, delightful, real hero

In such *aisling* poetry, the *spéirbhean* – the divine female, the sovereignty of the land – recovers the autonomous vitality and earthiness which had been subject to repression in the displacement of the divine, sovereign female by both political and ecclesiastical patriarchy. What we are seeing here is the re-emergence into public discourse of aspects of the cosmology of ancestral tradition that had been lost to view at official and learned levels of cultural representation but that had continued to be remembered and re-expressed creatively at the level of vernacular and popular cultural tradition. In the aftermath of the demise of the old social and political order during the seventeenth century, the Gaelic poetic voice of the Irish eighteenth century represents something of an amalgamation of ancestral themes, learned and popular, adjusted and applied to the circumstance of a newly emerging world. Especially prominent among these ancestral themes is that of the divine or otherworld female personification of the land of Ireland who shows herself to the poets and who bemoans her fate – she is in thrall to a foreign tyrant – while her true, royal spouse remains exiled overseas.

I have referred already to the possibility of seeing a relationship between the proletarian forms of the *spéirbhean* figure and that of the *Marianne* of French popular culture, despite the opposing ideological perspectives in which they function. The *Marianne* centrally personifies the spirit of the revolutionary Republic – and its attendant connotations of liberty, equality and fraternity – that informs the consciousness and the political rituals of the rural French proletariat. The *spéirbhean* figure of *Síle Ní Ghadhra, Móirín Ní Chuileannáin* or *Caitlín Ní Uallacháin*, generated by the Irish poets out of a creative renewal and reapplication of an ancestral ideology of royal rule, is given a comparable radical and revolutionary transformation in the political rituals and discourse that accompanied the activities of Irish, eighteenth-century rural insurgency.

In the course of that century, local unrest and agitation in respect of the enclosure and grazing of commonage in the interests of the new ascendancy and entrepreneurial classes, developed into a wider political ideology and a subversive practice that increasingly adopted the rhetoric and the imagery of the millenarian Jacobitism and found creative and vivid expression in the poems of the *Aisling* genres. Several decades prior to the French revolution, popular agitation in Ireland to defend the interests of the Catholic lower classes against encroachment and injury – in terms of land-holding and economic practice and the exaction of a tithe-tax to the benefit of the clergy of the established Anglican Church – was adopting the rhetoric and the imagery that informed the *aisling* genres of the contemporary Gaelic poetic output. Central to that rhetoric and imagery is the figure of the divine female sovereignty queen, then the personification in popular imagination of not only the royal spouse but also of a more democratic and proletarian sense of a common freedom and justice and solidarity that challenges not only 'foreign' oppressors but also the effects of commercialization and development within the native, rural world. Tenancies, rent and wages were the general grounds of grievance of the Whiteboy movement – an agrarian, oath-bound, secret society, strongest in Munster, that came to prominence from 1760. The name Whiteboys/ *Buachaillí Bána* arose from the choice of costume by the participants in the subversive activities of the society. Sometimes combining the straw disguise of the Wren Boy/May Boy/Straw Boy passage rituals with the Jacobite costume of the white cockade and the white cape, the rhetoric and rituals of these subversive groups declare their allegiance to a symbolic female figure that combines the age old sovereignty personification with the image of the refugee leader – the Prince himself, *Séarlas Óg*, in female disguise – as he is actually alleged, historically, to have escaped his Highland pursuers.[9]

The Whiteboy oath sought to bind the members in allegiance to each other and to Queen *Sadhbh*/Sive, to *Sadhbh Olltach*, or to Joan or Joanna Meskel, a surname suggestive, as *Ó Buachalla* notes,[10] of the intoxicatory powers of the female divine figure (c.f. Irish *meisce, meisciúil;* 'drunkeness', 'drunken' in relation to the etymology of the name of the Queen/Goddess *Meadhbh* (see p. 56).

We can see, in many of the *aisling* genre compositions, the reinterpretative amalgamation of the ancient royal sovereignty figure with the more proletarian non-sovereignty female personification of landscape, after a fashion that makes use of ancestral symbols and motifs in a new social and political discourse. The following texts are examples of a dynamic of retention and reinterpretation that eventually, in millenarian amalgamation of nationalism and localized politics, presents the figure of the exiled royal pretender, Prince Charles Stuart, as a Whiteboy insurgent in the struggle to assert traditional communitarian values and oppose the encroachment on the local community of the new order of social and economic life that was perceived as unjustly exploiting and oppressing the native population.

'CLANN SHADHBHA AGUS SHAIDHBHÍN'

Im shuan aréir go fuadarach faon, do chuala mé an slua ag teacht,
go trúpach, tréanmhar, luaimneach éadrom siúlach saothrach fuadrach,
bhí Sadhbh 's a clann ar fáil gan dabht, go buachach lansach luaimneach,
'Is dearbh', ar Sadhbh, do ráidh go deimhin, 'tá an báire ar Ghaill den ruaig seo'.

'Is éachtach liom ár nGaeil go fann, faoi ghéarsmacht Gall á gcloíochan,
's gach méithphoc reamhar go craosach teann, ag éigneart braindí 's fíona;
éamhaim ar chabhair na séimhfhear modhail do theacht le fogha aon oíche,
le faobhar, le fonn, le tréine lann do bhéarfadh scanradh baoth dóibh.'

'Bíogaidh suas, ná bídh bhur suan, bíodh faobhar is crua in gach claíomh libh,
Dibream scuaine an Bhéarla uainn, go tréan as cuantaibh ár sinsir.
Táid síbhrog áille chríche Fáilbhe ag éirí ar lár na hoíche.
Aoibheall, Áine, Sadhbh is Gráinne, a gclann, a gconách, 's an Stíobhart . . .'

Táid draoithe 's dáimh na gcríoch ag trácht ar ghníomh na sárfhear múinte,
Is Aoibheall áigh ag scríobh chum Áine an chliar bheith fáilteach rompu;
mo ghuí gach lá dem shaol go brách le hintinn Mháire ar úrneamh,
gach Buachaill Bán den tslua bheith slán, is Rí na ngrás dá gcumhdach.

THE CHILDREN OF SADHBH

Last night, lying in my restless slumber I heard the on-coming host,
Abounding in troops, powerful, restless, light of step, bustling to advance;
Sadhbh and her children were there too, of course, buoyant, keen, energetic,
'Certain it is', Sadhbh said with assurance, 'that this attack will rout the foreigners.'

'It is a mortal blow to me that our Irish people should be languishing vanquished under the foreigner's oppression
And every fatted buck of them, secure in their gluttony, with brandy and wine aplenty.

I implore the true gentlemen of proper manners to come on the attack
any night at all,
with vigour, with urgency, with such sharp and cutting force of arms as
would bring terrifying confusion on them.'

'Come awake, do not stay sleeping, but let your swords be sharp and bright
each one,
Let us forcefully drive out the hordes of English speakers from the
harbours of our forebears,
The lovely otherworld mansions of Ireland are coming to life in the night
bringing forth *Aoibheall, Áine, Sadhbh* and *Gráinne*, their children and their
prosperous well-being – and even the Stuart himself...'

The wise ones and the poets of the whole land are telling of the action of
the well-behaved heroes
And valiant *Aoibheall* is writing to *Áine* that the clergy are giving them
welcome;
My prayer each day of my life evermore is that, with Mary's help in
heaven,
Every Whiteboy of the company will be safe, with the King of Mercy
protecting them all.

The vision that the poet here has, in the course of his fitful sleep, is of both the liberating host coming to the assistance of Ireland and the Irish and of '*Sadhbh* and her children' as the symbolic personification of the land and people who are in thrall to unjust foreign rule. *Sadhbh* – in whose service the Whiteboys frequently proclaimed themselves, thinking of themselves as her children – calls, in the poem, on those children (the Gaelic Irish) to rise up and join with the incoming army of liberation so that Ireland and the Irish should no longer languish under foreign oppression. In the visionary transformation of a landscape cleared of its comfortably-settled English colonists, the ancestral female sovereignty personifications – *Aoibheall, Áine, Sadhbh* and *Gráinne* – are seen to emerge from within the landscape itself and its otherworld dwelling places, to repossess their hereditary territory together with *Sadhbh*'s children. Even the Stuart himself, the exiled leader, is envisaged here as coming into Ireland, not from the sea, but from the otherworld, where he is, in the imaginative dispensation of tradition, the rightful spouse of the sovereignty of Ireland.

The last lines of the above poem as quoted by Ó *Buachalla*[11] and reproduced here, are noteworthy on two counts. The first is the assertion that *Aoibheall* is writing to her sister figure *Áine* – *ag scríobh chum Áine* – with news of the great event that is taking place. This is possibly a unique image, that of the *literate* otherworld female, and is evidence of the bringing forward into the reality of an increasingly literate, eighteenth-century Irish world, of the symbolism of the otherworld sovereignty queen discourse. The other reason these lines are noteworthy is the amalgamation in them of sovereignty and liberation symbolism with the ideology and practice of Christianity. The poet claims that, in his vision, the Christian (Catholic) clergy are welcoming the overthrow of foreign rule and he invokes the aid of the blessed virgin Mary, mother of God, in his Christian prayer that the insurgents be safe in the keeping of the king of mercy, the king of heaven. This contrasts with the actual widespread and active hostility of most of the Catholic clergy, of all ranks, to the Whiteboy movement. Whiteboy leaders and their followers were excommunicated. They were denounced as 'loose', 'dissolute', 'desperate', 'abandoned' and 'accursed' by various bishops. With very few exceptions there was almost total opposition to and rejection of the movement, its arms and activities, on the part of the Churches. Despite this, there was a continued allegiance by many, in many districts in the south of the country, to the insurrectionary ideology and actions of a movement that drew its symbolism and its inspiration from a combination of the Jacobite discourse – of liberation from abroad – with the discourse of the female cosmic agency in the landscape. This revolutionary identification of the liberation of the plain people with place and with ancestral tradition finds vivid symbolic expression in the *Marianne*-like figure of the proletarian-named female personifications of territory. A poem by the West Cork poet and scribe *Seán Ó Coileáin*, who was born in mid-eighteenth century, expresses clearly this amalgamation of Jacobite and proletarian insurrectionary discourse in a poem that identifies the exiled royal leader with the indigenous commoner Whiteboy. The poem is quoted by Ó Buachalla[12] from a manuscript of the Royal Irish Academy, and is reproduced here with an approximation of the sense of the piece in my translation.

MAIDIN LAE GHIL FÁ DHUILLE GÉAG-GHLAIS

Maidin lae ghil fá dhuille géag-glais
daire im aonar cois imeall trá,
I bhfis trím néaltaibh do dhearcas spéirbhean
ag teacht ó thaobh dheas na mara im dháil . . .

★ ★ ★

Is sé dúirt le díograis 'Och uaill mo chroíse,
nó an bhfeicfead choíche mo Bhuachaill Bán?'

'Scoir den gháir sin, a bhruinneall ársa
's bí go sásta, cé fada tá

> *do Phrionsa rábach clumhail láidir*
> *trúpach gardach ar seachrán;*
> *atá anois go cróga 'gus buíon na hEorpa*
> *ar an gcósta go hiomlán,*
> *ag teach id phórtaibh le neart gan teora*
> *'s buaifid Fódhla don Bhuachaill Bán*
>
> *Ar gclos an scéil sin, do scaip a claonta*
> *'s do ghaibh a caomhchruit órga bhláith,*
> *do sheinn a géaga laoithe 's dréachta*
> *ríoga aosta ba mhór le rá:*
> *ní héin na míolta ach cnoic is coillte,*
> *aibhne is líoga in iomarbhá,*
> *do bheadh ag rince sna gleannta timpeall,*
> *le greann dá laoithibh dá Buachaill Bán*

ON A BRIGHT MORNING UNDER THE GREEN LEAVES

> On a bright morning when I was all alone
> under the green leaves of an oak near the strand
> I saw in my reverie, the vision of a beautiful woman
> coming to meet me across the southern side of the sea.

★ ★ ★

> Her fervent utterance was: 'Oh, my heart wails!
> or will I ever see my *Buachaill Bán?*
>
> Give over that cry, oh venerable maiden, and be contented now,
> Long though your Prince – famous, dashing, strong –
> has been wandering abroad, with his troops and his guards;
> He is even now, with the forces of Europe supporting him,
> strongly approaching the coast.
> Coming into your seaports with limitless strength, to win
> Ireland for the *Buachaill Bán.*
>
> Having received this news her complaining mood left her
> And she took hold of her beautifully-shaped golden harp;
> Her hands played ancient royal lays and
> verses of great note;
> It wasn't only the birds and animals, but the hills and the
> woods, the rivers and the rocks in their turn,
> That would dance in the valleys all around with joy at her
> songs for her *Buachaill Bán.*

We can note how the site of the poet's vision of the aisling *spéirbhean* is transferred from the more usual riverbank location to the shoreline, echoing the metaphor of overseas redemption. Here it is the female figure herself (the personification of sovereignty) who comes across the water seeking to be restored to her rightful royal companion, here represented as '*mo Bhuachaill Bán*,' 'my own Whiteboy (darling Hero)'. The amalgamation of the sovereignty-queen myth with the Jacobite vision of liberation is powerfully expressed in the next verse in which the poet addresses the 'venerable maiden' and tells her that her prince is returning to win Ireland for the Whiteboy *alter ego* of the exiled royal sovereign. The standard, colonialist, sexual imagery of the penetration and conquest of the person and the land of Ireland is here reversed, in that the Prince, with his European support, who is 'coming into your seaports with limitless strength' is her rightful spouse, the effect of whose ingress will be to invigorate and restore the sovereignty of Ireland and of the people of Ireland as represented by the Whiteboys – *Clann Shadhbha* (the children of Sive) – in other compositions. In expectation of such imminent liberationary reunion and repossession, the mood and appearance of the visionary female alters in line with the age-old hag/ beautiful young queen transformation trope. Her sorrow lifts, her body (i.e. the land of Ireland), is suffused with a joy, a gaiety, that in its expression in the images of royal music and trembling, dancing landscape and animals, combines the sexual and political overtones of sovereignty and liberation in a manner that is congruent with ancient tradition.

This sense of a sexual vitality and potency that survives displacement and domination is found also in a verse Ó Buachalla quotes[13] from *Liam Dall Ó hIfearnáin* in regard to *Caitlín Ní Uallacháin*, a verse previously published by Ó Foghludha:

Ó MEASAIMÍD NACH CALM RINN DEN BHUAIRT SEO I SPÁINN

Ná measaidís gur caile chríon ár stuaire stáid
ná caillichín 'na gcrapfaidís a cuail beag cnámh:
cé fada ag luí dhi le fearaibh coimhtheach gan suaimhneas d'fháil
tá saith an rí i gCaitlín Ní Uallacháin

SINCE THIS SORROWFUL BUSINESS IN SPAIN IS NOT SPLENDID NEWS

Let them not think of our handsome, stately lady as an ancient wench,
Or a little old woman shrivelled to a bag of bones.
Though she has long been given to lying down with foreigners without finding rest,
Caitlín Ní Uallacháin is ample mate for any king.

A verse[14] of *Seán Clárach Mac Domhnaill* in which the reunion is envisaged as happening between the persons of *Carolus* (Charles Stuart) and *Gráinne Mhaol* combines this celebratory invigoration with an image of bloody, retaliatory violence against foreigners:

A SHAOI GHLAIN DE PHRÍOMHSCOTH NA SÁIRFHEAR SAOR

> Beidh reacaireacht feasta, beidh aiteas, beidh dáin, beidh scléip,
> Ag flaithibh na Banba ar dtaisteal dá n-ardfhlaith féin;
> Beidh Galla ina gceathaibh dá leagadh le cáthadh piléar,
> 's beidh sealbh ag Carolus, geallaimse, ar Ghráinne Mhaol

O BRIGHT, EMINENT ONE OF THE CHOICEST OF INDEPENDENT GREAT MEN

Henceforth there will be poetic declaiming, there will be joyful fun, there will be poems, there will be gaiety,
Among the nobles of *Banba* (Ireland) once their own high-prince has travelled over;
Foreigners felled in droves by spraying bullets
And *Carolus*, I warrant you, in possession of his *Gráinne Mhaol*.

Other verses[15] of the same *Seán Clárach*, however, serve to emphasize, in the early modern, Jacobite context, the continuity of the *aisling* genre with earlier sovereignty personification and with traditional cosmology:

OÍCHE AN AONAIGH D'ÉIS MO FHLIUCHTA

> Do bhí an spéirbhean dhéidgheal mhiochair
> bhéaltais mhilis mhnámhail
> Is na mílte béithe aerga ó chnoic
> fé réim sa lios an tráth san. . .
>
> Do bhí ann Deirdre ghéigeal dhil,
> Éachtach oilte is Áine,
> 's an tsíbhean Bhéarra ó thaobh na toinne,
> 's Eithne ó thigh an Daghda. . .

FAIR-DAY NIGHT, FOLLOWING ON MY WETTING

The sweet, modest, tender soft-lipped, pearl-toothed fair lady,
Along with thousands of ethereal maidens from the hills, reigned,
at that time in the otherworld dwelling place of the *lios*

Beloved, bright-limbed *Deirdre* was there,
She of the prowess and the skill, along with *Áine*

And the otherworld female from *Béarra* beside the waves
And *Eithne* from the dwelling place of the *Daghda*

Another *Mac Domhnaill* poem[16] emphasizes even more emphatically the identification of the otherworld female with the landscape which she personifies and tells of how he pursued his vision of her from one landscape feature of otherworld association to another, ending up at a renowned otherworld hill in County Limerick. *Cnoc Fírinne* is the hill of truth, the feminine centre of cosmic reality, whose slopes are crowded with both the otherworld host and – it can be maintained in this poetic *aisling* discourse – the Whiteboy host as well. Thus we see the land and its people doubly amalgamated in this identification of the denizens of the otherworld with the Whiteboys:

OÍCHE BHÍOS IM LUÍ IM SHUAN

Nuair dhearcas í do bhíogas suas
go bhfionnfainn uaithi cérab as í...
Gur leanas í don tír ba thuaidh
go Sí na nGruagach cé gurbh fhada í.

Tím aníos arís de ruaig
go Sí Cruachna, go Sí Seanadh,
Go Sichnoc aoibhinn Fhírinn' fhuair,
mar mbíonn an slua le taoibh na beannaí

ON A NIGHT WHEN I LAY SLEEPING

When I saw her I started up
So that I might ascertain from her whence she came
And I followed her to the north country
To the otherworld dwelling of Warrior Heroes.

I quickly circled about to the south again
To the otherworld dwelling of *Cruachain*, to the
otherworld dwelling of *Seanadh*
To the delightful otherworld hill-dwelling of *Fírinne*
Where the hosts gather on the high slopes.

Brendán Ó Buachalla[17] refers to the belief of the plain people of Brittany in the mid-nineteenth century that *Marianne* was a flesh-and-blood human female who – though now quite aged – still lived among them. In Ireland too, in the eighteenth and nineteenth centuries and beyond, vernacular culture encompasses, manifests and renews, in the narrative creativity of popular verse and legend, a sense of the living presence, the intimate domestication of the divinely wise and powerful female *flaitheas* (sovereignty) and landscape figure of ancestral myth. *Nóirín* and *Meidhbhín* and *Caitlín* and *Síle*, as well as the named wise-women of legend and the ubiquitous, if anonymous, banshee figure are manifestations of such living presence and have a set of functions in cultural tradition that manages to combine, among other things, the aesthetic, the social, the therapeutic and the political. Another powerful invocation of the living presence of the otherworld female is the figure of *Aoibheall*, sovereignty personification and wise dispenser of justice at the Midnight Court at which the poet Brian Merriman found himself imaginatively present in East Clare.

Cúirt an Mheán Oíche/The Midnight Court
A decade before the proliferation in France, in the years following the Revolution, of female allegorical representations of Liberty and Justice, culminating in the figure of the *Marianne*, the goddess of reason, Brian Merriman's *Cúirt an Mheán Oíche* ('The Midnight Court')[18] achieved a revolutionary reinterpretation of the Irish sovereignty queen myth that made a profound mark on vernacular culture here. Using the literary device of the later medieval European court of love tradition, but embedding it in the native cosmological framework of the *aisling* tradition of love-vision, prophecy and the restoration of political sovereignty, he produced a poem which brings one of the deepest myths of Irish culture (learned and vernacular) to bear in an imaginatively creative and extremely novel way on issues arising from the contemporary social and political context. Written about the year 1780, *Cúirt an Mheán Oíche* opposes a spirit of health and mirth and vigour to the frustrations and repressions of a social order increasingly given over to calculation and caution. Merriman joins together in a novel unity, European literary motifs of the medieval love-court and the early modern female parliament with Irish motifs (literary and mythological) of a sovereign otherworld female whose nurturing presence is embodied in landscape. The resulting poem brings the energy of archetype to bear on contemporary social and political issues as Merriman confronts the 'new world' of his day with resources of language and metaphor rooted in an ancestral tradition, that challenges the hegemony of male values and male power, civil and ecclesiastical.

Claims made concerning the 'revolutionary' nature of 'The Midnight Court' in seeming to call for the abolition of marriage, for the exaltation of bastardy and for the casting aside of clerical celibacy have been refuted on the grounds that these themes are very frequently encountered both in the learned and popular traditions of medieval and early modern Europe. It is certainly true that their occurrence in his poem is not, in itself, solid evidence of Merriman's having been imbued with the notions of the European enlightenment, yet the poem is extremely radical in another sense in regard to these matters. Merriman's concern throughout the poem is with the flowering of human sexuality and while this, in itself, is not a radical departure in literature, what is startling in the Irish literary tradition is the informing of the call with the power and authority of the Gaelic sovereignty myth whose bona fide, or writ, in Ireland, runs back to insular Celtic times. The use to which Merriman puts the myth in late eighteenth-century East Clare is truly revolutionary, in that he invokes its characters, its images and its power not in the cause of tribal, dynastic or national sovereignty, but in the cause of the civil and psychological liberation of the individual at the personal level.

It has been remarked that romantic love is absent from 'The Midnight Court', but romantic love is also absent from the earliest examples of the *aisling* of a thousand years earlier, and it is to this *aisling* tradition (stretching back far beyond the eighteenth-century allegorical variety of the genre) that Merriman looks for the fundamental orientation of his poem. Early Irish offers surprisingly little literature of love in the conventional medieval European sense. The 'wooings', the 'elopements' and other forms of early Irish love literature present us not with lovers in personal roles but in mythological ones, so that what is expressed in the text is the course of erotic encounter rather than the working out of a personal relationship. This note is struck again very definitely, in 'The Midnight Court'. Once more the adjective 'revolutionary' can be used to describe what Merriman does to the *aisling* tradition of his day, and he achieves his effect very simply. By locating his dramatic monologues (which derive partly from the burlesque version of the *Roman de la Rose* tradition), in a court presided over by *Aoibheall* of *Craig Liath,* he is able by virtue of his poetic creativity of language, to transform the mythological tie between the sovereignty of Ireland and a rightful hereditary king, into a relationship between woman and man, and between both and the eighteenth-century Irish countryside, in terms both of society and psychology. From time immemorial in Gaelic tradition, the mythological role of love and sexuality was bound up with the notion of a divine mother who personified the land and its well-being. For Irish poets, from the earliest times to the eighteenth-century allegorists, the public welfare, the common good, of land and of people, was tied to the notion of mystical sovereignty and its embodiment in the person and authority of a rightful leader. By the eighteenth century, of course, real history had decreed that the liberation of Ireland as still envisaged by *aisling* poets such as *Aogán Ó Rathaille* and *Eoghan Rua Ó Súilleabháin* – the return for instance of a Stuart king in place of a dispersed native nobility – was a hopeless dream. The *aisling* poet, Merriman, also dreams of the liberation of the people, but what is important for him is a civil and psychological liberation of the individual, at the carnal level first rather than some impossible political liberation in the terms of a bygone age. Both Ó *Rathaille* and Merriman each have a vision of a restored Ireland and of a restored Irish people and both deliver their visions with eloquence and a profound sense of tradition. They do so, however, in very different ways indeed; the one with a backward-looking contemptuous regret, the other with a contemporary and dynamic comic gusto. It was not to any merely mortal royal liberator that Merriman looked for deliverance of country and people, but to the older, supernatural, 'female' sovereignty of the spirit of the land itself. Thus he seeks to ensure the return and perpetuation of fertility and prosperity for all, not in the restoration of the Stuart or any other royal line, but in the restoration of the primacy of '*fonn na fola agus fothrom na sláinte*' ('the urge of the blood and the lustiness of health'): the basic, healthy, animal, life instincts of the mature, adult, individual man and woman, free from conventional guilt or shame or repression. In effecting this transformation of the *aisling,* Merriman liberates sovereignty or love (in the person of *Aoibheall* of *Craig Liath*) from its mythological role, and brings it into play on the plane of the psychological and the naturalistic. In praising the allegorical *aisling* poems, Daniel Corkery says[19] that they are (in comparison to the Scottish Jacobite songs in English) in the heroic rather than the affectionate plane, with the result that we are dazzled by the splendour of their art rather than moved by their intimacy. Merriman deliberately chooses to move his *aisling* away from this heroic plane, not, however, to indulge the affections but to liberate the psyche in a work that is full and fierce and carnal, and that yet is free of all sentimentality or shame, so that we his readers are ourselves humbled and liberated by his vision and by the maturity of its expression.

Cúirt an Mheán Oíche radically articulates the feminine side of the human psyche that is resident in women and in men alike. Merriman's imagination, fuelled by feminine archetypal energy while consciously inhabiting the contemporary emergent world, looks to, calls for, demands, the psychic maturity and independence of individual human persons within that world, rather than the restoration of some bygone order of things. What is restored, in and by the poem, is the importance and authority of this demand, together with the prospect of personal psychic liberation from the distortions of an excessively patriarchal social order.

The traditional summons to the dreaming poet to attend the female assembly is delivered by a loathsome avatar of the radiant sovereignty queen who presides there. Thus Merriman combines European 'female parliament' genre with native 'sovereignty' myth and injects an ancestral Irish feminine imperative towards true justice into the work – and the significance – of the court assembled at Feakle.

The chief complaint laid before the court is one regarding the state of human relations in the contemporary social order. It is to be noted that the charge is here brought against particular types of women and men rather than against one entire gender. It is also to be noted that a literary stereotyping of female beauty is invoked by the plaintiff in pressing her claims. Thus gender and genre cross-cut and counterpoint each other. The human cry of loneliness and the human desire for union in the face of mortality and social sterility is the reality that is articulated. In response, the male mouthpiece of the prevailing social order can view the demands of autonomous woman and female psyche only as cosmic disorder and social obscenity and a preference, very masculine and very literary, is expressed for an alleged free-love alternative to the demands of a true union of hearts, sexes and psyches. The reality of human suffering within prevailing styles of marriage is symbolized further in the frustration of female sexual desire (even within the marriage bed itself), and the indispensable and irrepressible force of human sexuality (even within clerical ranks) is affirmed when the loss to human happiness and psychic well-being that the celibacy of the priesthood entails is proclaimed and lamented. At the end, *Aoibheall,* judge and female sovereign, delivers a judgement that seeks to restore primacy and legitimacy to the fundamentals of a truly human social order, an order that is expressed by her in the metaphor of a common voluptuousness indulged in for its own glorious sake.

I consider the kind of emancipatory liberation and empowerment of individual and community consciousness that Merriman's poem promoted in the figure of *Aoibheall* (hag-goddess of the north Munster landscape and sovereignty queen of the leading hereditary, north Munster O'Brien lineage), to be a 'major instance' of that creative reinterpretation of tradition that is, in terms of popular literary form, of a kind with the dynamic of vernacular reinterpretation of personifications of the otherworld female with which this work is, in general, concerned. Furthermore, the reception of Merriman's poem at the end of the eighteenth century and throughout the two centuries that have followed (during which time it has enjoyed continual popular acclaim in Irish language communities and, in translation, in the world of Irish consciousness), shows that its significance in transforming and transmitting anew the power of the archaic mythological figure of the hag-goddess cannot be confined to literary circles or to literary tradition. Himself steeped in the vernacular culture of his time, Merriman re-invigorates central symbolic and mythic themes of that culture in terms of their creative application to the social circumstances and the psychic realities of his day. He does this in a work that is primarily and unreservedly a work of the imagination, his imagination engaging with that of his contemporary audience and with that of succeeding generations of audience down to the present.

Bean Feasa/Wise Woman

If *Aoibheall*, territorial goddess of Thomond, operates in Merriman's poem and in the continued imaginative response to it in Irish speaking communities as an aristocratic source of wisdom and authority, we can point to the type of legend concerning the wise woman that is featured in Part Two, as manifesting a more proletarian resource of wisdom and authority which operates in the oral rather than the literary tradition of Ireland.

In discussing the meaning of the figure and the legends of the *bean feasa* (the Gaelic wise-woman), in such materials we must bear in mind both traditional or 'insider' or 'local' horizons of their semantic significance and the possibility of subsequent, multiple exegetic recontextualizations of these symbols and narratives. Such hermeneutic recontextualization serves to make traditional materials available in a contemporary and cosmopolitan discourse as the still-effective representations of cultural knowledge of, and collective insight into, the physical and social realities of the human condition. Ricoeur's definition of interpretation speaks of 'the art of deciphering indirect meaning',[20] in its multiple mediations through symbol, myth, dream, image, text, narrative and ideology. In the present case I focus on the meaning of the wise-woman as mediated in symbol, in narrative and in ideology, and try to show that the way the meaningfulness of wise-woman tradition was constructed in the tradition itself (in the narrative performance of legend) cannot be confined to that tradition, or to the past, but continues on in our own efforts at interpreting not only the traditional text but also our own contemporary life experience, in the context of our knowledge of such texts and their operation. Thus I operate with the idea that cultural meaning is never either bounded or totally coherent; rather is it a question of the continual construction and recreation of meaning in an ongoing process of symbolic and ritual representation that is continually giving fresh externalization and communication to the perceptions of meaningfulness that inform our lives, whether it is as participants or commentators, actors or analysts that we consciously register ourselves to ourselves at any given moment.

The archive of vernacular, oral narrative accumulated from the field-work activities of the Irish Folklore Commission collectors in the 1930s contains numerous accounts of how local communities kept alive the memory of local female healers, the most general native term for whom was *bean feasa* or 'woman of knowledge'. The term *bean leighis* (woman of healing) is also common. The role of the *bean feasa/bean leighis* is one of a set of female roles having close associations with the Gaelic ancestral otherworld that, along with popular forms of Christianity, constitutes the syncretic, vernacular religion of early modern, Irish culture. These female roles were activated at times of life-crisis in what was a predominantly patriarchal society, as a coping mechanism in the face of the trauma of major life transitions and afflictions. The power of these women – the *bean ghlúine* (the 'handy woman' or country midwife) the *bean chaointe* (the 'keener' or crying woman of funerary ritual) the *bean feasa* (the wise-woman) – to diagnose and minister to the stricken individual and the stricken community was held to derive from their close association with the native otherworld and the knowledge and skill which that association conferred. The *bean feasa* stands apart from the others in that the activation of her role is achieved in fictional legend rather than in the somatic reality of delivering actual children or reciting poetry over an actual corpse. The social and cultural interpretation of the figure and the legends of the wise-woman then, offers a challenge that can bring us far beyond the ethnographic sites and circumstances of her reported activities.

Biddy Early, the wise-woman of Feakle in County Clare, is the *bean feasa* who has hitherto received most notice in literature and social science. Lady Augusta Gregory, dramatist and literary colleague of Yeats, reported extensively on the stories circulating about Biddy Early and she recorded these first-hand at the turn of the last century. Professor Nancy Schmitz of Laval University used this Gregory material as well as the manuscripts of the Folklore Commission Archive, to produce an article in the *Journal of the Folklore Institute* entitled 'The Legend of an Irish Wise Woman'.[21] Schmitz attributes a shamanic character to the figure of Biddy Early and to the role of the wise-woman in general, on the grounds that wise-women were believed, in tradition, to acquire their knowledge and their power as a result of visiting the native otherworld and travelling with its spirit denizens, the 'fairies'. On this reckoning, the country midwife too (the *bean ghlúine*), would also have to be seen in shamanic light as very many accounts exist of visits to the native spirit world by the handy-woman that result in her endowment with increased gifts in her obstetric craft. I will leave the shamanic question to one side and will concentrate instead on the figure and the legends of the *bean feasa*, the wise-woman of Gaelic tradition, in an indigenous Irish context, conscious of course, that Scottish Gaelic vernacular culture has much to contribute.

A starting point is the acknowledgement that the Irish wise-woman is a healer – by predominantly symbolic means – of crisis trauma. Where the roles of midwife and keener focus on the life traumas of birthing and dying, that of the *bean feasa* focuses on the affliction traumas that arise from apparently inexplicable loss of health or property. When consulted about such trauma her diagnosis invariably involves an unrecognized transgressive disturbance of the balance of relationships between humans and otherworld spirits, sometimes also involving a disturbance, similarly transgressive but unrecognized, in the field of human social relationships. Examples would be the mysterious illnesses or injuries arising from the unwitting or negligent siting of a dwelling-house adjacent to a fairy ringfort or a fairy pathway, or the human and animal illnesses or crop failures arising from the sorcery of envious neighbours who feel themselves threatened by competitive and successful individuals or families in the matter of agricultural resources and productivity. Such diagnosis and its acceptance, involves the bringing into consciousness – for the victim and for the interpretative community of the story – of the hidden implications and the deeper motivations of behaviour in a society that is ideologically committed to communitarian values and that recognizes the dependence of its continued well-being on the maintenance of harmonious relationships with ancestral otherworld forces. Breaches of communitarian or cosmological harmony bring afflictive retribution in the form of, allegedly mysterious, loss of well-being. The fictional resort to the wise-woman is a narrative in which the community tells itself the truth about its relationships, albeit in coded and condensed form.

In the vernacular culture of the pre-modern Irish countryside, illness and injury are treated also, of course, by the herbalist and the bonesetter and to an increasing but very limited degree in the course of the nineteenth century, by the medical profession. Stories of resort to the wise-woman, however, remain a prominent part of the recorded memory of the largely elderly informants with whom the Folklore Commission collectors worked in the first half of the last century. The recounted practice of the wise-woman overlaps, to an extent, the actual practice of herbalism by both men and women and accounts of her diagnosis and advice often conclude with the instruction to administer, as drink or lotion, a herbal liquid, sometimes provided in bottled form by the wise woman herself. Some of the legends describe how she is to be seen gathering herbs, at dawn or dusk, accompanied, on occasion, by an otherworld spirit. The treatment the *bean feasa* proffers, however, ranges way beyond herbalism. An example of the fundamentally symbolic nature of such treatment is the detailed instructions provided by *Máire Ní Mhurchú*, the wise-woman of the Beara district of West Cork, to the man whose wife had been, in her diagnosis, 'swept' (abducted by the fairy otherworld host). Such otherworld abduction is commonly the explanation in pre-modern Irish vernacular culture for the condition of the sickly child, the wasting adult, even the sick animal. The unhealthy human or animal is understood to be a 'changeling' substitute left in exchange for the one who has been 'swept'. In the *Máire Ní Mhurchú* story in question, the *bean feasa* reveals the location of the abducted wife, across the bay in County Kerry, and gives specific instructions as to when and how she may be recovered. Not only does she prescribe such treatment but herself goes along with the rescue party and aids their escape from the pursuing spirits. The escape is not absolute or complete, however, since we are told that cattle belonging to the rescued woman's husband died every year during the next ten or twelve years. Such stories of otherworld fairy abduction and its consequences are now being revealed as coded discourse concerning such matters as post-natal depression, child and marital abuse, sexual non-conformity and psychic disturbances.[22] In relation to fairy abduction, we can observe hidden motives and oblique significations being given expression in displaced fashion, in the verbal performance of a narrative repertoire of legend that resembles in this respect the wise-woman repertoire and the repertoire of lament poetry of the *bean chaointe* (the keener at the wake), who also articulates that which otherwise cannot be talked of openly, such as the possible frustrations and tribulations that may have attended the married life of a bereaved spouse. Legends concerning the *bean ghlúine*, the country midwife, also appear to lend themselves to a hermeneutic involving coded symbolic displacement.

Even allowing for the traces of herbalist practice attaching to the figure and activities of the wise-woman, it is clearly the case that her central role is in relation to the healing of otherworld affliction by symbolic means. I have suggested earlier that the set of powerful females who are portrayed as operating in times of life-crisis in the patriarchal society of pre-modern Ireland – midwife, keener and wise-woman – have close associations with the ancestral Gaelic otherworld that, along with popular Christianity, constitutes the magico-religious field of late, pre-modern, Irish vernacular culture. I would argue that these occasionally powerful females are structurally parallel, in the cultural logic of ancestral tradition, to the mythic goddess of native Irish cosmology. Early Irish literature and the mythological legends of the pre-modern, oral narrative repertoire jointly attest to a continuing allegiance in the vernacular ideology and its narrative embodiment to the figure and jurisdiction in human affairs of a powerful, autonomous, female, otherworld agency who is a source of wisdom, authority and power in the vernacular understanding of and response to experience. In the case of the *bean feasa* especially we can, I believe, see how a transform of the goddess figure is represented as being actively available to the community in times of affliction as a kind of oracle who may be consulted in order to discover the true meaning of things and the appropriate course of action to be pursued in order to restore cosmic, social and psychic harmony.

If the knowledge of ancestral native cosmology, recreated and transmitted in the circulation of mythological legends in institutionalized storytelling, provides the pre-modern communities with the *figure* whom the wise-woman embodies in her dealings with the afflicted and her dealings, on their behalf, with the spirit otherworld (the unconscious) then I would argue that it is *knowledge*, too, that drives the transmission and re-creation of those legends. The knowledge involved here can be seen as a collectively, or communally-held, understanding of the dynamic of psychotherapy whereby the emotional distress of the afflicted victim is subjected in story to the kind of transference and transaction that enables a degree of resolution of the distress in a cathartic acknowledgement of, and in a partial insight into the origin and significance of the affliction. Painful or paralysed joints, loss of speech, swollen or ulcerated limbs, fevers, wasting sickness are, it seems to me – as much as fairy abduction is – code; code for a variety and range of emotional and psychosomatic disorders for which no cure is to be found in the hands of the bonesetter or the herbalist or the medical practitioner of the time. A coping mechanism is available, however, in the words attributed to the wise-woman and in the words that narrate her activities and the relief and therapy provided to fictional clients. Such words and narrations of purportedly 'real' persons and 'real' events are testimony to both the communal need to deal with emotionally disturbing experience on an ongoing basis and to the persistant utilization of the resources of an alternative cosmology to that of Christianity, in order to do so.

It is of interest that the wise-woman legends themselves incorporate the clerical view of the wise-woman as a witch figure and a danger to her community. Importantly, however, the stories present Biddy Early, of County Clare, *Máire Ní Mhurchú* of County Cork etc. as kindly, well-regarded women, always ready to help those who seek their aid. Their powers and their knowledge are clearly shown as grounded in their access to the *native* otherworld and not, as in the clerical view, to an anti-Christian diabolic order. This mistaken clerical view is portrayed in story after story showing the wise-woman as a mediator (on the community's behalf), with the *native* otherworld, rather than with any version of the Christian supernatural. In many stories her power is shown to be equal to or better than that of the priest in respect of the diagnosis and healing of affliction; often the priest is taught a lesson that silences his criticism of the wise-woman and the community's reliance on her in times of crisis. Thus the legendary wise-woman successfully opposes the male agent of the male divinity of the patriarchal world religion, unlike the human *bean chaointe*, who succumbs during the actual history of the nineteenth century, to the direct and sometimes vigorous opposition of parish clergy to her funerary performances.

Here, again, I should like to emphasize the fictional nature of the *bean feasa* and the resorting to her that the wise-woman legends recount. Despite extensive documentary research, Nancy Schmitz was unable to establish the historical existence of Biddy Early in County Clare. Likewise, Máirtín Verling reports an inability to locate *Máire Ní Mhurchú* in the historical records of Beara,[23] despite the reporting, by several informants, of familiarity with her whereabouts. Indeed the stories show the wise-woman as operating across the countryside at times and places that conflict with merely human powers of travel. Instead, what we encounter is a sense of the embodiment in the figure of the wise-woman of the landscape goddess of Irish ancestral cosmology, omnipresent guardian of her territory and personification of its well-being in cosmic harmony. The widely attested motif of 'travelling with the fairies' that is attached to various wise-woman figures, also strengthens the *bean feasa*'s connection to the goddess and to the native otherworld.

James Dow's discussion[24] of the universal aspects of symbolic healing suggests that a culture's 'mythic world' is particularized by the healer, in the course of the curing process, so as to give rise to transactional symbols on to which the patient attaches emotions in a fashion allowing their therapeutic manipulation. In the case of the Irish *bean feasa* tradition, both the healer and the patient appear to be symbolic fictions; they are brought to life and set to fictive, therapeutic work in the narrative accounts of the resort to the wise-woman in time of affliction and crisis. I have already suggested that the afflictions recounted in the wise-woman legends are coded projections of the real distresses of an emotional and psychosomatic order for which no treatment is available to the community in which the legends circulate. That they continue to circulate in transmission over time and that they are recounted in a fashion that suggests they are literally, true stories, can be taken as evidence that they are (of themselves and in their continual re-creation in narrative performance) important testimony to the collective awareness in the community at an unconscious – if creatively imaginative – level of the necessity of giving expression to the incidence of, and to the symbolic resolution of, stressful and afflictive experience as an ongoing part of human life.

What I wish to draw attention to here is the way in which the Irish vernacular wise-woman tradition, while exhibiting a structural parallel with ancestral myth and cosmos in terms of the figure and significance of the *bean feasa*, exhibits also a functional parallel with western psychotherapy in offering individuals an opportunity of engaging with a discourse in which their emotional distress is contained and projected in terms of a symbolic coding which furnishes them with the opportunity of distancing and transacting their painful emotions, as if by proxy, in the distancing and transacting portrayed as being achieved by the afflicted victims in the wise-woman stories. Such stories, in their continued narration and transmission, continually remind the community that meaning can be put on all life experience and that, in imagination at least, a way of coping is available that both does and does not work all the time, as in the story of the girl who was struck dumb and who has her speech restored through a visit to the wise-woman. In narrative imagination the girl can both a) speak with the wise-woman out of her dumbness and b) continue to remain intermittently mute in the aftermath of her cure, illustrating the complex and ambiguous nature of the communal credence afforded to the legends in question – a complexity and ambiguity paralleled in the truths by means of which psychotherapy operates today.

Wise-woman tradition constitutes, I think, a kind of communal or public therapy in the case of traditional communities who are generally held, in current thinking, to lack any public space or mediated communication. I think it would be a mistake to overlook the capacity of traditionally institutionalized, vernacular, oral narrative performance (for example, Irish storytelling) to provide a forum where private afflictions (which may have remained unspoken in any *actual* social context) could be made publicly amenable to a psychotherapeutic dynamic that operated, in a collective and largely unconscious way, to the benefit of the emotional and psychic health of the individual members of the communities to whom the wise-woman symbolically ministered. Healing rituals usually take place in public and it is in the public arena of oral narrative performance that I am claiming similar ritual status for the legends of the *bean feasa*. In them I see a communal insight into both the creation of cultural meaning and into the interpretation, in decipherment, of its narrative externalizations to the benefit of imaginative and mental life.

In speaking of such interpretation as an art of decipherment (see p. 71), Ricoeur draws attention to the imaginative creativity of any authentic hermeneutic. Such creativity initially characterizes both the indigenous, symbolic construction of meaningfulness and its subsequent reconstruction, transformation and transmission in tradition. It must also be present in authentic philosophical or anthropological exegesis and commentary and in the authentic application, to therapeutic effect, of such exegetic understanding of the dynamics of the construction of cultural knowledge and its imaginative renewal. Taking this view the relevance of the traditional narratives of Irish cosmology and mythology as resources of creative imagination once again becomes apparant, since what they recount is, finally, not arcane and peculiar, but can be taken as a symbolic representation of common life experiences arising from the human condition. In representing how one cultural tradition made those experiences meaningful and suggested ways of transcending the darker aspects of that meaningfulness, the Irish stories we consider yield valuable insight into the operations of culture process as these impinge on the life of the imagination and of the psyche.

'Telling Tradition'. Bess Cronin, singer and storyteller, performing at her fireside in the townland of *Lios Buí*, Co. Cork.

PART TWO

*Stories of the Cailleach and
the Wise-Woman*

Introduction

Central to the stories presented in translation in this Part (and, in their original Irish-language versions in Part Three) are the figures of the *cailleach* and the wise-woman as prototypes or original, archetypal condensations of ranges of meaningfulness that have been traditionally constructed and transmitted in mythological and legendary Irish narrative. Who this *cailleach* figure is or is understood to be, for the communities in which the stories were told, is a product of the complex amalgamation of cosmological, religious and literary ideas and images that changes and develops through time. The two ideas/images that are emphasized in the perspective in which the *cailleach* and wise-woman stories are dealt with here are a) the idea/image of the divine personified female sovereignty principle and b) the idea/image of the human old woman, who has otherworld or supernatural associations. The connection of the *cailleach* figure as sovereignty principle with southwest Munster arises from the prominence of the medieval poem in which 'The Old Woman of Beare' – calling herself *cailleach* – envinces something of the identity of a displaced and Christianized sovereignty queen. That connection with Beara and the South West is diluted, however, in the case of stories of the *cailleach* which derive from the narrative tradition of other areas in Ireland and Gaelic Scotland. Though the wise-woman stories presented here are taken only from the narrative tradition of counties Cork and Kerry, this does not suggest that the figure of the wise-woman in Irish tradition should be understood as standing in a special relationship to the *Cailleach Bhéarra*, but rather to the generalized sense of the *cailleach* as an archetypal figure of Irish myth and legend.

The term *cailleach*, of course, has its own complex etymological history that reflects the way in which it has carried competing cosmological, religious and literary connotations. These have been succinctly outlined and discussed by Máirín Ní Dhonnchadha in an article[1] that convincingly proposes a line of semantic development for the word *cailleach* that originates with its derivation from the latin word *pallium*, meaning 'veil'. In its primary meaning of 'veiled one' *cailleach* is shown to be a term relating to a Christian categorization of women who were either 'spoken for' in marriage or consecrated as nuns and thus 'spoken for' in marriage to Christ. In this context *cailleach* also developed the sense of denoting the married woman who moves (as in widowhood) from human sexual union to embracing the status of consecrated celibacy, as a nun. It is this latter sense of *cailleach* that is counterpointed (to such moving literary effect) in the ninth-century 'Lament of the Old Woman of Beare' with its pre-Christian sovereignty queen personification of territory and landscape. The sense of *cailleach* as 'supernatural figure, hag-witch', develops through its association with manifestations in medieval Irish literature of the terrifying, destructive aspect of the sovereignty queen as death-goddess. These, in Ní Dhonnchadha's words, invest the term *cailleach* 'with memories which overbear its primary meaning and ordinary significations', and allow for the emergence in Modern Irish of the unqualified term *cailleach* as a word for the female 'supernatural figure, witch'.

Cailleach Bhéarra

The *Cailleach Bhéarra* of modern Irish and Scottish Folklore of whom stories presented here speak, is a figure whose cosmological and mythological import can be taken to include the senses of sovereignty personification and old woman or hag of supernatural association. In terms of both medieval mythology and modern legend she is, clearly, an archetypal figure.

Reference to *Cailleach Bhéarra* in both medieval materials and in modern scholarly surveys of the medieval Gaelic world is pervasive. She appears as an unstable and yet pre-eminent presence whose status is attested equally in Irish and Scottish Gaelic tradition and in the modern scholarship of these traditions. Professor Mac Cana's reference to her in his survey[2] of Celtic mythology is typical both in its emphasis and in its qualification. He speaks of *Cailleach Bhéarra* as being 'as famous in modern Irish folklore as she evidently was in the early literary tradition'. The textual basis of her earlier fame is clearly of an implicit nature only, yet Mac Cana just as clearly accepts the ascription to her by early tradition of a cluster of roles: a geotectonic role in landscape formation; a status as divine ancestress with numerous progeny of tribes and people; the characteristic of being an epitome of longevity in passing repeatedly through the cycle of youth and age; and a role as sovereignty symbol in, for example, her representation in the medieval materials, under the name *Buí*, as the wife of *Lugh*, elsewhere himself the model representation of kingship. The Scottish scholar, J.G. MacKay, has referred to her as 'the most tremendous figure in Gaelic myth today'[3] while Professor Wagner – thinking, surely, not only of the famous ninth-century poem – calls her 'the most famous old lady in Irish literature'.[4] Ann Ross, too, has accorded her considerable prominence, not only in her book *Pagan Celtic Britain*[5] but also in her 'The Divine Hag of the Pagan Celts'.[6]

Attempts to identify the nature and the significance that *Cailleach Bhéarra* carries within the Gaelic world, quickly lead one to the realization that we are dealing with an extremely complex figure. At different stages and at different levels of Gaelic tradition, the figure of *Cailleach Bhéarra* has been used to represent various different clusters of cultural meaning so that we are faced with a multiplicity of forms and functions which prove very difficult to distinguish and whose historical and/or functional relationship to each other continues to be obscure to a great degree. In one viewing, *Cailleach Bhéarra* would appear to represent a version of traditions of a mother-goddess emanating from the worlds of Indo-European and even old European cosmology. In another she appears as a representative figure of the Divine Hag of the Celtic and early Irish worlds who has close connections with the sovereignty queen tradition. *Cailleach Bhéarra* can also be seen as a version of a supernatural female wilderness figure, peripheral to – and usually inimical to – the human world. Indeed in modern Gaelic folklore of Scotland and Ireland she is most frequently understood as one of a range of such wilderness figures and it can be asserted that these owe their existence (at least in part), in Gaelic traditions, late and early, to the influence of Norse cosmology in its personification of the forces of wild nature. I believe this is an aspect of *Cailleach Bhéarra* tradition that has not, hitherto, been generally acknowledged to a sufficient degree.

An examination of Scottish material relating to the supernatural female bearing the names *Cailleach Bhéarra/Bheurr* reveals a multitude of association between her and the forces of wild nature, especially the storms of winter, the storm clouds and the boiling winter sea. She is also very much the spirit of the high ground, of mountain and moor, and is seen frequently to personify wildlife, for instance the life and wellbeing and fertility of the deer herd. Norse folklore is pervaded with creatures representing the forces of wild nature and in Scottish tradition *Cailleach Bheurr* is frequently said to have originated in Norway, from where she allegedly carried the rocks out of which she formed the coasts and mountains of the Scottish mainland and of the Western Isles. If many of the Scottish legends of *Cailleach Bheurr* contain such motifs of Nordic provenance there is equal evidence of a Norse element in the make-up of other varieties of Scottish hags of the peripheral wilderness who also personify wild nature and are held to threaten human life. Such personages, but especially *Cailleach Bheurr*, are credited with the formation of various aspects of the physical landscape and are often said to reside in a cliff or a sea rock where they rule the waves of the sea.

The *Cailleach Bhéarra(ch)* of the Irish Beara peninsula is locally associated with a standing stone in the vicinity of Eyeries. Eyeries is a placename that Roibeárd Ó hUrdail suggests may be of Scandinavian origin in being derived from the Norse *eyrr* which means 'a gravelly beach', and is found in well-known placenames of the Scottish coast (c.f. Ayr), in the Western Isles and in the Isle of Man. At the tip of the Beara peninsula is *Oileán Buí*, named for *Cailleach* or *Sentainne Bérri*, one of whose earlier names was *Buí*, and which bears also the Norse-derived name 'Dursey'. There is little doubt that the south-west Irish coast is rich in Norse association; *An tOileán Thiar* (Blasket) and *Carraig Aonair* (Fastnet) are two other major south-western locations seen as having Norse-derived, alternative names.

Cailleach Bhéarra's reputation as a figure of significance would, then, appear to span the worlds of Celtic mythology, Gaelic medieval literature and modern Irish and Scottish folklore with, in each case, a possible Norse connection. Eleanor Hull and Alexander Hagerty Krappe have both written valuable articles on aspects of *Cailleach Bhéarra* in later popular tradition. Hull[7] raises the question of whether the myth of *Cailleach Bhéarra* might not be a comparatively late one since she is, according to Hull, unknown outside the Gaelic world and within that world gets no mention in mainstream medieval sources such as *Sanas Chormaic, Cóir Anmann, Dindsheanchas,* or *Acallamh na Senórach*. She is mentioned, we may note, in *Aislinge Meic Conglinne* and also in the *Expulsion of the Déssi* (both twelfth-century tales) and under her earlier name, *Buí/Boí*, she appears in the *Metrical Dindsheanchas*, a twelfth-century compilation of the lore of prominent places. Despite this relative dearth of mention, Hull concedes that *Cailleach Bhéarra* tradition, especially in its geotectonic aspect, might well have an earlier and more distant source than the boundaries of the Gaelic world. Krappe takes that earlier, distant source for granted[8] and sees *Cailleach Bhéarra* tradition as a Gaelic reflex of a theme or themes whose provenance is wider and older than the entire Celtic world:

> La Cailleach Bheara est une ancienne déesse agraire et chthonienne équivalent gaélique de la Déméter grecque, déesse de la fertilité mais aussi de la mort. S'est rattachée à elle une légende développée d'un ancien rite qui, en Phrygie, courait sur Lityerse.[9]

Hull in fact quotes in translation from the text of a modern Irish narrative (published by Douglas Hyde[10] in *An Sgéulaidhe Gaedhealach*) that seems to echo the Phrygian tale of how, in a reaping contest, Hercules eventually overthrows Lityerses, son of Midas, who in those days reigned over the corn-harvest on the banks of the Maeander river in Asia Minor.

In such a context one must recall Gerard Murphy's remark that 'many Irish folk-tale motifs are as old as the days of primitive Indo-European unity',[11] and the contention, on archaeological rather than on literary or linguistic grounds by Jan Filip, of a significant degree of continuity into the Celtic world from the late stone age in the matter of the *Magna Mater*.[12] If early twentieth-century storytellers in the west of Ireland have – as an authentic part of their traditional repertoire from medieval and earlier times

– an account of how a local champion overcomes the female divinity of the corn harvest in a reaping contest, then it would appear that Gaelic oral narrative tradition (in Ireland at least), was still, into the present age, carrying forward an extremely ancient formulation of that pattern of opposition between otherworld supreme divinity and semi-divine/semi-human hero whose outline in Irish mythology O'Rahilly tried to establish.[13] Not only that, but Hyde's text (if genuine), could well supply the affirmative answer to Tomás Ó Cathasaigh's question[14] in *The Heroic Biography of Cormac Mac Airt* as to the existence of an (as yet) unrecognized 'otherworld goddess *vs* hero' opposition as predicated in the syntagmatic and paradigmatic relations inherent in O'Rahilly's theory. A second source of such 'goddess *vs* male hero' opposition is alluded to by Máire MacNeill, in *The Festival of Lughnasa*, when she speaks[15] of the shadow of a female person – sometimes called *Ana/Áine,* sometimes *Cailleach Bhéarra* – looming behind the male divinity of *Crom Dubh* from whom, in the *Lughnasa* legends, *Lugh* ultimately wins the harvest. Again popular tradition would appear to be preserving the names and the older strands of meaning – as chthonic and fertility goddess – of a figure who, at the learned and aristocratic level of tradition, is long-since transformed in function to sovereignty queen.

At the learned, political and literary level of Irish tradition, the chief significance of the female divine develops away from the ancient chthonic and harvest associations and – through the figures of the goddesses of war and death – is ultimately invested in figures representing the sovereignty of the rightful ruler and the personification of the territories and even of the whole land of Ireland itself. The medieval conception of such sovereignty figures persists into the eighteenth-century *aisling* genre of modern Irish poetic tradition. The allegedly repetitive and clichéd nature of the eighteenth-century tradition was (as I suggest in, pp. 67–70) to be radically revitalized by Brian Merriman who, in calling on – in *Cúirt an Mheán Oíche* – the medieval form of the sovereignty myth, liberated into the modern Gaelic world the powerful, full-blooded personification of sovereignty in the guise of *Aoibheall* of *Craig Léith*.

One of the chief methods known to us in which *Cailleach Bhéarra* is established in medieval tradition in the ranks of the sovereignty queens, is the use of her name to identify the subject of the celebrated Old Irish 'Lament of the Old Woman of Beare' (see pp. 48–52). In the second quatrain of this poem the line '*Is me Caillech Bérri Buí*' is rich in ideological import with its overtones of Christian religion, Celtic mythology and localized political topography. *Buí* was claimed as divine ancestress by the *Corca Loigde* (a leading tribe of the *Érainn* of West Munster), whose territory once included the whole of the Beara peninsula and the chief residence of whose over-king was at Dunboy (*Dún Buíthe*). Such political use of the significance of *Cailleach Bhéarra* in the realm of poetry is presumably paralleled by her similar utilization in prose, as in the subject of the now lost tale *Serc Caillighe Bérri do Fothad Cannaine* where, we may assume, the desire to shape political reality produces a further claiming of her as ancestress and divine legitimatrix on behalf of aspirants to political authority.

The author of the ninth-century Lament proceeds to exploit ideological ambiguities in inventing the figure and name-form of the aged female who is at once the lingering representative of a profane, native eternity of earthly sovereignty *and* the Christian nun finally embracing the prospect of an eternity of the heavenly sovereignty of the male Christian god. In his 1953 edition of the poem Gerard Murphy wrote:

> Her name which is *Sentainne Bérri* ... has already become *Caillech Bérri*. *Caillech Bérri* would once have meant 'The Nun of Beare' but had doubtless at the time the poem was written already, in ordinary speech, become the equivalent of an obsolescent *Sentainne Bérri* which could mean only 'The Old Woman of Beare': *sentainne* is obsolete in Irish today and *cailleach* for long has meant, not 'nun', but 'old woman'.[16]

Sentainne Bérri then is an ancient ascription of the divine female that gives her a localized mythological and quasi-political association with south-west Ireland and in particular with the Beara peninsula at whose tip lie both *Tech nDuinn* (The Bull Rock, *Donn's* house, the otherworld realm of the dead) and Dursey Island (*Oileán Buí*) a kind of headquarters location of the premier, female otherworld agency.

We can note that Heinrich Wagner would accept the identification of the earliest name for *Cailleach Bhéarra* (viz. *Boí/Buí*) with a derivation from the Indo-European form **Buvyā* meaning 'white cow-like-one' – this being, Wagner claims, a characteristic appellation of Indo-European manifestations of the *Magna Mater*.[17] On Professor Wagner's terms, then, the river Boyne (*An Bhóinn, Boänd* (OI), Buvinda (Gr), Govinda (Skt)) is named, ultimately, for the female divine who herself begins to become known as *Cailleach Bhéarra* at about the late-eighth or early-ninth centuries when the famous Lament was composed. In considering prose narrative versions of *Cailleach Bhéarra* legends, a further remark of Gerard Murphy's regarding the Lament is crucial:

> The change from *Sentainne Bérri* to *Caillech Bérri* doubtless first occurred colloquially among the illiterate. When it had firmly established itself, the learned may have invented the legend that the Old Woman of Beare became a nun and received the *caille* or

nun's veil ... thus justifying the title *caillech*. In quatrains 11, 12 and 22 of the poem, the Old Woman of Beare is clearly looked upon as a nun.[18]

From other quatrains of the poem it is equally clear that the Old Woman of Beare has been the consort of kings and, thus, the embodiment of the sovereignty principle in much the same way as *Gormfhlaith* and *Liadain* embody it in the poems attributed to them. Using the traditional associations of the *Cailleach* or *Sentainne Bérri* as mother-goddess, as shaper and guardian of the land, and as sovereignty figure, the author of the Lament is able to express, to quote Professor Mac Cana, 'the deep incompatibility between Christianity and the world of pagan belief', something that Mac Cana calls 'one of the great crucial themes of the Irish past'.[19] Most commentators on the Lament see this contrast, or opposition, to be something pivotal in the poem and a major source of its imaginative tension. Such imaginative tension, generated between native and Christian ideology and motif, is a source of a good deal of Irish artistic output – visual as well as literary – in the medieval period. Whether this ambivalence of cosmology inherent in the Lament itself – and, for example, in poems such as 'Hail *Brigit*', attributed to Orthanach Ua Coíllámha in the early ninth century – , found any similar expression then in prose tales featuring *Cailleach Bhéarra* in the colloquial repertoire of the bearers of popular Gaelic tradition, we can now never know in any direct way. We can, however, examine what has come down into modern times, amalgamated in complicated ways with later and with learned material, as the popular traditional repertoire of the last generations of *scéalaithe* and *seanchaithe* in the Gaelic world.

Cailleach Bhéarra is prominent in this repertoire, both in Ireland and in Scotland, and some attempt can be made to impose order on the multiplicity of significance which she seems to possess in this material. One may attempt to establish the developmental stages in the narrative and other history of the person and the legend of *Cailleach* Bhéarra, or one may in synchronic or structural terms, attempt to construct a model showing the relationships to each other of the various aspects of *Cailleach Bhéarra* tradition. Such a structural model has been proposed by Paul Friedrich to cater for the significance and development of *Aphrodite* through antiquity.[20] By means of his model Friedrich is able to resolve apparently opposing aspects of the *Aphrodite* tradition; for instance, the sexuality and purity that are, in her texts, simultaneously affirmed. The apparent absence of any substantial early corpus of *Cailleach Bhéarra* myth or legend probably means that textually-based work on her earlier significance (parallel to Friedrich's on the significance of *Aphrodite*), is less likely of accomplishment. Nevertheless, in the case of

Cailleach Bhéarra and her surrogates, we should regard them as possessing separate – and perhaps structurally opposing – clusters of cultural meaning in the context of the Indo-European, the Celtic and the Gaelic worlds. The early, Indo-European heritage in the *Cailleach Bhéarra* character can be seen (in the more modern material), primarily in the earth mother and fertility goddess aspects of her figure. Similarly, in relation to a more specifically Celtic heritage of significance for the Divine Hag, we should highlight the primacy of the Hag of War and Death aspect, which also has strong overtones of a powerful sexuality. The aspect of the tradition developed latest and only at the learned and literary level is that of sovereignty goddess, divine consort of the rightful ruler. It is this aspect which has, however, made the term *Cailleach Bhéarra* or a rendering of it, well-known throughout the later Gaelic world as a name for the subject of a large corpus of legend regarding various manifestations of a supernatural female ancient.

The significance of *Cailleach Bhéarra* in modern Irish and Scottish folklore has, thus, to be understood in relation to two separate, yet related, levels of tradition: the literary, learned traditions of the early middle ages in which the term *Cailleach Bhéarra* is established as the name of a sovereignty queen in politics, in prose and in poetry; and the common, popular, unlearned level of Gaelic tradition (concerning which there is little direct evidence until modern times) which seems to have contained a range of manifestations of an ancient female divine with the general characteristics of the Old European *Magna Mater*. Since the middle ages and due partly to the fusing of the learned with the unlearned traditions in the social upheavals of the early modern period, versions of the name *Cailleach Bhéarra* have come into widespread use throughout the Gaelic world, in Ireland and Scotland, as names for *Magna Mater*-type female supernaturals, in materials placing a marked emphasis on the Terrible Mother, the wilderness-personifying and the threatening side of their nature. In Ireland the forms *Cailleach Bhéar(r)a* and *Cailleach Bhéar(r)ach* are the usual ones found in oral tradition. In Scottish tradition the range of oral variants includes *Cailleach Bhéarra, Cailleach Bheur, Cailleach Bheurr, Cailleach Bheurrach, Cailleach Beartha, Cailleach Bheathrach* and it appears that in the transmission of the name at the non-literary level, a degree of folk etymology has come into operation that draws on conceptions of a female nature and wilderness spirit owing something to the influences of Norse mythology. The second element of the name in Scotland is often understood by tradition-bearers and scholarly commentators alike to mean 'keen', 'sharp', 'pointed' (< *beur*) or else 'quick-witted', 'sharp-spoken', 'eloquent' (< *beurra(ch)*).

In Irish tradition too, the oral form *Cailleach Bhéarrach* and the allied form *Cailleach Bhiorach* also suggest the operation of an element of folk etymology in non-learned transmission of the name *Cailleach Bhéarra* as a term for a female supernatural who is perceived as much a wilderness spirit as a sovereignty queen. A detailed analysis of the full range of the forms of the name would prove instructive. I suggest that it might well reveal that a majority of the hags known to popular tradition over Ireland and Scotland carrying a name-form suggestive of identification with the Béarra of the poem, should instead be understood to be named from a female personification of the peripheral wilderness whose chief feature is that of being *biorach,* 'sharp', 'shrill', 'inimical'. The form *Berach/Beorach* was a relatively common personal name in early Ireland and the forms *Cailleach Bheurr/Bheurrach* are perhaps the most widely encountered forms in the Scottish material. It is surely relevant that the forms '*An Chailleach Bhéarrach*', '*leis an gCailligh Bhéarraigh*' are the oral forms occuring on the Beara peninsula itself to refer to the 'Old Woman of Beare beside Dursey'. It may be argued that, at the level of popular oral tradition even in Beara itself, the connotations of *Cailleach Bhéarrach/Bheurrach* are primarily those of the generalized wilderness figure rather than of the Divine Hag cum sovereignty queen of learned tradition. George Broderick's suggestion[21] that the Manx traditional song about *Berrey Dhone* is possible evidence that *Bérri* was there the hag's original name and not merely a toponym, is of the greatest interest and needs to be taken into account in the wider context.

We can look at some of the non-sovereignty legends attached to the figure of the *Cailleach Bhéarra* in later tradition as examples of narratives that carry the retention and the reinterpretation of the ancient figure of the divine otherworld female down to the brink of the present day. Elsewhere I have suggested broad categories of classification for the non-sovereignty queen legends about *Cailleach Bhéarra* as follows:[22]

1. Creator and dominator of landscape.
2. Extraordinary facets, physique, nourishment and hygiene.
3. Suggested physical eternity but shown to be finite.
4. Conflict with and displacement by Christianity.

In respect of category 1 we can note how the material, nurturative aspect of the otherworld female is inherent in her being presented as creator and shaper of the physical landscape; islands, lakes, hillsides, rock-formations, thunder, storms, wave power, all attest to her geotectonic power. In this fashion the non-sovereignty queen hag-goddess also personifies landscape and territory and is represented as even constituting, corporeally, the very fabric of landscape in the identification of physical features with aspects of her body: the Paps of *Anu, Dá Chích Anann* (a mountain range in Kerry); *Brú na Bóinne/Cnogba,* Newgrange and Knowth burial chambers (the latter being 'the telluric womb' of the goddess in the words of Tomás Ó Cathasaigh).[23] The negative, destructive aspect of the hag-goddess is attested to in widespread legends regarding the dangers to humans and to human well-being that are associated with travel through certain landscapes such as mountain passes or remote valleys, or with being abroad in the night when the outdoors is best left to the otherworld forces.

The legends of the second category of non-sovereignty queen material relating to *Cailleach Bhéara* present her as a gigantic presence covering the land and passing through it continually in a way that makes her everpresent and identifies her with the fertility of the natural environment and its creatures. In south-western coastal regions, legend presents her as subsisting on a marine diet (seaweed, salmon and wild garlic), which she is able to harvest over a huge stretch of terrain. This sense of ceaseless movement across the landscape is also expressed in the detail that she was forever washing her feet and legs so as never to carry the mud from one puddle to the next; she is not to be fixed or confined in identification with any single location, but is a shifting, dynamic, vital force within and across the physical landscape.

Category 3 type legends present the figure of *Cailleach Bhéarra* as the epitome of longevity. Together with the yew tree and the eagle she is said to be among the three longest-lived phenomena of tradition, the length of whose days defies human reckoning. If any measure is set on the existence or life-span of the hag-goddess, it is in terms of fitting her into a framework of mythic history starting from the baseline of the Biblical Flood. Since the compilation of mythic, pseudo-history – culminating in the twelfth-century work, *Lebor Gabála Érenn* (The Book of the Invasions of Ireland) – was an attempt at achieving an accommodation between Biblical Christianity and archaic ancestral cosmology at the literate and learned level of cultural tradition, it is not inappropriate to suggest that at the vernacular level of traditional culture also, the figure and person of the hag-goddess (hitherto conceived of as immortally ever present and co-terminal with the physical), should now be envisaged as having a pseudo-historical beginning. She is correspondingly envisaged, at both the learned and vernacular levels as being ousted, at the end, and displaced by the Christian male divinity, in terms of the 'victory' of the saint and the cleric over the hag-goddess in the legends of category 4 – legends that, as it were, re-present the matter of the 9th century Lament of the Old Woman of Beare.

The category 4 legends, regarding *Cailleach Bhéarra* displacement, banishment and petrification, show both a feminization of the Christian representative who wins out over the hag-goddess (the female St Gobnait, herself the product of Celtic/Christian syncretism), and the internalization into the secular cultural tradition of patriarchal Christianity of the otherworld divine female figure, that we have seen in Part One expressed so powerfully at the learned and literary level in the early medieval era. I deal below with the legend of the servant boy of *Cailleach Bhéarra* who persisted in going out to turn hay on a day when, by her estimation, rain was a certainty. On being scolded by her for setting out to turn hay on a wet day, he questions her certainty as to the weather forecast. When she declares her basis of certainty to be what the scaldcrow and the deer communicate to her — in terms of a communion of nature — the boy, speaking with the secular voice of a patriarchal Christianity, then says:

> Ná creid feannóg is ná creid fia
> 's ná creid briathra mná;
> Más moch mall eirgheas an ghrian
> Is mar is toil le dia a bhéas an lá.

> Believe not the scaldcrow nor the deer
> And place no store by the word of a woman;
> Whether the sun rises early or late
> The day that ensues will be as God disposes.

Further examples of the displacement of the goddess, in category 4 type legends and also in respect of her sovereignty queen persona are examined in this Part (pp. 142–60).

Though there are relatively few instances known to us of the 'political use' of the figure of *Cailleach Bhéarra* we have a general understanding of how the names and alleged exploits and associations of many eminent figures, lay and clerical, profane, sacred and divine, were put to use by the composers, compilers and transcribers of medieval Irish genealogies, origin legends, saints' lives, praise poems and so on. We should also, I believe, allow for the operation of a similar kind of judicious exploitation of traditional lore and the traditional associations of aspects of that lore, in the creative performances of both medieval and modern storytellers at the popular or folk level of tradition. In particular, in relation to the figure of *Cailleach Bhéarra* and the associations attaching to her in Irish and Scottish Gaelic tradition, we have, I believe, evidence of skilful manipulation by the modern traditional storyteller that bears comparison, in its own way, with the manipulation of aspects of *their* common heritage by the learned practitioners of the medieval material. In either case, we can perceive (along with the recounting of central motifs associated with traditional figures), the ordering of the material, and presumably its delivery in the case of the taletellers, after a fashion that gives creative expression to current imaginative tensions and to the contemporary social and cultural status quo.

Bean Feasa/Wise Woman

Wise-woman legends in Irish tradition may be taken as evidence of an allegiance, in the popular culture of the early modern era, to the generic figure of the *cailleach* as a spirit-personification of the native otherworld. The assertion of such an allegiance carries different meanings in different approaches to the study of tradition and traditional materials that have succeeded each other as dominant paradigms in twentieth-century scholarship. We can identify three separate approaches within that scholarship, that bring with them separate assumptions and procedures to elucidate the materials being studied. These approaches are: firstly, the so-called Finnish or historical/geographical method where the emphasis is on the reconstruction of diachronic lines of textual transmission; secondly, formalist or structural analysis where there is more concern with the patterning of synchronic relationships, of both a textual and a symbolic nature; and thirdly, a contextual approach which emphasizes the continual construction and articulation of meaning within a dynamic of discourse. In summary, there are three separate central concerns – with Figure, with Function and with Process – each of which can be used in the study of narrative materials dealing with the huge subject of the supernatural female in Irish tradition and in particular with narrative of the wise-woman.

Some examples may be mentioned. The concern with Figure and with the identity of specific figures within the reconstructed lines of textual and cultural transmission is to be found in the treatment of 'banshee' legends by Patricia Lysaght[24], (see pp. 53–4). Here it can be claimed that, within a historical/geographical paradigm, the 'banshee' of late nineteenth- or early twentieth-century legend is the sovereignty queen of early medieval literature, albeit in her destructive transform. In terms of a concern with Function on the other hand, and a delineation of the structural relationships that characterize function, we can point to much of Évelyne Sorlin's analysis of the traditions of midwives and corpse washers and keeners, wherein she demonstrates their structural analogousness to the Celtic Goddess.[25] My own depiction of the patterning of the rituals of the Merry Wake aims at establishing a structural closeness or similarity between the *bean chaointe* (the flesh-and-blood keening-woman) and the 'banshee' figure of legend, in respect of the function that each performs in 'crying' or 'performing' death into and out of the community.[26]

Finally, in terms of a concern with contemporary context and the process of constructing and articulating meaning within that context, Timothy Corrigan Correll presents a dialogic analysis of turn-of-the-century discourses surrounding Irish folk healers, including the wise-woman. Corrigan Correll[27] aims to demonstrate how stories collected by Augusta Gregory about fairy healers and folk medicine[28] give expression to social and political pressures arising from the opposition of traditional and newer forms of ideology and authority in rural Ireland at the end of the nineteenth century. In this broader view, wise-woman legends continually re-interpret ancestral symbolic materials in the light of prevailing political and social conditions. It is also necessary, however, to address the 'microdynamic' of re-interpretation, in terms of the rhetorical and other performance characteristics of specific performance contexts, in order to complete the picture from the point of view of the Process paradigm. Some of these issues are addressed in the commentary which I attach to each of the wise-woman legends included in this Part.

The eighteen texts included here derive from a variety of locations – *Corca Dhuibhne* and *Tuath Ó Siosta* in County Kerry, *Cléire* and *Cum Sheola, Cill Uird* and *Béarra* and *Cairbre* in County Cork – and were recorded in the 1920s and 1930s by different, male, Irish Folklore Commission collectors. The context and circumstances of their collection are, for the most part, those commonly associated with the field activities of the Irish Folklore Commission collectors. Such fieldwork is itself, of course, a part of the cultural process that constructs and transmits the meanings that we may assign to the texts in question and, more generally, to traditions of the *bean feasa*. Its role in the dialogic dynamic of the representation of tradition should not, at any point, be overlooked, though its close analysis – even in respect of this very limited corpus of text – is not attempted here.

Figure
The figure of the *bean feasa*, the woman of knowledge, presented here is referred to by name in a majority of these texts. The specific names themselves are *Eibhlín Ní Ghuinníola* of *Corca Dhuibhne*, *P. Ní L.* of *Tuath Ó Siosta*, *Máire Liam* of *Cill Uird*, *Máire Ní Chearbhaill* of *Cairbre* and *Máire Ní Mhurchú* of *Béarra*. The question arising in a paradigm one perspective – the concern with historical-geographical transmission – would be with the *real* identity of this legendary female figure. Is she really the *Magna Mater* of Old Europe, is she the Celtic sovereignty queen, is she the *bean sí*, is she the non-sovereignty queen *cailleach*, the generalized landscape figure of Irish and Scottish Gaelic oral narrative tradition? In only one text of these eighteen can we be sure of the answer. *P. Ní L.* of *Tuath Ó Siosta* tradition was, 'really' a flesh-and-blood woman, a 'neighbour' who was wont to fall into trance when attending wakes and who was said by other neighbours to bring knowledge and wisdom with her from the otherworld on returning out of these trances. She is also the clearest and, possibly, the only case where the term 'shaman' might be provisionally invoked in a tentative way, in the light of this reported experiencing by an actual individual of a journey to the

otherworld during the regular public performance of trance, at the sacred assembly of the wake.

Apart from *P. Ní L.*, all the other texts appear on examination to present us with figures of legend rather than of flesh-and-blood, figures whose symbolic identity remains a matter of interpretation according to prevailing hermeneutic fashion. If, in the current era of cultural construction and dialogic process, we relinquish any aim of showing that the *bean feasa* is *really* a figure surviving from an earlier era, then also, bearing in mind the necessarily grounded nature of the creativity and renewal associated with the processes of cultural construction, we can recognize the sense of the generic otherworld female still informing accounts of the *bean feasa* in these Kerry and Cork texts of nearly three-quarters of a century ago. This contention is strengthened by the use of the term *cailleach* to refer in a generic way to the figures of such as the wise-woman and the healer, and especially its use in the discourse of male ecclesiastical figures who are frequently portrayed as opposed to the activities of the *bean feasa* and the *bean leighis*. On the legend of the priest's stricken horse, Pádraig Ó Héalaí refers to a variant of the legend from County Galway where the priest calls the healer a *deabhal caillí* (a devil of a hag), noting, however, that this is a term of ecclesiastical vulgar abuse rather than a serious implication of diabolical association.[29]

Function

In terms of Function we should distinguish between the functional role played by the figure of the wise-woman in the plots of the narratives concerning her, and the more formalist or structural function that she plays in the patterning of the cultural discourse in which her representations feature. In relation to the former, perhaps more superficial sense of her function, we can note that the wise-woman of these eighteen texts:

- locates the whereabouts of stolen and lost animals
- diagnoses, explains and prescribes for a variety of physical ailments
- diagnoses otherworld ailments and effects, or prescribes their cure
- diagnoses otherworld injuries and prescribes cure, while claiming to have herself prevented more serious – or even mortal – injuries on the occasion of their infliction
- foretells death or diagnoses an otherworld ailment which results in death
- diagnoses otherworld abduction of adults; prescribes for and participates in, the complex procedures whereby the abduction is reversed

The afflicted parties include parish priests and curates, a landlord *(taoiseach agus tiarna mór)*, neighbours (farmers and farm wives), craftsmen and servants. Thus, the knowledge, power and authority of the wise-woman is represented as active within narratives that reflect both the historical tensions and oppositions of the fields of social and political relationship in the past and the prevailing tensions in the social and political circumstance of the cultural sites in which these texts were recorded. In the context of a concern with paradigm two issues of structural relationship and functional parallelism beyond the plot-pattern, however, I would argue that an analysis of these texts can lend support to my contention[30] (see pp. 71–2) that, in the popular culture of early modern Ireland, the figure of a powerful, autonomous female agency (analogous to the non-sovereignty queen roles of the *bean sí/cailleach*), symbolically underlies and underwrites culturally, the ritual operations and services of real human females in times of social and individual crisis. This symbolic underwriting in structural analysis finds imaginative narrative expression in legend form in the narrative portrayals of the otherworld associations assigned by tradition to certain representative female figures; in this case healers and sources of healing knowledge and, in other cases, midwives and keeners.

In this reading of the function of the narrative *bean feasa*, she serves a structural role within the cultural logic of Irish tradition that bears comparison with the functional–structural operation of the Azande poison oracle, as classically described by Evans-Pritchard for the culture of Southern Sudan.[31] In order to draw out this comparison properly one would need to compare the cosmological settings in which both the Irish *bean feasa* and the Azande poison oracle are operated. While this is a subject to be pursued more fully at another time, there is a crucial point here that I wish to emphasize. Both the *bean feasa* and the poison oracle are imaginatively sophisticated institutions of their respective cultural processes and are resorted to and manipulated in the face of affliction, uncertainty and stress at a time when traditional wisdom is able to offer the prospect of some kind of relief. Both are founded on a common knowledge and perception of certain physiological and psychological realities. For the Azande this involves 1. the knowledge that certain substances are unpredictably poisonous, in certain doses, and 2. the perception that daily life can proceed without a basis in 'absolute certainty' for important decisions. For the Irish it involves 1. the knowledge that some individuals (for instance, P. Ní L. of *Tuath Ó Siosta*), can publicly enter alternative states of consciousness, on occasion, and 2) the perception that certain individuals have a greater talent than others for being psychologically astute as to what motivates human behaviour. On the basis of these physiological and psychological 'cultural realities', Azande and Irish cultural traditions developed symbolic cultural institutions that could be manipulated creatively to interpret and to deal with troubling experience, in ways that draw on ancestral values and ancestral forms of authority. In one case, the response is ritual/behavioural; in the other legendary/narrative. Central to both oracular-diagnostic-therapeutic institutions is imaginative creativity and cultural re-construction. In the Irish case the chief implication, for the study of wise-woman legend, of this way of thinking, is the realization that the existence of *Biddy Early, Máire Ní Mhurchú, Eibhlín Ní Ghuinníola, Máire Ní Chearbhaill* etc., is an existence in interpretative legend, in imaginative creativity, in cultural process. Just as Nancy Schmitz was unable to identify a historical *Biddy Early* in Thomond,[32] and Máirtín Verling was unable to pinpoint a historical *Máire Ní Mhurchu* in Béarra,[33] despite in each case extensive documentary enquiries – so the figure of the wise-woman will forever evade the exact co-ordinates of history and empiricism, living and functioning instead, in the narrative and ritual realms of cultural creativity and renewal.

Process

Moving to the third paradigm, which is concerned with the contexts wherein cultural meaning is continually constructed and transmitted within a dynamic of discourse that gives expression to both cultural innovation and to competing historical, social and political forces, we should again try to distinguish between two kinds of perspective. One is the deductive perspective of the analysis of the west of Ireland healing discourse within which Corrigan Correll embeds the *Biddy Early* material collected by Augusta Gregory. Here we can perceive, historically, the social and political contexts within which healer and wise-woman legends give articulation to the competing sources of knowledge and authority that existed in Thomond and throughout rural Ireland at the turn of the last century. The second is an inductive perspective in which one can try to discern in the words and the performance of the recounters themselves, their own sense of the creative and imaginative process: the process whereby the legend-institution of the resort to the wise-woman is renewed and brought forward into the modernizing world of the twentieth century.

Attention should be drawn to a few passages in the texts that suggest one particular aspect of the conscious process of imaginative renewal that accompanies the recounting of *bean feasa* tales. In the case of the seven *Máire Ní Mhurchú* texts recorded from the *Béarra* informant, we see a constant effort on the informant's part to substantiate and legitimize his narrative by invoking the authority of his own neighbours and relatives, for whom these legend accounts of the activities and pronouncements of the *bean feasa* were, allegedly, true: '*Ach d'inis mo mhathair féin domhsa go minic*' ('But my own mother often told me'); '*Ní raibh aon bhréag ansan – Bhí san chomh fíor agus atá an ghriain ag taithneamh ar an aer*' ('That was no lie – It was as true as the sun shining in the sky'); '*Táim chun insint díbh arís go raibh fianaise mhaith age an mhuintir a bhí ar an mbaile go rabhas-sa mar gheall ar Mháire Ní Mhurchú, mar d'aithn mo mhathair féin í chomh maith is a d'aithn sí aon bhean eile do bhí ar an mbaile*' ('I am going to tell to you again how the people of my home place had good evidence for *Máire Ní Mhurchú*, because my own mother herself recognized her as well as she recognized any other woman that was in the place'); '. . . *go b'fhíor na scéalta mar gheall ar Mháire Ní Mhurchú: nár scéal dúirse dáirse ab ea iad in aon chor; ná scéal gur 'nis bean dom go ndúirt bean léi*'. ('. . . but the stories about *Máire Ní Mhurchú* were true, that they were not tell-tale-tattle by any means, nor the kind of gossip that goes from mouth to mouth').

One text from *Corca Dhuibhne* has the narrator's grandfather as the one who resorts to the wise-woman, to locate and recover a stolen horse. Another has the narrator say that it was his own father who used frequently recount stories of the wise-woman *Eibhlín Ní Ghuinníola* that he, in turn, heard from his father-in-law. A text from *Cairbre,* County Cork tells how the narrator's mother's aunt used to visit a house where the wise-woman *Máire Ní Chearbhaill* came every day. Another text from the same informant has the brother-in-law of one of his own neighbours as the victim of the otherworld injury upon which *Máire Ní Chearbhaill* pronounces. The *Cairbre* texts featuring *Máire Ní Chearbhaill* are in English with *Máire* herself speaking Irish in them. This gives her, perhaps, an arcane authority rooted in the ancestral world but also emphasizes the contested nature of the knowledge and power which she represents in a cultural context which was by then, largely English-speaking. Overall, these texts convey a sense of an ancestral worldview that is sensitive to and representative of the culturally constructed and provisional nature of reality, which accords well with much of today's thinking about, and theory of culture and cultural tradition.

The stories presented here in Part Two consist of sixteen texts relating to the *cailleach* and eighteen texts relating to the *bean feasa*/wise-woman. They vary in length from a few lines long to substantial tales. The narrators from whom they have been recorded are, with two exceptions, male. One *cailleach* item (no.4) was recorded from a woman in North County Mayo while the *cailleach* (no.5) story was recorded from schoolchildren in Dunquin, County Kerry. The *cailleach* stories come from western areas of Ireland and Scotland with the following distribution: Cork 1, Kerry 2, Galway 7, Roscommon 1, Mayo 3, Mull 2; while the *bean feasa* stories are confined in origin to Cork (13) and Kerry (5).

The stories form a somewhat eclectic anthology of texts. They are presented here because of their intrinsic interest and value as examples of

Irish Folklore, but also because they illustrate, in a perspective which this book attempts to establish and communicate to the general reader, the 'literary' riches of traditional narrative and the relevance of Irish narrative tradition to questions of the literary representation of the feminine. They are presented and interpreted here at a remove from the repertoires and actual narrative practices that prevailed for their narrators and primary audiences and it is likely that these legends vary considerably in the degree to which they were commonly known and told in the communities from which they come. Placed together, they cannot be taken to reflect directly the oral repertoire of any one community or district, and important questions remain unaddressed here regarding the distribution of particular stories and their frequency of occurence in the folklore record and – most interestingly – in their possible continuance in the practice of storytelling today. Also unaddressed are issues arising from the use in these stories of motifs of European and wider international folklore provenance. The emphasis here is on the way these texts can be interpreted in a way that attempts to remain faithful to broad patterns of Irish tradition.

What the stories represent, in general, is evidence of the retention and reinterpretation in Irish Folklore and narrative tradition over a long period, of a sense of a female aspect of experience and imaginative life available to all who encounter these stories, whether as hearers or readers. That we have these stories mainly from male narrators, collectors, editors and translators (including the present writer) will, I hope, be taken to suggest not an oppressive detraction from or usurpation of female expression, but rather an indication of how in the historically masculine world of literary and folkloristic scholarship, feminine voice finds insistent expression in sometimes surprisingly authoritative fashion. In locating stories about the *cailleach* and the *bean feasa* in the manuscripts of the Irish Folklore Commission collections and in publications deriving from other collectors of oral narrative featuring these figures, no conscious emphasis was put on the gender of the narrator, so that, while there can be no possible claim of statistical reliability, the preponderance of male informants is thought-provoking in itself.

It is as thought-provoking material that these stories and their treatment here are offered. Featuring, until relatively recently, in the imaginative life of the communities from which these texts derive, the figures of the *cailleach* and the *bean feasa* (together with their imaginative functions which the attached commentaries attempt to suggest) can be seen to both constitute and contribute to cultural resources for not only their communities of origin but also for contemporary readers. The categories into which the texts are placed in this section is intended to aid the appreciation by the reader of their significance in the framework of interpretation aimed at in Part One. It is not contended that this exhausts their significance or does full justice to it in any comprehensive or historical fashion. The reader is simply invited to begin to explore the meaning of these traditional stories along the lines suggested (often merely hinted at) here. In many cases fuller and, no doubt, alternative commentary and interpretation will suggest itself. The meaning of myth and legend can never be fixed or finished since it is the symbolic expression of the engagement of creative imagination with the ever-dynamic experiences of the human life of individuals in the world. The symbolic expression of what individual experience signifies proceeds in terms of collective as well as individual representation, and the stories we address here are reflections of enduring aspects of some of the collective representations that have been constructed in popular Irish cultural tradition. They were and are meaningful within a universe of discourse that is as wide and as complex as life itself. As a record, however slight and however arbitrarily assembled, of an element of that discourse, they are presented here as a contribution to the field of Irish studies.

STORIES OF THE CAILLEACH

Intimations of a female-centred cosmos

1. **The *Cailleach Bhéarrthach* and the cold of May-day Monday**[34]
    There was a woman long ago that they used to call *An Chailleach Bhéarrthach*. She was very old and she had travelled nearly the length and breadth of Ireland. She always had a large herd of cows and she had goats sometimes and I suppose that she had sheep. She used to travel from place to place, with the animals, from county to county. She didn't stay settled long in any one place but always moved on. The animals all gathered together at night, gathered into one great assembly, every evening, but they never stayed long in that one place or on this hillside. In the course of her travels she eventually came to a place they call *Néifinn* Mountain, in County Mayo, and she drove out her beasts there in the morning. When evening came, there wasn't any two of the beasts gathered together. They were scattered over and hither, and every one of them stayed at night-time in the place where they had been during the day. They had eaten so much that they didn't want to move any farther that evening or gather all together. And the *cailleach* stayed for many years after that day at the foot of *Néifinn* Mountain with her beasts.

    There was a man in the place who wanted to hear news and stories from the *cailleach* because he knew that she had lots of old knowledge of all sorts. He knew that she was so old that she had seen and heard and knew about all that had happened for hundreds of years past. He asked her if she could give an account of how cold it was on a day that came hundreds of years before that, that was awfully cold. The time of the year when that day had happened was *Luan Lae Bhealtaine*, the first day of summer. The *cailleach* told him that she had no account to give of the cold that was there on that *Luan Lae Bhealtaine* but that he should go to the Eagle who was in a certain place – in the ruins of an old forge – and that maybe he'd know what cold there was. She said that the Eagle was three hundred years older than herself and that the Eagle knew about a lot of things that she didn't know about.

The man went off and never rested until he came to the old forge and he found the Eagle there before him. He spoke to the Eagle and asked him if he could tell him how cold it was on *Luan Lae Bhealtaine*: that no day ever came since that was as cold as it and that it was hundreds of years since it had happened. 'I'm here with seven hundred years', said the Eagle. 'This anvil that is in the forge was new and the peak that it had then was as thick as any peak that was ever on any anvil. When I used to eat my food', said the Eagle, 'I used to rub my beak on the peak of the anvil, on both sides, over and hither, in order to clean my beak. The peak now, today, is so worn and slender from my rubbing my beak on it after my meals for so long that it is as thin as a pin.' 'I have no account of how cold it was', said the Eagle, 'it happened hundreds of years before my time.' 'Go on', said the Eagle, 'to the Otter of the Rock and maybe he can tell you or give you an account of the cold of *Luan Lae Bhealtaine*.' He went off and went to the Otter of the Rock and the Otter was there on the Rock when he got there. He asked the Otter could he tell him how cold was the *Luan Lae Bhealtaine* that came long ago.

'I'm lying on the Rock here for five hundred years', said the Otter, 'and I have the Rock worn down so deeply that no trace of me is visible on any side of the Rock when I am lying on it. I have no account to give you of the cold, but go to the Half-Blind Salmon of *Eas Rua* and if he has no account of it to give you then you will never get an account of it anywhere.'

The man went off again and didn't stop until he came to *Eas Rua* and the Salmon was there. He called the Salmon and the Salmon came to him and he asked him if he could tell him how cold it was on *Luan Lae Bhealtaine*. 'I'm able to tell you that', said the Salmon. 'I was here', said the Salmon, 'in the same place I am now, in *Eas Rua*, and I leaped up out of the water to catch a fly. And in between my leaping and my landing back in the water there came such thick ice on the river here that it held me up when I fell back. I stayed there, fallen back on the ice, until a seagull came and took the eye out of my head. And blood came out of my head, from the socket of the eye, and the blood melted the ice and I went down again into the water. And that is the cold that was there on *Luan Lae Bhealtaine*.'

This story presents us with the figure of *Cailleach Bhéarra* as that of a very ancient female who, for the purposes of this tale, and in the communal consciousness of its narrator and its traditional audience, has become localized in the Nephin Mountains area of County Mayo. While she is now perceived to be resident as a landscape figure in this district with her flocks and herds of beasts – of whom she is as much a personification as she is of territory – it is made clear to us that all of Ireland is her domain, through the length and breadth of which she has continually moved with her animals, never staying long in any one place. At evening time, we are told, the animals used gather together, into one great assembly, ready to relocate the next day in a continual and perpetual redispensation of her sacred presence, a presence pulsing throughout her territory as a cosmic vitality in landscape and in its life forms. Her localization, together with her sacred animals, in the Mayo mountains renders her closer and more accessible to human consciousness and human communication. The 'man' in the place where she is now permanently available, as it were, is the representative figure of human consciousness with its questions and its cosmic curiosity about 'all that had happened for hundreds of years past' – a formula for a time-span of immense geological proportions.

The question this male representative of human community and communal memory puts to the *cailleach* concerns how cold it had been on a day that is styled *Luan Lae Bhealtaine*. *Lá Bealtaine*, Mayday is the first day of summer, the light half of the year, to be understood here as a kind of unique, first human day of all time that is humanly reckonable. In this instance the sense of 'primal' or 'only' day as a meaning for *Lá Bealtaine* is reinforced by the presence of the word *Luan* preceding it. *Luan* is Monday, a day with its own special qualities of uniqueness. There are traditional prohibitions attaching to Monday in the matter of undertaking certain kinds of work – for example shearing – or of commencing any work at all (*Lomadh an Luain*: 'an unlucky shearing' but also 'general misfortune'). Also, *Lá an Luain* means the Last Day, the Day of Judgement, the final day of all, so that the conjunction of last and first days of all, in the name *Luan Lae Bhealtaine*, reinforces the emphasis on the primal, cosmological connotation of the 'coldest day that ever came out of the heavens'.

The *cailleach* says that she has no account to give of how cold it was at the beginning of time but advises her questioner to go to the Eagle for an answer. The Eagle, who we are told, is as old again as the *cailleach*, also fails to supply the answer and sends the questioner to the Otter of the Rock who is, in turn, twice as old as the Eagle. He too is unable to supply the answer but says that if the Half-Blind Salmon of *Eas Rua*, to whom he directs the questioner, is also unable to answer, then the answer can never be ascertained. Thus the Salmon of *Eas Rua*/the Red Falls (or Cataract or Swift Current) is a kind of ultimate point of reference, drawing on the senses of being both the ultimate point of primeval creaturedom and the original source of sacred wisdom.

On the one hand the human questioner looks to the *cailleach,* who also has human-like form (even if giganticized). The *cailleach* looks to the Eagle who, being a creature of the rock fastness, soars over the landscape in which she herself reigns. The Eagle in turn, looks to the Otter of the Rock, a creature partly of the land and partly of a marine environment. Finally, the Otter looks to the Salmon, creature of the waters and voyager through the oceans, a kind of fully marine, ancestor symbol of all life thereafter.

On the other hand, *Eas Rua* is one of the places at which *Fionn MacCumhaill* is said to have encountered the magic Salmon of Knowledge from whom he absorbed his endowment of divine seerdom and clairvoyance. The *Eas Rua* of the Finn tradition is in County Donegal, but the salmon of *Eas Rua* is known generally within Irish tradition and features in this present tale as the final arbiter of human understanding of the origins of landscape and cosmos. 'I am able to tell you' he says; 'I was here.' He proceeds to tell how he survived the Ice Age which caught the whole world in its grip. This survival was not without cost; it required the loss of one eye and the expenditure of his heart's blood so as to bring his entrapment on the frozen surface of the pre-human, even prefaunal world to an end and to enable him to live on and bear witness in this tale to 'the cold that was there on *Luan Lae Bhealtaine'.*

This story appears to suggest that the *cailleach,* the hag-goddess, has an entry point into history and has not been the eternally present force in landscape and cosmos that other tales concerning her might suggest. Two observations seem apposite in this regard, two that, perhaps, merge into a single understanding of the eternal presence of the divine female agency, after all. Firstly, we can place her along with the Eagle and the Otter as one of the trio who are of fabulous age, in comparison to humans and who are, to all intents and purposes, ageless. Triadic traditional wisdom widely features the *Cailleach Bhéarra* along with the Eagle and the Yew Tree in a well known formulation of the three longest lifespans. Thus, in this tale we can take the sending on back of the questioner – from *Cailleach* to Eagle to Otter – as a kind of referral among the equally ancient (in human terms), despite the estimations of relative ages in hundreds of years. Secondly, we can note that the Salmon's survival on the ice is due to having his eye plucked out by a bird (a sea-gull, in this instance) with the result that his blood (cold and all as a fish's blood is taken to be) warms the ice sufficiently to melt it and to enable the Salmon's escape back into the lifegiving waters. Who is this sea-gull and what does it represent? Could we take it that the scavenger sea-gull, the solitary flier, wheeling over the ocean wastes, is a marine transform of the similarly scavenging raven, who in Irish mythological tales appears presiding over fateful encounters on land. The raven-goddess *Mórrígan,* who appears to the Ulster hero *Cúchulainn* in the epic tale of *Táin Bó Cuailnge* and as the *Badhbh* or Raven form of the banshee in later tradition can be mentioned here as instances of the presence, in avian scavenger form, of the hag-goddess at crucial points of mythological and cosmological import. Thus, we can plausibly take the motif of the life-saving injury inflicted on the primal salmon of knowledge by the seagull, to be an instance of the fierce protection afforded to life-forms by the divine cosmic agency, who here combines, as it were, her destructive and nurturing powers in a context – the beginning of time – when in consciousness and in cosmological record, the primal unity of cosmic force has not yet fully divided into its binary opposition of helpful and harmful halves.

Following his terrible, but life-sustaining injury, the Salmon 'went down again into the water' bearing with him knowledge of the extremities of existence and of the terrific redemption which he has undergone in his encounter with the avian transform of the hag-goddess who now, 'in the present day' of this narrative reigns as a territorial sovereign at the foot of Nephin Mountain, but has connections, in cosmological imagination and in narrative repertoire and performance, with the furthest reaches of the universe, in time and space, and with the roots of consciousness.

2. *Cailleach Bhéarra's* Shower of Stones[35]

There are two hillocks up in *Poll*, a grassy mountain upland at the far end of the parish of *Magh Cuilinn*. There is a great pile of fairly big rocks on top of one of the two hillocks. In olden times, when the *Cailleach Bhéarra* was at her best, a row broke out between her and another *cailleach*, another *Béarra* woman, who could also fire a stone as accurately as any man of that time. Anyway, they gathered up piles of rocks on the tops of the two hillocks one evening and they were all set to pelt them at each other on the following day.

They rose at dawn and started to shower the rocks on each other, all unknown to the people of the place, who were asleep for themselves. They were attacking each other, with no idea of which of them would be the victor, when the *Cailleach Bhéarra* started to fire her own rocks away beyond the other *cailleach*. She, for her part, kept on trying to injure *Cailleach Bhéarra* and kept striking her with great lumps that wrung sobs from her heart. She was that frenzied that she never noticed that her supply of rocks was almost used up and that her rocks were now nearly all across on the *Cailleach Bhéarra's* hillock. She hadn't understood, either, the trick *Cailleach Bhéarra* was playing, throwing her own rocks away past her so that they landed far out of her reach down the slopes. The *Cailleach Bhéarra's* plan was to leave the other *cailleach's* hillock with no rocks on it.

When she found that this was the case she attacked the other *cailleach* again and she was pelting her until she had her beaten into a pile of bones on the top of the hillock. When the people of the place arose that morning, they found *Cailleach Bhéarra* stretched on the top of one hillock and bleeding badly. She had buried the other *cailleach* under the pile of rocks on the hilltop.

Anyone who comes to that district today can still see the pile of rocks fixed on the hilltop – with no other rocks anywhere near them. The rocks that *Cailleach Bhéarra* threw down the slope of the hill aren't to be seen at all, as they have been swallowed into the marshy land that's there. That, now, is the reason why those rocks are at the top of that hill until today.

In this story and the following, we see the attribution to *Cailleach Bhéarra* as shaper of landscape, of features of the physical environment, whether 'natural' or 'man-made', i.e. artefactual. In the first story, of the rock pile on the hilltop near Moycullen, in County Galway, we see how the legend has two individual versions of the *Cailleach Bhéarra*, opposed as a kind of narrative device. Both are otherworld females with associations with Beara, the traditional heartland of the hag-goddess of legend, and both can 'fire a stone', that is to say bring about geotectonic changes in the environment and settle the rocks of the landscape into their 'home' form. We can understand the duplicated *cailleach* figure here as a representation of the generalized, universal, sovereign dispensation of the otherworld female agency 'in olden times' when, as the text has it, 'the *Cailleach Bhéarra* was at her best'. The pelting match that takes place between the two takes place 'at dawn' and 'unknown to the people' who 'were asleep for themselves', or had not yet come to awareness, had not yet settled or got to know, the physical characteristics of the territory in which these cosmologically dynamic events are taking place at the dawn of consciousness. The 'row' – and its greviously injurious outcome – is a metaphor for the terrifying cosmic energies that have gone into the rendering of the physical landscape of human times into its shape and form, energies beyond the tolerance of humans who live their lives in smaller and, hopefully, safer compass. The physical features of landscape today, however, and legends about its formation, remind the human community of the otherworld dimension of their environment, a dimension available to them in the legends and other imaginatively creative narrations of cultural tradition. Underneath, as it were, the tranquil appearance of 'the grassy, mountain upland at the far end of the parish' lies the profound energy that, in frenzy, can be said to 'wring sobs' from the heart of even the divine agency and leave her 'beaten into a pile of bones'. In the perspective that encompasses a 'sacred' landscape such as this, the people, in imagination and its narrative expression, are constantly finding *Cailleach Bhéarra* stretched on the hills and requiring their therapeutic narrative performance of her story, so that she may live on, in their consciousness and their cultural tradition. In this engagement of imagination with landscape it is fitting that the story should end with the apparently simple statement: 'That now is the reason why those rocks are at the top of that hill until today.' Their continued existence, even as physical features of the 'natural' environment, it is implied, depends on the narrative continuance of the legend of *Cailleach Bhéarra* and the concomitant imaginative re-endorsement of the truth of the worldview to which such legends give expression.

3. **The *Cailleach Bhéarthach* and the Walker**[36]

There was a man there long ago, during the time that *Cailleach Bhéarthach* lived at the foot of the *Néifinn* Mountains in County Mayo, and he thought that he was as good a man for walking as there was in Ireland. But he knew that the *Cailleach Bhéarrach* was that little bit better than him. He decided to go and speak to her and take her walking to see what walking she was able to do more than himself. And he came to her and he said that he had business to do in Galway and he asked the *cailleach* would she come with him, that maybe there was something she might want to buy inside in the town. She said she would go along with him, to Galway, that she needed a pair of teasing cards, to card her wool and that, since he was going there, they would go together. She said it was much better company to have the two of them walking together rather than having one person walking on their own.

They got themselves ready and they started off on the walk and it didn't take them a very long time until they were inside in Galway. They had their dinner and the *cailleach* bought her teasing cards. When they had all the things bought that they required – bits and pieces – they set off for home again. They were walking on strongly – sometimes half running, half trotting and it wasn't long until they were almost back at the foot of *Néifinn*. But they came upon a big river that faced them on their journey. The roads weren't there that time, like they are since then. And they met up with another man who was going some of the way in the same direction they were going themselves. When they got to the river the *cailleach* made a run, carrying off with her, under her arm, the man who was her companion for the day, and gave a leap across the river. When she brought her companion across the river under her arm, the other man wasn't able to jump across at all – not even half-way. And the spot where there was a waterfall and a fording place to cross over by, was nine or ten miles away from them.

The *cailleach* and the man she took across under her arm, had, indeed, made a great shortcut.

'What harm did I do you', said the man she had left behind on the other side, 'that you wouldn't bring me across as well as the other man?' 'You did not do me a bit of harm', she said 'but let those things stay unreconciled.' She left him there, though he had never done anything to her, because she thought that it wouldn't be right for her to be coming to the aid of every last person.

When she was parting from the man who had been her companion for the day – the *cailleach* was going on a bit farther – she knew well that he was knocked out after the walking. She asked him: 'Has your wife much butter in the house?' 'She has some', he said, 'she has a few crocks of butter.' 'Well, when you get home tonight', said the cailleach, 'tell your wife to fetch a crock of butter and to put it with its bottom facing the fire and its mouth facing away from the fire. And let you put the soles of your two feet', she said, 'on top of the butter at the mouth of the crock and stay like that until tomorrow. If you don't do that', she said, 'you'll be dead before tomorrow morning.'

He did as the *cailleach* instructed him. He told his wife, when he came into the house, to lay a crock of butter on the hearth with its mouth facing away from the fire. Then he took off his shoes and stockings and put his two feet onto the butter in the mouth of the crock. And in the morning, every last morsel of the butter had soaked into his feet. And only for that he was dead from the exertion of the day's walking with the *cailleach*.

When the *cailleach* had arrived home, she took a can with her and milked her goats; and she had them all milked and settled down before the sun set at the foot of *Néifinn* mountain in County Mayo.

The figure of the *cailleach* with which this tale opens, is that of a neighbour who, like everyone else in the district, farms sheep and teases their wool for cloth-making and goes to town for supplies. It was the time, 'long ago', when people walked great distances on business like this and had a distinctive 'walker's' gait, or lope, which enabled them to cover ground rapidly on the cross-country walking routes that were marked out by the passage over them of generations of local people. On such journeys, company was generally desirable, companionship giving rise to talk and the diversion of being imaginatively entertained in a fashion that shortened the road. The *cailleach* here is, like any neighbour, glad of the company on the proposed walk to Galway and back.

Since this narrative was recorded in Carna, County Galway, from where

Galway City would indeed be the local market town to which people would walk for supplies, we can recognize the sense in which the action of the story is, as it were, transplanted so as to have 'the walk' taking place from central Mayo down to Galway – a huge distance, greater than could apply to the 'real' world of historical, human society, west of Lough Conn – for whom Crossmolina or Castlebar would have been more realistic market-town destinations. The discrepancy is reduced somewhat by the suggestion of the male character himself that 'he was as good a man for walking as there was in Ireland', capable perhaps of even such an immense walk, and by his acknowledgement that the *cailleach* is even better than him, putting her off or beyond the human scale of things from the outset. In fact, his plan to 'take her walking' is presented as an attempt to gauge how far off or beyond the human scale is she, how different she and her world is, to humans and the human world.

They undertake the journey to Galway, dine, do their shopping and set off home again, without incident or with no apparent difference between them. However, when they meet up with another 'ordinary' man and come, together with him, to the place where they need to cross a broad river, the difference and the deviation become very apparent. In running at the river and clearing it at a jump, carrying her neighbour-companion under her arm, the *cailleach* emerges from her apparent role as human neighbour and enters into her true identity as sovereign landscape figure whose writ runs across rivers and mountains and all other aspects of her territorial domain. She operates, within the landscape of that domain, at a scale and swiftness that is beyond the human, that, literally, leaves the human behind, as the other man is left behind. The story emphasizes for us that the ordinary human is 'left behind' not because of hostility or maliciousness towards him on the *cailleach's* part, but because that is the nature of things, given the unreconcilable differences that exist between the sacred, otherworld domain of the hag-goddess and the ordinary, everyday world of human society and human life-ways. Her companion on the journey to Galway and back has, exceptionally, been afforded contact with, and has been supported on the journey by the cosmic forces that reign in that otherworld and whose personification the *cailleach* is. Without that support, such a journey would have killed him and he is, in fact, even having been supported, prostrate in its aftermath.

The hag goddess, before returning him fully to the human order, counsels him on how to protect himself from the ill-effects of such close involvement with the energies of the otherworld. He is to resort to the help of his wife (normally a more fitting female companion for man than the *cailleach* is, no doubt) and through *her* domestic and cultural operations–and resources as butter-maker—he is to treat and cure his body in respect of the superhuman demands that have been made of it and to which it has been subject, in a way that would, normally, prove fatal. 'You'll be dead before tomorrow morning', the *cailleach* tells him, unless he has resort to the healing goodness of the butter which is, of course, cultural produce that derives from the cattle herds whose fertility is personified so often in these stories, by the hag-goddess as sovereignty queen not only of territory but of herds and flocks and, on occasion, as we shall see, of the corn harvest also. In casting off his shoes and stockings and putting his two feet into the butter for the night, the human male hero of this story is planting himself in the otherworld that the *cailleach* represents so that he can draw sustenance into himself from it and recover from his superhuman exertions. Butter here is the 'crock of gold' that enhances and sustains human life as nourishment, not only for the body but, in narratively creative ways, for the imagination and the life of the spirit too. Women, in traditional Irish farming communities, were the ones who milked the cows and made the butter and it is through his marital access to this female realm of practical activity that the 'hero' of this tale is able to recover from the danger and the possible harm of entering too deeply into the otherworld female realm. In the person of his wife he is enabled to have an appropriate and harmonious relationship with the Feminine which, in the course of this tale is a source of both destructive and nurturant power in his life, mirroring the two aspects of the *Magna Mater* figure that we see running through the repertoire of Irish traditional narrative at both learned and popular levels.

4. **The mark left by *Cailleach Bhéarra*[37]**

Isn't it a great wonder how a child isn't able to walk as soon as it's born, along with every other kind of young. Not to compare a child to a calf or a lamb, but neither of these is born more than an hour, before it's able to walk and the child will be two years of age before it's able to put a foot under itself.

They say that it is *Cailleach Bhéarra* who is responsible for that. At a time that a certain child was born – but I don't know which child – she put her hand to the small of his back and that left children, ever after, unable to walk quickly, when they have come into the world.

Cailleach Bhéarra left that handicap on them.

This brief text is itself more a comment than a narrative and was written down from a female informant in north County Mayo in 1941. It poses, in an apparently simple way, the question of why the human infant differs so greatly from the young of farm animals in lacking an ability to walk for so long after birth. The implications of this question, in terms of biology, physical anthropology, traditional cosmology and theology are, of course, considerable. Whatever the evolutionary realities of hominid brain development with concomitant cranial enlargement and its obstetric consequences, the general helplessness of the human infant at birth is regarded, in this text, as a handicap deriving from an injury suffered by the first human child, when the hag-goddess 'put her hand to the small of his back' in the course, presumably, of the primal human birthing at which, as divine personification of nature, she presided as a kind of cosmic midwife. In that primal birthing, human beings, human life, society and culture emerge from nature and live in symbolic reality, in imagination – and in imaginative, creative narrative – in relation to, but also apart from, the cosmos and the cosmic natural forces that frame human experience and the world of meaning that humans derive from both experience and imagination.

What this little text presents, by implication, is a kind of nativity scene of human, rather than divine, incarnation: 'man' is born out of the world of nature, in contrast to the Christian nativity scene which represents 'god' born into the human world. From the outset the difference between the human infant and other young is asserted to be 'a great wonder' and, in its brevity, the text explains clearly that it is due to the imposition of a handicap on humankind by nature itself, in the guise of its hag-goddess personification. This handicap is, of course, also capable of being regarded differently; not as a handicap at all but as a sign of the delicate complexity and the sacred potential for imaginatively transcendent social and cultural life, that is the human endowment. Either way, this Mayo text is one whose brevity and slightness detracts little from its intriguing cultural and cosmological suggestiveness.

In other North Connaught texts dealing similarly with the question of the human infant's ability to walk and the impairment of this by *Cailleach Bhéarra*, we learn that the marks of the *cailleach*'s fingers can be seen, to this day, on the thighs and waists of adolescents, a permanent reminder of her primal encounter with humankind. The attribution, in this way, to the activities of *Cailleach Bhéarra,* of the growth/stretch marks that occur as a feature of the 'landscape' of the human body, matches, in the individual, corporeal sphere, the attribution to her of the origin of features of the physical landscape, such as the huge, scrape-like skrees that are seen on the sides of certain mountains. In each case the features involved are manifestations of an evolutionary or developmental dynamic – the one biological, the other geological – the energy or life-force of which the landscape hag-goddess *Cailleach Bhéarra* represents. Isomorphism between the human body and the physical universe is a feature of archaic cosmologies and we have, in these Mayo and Sligo legends, the suggestion of the similar manipulation of both the physical landscape and the human body by a supernatural female figure from whose oppressive clutch humanity has, with difficulty, emerged.

Lévi-Strauss held[38] that, in mythology 'it is a universal characteristic of men born from the Earth that, at the moment they emerge from the depth, they either cannot walk or they walk clumsily', and that traditional narratives that relate the origin and continuing existence of such ambulatory impairment bear witness to the persistence of the notion of the autochthonous origin of humankind, sprung from the soil as the products of the plant world are, as much as deriving from the conception and gestation processes of the animal and human world. *Cailleach Bhéarra*, the personification of the fertility and vitality of both worlds is, in these legends, as in so much of ancestral Irish and Scottish Gaelic tradition, intimately connected, in primal ways, with human consciousness and cosmology as these attempt to register, record and represent the meaning of experience.

5. *Cailleach Bhéara (Dún Chaoin)*[39]

There is much telling of this *cailleach* from *Béarra* in the folklore of the older people of the *Gaeltacht*. It is said that she lived on the summit of *Cnoc an tSídhe*. By all accounts that's where she had her cabin even though you would think she would be blown away from there, out to *Carraig na hIngeanach*, in *Inbhear Scéine*, with the wind and the bad weather.

> What she had to eat was:
> Real, pure *madhbhán* from Whiddy
> *Duileasg* from the harbours of Cape Clear.
> Fish from above in the Laune
> And wild garlic from *Bealach Bhéimis*.

It's little wonder she lived so long, if the stories that are told of her are true.

She had the reputation of great wealth also and people were anxious to steal it from her, since there were people that time who wouldn't be long doing just that. She understood that herself as much as anyone and what did she do, this day, but go down to *Scéic* in *Cuan Leitid* and steal a lobster out of a pot that was there. She brought it home alive in her apron and she put it into the box where her money was.

The following day, when she was away collecting food from the different places, a thief went up the hillside and stole in through the window of the *cailleach*'s house. He wasn't able to locate the money, high or low, until he noticed the box in under the old bed. He dragged it out. It wasn't too big but there was great weight in it. 'It's full up with gold, of course', said the thief to himself. He noticed that there was a sizeable hole in the side of the box. 'Isn't it a pity, you filthy old *cailleach*', says he, 'that you didn't think to mend that hole – but 'tis an ill wind that doesn't blow for someone's benefit.'

With that he thrust his hand into the hole and he started to grope around inside in the box looking for the gold. What did the lobster do but seize the hand in between his two claws and squeeze hard on it. No matter how the thief turned and twisted he couldn't break the grip or pull out his hand. When the sun was setting that evening the *cailleach* arrived home. 'You did well, lobster', said she and she killed the thief with an axe.

This text is noted as having been supplied by schoolchildren from *Dún Chaoin* in Dingle in 1933. It combines the motif of the intimate connection between *Cailleach Bhéarra* and the landscape of the South West (which she personifies), with the representation of her as a potential enemy of the people; in this case, a murderous enemy to those who would harm her. She is portrayed as having great wealth, by repute, though in this text no great wealth other than the fruits of nature is featured: garlic and seaweed, fish and lobster, from inland mountaintop and river, from sea shore and sea-bed, from the length and breadth of her natural, territorial domain. People of the district are said to have been anxious to steal her wealth from her and we can understand this as expressing the desire of those in human society to exploit, and benefit to the maximum from the natural environment and its resources. Aware of the risk of being robbed, she helps herself to a lobster from a pot set within her territory, by presumably human agency and brings it home 'in her apron' (indicating her own lack of technology), to her house on the wild top of *Cnoc an tSidhe* ('The Hill of the Fairy Mound/otherworld') She puts it, we are told 'into the box where her money was' and where, in our reading of the significance of the episode, it constitutes or represents the wealth (of nature) with which the *cailleach* is abundantly endowed.

The thief who comes to her house, to plunder it, next day, when she is away gathering her food from the wild landscape, believes that her wealth consists of gold, since he is someone, apparently, without an appreciation of her significance as hag goddess of the landscape, and without proper respect for the natural forces of that landscape which the lobster – freed, as it were, back into the caring domain of the *cailleach* from the murderous pot of the lobster-catcher – here represents. In his greed and cosmic blindness the thief comes to grief, trapped on the wrong side of nature and subject to the terrible penalty that nature exacts of the disrespectful and the foolish. She killed the thief, with an axe, on her return.

This text appears to present the *cailleach* as a potential danger to human well-being, irrespective of any question of cosmological allegiance to either ancestral or Christian worldview. However, it restricts the threat that the *cailleach* represents to those who would, for their own part, seek to injure her or move actively against her.

Victories of a male–centred social order

6. **The *Cailleach Bheurr* and *Loch Bà*–I**[40]

    In the olden times, on the Headland of Mull, there lived a woman whom the people called *Cailleach Bheurr*. She didn't hail from the people of this world, since we are told that *Cailleach Bheurr* was a young girl when Adam and Eve were still enjoying the pleasures of the Garden of Eden. She tells us, in her own words, 'When the ocean was a forest with its firewood, I was then a young lass.' Let that be, as it may, and far be it from us to doubt it, but it seems that *Cailleach Bheurr* evaded death in a way that no one was ever able to do, before or since.

    On the western side of Mull there is a beautiful lake that shows its blue waters to the heavens from the time the sun rises in the east until it sets in the western harbour. The waters of the lake lie smooth and calm, with never any tossing waves from the first time ever the *Cailleach* knew the Isle of Mull. But the story goes that something very unusual happened at *Loch Bà* every hundred years.

    When the *cailleach* came, each time, to within two years of another century, a great change used to come over her appearance. She used to start to grow old and grey and pale and stooped, like other old people. However, unlike other old people, she had the ability to transform herself into a young girl again without much difficulty. She did this by immersing herself in the waters of *Loch Bà* before any living thing, animal or bird, would have welcomed the sunrise. Thus, whenever she had put down a hundred years of life, she would cast aside from her the appearance of age and she would again be an elegant maiden.

    One of the days, at a time when another hundred years was all but up and when the *Cailleach* was thinking that it would be best for her to immerse herself in the waters, she was descending calmly to the shore of *Loch Bà* just as the sun, with its golden rays, was rising in the east. When she was standing on the edge of the lake and just ready to immerse herself, what did she hear from a distance but the barking of a dog. Since *Cailleach Bheurr* was unable to keep it at a distance, the noise echoed off the cliff and the crags around *Loch Bà*, all at once, answered back loudly. The *Cailleach* stood there, where she was, listening to the noise, and, after a while, when the life was going out of her, she called out in a loud voice, gave a step from side to side, tottered over and back and fell down on to the ground with a great crash. Just as the life left her, she called out aloud:

> It's early the dog spoke, in advance of me,
> The dog, in advance of me; the dog, in advance of me.
> It's early the dog spoke, in advance of me,
> In the quiet of the morning, across Loch Bà.

Further evidence of the identification of the *cailleach* of this story with the archaic female sovereignty personification of landscape in the Celtic, and possibly pre-Celtic, ancestral, cosmological tradition can be glimpsed in the assertion, 'in her own words', that she was alive in a predeluvian era 'when the ocean was a forest with its firewood' – something which is referred to in more detail in the second version of this story below. The concept of the ancestral otherworld, the sacred, cosmological domain that surrounds and underlies human experience of physical reality, as a domain located beneath water, constitutes a recurrent theme in the allusions to the otherworld at the learned and literary level of early Irish tradition.

We can also note the sense in which the name of the lake, from beneath whose waters the hag-goddess finds cyclical renewal in these two texts, is evocative of the personal name *Boí* of the divine, territorial, sovereignty queen/spouse of the divine *Lug*, himself the model and epitome of the king-god of Celtic mythology. *Boí* is understood to be etymologically related to the Indo-European word for cow (Mod. Ir. *bó* and Sc Gael. *bò*; gen. sing *bà*) and to be evocative of the primordial cult of the cattle divinity (sacred bull; sacred cow). *Loch Bà* is thus a name tinged with ancient and important associations within Gaelic ancestral tradition in which the vernacular *Cailleach Bhéarra/Bheur(r)* of Irish and Scottish folklore legend can be taken as a figure of mythology and cosmology who is a transform of the *Boí/Buí* prominently associated with the Beara peninsula in early literary tradition. 'The Lament of the Old Woman of Beare', dealt with in Part One, had, in the ninth century, articulated as much, in the line in which the Old Woman names herself as *Cailleach Bhéarra Buí*. Regarding the exact translation of this there is scholarly debate but no dispute as to the co-occurrence, in the name, of the literary and cosmological elements that we find still conjoined in these Scottish texts of a millennium later, which we are dealing with here.

We also note again the sense in which the sovereign presence of the hag-goddess in the landscape of *Loch Bà*, represented in her 'noise' (cosmic energy) when 'she called out in a loud voice', is overridden and 'deafened'/displaced by the overwhelming, loud, noise (energy) – echoing from the crags and the cliffs – of the culturally-domesticated herdsman's dog, who has barked before she was able to reach the renewing medium of the lake waters. The landscape is now 'speaking' with the voice of human society and her reign in it, as the personification of the pre-human, 'natural' world, is at an end. In 'the quiet of the morning', at sunrise, across *Loch Bà*, a momentous cosmological shift occurred in mythology and in the imaginative consciousness of the tradition to which the eleven-year-old narrator's story here gives renewed expression.

7. The *Cailleach Bheurr* and *Loch Bà*–II[41]

Now, believe it or believe it not, but there were giant creatures there in olden times. The Bible tells us that. If you look at the sixth chapter of Genesis, you will see that there were giant creatures there in olden times.

But there was this giant creature there, the last of these giant creatures that was in Mull, the *Cailleach Bheurr*, who was settled on the island of *Earraid*, as we call it today. That island is well celebrated in books in English today, but at that time there was no one settled there except for the *Cailleach Bheurr* and the three cows she had, who used to graze there every morning. Now she must have been fearfully huge. And we are told, it has come down to us by word-of-mouth, that she had only one eye and that it was in the centre of the forehead.

But there was this day and she was gazing out to the west and she said: 'When the ocean was a forest, full of trees, I was, at that time, but a young girl.' Now when that female one spoke – and it's very rarely, indeed, that she did speak at all – when she did speak, everyone in her own chief – territory heard her and, maybe, people in other territories too.

Now you will be thinking that it can be said that maybe the *Cailleach* was telling lies when she said that the ocean was a forest of trees at the time that she was a young girl. But why shouldn't we believe her? Isn't it likely enough? If every one of you hasn't actually seen the *Torranach* sea-rocks, you will all have heard reports of them. Looking out from the island of *Earraid*, past *Rath (?) na Dubh h-Irtich*, there are dangerous sea-rocks out there, stretching out for seventeen miles. And, in the olden times, couldn't those sea-rocks have been hilltops? Mountain moorland that subsided because of an earthquake or a great upheaval like that. And we are unable to say that *Cailleach Bheurr* wasn't correct when she proclaimed: 'When the ocean was a forest of trees, I was, at that time, but a young girl.'

But *Cailleach Bheurr* was dependant on this one thing. At the end of every hundred years she was obliged to bathe herself in the waters of *Loch Bà* – up at the other end of Mull. You will all have heard talk of *Loch Bà*. It is a most beautiful lake, both very long and very deep. And when she bathed herself – and it was always at Maytime – as soon as ever she bathed herself, her youth was renewed and she became a young girl again. Now, perhaps you are doubting that much, but, do you know, it's many the strange thing happens in life and it's many the strange thing that happened long ago that we know nothing at all about, except as it has come down to us, concerning it, by word-of-mouth.

She had three cows and she used to go out of *Earraid* with them every day and drive them to pasture down through Mull until she reached the Headland of Kintyre. Now that must have been the desperately long journey the cattle had, going down to the Headland of Kintyre and grazing there until it was time for them to be on the road back again. But it wasn't such an extraordinary thing at all when you think of the kind of female that *Cailleach Bheurr* was, and her complaint against *Crùlachan*. You know of *Crùlachan*; it's not too far from *Gleann Mór* in Mull.

> Dark, deep *Crùlachan*
> The deepest loch in the world
> The Straits of Mull used to reach as far as my knees
> But *Crùlachan* used to reach to my thighs

That is what she used to say herself. And why shouldn't we believe her? How do we know that it wasn't true?

Now there was only one place where *Cailleach Bheurr* watered her cattle-herd when she was away from Mull itself. This was a well halfway along the road she took to the Headland of Kintyre. I don't remember what its name was but, indeed, there was such a well there. And there was a great stone lid on the well and as soon as she arrived there in the morning, she would lift off the great stone so that the herd could get a drink at a time when they were thirsty. But if she didn't place the great stone lid back onto the well before the sun went down, the water would flow out of it and would flood the whole world. It would pour out of this well and cover the whole world with a flood. Well, she was [there] this one time, when she was growing old and growing weak, like any elderly woman. When she was sitting down next to the well, she started to fall asleep. But something shook her awake with a start. The water was coming roaring out of the well and the sun was just going down. Only the smallest bit of it was still up. She sprang up and she shoved the great stone lid down onto the well and she saved the world from being flooded. But though she prevented the whole world from being flooded, there is still a part of it flooded there, all the time; and that is *Loch Obha*.

There it is for you now; that is how *Cailleach Bheurr* was. But, the poor creature, she came on that time and brought her herd back to *Earraid*. Now the summer was coming and it was nearly Maytime and it was very close to the time for her to go and bathe herself. Now she had to bathe herself early, before she heard the bark of a dog or the chirping of a bird in the bushes. If she were to hear either of these things, it would be all up with her, she would be finished.

And early this day, she was going down the slope of the bank to the side of the loch and she was walking at her leisure, with a stick, making her way down to bathe herself. And just as she was at the water's edge, the dog that belonged to a shepherd who was not far away from there barked. No sooner had she heard the dog's bark than she fell down like a heap of bones. Now the shepherd had known very well that it was time for the *Cailleach* to come there and he was constantly seeing to it that the dog was kept in at night, so that she would get the chance to bathe herself. But that night the dog had been out and it was in that way that he barked, when he saw the *Cailleach* going down the hillside. And she fell down in a heap of bones. The shepherd ran to where she was, as quickly as ever he could, to see if there was anything he could do for her. But she was at the point of death and she was singing to herself a grievous, lonely, sorrowful song. Now I can't sing, but the song went something like this:

> It is early today the dog spoke
> The dog spoke, the dog spoke,
> It is early today the dog spoke,
> This quiet morning, across *Loch Bà*.

That was how the song went. There was a great number of verses – but that was the tune to it.

Now, anyone who doesn't believe that story has only to go up to the *Barrachan* – you all know the *Barrachan* – and row up along *Abhainn na Slat,* and you can see there, on the left, the steps that *Cailleach Bheurr* had to go up, to the place where she lived. And they call it *Cailleach Bheurr*'s Ruin to this very day. Now whether you think this worth believing or not, I don't know, but that is how I heard it and if I am telling a lie, then it is as a lie it came to me.

This version begins, as the other does, with an invocation of Biblical authority to locate the *cailleach* in time and in character. The other version tells us that when Adam and Eve were in the Garden of Eden, *Cailleach Bheurr* was living in Mull. This version refers us to the Book of Genesis also, to Chapter Six specifically, in order to show that – from the Christian point of view – *Cailleach Bheurr* is a heathenish, primordial, 'giant creature', linked to wild landscape and, possibly, to marine wilderness also (*fuamhairean*<*famhair:* 'giant'; c.f. Ir *fomór:* 'sea demon'). She is said to be the last of these primordial natural agencies in this part of the world (Mull) and she is presented to us as having a solitary existence – apart from her three cows.

We are told that one day, gazing out to the west, across the ocean from the island of *Earraid*, her home place, she recalled and recounted how at the time she was a young girl, the ocean was a forest, full of trees. This attests to two aspects of her identity as primordial, divine, landscape personification. One has to do with the geological ages through which she has endured as living witness to the formation and transformation of landscape by natural forces. The other has to do with her association with the ancestral otherworld, conceived of as located beneath water. It is as if her vision, looking out across the ocean from *Earraid*, on the day she speaks in this fashion, penetrates the waters and uncovers the deeper reality of the otherworld realm. That the possibility of such a vision – at least in its geotectonic dimension – is shared by the human narrator of the *cailleach's* words, is evident in the argument he offers his listeners regarding the possibility that the sea-rocks to the west of *Earraid* were, at one time, the hilltops of a now submerged landscape. The enduring presence in the physical world and in the ancestral realm beyond it, is thus proclaimed doubly by the combined assertion of such by the *cailleach* figure herself and by the narrator of the story featuring her.

The enduring presence of the *cailleach*, as personification of the physical realm, is here presented, as in the other Scottish tale, as being dependent on a cyclical renewal of her vitality by means of immersion, every hundred years at Maytime, in the waters of *Loch Bà*. We can note how the narrator invokes oral tradition – 'word of mouth' – as the justification for our acceptance of the truth of this 'strange thing'. Ancestral tradition, as transmitted in the continued narration of stories, is thus presented as a kind of knowledge of a deeper order of reality, lying outside of the range of everyday human experience, but accessible to the creative imagination as this expresses itself in verbal art. This is emphasized also in the presentation of the ability of the *cailleach* to journey across great reaches of landscape, with her cattle, in a way that far exceeds the human scale of travel. Such huge journeys are commensurate with her huge stature, as evidenced in her own assertion that, when she stepped into the waters during her travels, the waters of the Straits of Mull used reach only to her knees while the waters of *Crùlachan*, 'the deepest loch in the world', reached only as far as her thighs.

Throughout Gaelic ancestral tradition in Ireland and Scotland, the geotectonic powers of the *cailleach* are attested to and remembered in stories that attribute to her the origin of landscape features such as lakes, rock formations, islands, hills and valleys. Here we see the origin of another lake attributed to her, *Loch Obha*, though in a way that presents her as being herself subject to the frailty of age within the cycle of her periodic renewal and subject to cosmic forces greater than herself, at least at that time of her cycle of endurance when renewal is most necessary. The import of this motif of how, on one of her journeys through Mull she almost caused the whole world to be flooded but prevented the disaster just in time, can be taken to be an indication of how Gaelic, ancestral, imaginative tradition conceives of *Cailleach Bhearra/Bheurr* as a creature actually and narratively distinct from, though personifying, nature. As such, she is in need of the renewal of her vitality by means both of her own periodic immersion in the primordial waters of *Loch Bà* and the 'immersion' of the consciousness of the narrator's audience in periodic recountings of her doings. 'There it is for you now; that is how *Cailleach Bheurr* was, the poor creature', our narrator says, as if alluding, for an instant, to the imaginative collaboration of communal narration with landscape, in the creative constructing of the meaningfulness of the figure of the hag-goddess in traditional accounts of human experience of cosmos and its energies.

The story goes on to tell, as the previous Scottish story did, of how her attempt to renew herself once again in the vitally restorative waters failed by reason of the shepherd's dog barking before she was able to immerse herself and achieve renewal. We should note that the shepherd, the representative of human society, is said to have known that it was time for the *cailleach* to enter the waters 'safely' and that 'he was constantly seeing to it that the dog was kept in, at night, so that she would get the chance to bathe herself'. This suggests that a kind of harmonious balance has existed, over many cycles of renewal of the *cailleach*, between the human and otherworld orders. Moreover, it hints again at the type of imaginative tradition that allows the power and mystery of the cosmos to be engaged with in meaningful ways by a human consciousness that both personifies wild nature and natural energies in the figure of the hag-goddess and keeps her alive in the narration of the traditions concerning her in a repertoire of ancestral tales.

In these two Scottish tales, the barking of the dog, the domesticated animal-artefact which symbolizes the cultural realm of a human world, rings the death-knell of the *cailleach* and, in one sense, marks the closure of her reign. The traditional narration and transmission of these tales – of how and when her reign ended – can be said, however, to extend that reign into 'later' or ever-present human consciousness. The final paragraph of our text can be taken to assert this extension of the presence and significance of the *cailleach* in the landscape (physical and imaginative) of 'contemporary' life. If you do not believe his story, our narrator says, then you have only to go and see, and to listen. Stories such as these, it is implied, bring us to where the hag-goddess is, show her to us and tell us something very real and true about the world and our lives in it.

8. **The *Cailleach* of *Gleann na mBiorach* and the Black Bull**[42]
In the old time a hag lived in *Gleann na mBiorach* in County Kerry. She had neither house nor home; only a cavern that was under a huge rock on the side of the valley. She was there in that place for as long as anyone in the community could remember and she hadn't changed in even the smallest way throughout all that time. She had no means of livelihood that anyone had any knowledge of and she was never seen to be more than a perch from the mouth of the cavern. No one had ever seen either food or drink going into where she was and all believed that she was an enchanted hag. Not one of them, old or young, and even if they got gold and silver for it would go through *Gleann na mBiorach* after nightfall. There wasn't any night of the year when the people didn't hear a great barking in the valley as if hundreds of dogs were fighting inside.

One day, before sunrise, an old man called *Murchadh Ruadh Ó Conchubhair* went through *Gleann na mBiorach* carrying a sheaf of oats to feed to his black bull that he had grazing in the valley. When he looked up at the mouth of the hag's cavern, as he passed it by, he saw above it a heron with a great long eel in its mouth. The heron let the eel fall at the mouth of the cavern and, almost at once, a white dog came out from the cavern, caught up the eel and carried it back inside. *Murchadh* noticed that the white dog had eight legs and he was amazed and very frightened by this. 'By my soul', said he, 'the people's judgement is correct; she is indeed an enchanted hag inside in that cavern.'

The black bull was listening to *Murchadh Ruadh* saying that much and he pricked his ears, gave a little bellow and said, '*Murchadh Ruadh*, do not be amazed or frightened, but listen to my words because they are the truth. The grey hag is in that cavern since the time of the *Fir Bolg* and it is she who brought about the great destruction that befell the cattle of all this land: perhaps you have not heard of the full extent of the destruction that plague caused. It didn't leave a bull or a cow or any other horned creature in the countryside except for myself and one young female who was in this valley and it is from us are descended all the cattle of the land.

'There is one way only to overcome the hag and her son, the eight-legged dog. Gather up enough of my droppings as will make a great heap of firing. When you have dried it, pile it up in the mouth of the hag's cavern and set fire to it. This will bring her out, herself and her son, the eight-legged dog, along with her. The heron is the hag's mother. Protect yourself against her or she will leave no eye in your head. Bring a flail with you but do not strike the hag. Attack the dog and the heron if they come near you and I myself will battle with the hag.'

'Well, by my bonded word, but I will do as you say', said *Murchadh Ruadh*, 'but, whisper here to me! Will I tell other men that you spoke to me?' 'Indeed and I don't care', said the black bull, 'because when I kill the grey hag, along with her son and her mother, my term on earth will be over – but it would be best for yourself not to speak of it.'

Murchadh Ruadh was filled with great anxiety as he went home that day. The following morning he called to his wife and told her to get him the loan of a flail. 'What use have you for a flail?', said his wife, 'You have neither oats nor wheat to thresh.' 'Isn't it all the one to you what use I have for it; but get it for me', replied *Murchadh Ruadh*.

Murchadh ate his meal then and, after it, took himself off to *Gleann na mBiorach* and gathered up a great deal of the droppings of the black bull. He piled it up on a great rock to dry. He came home then again and he asked of his wife if she had got the flail for him. 'I got it', she said, 'and it's there in the corner, and I'm to give it back tomorrow, if I live that long.' 'Indeed, that is proper', he said 'that is, if it isn't broken.'

The following day again he went to *Gleann na mBiorach* and he made a heaped up pile of the dried droppings in the mouth of the hag's cavern and set fire to it and it wasn't long until it was ablaze and the smoke from it was going down into the cavern.

Murchadh took a firm hold of his flail and moved back out into the valley from the mouth of the cavern and it wasn't long until he heard barking and coughing inside it. Soon after this the hag and the white dog came outside. The black bull sensed that they were coming and he rushed at them at great speed and attacked the eight-legged dog. The hag clapped her palms together and called out, 'Get a grip on him, my pup, get a grip on him or else you and I will be swept away; that bull in front of you now is *Domblas Mór*, a great enemy, whom I have continued to persecute since the time of the great cattle-plague.'

'Indeed, that is so, you horrible hag', said the bull, 'You killed thousands of head of cattle and you left hundreds and thousands of people in want, without milk and without meat', said the black bull.

The dog gave a leap then and he tried to get a grip of the bull's nose. The bull put his two horns under him and tossed him up into the air just as you would throw up a little pebble and, when he was falling back down, *Murchadh* drew on him with the flail and struck him a blow in between the two eyes that split his skull. But the eight-legged dog wasn't dead. He attacked the bull a second time and tried to manoeuvre him to the edge of the cavern. The bull was too clever for him, though, and threw him up into the air a second time, this time higher than before. As he was falling back down *Murchadh* was ready again to strike another blow. As he was just about to strike, however, the heron came and tried to stab him in the eye. It wasn't in the eye she struck him, however, but in the middle of his forehead and she toppled him head over heels. The hag ran in and got a grip on him and started to shake him and choked him until he was sure that the life was going out of him. He would have died, but that the black bull came and lashed a kick at the hag that put her across to the other side of the valley. She came across again swiftly and said to the black bull: 'Let the fighting to *Murchadh* and myself!'

'I'm satisfied', said *Murchadh*, 'but you got an advantage of me when I was knocked down with the blow from the beak of your enchanted mother.' With that he drew on the flail and struck her a blow on the forehead, so that she let a scream out of her that was heard seven miles from the valley. Meanwhile the eight-legged dog was stretched out as if dead, but when he heard the hag's scream, he rose up and gave a leap. He got a savage grip on *Murchadh*'s throat and was choking him until the black bull ran in with his mouth agape, fastened on to the dog and crunched up every bone in his body into little pieces.

'I grant you the victory and my seven thousand curses along with it', said the hag and she dropped down dead on top of the eight-legged dog. The heron came down, screaming loudly and made to attack *Murchadh*, but he was on his guard and he broke her neck with a blow from the flail, so that she fell down dead on top of the other two.

'My word, but you are a proper warrior', said the bull to *Murchadh*. 'Follow me now and I'll show you a treasure of gold and silver.'

Murchadh followed him into the hag's cavern and such a sight as met his eyes was never seen by anyone before that. A huge golden table stood at the centre of the chamber and a heap of gold and silver pieces on it. 'Now', said the black bull, 'carry away with you as much of the gold and silver as you will need for the rest of your life and if anyone questions you about it tell them that you sold me for a big price, because no one will ever see me again from this day out.'

'I am truly sorry for that', said *Murchadh*, 'you were a good friend. But since it can't be helped, I wish you a thousand blessings.' 'There is a leather bag under the table', said the bull, 'fill it up quickly and be going.'

Murchadh did this and when he had emerged from the cavern a great fall of earth and stones blocked the entrance to the cavern.

It was late on in the day when *Murchadh* arrived home. The striker of the flail was broken. 'Wherever were you and however did you break the striker of *Páidín Shéamais's* flail?', asked his wife. 'I broke the striker beating my wild and disobedient bull', said *Murchadha*, 'and I have sold him to a lord from Connacht. I am now too old and too weak to control him any longer.'

'What amount did you get for him?', asked his wife. He brought out the great bag and he said: 'Look, this bag is filled with gold and silver; this is the most any man ever obtained for a bull.' 'You are my heart's love', she said 'we are rich for all time.'

Murchadh and his wife lived the good life after that, but when he knew that he was near death, he sent for a friend and told him the whole story from start to finish. The story went from mouth to mouth until my grandmother heard it and it was from her that I got it then.

This tale was first published, in Irish, by Douglas Hyde. He had obtained it from a correspondent of his, an inmate of the workhouse in Athlone, who, at Hyde's bidding, kept a look out for bearer's of tales and legends among the other inmates and wrote down from them versions of the narratives that he was able to get them to recount. This particular story was collected from a Roscommon inmate, named *Mac an Ultaigh*, and situates the location of the events it describes in County Kerry, at a distant remove, as it were, from the ordinary context of life in the west of Ireland. The strangeness of the story's setting is emphasized also by the use of the phrase 'In the old time', to begin the narrative. Here again we have a switching between mythological time or timelessness and the era of history, especially history reckoned in terms of eras of technology and technological development.

In that 'old time', the time before history and at the dawn of human existence, when culture and memory first come into play, a hag, we are told, a *cailleach* – with the implicit connotations of the divine, ancestral otherworld female elder – lived in County Kerry, in a valley called *Gleann na mBiorach*. *Gleann na mBiorach* means the Valley of the Horned Herds, herds of animals such as cattle and deer with whom the figure of the *cailleach*/hag is associated in Gaelic tradition, in both Ireland and Scotland. In Scotland many legends exist that feature and name the *cailleach* as a Deer-Goddess, a personification of the life and fertility of the wild horned creatures, whose presence animates the Highland landscape. In Ireland there is an ancient tie between her and the bovine order, as the name of the most sacred or otherworldly of the Irish rivers – the Boyne/*An Bhóinn* – attests. Evidence of the hag-goddess's personification, in the Irish tradition, of the fertility of the domestic, rather than the wild herds and flocks is also to be found in the milk and butter symbolism of customs associated with the feast of *Imbolc*, on 1 February. This is when St Bridget is venerated; she being the Christianized version of the mother goddess, Brigit, the 'exalted one', who was fed on the milk of magical, otherworld cows and whose own cows were later milked three times a day. *Imbolc*, the earliest name for the Celtic festival of 1 February, the start of spring, is itself a word meaning 'lactation in sheep', which again emphasizes the connection between the figure of the female supernatural and the vital and reproductive life forces of the animal kingdom.

In *Gleann na mBiorach*, we are told, the hag of this tale has neither house nor home. She is of a larger order than can be accommodated in any human dwelling and lives, instead, inside a huge cavern under a great rock on the side of the valley. Her abiding, seemingly eternal presence – she is there, unchanging, since way before the human era – is literally in the landscape. She is said never fully to emerge from the cavern, into the human world, above ground, as if the story wishes to emphasize her otherworld nature in the mythological narrative context of the famous division of Ireland at the displacement of the reign of the divine *Tuatha Dé Danann*. They withdrew underground, into the landscape, leaving the ground clear, so-to-speak, for occupation and development by the succeeding Gaelic Irish settlers. These settlers cleared and stocked and tilled the land and had their livelihood from their labours. For her part, we are told that she had 'no means of livelihood that anyone had knowledge of', indicating that unlike the human population, she does not rely on culture, technology and artefacts to maintain herself, but exists as a kind of cosmic force and presence within nature itself. As such, she is a terrifying figure in the eyes and understanding of the people and not even gold and silver, we are told, as if these are the ultimate fruits of the cultured civilization of humans, would induce any of them to venture into her realm, especially by night when her association with wild nature is emphasized in the fearful animal noises that fill the valley.

One man grazes a black bull in *Gleann na mBiorach* and it is not difficult to perceive the symbolism that both bull and man represent. The bull, grazing the valley of the horned animal kingdom, under the terrific tutelage of the hag/*cailleach* is charged with something of the mythic significance of the great *Donn* and *Findbhennach*, the black and white, dark and light bulls of the *Táin Bó Cuailnge*, the main epic of Old Irish literature. The black bull's owner and human master is the old man, we are told, whose name is *Murchadh Ruadh Ó Conchubhair*. This name also carries echoes of symbolic and mythical import. *Ó Conchubhair*/O'Connor is the royal name of Connaught in medieval times. *Ruairí Ó Conchubhair*, who died at the end of the twelth century, is remembered as the last High King of Ireland and, in the eighteenth century, the family estates of his lineal descendants were at Belanagare, in County Roscommon, from where comes our text. The *Ó Conchubhair* chief protagonist of this text can be seen as a representative, even a royal, figure and his sobriquet, *Ruadh* (red-haired), emphasizes this to the native ear and eye in that the association of red bodily marking with representative leadership is well established in popular symbolic tradition.

Murchadh Ruadh Ó Conchubhair is presented to us in a dual capacity in the course of the story. At home, with his wife and especially in the aftermath of his victory over the *cailleach*, he is portrayed as a small-time farmer, ruling his household in the manner of a peasant patriarch appropriate to the rural, nineteenth century, Irish world. In *Gleann na mBiorach* however, in relation to his black bull and, above all, in relation to his encounter with and conquest of the *cailleach*, he has the character of an allegorical and mythic figure, representative of the human order and of the forces of culture and society by comparison with the cosmic forces of the natural order that find expression in the person of the *cailleach*, her mother and her son. In the course of his fight with the *cailleach* he is recognized by her – and recognizes himself – as her true and proper opponent in place of the black bull, whom both the title of the story and the bull's own estimation of the situation, might lead us to perceive as her natural, true antagonist. However domesticated and however symbolic within the human cultural world, the black bull remains animal and horned animal by nature, something won from the wild and transformed into a kind of living artefact, a living piece of technology, despite his primal identification with the realm over which the *cailleach* reigns. At the beginning of our story, however, none of this is obvious, or at least communicated in the narrative. We simply find the old man going one day before sunrise to feed his animal a sheaf of oats. And yet we can register, along with the native ear, that to be in *Gleann na mBiorach* before sunrise, is to be dangerously placed on the margin of the fearful world of mystery and power that the *cailleach* inhabits. We are, narratively, back in prehistoric times with the early pastoralists, winning a living from and establishing a cultural dimension in a hitherto undomesticated landscape.

Murchadh, on the threshold of this new day, witnesses for himself – and for us, as audience/readers of the narrative – the extent of the mystery of the forces of the natural world that amaze and frighten him, in the forms and activities of the heron and the dog at the mouth of the *cailleach*'s cavern. Both heron and eight-legged dog are figures charged with otherworld associations in native Irish tradition and they confirm for *Murchadh,* and for us, too, the mythological and archetypal significance of the events about to unfold.

Witnessing the events at the mouth of the hag's cavern has brought *Murchadh* to the threshold of the otherworld. The eel, carried into that otherworld in being taken into the cavern, is itself an emblematically liminal creature in Irish tradition – part fish, part animal, believed to undergo reincarnation and, on occasion, to speak. Here, however, it is the black bull who speaks, confirming for *Murchadh* and for the narrator's audience, that the story is leaving the realm of ordinary human life and entering a mythological mode where other creatures do, indeed, have the 'power of speech' – implying, of course, domains of knowledge of the natural world and its 'history' that are not normally accessible to human consciousness. It is in this sense that the bull says to *Murchadh* not to be amazed or frightened, but to listen to the truth. This truth concerns the history of the domestication of wild animals in the archaic past, a history not fully contained in Ireland or Irish prehistory, but pertaining to the universal human story and human condition. Being 'here' since the time of the *Fir Bolg* – who in Irish tradition reigned in Ireland even before the arrival of the semi-divine *Tuatha Dé Danann,* who themselves preceded the human Irish – the *cailleach*/goddess of the wild landscape (who also personifies the life of its fauna), is perceived by the bull-representative of the domesticated animal order (the cattle herds), to have been responsible for the apparent failure of the earliest efforts at stock-raising in Ireland. The plague, for the introduction of which and the consequent destruction of the earliest pastoral Irish culture, the *cailleach* is blamed, is a metaphor for the impersonal forces of the landscape and the cosmos in the face of which human society has had to struggle to establish itself and endure. Having being nearly wiped out, pastoralism spread once more 'in the countryside' as the ingenuity and tenaciousness of people triumphed over the natural order. The black bull is the progenitor and, as it were, bovine/taurine, patriarch of the domesticated animal kingdom, and we get the merest glimpse of the 'young female' who, as his primal partner, is an equally essential element in the construction and the well-being of the pastoral order. This slighting of the status of the female in the bull's worldview is allegorical and similar to the displacement and devaluing of the female in human culture, as represented by *Murchadh's* behaviour and attitude in respect of his wife. That slighting displacement, is what constitutes the whole point of this story: the *cailleach*, the hag/goddess of wild nature is vanquished and, as it were, extinguished, in the victory of man and male society in the world.

It is the bull who prompts *Murchadh* as to the means of achieving this victory over the *cailleach* and the projections of her in nature (the heron) and in imagination (the eight-legged dog). The instruments of that victory are to be – as is the bull himself – the products of the cultural transformation of nature into artefact and technology and social relations. We can see the black bull – in the heightened, liminal perception we share as audience of the narration, with *Murchadh* – on the threshold of an otherworld, mythic order as essentially a cultural being, a living artefact, distanced from his former state as natural phenomenon, as wild beast, as manifestation of the cosmic forces the *cailleach* personifies. Equally, the cattle droppings used as firing and the flail borrowed from a neighbour are cultural work – technology and social relationship – brought into action in order to overcome and defeat nature in this showdown battle with the *cailleach* and her allies, just as they act to transform and transcend nature in the course of their use and operation in everyday life. The flail – its handle and striker, two lengths of stick taken from trees; its thong a strip of hide (perhaps eel-skin) taken from the body of an animal – comprises the application of human ingenuity and intelligence to the adaptation, organization and transformation of the natural world, in this case in the cultural process of producing bread, the staff of life, from the fruit of the corn harvest. Corn, being the result of the domestication of wild grasses, is akin to the domesticated herds whose waste products (rather than their seed) are capable of creating no less a staff of human life: the fire that warms and cooks and also symbolizes the heart of the social unit. The fire is the central focus of domestic life and the centre-stage location for the creative performance of imaginative narrations of which this story of *Murchadh Ruadh* in *Gleann na mBiorrach* is itself an example.

In the preparations for the battle with the hag, the bull sees himself as the hag's chief adversary. 'I myself will do battle with the hag', he proclaims. Two observations seem pertinent here in the light of the way the narrative is structured and develops. Firstly, the battle is taking place 'now' because *Murchadh* has, as it were, stumbled onto or found himself unwittingly present at the liminal threshold of the hag's cavern, the mythic otherworld order (knowledge about which was, hitherto, not available to him in the ordinary course of social life). Possessing this knowledge now sets *Murchadh* in the role of mortal enemy of the *cailleach,* destined somehow to attempt to face her down and dominate her in a kind of once-off, yet mythically eternal and recurrent showdown between the worlds of culture and nature. Secondly, the bull, part natural, part cultural in his being and already privy to the cosmic knowledge of the *cailleach*'s domain, is superseded as chief adversary by *Murchadh*, once *Murchadh* attains this knowledge, admittedly with the bull's/nature's assistance. *Murchadh*'s increased knowledge occurs in the heightened mode of perception that goes along with his realization of his positioning on the liminal boundary of culture and cosmic consciousness at the entrance to the hag's cavern. His initial reaction to the realization of what this destiny brings, is to ally himself enthusiastically to the bull as chief protagonist of the cultural order in the forthcoming struggle, and also to wonder what the consequences will be for himself in the human social world, given what he is experiencing and participating in at the liminal and mythic moment. The fact that the black bull sees himself as chief enemy of the *cailleach* is again underlined for us in his comment regarding the coming to an end of his earthly existence when he has himself killed the 'grey hag' and her mythic retinue.

Murchadh's question to the bull, 'Will I tell other men that you spoke to me?', is capable of being taken as expressing *Murchadh*'s awed awareness of the privileged position he finds himself in, privy to a kind of sacred animation and consciousness on the part of the natural world which is not properly part of the ordinary knowledge of humans and human society. Also, his question can be understood as indicating a reluctance on *Murchadh*'s part to share this sacred knowledge: 'Must I tell?', he seems to imply, as if there is in him (as representative human figure) something of a calculation as to how to take advantage of what he has learned. The black bull, symbol of an already achieved degree of advantage and exploitation on the part of humanity over nature in the domestication of cattle, suggests that to which his very existence as a domesticated beast bears witness: that it is best for *Murchadh* not to share his secret knowledge (and thereby his power) with 'other men'. This will, in the course of the narrative, be seen to comprise part of the deception that, the story suggests, lies at the heart of society, both in respect of relations between the sexes and of relations between society and the life of the natural resources it exploits and consumes.

Going home, with his sacred, secret knowledge, *Murchadh*, we are told 'was filled with great anxiety'. We gather that he does not share this knowledge with his wife who queries him the following day in respect of his telling her to get him a flail on loan. It is clearly the case that *Murchadh* is a pastoralist and a symbolic personification of a technology and a lifestyle that is perceived as being pre-agricultural – though existing side by side with the tillage agriculture which provides the sheaves of oats with which *Murchadh* supplements his animals' grazing. In acquiring a flail from his agriculturist neighbour, *Murchadh* is, as it were, acquiring the technology of agriculture to add to the technology of pastoralism as an armoury with which to wage war on the female personification of the vitality and productivity of the natural order. I have already noted how not only technology, but social relationship is also pitted against the *cailleach* here – the relationships and the advantages flowing from the bonds of kith and kin, of neighbour and wife. We can note also that while *Murchadh's* wife remains unnamed for us, we learn that the name of the neighbour agriculturist from whom *Murchadh's* wife borrows the flail is *Páidín Shéamais,* a name identifying its male bearer in the patriarchal order of descent reckoning: *Páidín,* son of *Séamas. Murchadh's* wife, surely with her own feminine prescience and premonition – in the absence of her husband's sharing with her of his sacred secret – registers for us her sense of being involved with events of moment. The flail, she says, must be given back by her to its owner, the agriculturist, the following day – if, as she says, 'I live that long'. One senses here, again, something of the paradigmatic nature, in the history of cultural and community consciousness, of the events that are unfolding. The seemingly final domination of landscape and of the forces of nature by the combined power of pastoralism and agriculture – in historical reality the result of long centuries of settlement and technological innovation – are in this story brought to a dramatic, almost momentary, mythological turning point in the confrontation of the *cailleach* landscape figure, on the threshold of her mysterious world, by the symbolic figure of the male human who represents the world of that cultural and social order that has been established in the face of wild nature. The words 'if I live that long' are those of an actor, or participant in these mythic events who registers also something of the consciousness and cultural knowledge of the audience for whom they are being narrated. *Murchadh's* response to his wife's words also has something of this mixture of participation and reflection. It is fitting, he says, to give back the flail, i.e. to restore to normal the differential distribution of technology and lifestyle which are, for the purposes of the symbolic confrontation, all gathered together, pooled and put at the disposal of the symbolic representative of the social cultural order. In the aftermath of the confrontation, the flail will be given back: 'that is', says *Murchadh,* 'if it isn't broken'. The prospect of breaking the neighbour's flail is glimpsed by *Murchadh,* by his wife, by the narrator and by the tale's audience, and is a prospect that contains the element of uncertainty regarding the victorious outcome of the confrontation of man and *cailleach,* as well as an element of foreknowledge that things will, in any case, be changed utterly, whatever the outcome. The broken flail can be a metaphor for the fracturing of an older dispensation in the affairs of culture and social life, in relation to environment and landscape and their exploitation in the cause of human wealth production. (This sense of the fateful alteration in consciousness and in relationship is communicated more palpably and more unambiguously towards the end of the narrative.)

On the appointed day battle is joined at the mouth of the hag's cavern. She recognizes the finality of the encounter and the representative identity of her opposition, and she names the black bull, to her son, as *Domblas Mór*, her great enemy since ancient times. She affirms that unless she can restrain and conquer this great enemy (the socio-cultural forces of domestication), she and her powers will be 'swept away' in the victory of human technology over nature, which will threafter provide the 'hundreds and thousands of people' with their symbolic, and actual, 'milk and meat'.

The battle follows a kind of pattern where the initial attacks on each other by the bull and the dog are succeeded by the direct confrontation of *Murchadh* and the *cailleach*. It is the bull who finally disposes of the (male) dog while *Murchadh* dispatches both the *cailleach* and her (female) heron-mother. This narrative alignment conveys the sense of male, patriarchal success that encompasses not only the symbolic victory of *Murchadh* the warrior, but also of *Murchadh* the duplicitous entrepreneur, who conceals the source of his wealth and lives 'the good life' on the basis of a deception that amounts to a self-deception which lasts 'through all time' until he knows 'that he is near death'. Once again, we have that narrative mixing of mythological and historical levels whereby condensed significance is assignable to both the symbolic and the psychological domains of both the narrative itself and the interior lives of the narrative's audience.

At the moment of victory, following the symbolic violence of the confrontation in which the hag, her mother and her son fall in a broken and vanquished heap, it is the bull who confers on *Murchadh* the title of 'proper warrior'. Not only is *Murchadh* thus hailed by his creature, but he is brought by the bull into possession of the treasure of the hag's cavern. This gold and silver treasure can be taken to be the wealth that technology and trade extracts and develops from the resources of the landscape. In taking possession of this hitherto untold wealth, *Murchadh* bids farewell to his bull-friend, relinquishing, as it were, his intimate and mysterious knowledge of and relationship with the animal realm, in return for the ability to turn the natural world into the wealth of a social order that reckons worth in pieces of gold and silver and confers status and power on the rich. *Murchadh*'s wife's words, 'we are rich for all time', is an aspect of the cultural illusion and self-deception that *Murchadh*'s triumph plays on his world and on himself. Central to the illusion-deception is the notion that it is through *Murchadh*'s own efforts as stockman and trader that he has prospered. The lie that *Murchadh* tells of how he came by his great wealth is being told to himself as well. He hears it (on the surface level of plot), from the bull, who encourages him to use it as a cover for helping himself in individualist greed to as much of the treasures of nature as he could ever want. But the black bull, *Domblas Mór*, the binary complement to the *cailleach*/goddess of horned creatures, is no longer a guide to *Murchadh*, especially in relation to behaviour in the fresh, new human order that is henceforth to prevail outside the otherworld cavern the entrance to which is now lost to social consciousness. In the new reality dawning on *Murchadh* as he stands by the golden table at the centre of the cavern chamber, the black bull is already relegated from symbolic representative of domesticated – but still mysterious and potent – cosmic creatures to being no more than a vehicle, an instrument, an object for the conveyance of wealth out of nature and into the possession of *Murchadh*, the symbolic agent of human and cultural lordship over nature. The very last glimpse we are given of the great *Domblas*, the father of all the bovine nation, is his transformation (in *Murchadh*'s perception) into a leather container, to be stuffed as fast as possible with the treasure-spoils of conquest. This conquest – of the hold of natural processes over the experience of social life – is one that brings *Murchadh* and the sociocultural order he symbolises, to a major turning point in the imaginative history of cultural consciousness as articulated in Irish traditional narrative. The landscape has been altered. Technology and social relationships of an earlier era have been strained and smashed. The broken flail (a metaphor for the breaking of the communal bonds of a pre-capitalist social order, as much as an icon of obsolete technology), is cast aside as something of no consequence, in the light of the wonderful news *Murchadh* has for his wife when he arrives home 'late in the day'. The lateness of the hour on the plot's surface is matched by a 'lateness – or a profound progression – in cultural development at the deeper levels of the narrative. This development – in culture, in consciousness, in self-knowledge and self-representation – involves the political and ideological fiction that *Murchadh* has lost control of wild nature and has relinquished his command of its resources in return for the wealth obtained in a bargain struck with 'a lord from Connacht'; a bargain delivering to him 'the most any man ever obtained for a bull'.

As we noted at the outset, this story though set by its narrator in County Kerry, derives from the narrative tradition of County Roscommon and the West of Ireland. In having *Murchadh* say that he has sold his 'wild and disobedient' bull to a lord from Connacht, the story, in the consciousness of both narrator and audience, can be taken as giving symbolic expression to both the prevailing patriarchal and peasant social order and the culturally constructed fiction on which that order was developed. *Murchadh*, the Ó

Cochubhair lord of Connacht, is legitimating in a traditional way his own royal prerogative to rule in his territory. This prerogative traditionally derives from an encounter with an otherworld female whose conferral of sovereign victory on him is accompanied, not by the blessing of the sovereignty queen of learned cultural tradition, but by the seven thousand curses of the hag-goddess of landscape who is brutally slaughtered in the cause of economic exploitation and social domination within a new order of culture. The story, therefore, draws on a central motif of Irish tradition and uses it in a complex way to echo both the medieval sovereignty of a traditional ruling dynasty of Connaught and the later mercantile and Big House sovereignty of the early modern and modern peasant – capitalist eras, whose 'lords' dominated landscape and society on the basis of aggressive wealth extraction rather than nobility of lineage. That our text is, arguably, capable of bearing such a complex exegesis, is testament to the complex and sophisticated nature of the popular oral narrative tradition of which it is a splendid example.

9. **The *Cailleach Bhéarach* and *Donnchadh Mór Mac Mánais*[43]**

In the olden times, a *cailleach* and her daughter along with her, came to Glenamaddy. No one at all knew where they had come from and they weren't asked for any account of themselves.

The *cailleach* had considerable wealth and it wasn't long before she demonstrated that. She bought a big house, an estate, horses, cows and sheep and she began to farm. She used take on no labourer except one who would contract with her for the half-year and he wouldn't have any pay coming to him at the end of the half-year if he wasn't able to keep up with the *cailleach* in every kind of work that she undertook. And the only kind of food he would get would be oat-meal bread and porridge.

Now the *Cailleach Bhéarach* was an enchanted *cailleach* and no labourer could keep up with her at work and it's many the grand young man she killed. No young man was able to spend a second week with her; they used to go back home and they used to die.

One day *Donnchadh Mór Mac Mánais* heard a great account of the *cailleach* – that no man in the whole country was able to match her at work – and he said that it was miserable men they were who couldn't keep up at working with an old *cailleach*. 'I'll go to her tomorrow', he said, 'and if I don't defeat her, I'll drown myself.' Now this same *Donnchadh* was as strong as a stallion and as fleet-footed as a deer and there wasn't a market or a fair that he wouldn't clear with an ash-plant if he was angry – and seldom he went anywhere without the same weapon.

The Cailleach and the Wise-Woman   133

The following morning *Donnchadh Mór* went to the *cailleach*'s house and said to her that he heard she was looking for a labourer. 'I'm in want of a man', she said, 'but there's no good in the men that are in this place; they are not worth their salt. Lots of them settled with me for the half-year but not a single man of them stayed with me the second week.'

'I'll wager you my life against a fat sheep that I'll stay with you a half-year if you will give me good pay and give me enough to eat', says he. 'I'll make the same bargain with you that I made with the other men' said the *cailleach*.

'What bargain is that?' said *Donnchadh*. 'Sixty florin pieces and the same again at harvest and a fat sheep at *Lá Samhna* (1 November), if you are able to toss her over the wall of the field on that day; but if you aren't able to keep up with me at the work, there won't be any pay for you.'

'I think it's joking me about the fat sheep you are', says *Donnchadh*, 'but since it is a joke, make it a good joke – say a score of sheep and I'll strike the bargain with you.'

Even though she was an enchanted *cailleach* she didn't imagine that any man in the world could toss a fat sheep over a stone wall that was twenty feet high. On these grounds she said, 'Let it be the score, and, as well as that', said she, 'do you know what food you will get to eat in my house?'

'Indeed I do not', he said. 'My appetite is not very big; it is not hard to satisfy me.' 'You will get oat-meal porridge, bread and mash and pig meat on Easter Sunday.'

'I'm satisfied with this bargain', he says, 'and I'll come to you tomorrow morning, if I am still alive.'

Donnchadh went home and told his mother about the bargain he had struck with the *cailleach*. '*A chuisle mo chroí*' ('pulse of my heart'/'my darling'), said his mother 'she is the unlucky *cailleach* for many; no man that went to work for her but is in the grave today.'

'You will see yourself, mother, that I will put her down before another month passes. I always heard that prudence was better than strength, and I have both strength and prudence.'

In the morning, on the following day, *Donnchadh* went to the *cailleach*'s house. When he entered with a greeting there was a dish of porridge on the table and she said to him, 'Sit down and eat – an empty belly doesn't make for hard work.' *Donnchadh* sat down but he didn't eat much. The *cailleach*'s daughter came into the room and she had an appearance that was as ugly as death, but *Donnchadh* started to praise her and to say that he was lucky to be in service at a house where there was a lovely girl like herself.

'Stay quiet', she said, 'maybe my mother is listening.' 'Even if the whole community was listening', he said 'I would sing the praises of a lovely girl.'

It wasn't long till the *cailleach* came and she said, 'Come on, we will go to dig stubble fields today.' They went out into the fields and they began to dig. The *cailleach* worked on a half-ridge out in front and *Donnchadh* worked on a half-ridge behind. It wasn't long before the sweat was running down off *Donnchadh Mór*. He kept up with her for the day but he had never before worked such a hard day in his life and he was almost dead by evening.

He planned to escape away home that night and he would have gone if it wasn't for the daughter of the *cailleach*. When she got the chance of being away from her mother she enquired of *Donnchadh* as to how he had got on during the day. He told her that he could not endure the length of another day only that he was in love with herself. She answered that if he was in love with her that she was also in love with him and that if he remained on, that he wouldn't have to do any hard labour any more and that she would make him as strong as a lion.

The *cailleach* had a black hound and whoever drank her milk would be as strong as sixty men. On the morning of the day following, the daughter soaked *Donnchadh*'s bread in the milk of the hound and when he went digging with the *cailleach* that day he was easily able to keep up with her. The second day he was stronger and on the third day he was able to beat her [at the work] without harm to himself. He was getting stronger from day to day and he'd have a ridge the whole length of the field dug before the *cailleach* would be half-way. She used be furious and finding fault with her spade every day.

She went to a magician blacksmith and told him to make her a new spade. He did so but she wasn't able to beat *Donnchadh* with any kind of spade because the daughter was soaking his bread with the black hound's milk and he was becoming stronger every day.

One time they were digging together in the field and *Donnchadh* went forward in front of the *cailleach* and that angered her. 'Stay behind me', she said. 'I will not stay behind', said he, 'if you are not able to stay in front of me, then give me the lead.'

'I never yet let any man lead me and you are not going to get the lead of me', she said. 'Stay behind me', said *Donnchadh*.

At that she blazed with anger and she made an attempt to strike him with the spade, but he caught a hold of the handle of the spade, pulled it from her and threw it seven perches outside of the field. Then she got a throttle-hold on him and made to try and choke him. He knocked her down, but he wasn't able to loosen the grip she had on his throat and she would certainly have choked him, only that the daughter arrived just in time to save him and she broke the *cailleach*'s grip. She made peace between the two of them and took the mother away home with her.

After that they worked well together until the time came for mowing the hay. The *cailleach* fixed a scythe for herself and *Donnchadh* fixed another. On Sunday evening the *cailleach* said: 'We will be scything tomorrow.' 'Right you are', says *Donnchadh*, 'I'm ready.'

That night the *cailleach*'s daughter said to *Donnchadh*: 'You are going scything tomorrow and you must take care of youself. I will put down harrow spikes in the path of my mother and you won't have any trouble in keeping up with her.' 'Thank you kindly, *a chuisle mo chroí*', said *Donncahdh*, 'I'll be able to keep up with her easily.'

'You won't', she said, 'My mother has a scythe that keeps its edge for the whole time that the hay is being saved, until the last of the hay is mowed; but if it looses edge just once then it's no better than any other, ordinary scythe. The edge on my mother's scythe is a very special edge. Every season, before she starts to mow with it, she brings it to a stream of water. She puts the blade into the water. Then she releases strands of wool to float down with the stream and she's not satisfied unless every strand of them is sliced by the blade of the scythe when they come as far as it.'

On Monday morning the *cailleach* and Donnchadh went to the meadow to mow. The *cailleach* began on the first wynd in the place where the spikes were shoved into the ground by her daughter. It wasn't long until she met up with one of them. She cut it but lost edge on her scythe. 'A tough kind of dock', she said. 'It was', said *Donnchadh*. She came to another one and she did the same thing to it. 'Upon my soul', she said, 'the docks in the meadow are very strong this year.' 'They are very strong, indeed', said *Donnchadh*.

She went on another bit but her scythe wasn't mowing well for her and she called out: 'Edge, *Donnchadh*.' She put up edge but she hadn't gone five yards when she shouted out again: 'Edge, *Donnchadh*.' He gave her time to put up edge once more but after a few minutes she called again, 'Edge, *Donnchadh*, hay is cut down by edge.'

'Not so, *cailleach*', said he, 'but by a good man and a sharp scythe. And if you don't move out of my way I'll take the shins off you.'

'Give me a chance to put up the edge this one time more and if my scythe fails me again before I have this wynd finished, I'll make two halves of the blade.'

She put up more edge and she started to mow but she hadn't gone twenty feet when the edge was gone again. She was furious and she made to break the blade across her knee, but the blade twisted and she cut the knee very deeply and had to send for her daughter to carry her home and she didn't come near *Donnchadh* again until all the meadow was cut.

Donnchadh made good progress then until the corn was ripe. The *cailleach*'s knee was healed by then and she was able to work again.

On Sunday evening she said to *Donnchadh*: 'Be ready, tomorrow morning, we will be reaping the corn.' 'I am ready at any time', he answered.

The daughter said to *Donnchadh* that night: 'You are going reaping corn tomorrow. Be careful of yourself or my mother will defeat you at that work.' 'There is no fear of me', he said, 'I am able to reap twice as much as her.'

'If it wasn't for one thing, you surely could', said she, 'but you don't know that there is a beetle in the handle of my mother's sickle and, for as long as it remains there, no-one in the whole world will be able to keep up with her.'

'A *stóir mo chroí* ('my heart's treasure'), said *Donnchadh*, 'I would be dead long since only that you are helping me, but we will have good days yet when your mother is in the clay.'

On Monday morning the two went to the field and they started to reap the corn. The *cailleach* took the first swathe and Donnchadh was at her back reaping behind her. It wasn't long until she had gone out ahead of him and he wasn't in any way able to keep up with her. When she was about twenty feet out in front of him she called out: '*Donnchadh*, I think there is something the matter with you today.'

'What's that you say, *a chailleach?*' said Donnchadh and at the same time he ran towards her and snatched the sickle from her grasp. He pulled the handle out of it and the beetle fell out onto the ground. 'Ha! Ha! a *chailleach bhradach* ('thieving'), you are caught now, but I'll put an end to your magical tricks; many the young man you killed with them but you won't kill me.'

The *cailleach* made an effort to try and pick up the beetle but Donnchadh stamped his foot on it and put out its guts through its mouth. 'Now, *a chailleach*', he said, 'get on with the reaping.'

'I won't reap more', she said, 'but I'll bind after you – sit down and take a rest.'

'I have no want of rest', said *Donnchadh* 'and the sooner *Lá Samhna* comes the better I will like it.'

'You are free to go tomorrow and you will get as much as if you stayed on until *Lá Samhna*. If you will give me your word that you will keep my secret until I die – and that time isn't long away from us, because I am very old – I will give you your pay tomorrow and I will let you go.'

'What is your age?' asked *Donnchadh*. 'I am more than nine times twenty years old', said she, 'and if you promise me that you won't tell out my secret, I'll tell you the story of my life.'

'Upon my word', said *Donnchadh,* 'the ear of no-one living will hear your secret from me for as long as you are alive.'

Then the *cailleach* began and she told like this.

> When I was a young girl, I fell in love with a neighbour's son, and he promised that he would marry me, but in the end he deserted me and he married another girl. One night, I stole away from my father's house and I went to the house of a smith magician and I enquired of him if he could give me magical powers. 'I'll give them to you and welcome', he said. 'Here's a *casarán* and a *biombal;* carry them to the base of an apple tree that is in your father's garden. Throw them into the well that is at the base of the tree and you will get the power of magic.' I went and I threw those things into the well and, on the spot, a black hound and a beetle came out of the well. I have the hound still but, to my sorrow, you have killed the beetle on me. There is a powerful significance in the hound's milk – anyone who would drink it, he would be as strong as a lion, and – anyone who carried the beetle with him – no one could overcome him at work or labour. I wasn't long drinking the hound's milk until I was very strong indeed. I went, by night, to the house of the young man who had deserted me and I killed him and his wife and no one at all suspected that it was I who committed that crime. I stayed on in my father's house until I was heavy with child, unknown to them. Then, with the shame of it, I left house and home. My black hound followed me and I stayed that night in the house of the smith magician and it was there that my daughter was born. The following morning the smith asked of me where I would go. 'Anywhere at all, to hide my shame', I said. Then he gave me man's clothes to

put on and he changed me in appearance so that my own father or mother wouldn't know me. I spent twice twenty years with him, blowing the bellows and helping him in all his work. One day, I was striking for him with the heavy sledgehammer and I struck him on the thumb. That angered him and he struck me with a magic rod and turned me into a sow and sent me to Knockmeagh, for a hundred years. When I was let go out of there, I was sent back to the old smith and I was given a purse filled with gold and with silver. I discovered my daughter, my hound and my beetle there before me with no change in them and no change in myself. I brought them with me here to this place. I bought it and settled down in it. There you have my story, now and I beseech you not to let it out of your mouth for as long as I remain alive.'

'Indeed I won't', said *Donnchadh*.

Harvest went by and *Samhain* came. On the morning of *Lá Samhna*, the *cailleach* paid *Donnchadh* the cash and told him to come with her to the sheepfield in order to throw the sheep over the wall.

When they came into the field, he caught hold of the heaviest sheep that was there and he threw it over the wall like he would throw a pebble. He was throwing them over the wall until he had thrown a score of them.

'Upon my word', said the *cailleach*, 'your half-year's pay is no bad pay.' 'It's not better than I earned', said *Donnchadh* and, with that, he drove his twenty sheep in front of him and went home.

It wasn't long after that until the *cailleach* got sick. The old women of the place came to tend her. 'How old are you?' said one of the women. 'More than nine twenties of years', she said. 'And how is it that you are so lasting.'

'The morning breeze never blew on my empty stomach; the dew never wet my foot before sunrise; I consumed hot and I consumed cold and that's the reason why I'm so lasting.' But we know that this was a lie in her mouth when she was dying.

That night there came a great storm, and thunder and lightning and the *cailleach*'s house was knocked to the ground. The *cailleach* was killed along with her daughter and her hound. On the morning of the following day there were hundreds of dogs round about the house and from that day to this there is no other name on that place but Glenamaddy.

While the story is set 'in the olden times' we are given to understand that the *cailleach* – together with her daughter – arrived into the district in question from somewhere else, neither giving nor being asked for, any 'account of themselves'. Such account is given, however, by the *cailleach* herself in the inset tale towards the end of the story, when she has been vanquished by the male hero, *Donnchadh Mór Mac Mánais*. That biographical inset tale account serves to explain, as it were, the character of the *cailleach* of the frame tale, a character fatally inimical to the well-being of the succession of young men who work with her as farm labourers. What she represents in the frame tale is a version of the archaic, territorial, sovereignty queen with emphasis on the fierce, martial, destructive side, the terrible hag aspect of her divine sovereignty. This mythological figure is set in a socio-historic framework of Big House and landlord Ireland, with the *cailleach* as a member of the landed gentry, though herself participating – indeed, symbolically heading up – the work of the estate. In the inset tale the mythological figure of the hag-goddess is set into a psychic and symbolic discourse wherein the origin of her fiercely destructive disposition towards the line of males is presented as arising from a form of primal abuse that mirrors, and is mirrored in, her own and her daughter's devious defeat and vanquishment by *Donnchadh Mór*. This tale, overall, constitutes a startlingly dramatic and sophisticated presentation of the issues of male–female relationship in terms of both archetypal and cultural-historic patterns, blended in a fashion that would do credit to a practitioner of the modern short story. And yet the text we are dealing with here comes to us from an oral tradition that has transmitted and adapted the figure, and the significance of the hag-goddess to the consciousness of modern times and, as such, shows clearly the imaginative potential and personal relevance of traditional legend for the representation/articulation of contemporary concerns and for their symbolic realization in creative narrative.

At the outset of the story, when the *cailleach* is presented as a kind of female landlord hiring farm labour by the season, we are told that the contracted males would have 'no pay' coming to them, at the end of the half-year, if they proved unable to keep up with the work. That this is no ordinary farm-work and that this is no ordinary, albeit female, landlord is signalled in the fact that the only kind of food she provides for her labourers is 'oat-meal bread and porridge'. The cereal diet symbolizes her personification of the life and fertility of crops and, indeed, the whole of the plant or vegetable kingdom, just as in other stories she is the personfication of the animal kingdom in her symbolic association with cattle or deer. We can note in passing the use of the term *cailleach* to signify the last sheaf of the corn harvest in Irish and Gaelic Scottish tradition and the existence of traditional customs concerning the 'last sheaf' and the avoidance of it among farmers and farm workers. Our narrator tells us that she was an *enchanted* (i.e otherworld) *cailleach* and that young men having association with her went to their deaths as a result. It is in the understanding of the hag-goddess sovereignty queen in Irish tradition that the associates (i.e. spouses) of the sovereignty queen – the kings and heroes to whom she is serially joined in the *hieras gamos,* the sacred marriage of female, territorial sovereignty principle with chief male mortal – go from her in death in the sense that they pass away in the course of time and human mortality while she endures as the divine eternal female agency of the cosmos and its vital and renewing forces. The *Cailleach Bhéarach* of Glenamaddy – whom we will later see to be a primally abused and mistreated female in her youth – is the age-old, divine, otherworld female; part divine personification of territorial sovereignty, part harvest goddess, operating here as a vengeful and destructive agency in reaction to the wrong done her long ago that parallels, as it were, the violation of the sovereignty queen of medieval myth in her reduction to prize trophy of the competing dynastic lineages. Both frame tale and inset tale deal again with the overthrow and expulsion of the autonomous otherworld female, something that in Part One we have seen personified in the figure and the fate of *Mongfind,* a millennium earlier in narrative chronology.

Donnchadh Mór Mac Mánais is the archetypal male who faces and opposes the hag-goddess in this recounting of the displacement – expulsion theme, though at the beginning of our text he is presented as being unaware of the mythological depth of his own or the *cailleach*'s identity. In the course of the story he acquires some knowledge of his role akin to the role-realization acquired by the young curate in the *Ana Ní Áine* tale (see pp. 149–60 below). Unwittingly, he expresses from the beginning, the sense of a mythological or archetypal showdown in his crude reaction to hearing that 'no man in the whole country was able to match her at work'. He reacts as if driven, somehow, to the confrontation: 'I'll go to her tomorrow ... and if I don't defeat her, I'll drown myself.' We are told that the same *Donnchadh* is 'as strong as a stallion' and 'as fleet-footed as a deer', pitting his combatative, male, animal or faunal strength and identity against her fertile, female, vegetable and floral vitality and resources. His warrior dominance is again articulated, in an initially unreflective way, in the assertion that, when angry, he could with his ash-plant weapon, clear the market-place or the fair-ground of his competitors. We might wonder here also as to the possible significance of his reported use of an ash-plant as his weapon, since the term *caillichín* (lit. 'little old woman or *cailleach*') is a name for a fighting stick in the tradition of the faction-fighters. *Donnchadh Mór*'s consequent defeat of the hag-goddess – and his incorporation into himself of her former natural and vegetable/plant – kingdom dominance – is here pre-figured in the representation of him as local strong man in the early-modern, historical era, with its faction-fighting on fair days and the *caillichín*, the ash-plant, as the instrument of aggression and domination.

In the way they strike the bargain, both *Donnchadh Mór agus* the *cailleach* sound a note of aggression and domination. Each has the expectation – unreflective and pre-conscious – that they will prevail, as is their wont, over the other. Two small points can be noted as evidence of the projection by the narrator of the ancient opposition of hero and goddess into a more modern setting: meat will be added to the hero's otherwise cereal diet at Eastertide (indicating the presence of Christianity), and the hero's wages will consist, in part, of 'sixty florin pieces' (denoting the cash economy of the early modern period). In expressing his satisfaction with the terms of the bargain struck, *Donnchadh* says that he will begin work on the following day 'if I am still alive'. We have already seen, in the text concerning the *Cailleach of Gleann na mBiorach,* how a similar phrase ('if I live that long'), is capable of being understood as bearing witness to the telescoping of the history of settlement and of cultural development, into a turning point of mythological import wherein representative figures (male–female; technological–natural; Christian–ancestral), stand opposed in a showdown confrontation the outcome of which the audience (and the later readership of which we ourselves form a part), are already aware. In this tale, *Donnchadh Mór* and what he symbolizes will indeed live long, in the aftermath of the defeat and displacement of the divine female agency.

Donnchadh Mór's victory over the hag/*cailleach* – his mortal enemy – is achieved his being able to benefit from other aspects of his relationship (as male) with the feminine. These are a) his relationship with his own mother, a structurally parallel figure to the mother-*cailleach* of the story, and b) his relationship to the *cailleach*'s daughter, who is portrayed in the tale as a hag-like young female whom he deviously and deceitfully 'embraces', thereby benefiting immensely – and crucially – in his struggles with her mother. The nurturing warmth evident between *Donnchadh Mór* and his own mother – she calls him '*A chuisle mo chroí*' – is reflected in his seduction, as it were, of the *cailleach*'s daughter. In early Irish tales of the hero's encounter with the hag-goddess, sovereignty is won by means of an 'embrace' (kiss or coition) and, in this 'modern' story, *Donnchadh Mór* consciously employs what he terms 'prudence' (the Irish term is *stuaim*) in order to acquire for himself the means of attaining sovereign victory over *Cailleach Bhéarrach* and her daughter; the latter a victim of abuse by *Donnchadh,* in that she shares in the defeat and displacement inflicted on her mother on the feminine, despite her espousal of him – which he has brought about by 'prudence', i.e. trickery. Insofar as the *cailleach*'s daughter in the frame tale can be taken to represent the youth of the *cailleach* herself, we can see how the inset tale (narrated as autobiography by the *cailleach* subsequent to her defeat), prefigures the fate of her own daughter in the frame tale in a way that suggests the cyclic and enduring exploitation and abuse of female by male that is the antithesis of harmonious male–female relationship.

The story of how *Donnchadh Mór* with the clandestine help of the daughter (whose name we never learn), gains triple victory over the *cailleach* in the triple confrontation/opposition arising in the digging, mowing and reaping 'contests', is the story of how the crafty hero takes advantage of the innocent goddess in a way that leads both to her displacement (in the frame tale), and to her becoming a principally destructive and vengeful agency (inset tale shading and feeding into the frame tale). The *cailleach*'s resort to the magician blacksmith in order to have a new spade made for herself once *Donnchadh* starts to outdig her, further blends the matters of both tales (frame and inset); we are able to sense the figure of the magician blacksmith of the frame tale as the smith-magician to whom the youthful *cailleach* resorts, in the inset tale, following her desertion by the young man who had promised to marry her.

In the symbolic logic operating within this story it is possible to see such identification not only between the two smiths but between the smith and the two versions of the abusing male: a) the nameless young man who deserted the young *cailleach* and b) *Donnchadh Mór* who similarly deserts/abandons the *cailleach*'s daughter. In this light the smith-magician into whose power, and life, the young *cailleach* places herself, is equally the father of her daughter along with the nameless, deserting young man, and the cruelty and capriciousness of the 'punishment' inflicted on the *cailleach* when she inadvertantly angers the smith-magician, mirror the fate *Donnchadh Mór* inflicts on the *cailleach*'s daughter, in bringing about her death along with that of her mother, in the great cultural and cosmological transformation that his 'victory' represents.

In thanking the *cailleach*'s daughter for informing him of the beetle in the handle of her mother's sickle *Donnchadh Mór* addresses her endearingly, '*a stóir mo chroí*', reminiscent of his own mother's remarks when she was warning him of the dangers of having any dealing with the *cailleach*. Having asserted to the *cailleach*'s daughter – who is his saviour – that 'we will have good days yet when your mother is in the clay', it turns out that *Donnchadh* is happy to consign both mother and daughter to 'the clay', once he has been paid the money of the bargain and has driven away with him the twenty most valuable sheep. Money and wealth here appear to extinguish other values arising from the hero's intimate relationship with the feminine – in terms of his allegedly loving involvement with the *cailleach*'s daughter – and we can note the somewhat similar role that wealth plays in the inset tale when the

Bronze Age Co. Armagh hillfort on neolithic era habitation site. Legendary burial place of *Macha* and mythical centre of *Ulaid* sovereignty.

2. 'Red Woman' (Katherine Beug). A painting redolent, for this writer, with many images and motifs from the stories of the *cailleach* and the *bean feasa*.

Oileán Buí/Buí's Island/Dursey (Cambridge University Collection of Air Photography). As is *Cnogba*/Knowth, the great megalithic tomb on the River Boyne (*Bóinn*) in Co. Meath, *Oileán Buí* is named after the mythical female personification of territorial sovereignty. The village on the island has the name *Baile na Cailli*/The Townland of the *Cailleach*.

4. '*Loch Bá*' (Photograph by James Westland). "You will all have heard talk of Loch Bá ... a most beautiful lake, both very long and very deep ... that shows its blue waters to the heavens." Isle of Mull site of *Cailleach Bheurr's* renewal and demise.

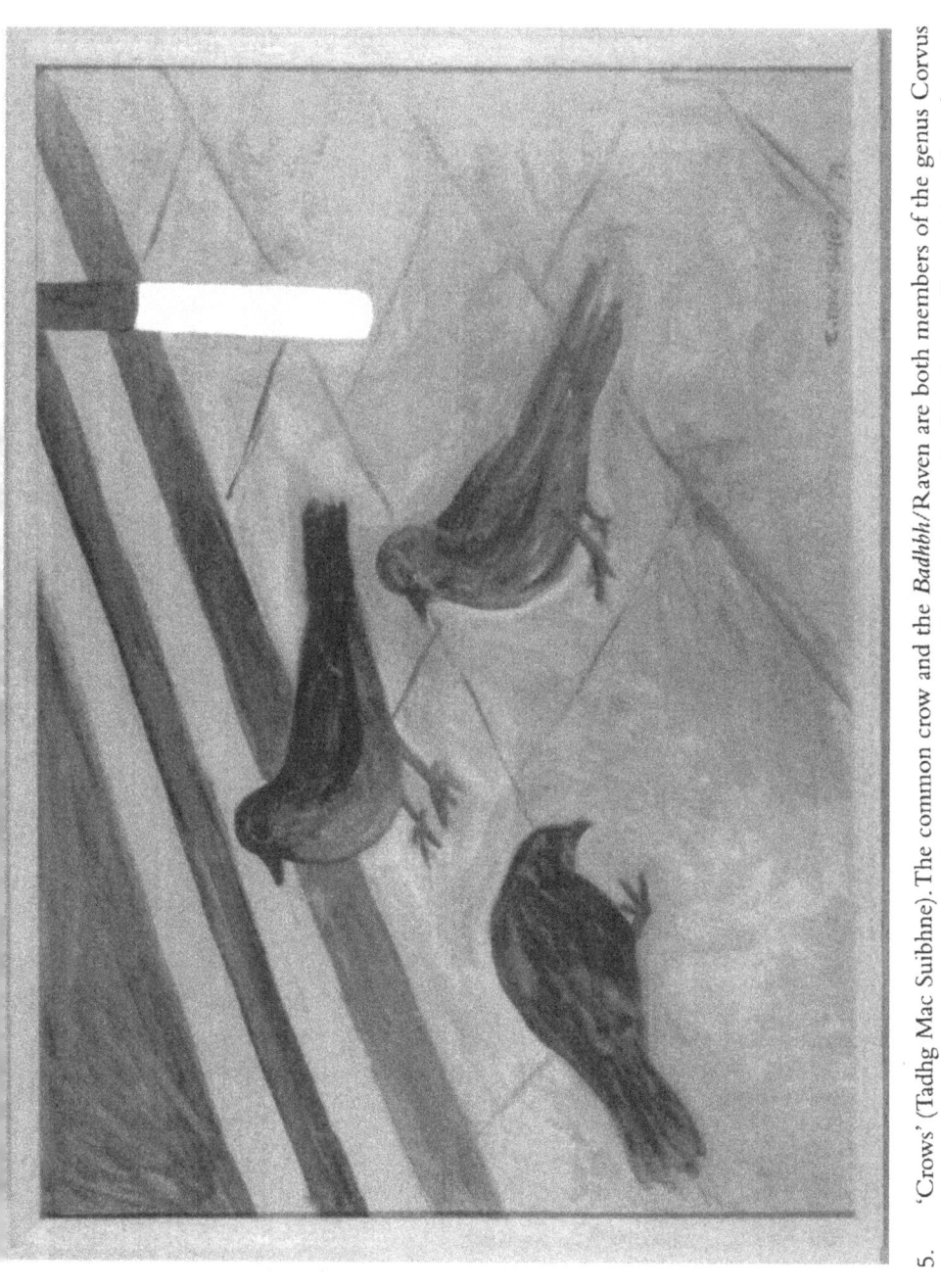

5. 'Crows' (Tadhg Mac Suibhne). The common crow and the *Badhbh*/Raven are both members of the genus Corvus that poets and artists use in symbolic ways: messenger of the gods or god of death, guardian spirit, culture hero or anti hero.

6. 'Sacred Animal' (anon.) This bull with anthropomorphic features is another example of the arti[st's] use of nature symbolism.

7. Edvard Munch: Two Human Beings. The Lonely Ones, 1899 Woodcut. Munch Museum, Oslo © Munch Museum/Munch-Ellingsen Group/DACS 2003. Photograph © Munch Museum (Andersen/de Jong).

8. 'The *Cailleach*/Kilcatherine Stone (Photograph by John Eagle). Even in her petrified state, she still speaks eloquently to us.

cailleach is 'given a purse filled with gold and with silver' in apparent recompense for the abuse and punishment she has suffered in the form of a one-hundred-year animal existence on the otherworld hill of Knockmeagh (*Cnoc Meadha*) west of Tuam in County Galway. That existence was an outrageously disproportionate punishment, inflicted as we have seen, in retaliation for an accidental offending of the smith-magician on her part, when she strikes him on the thumb with a hammer in the course of assisting him at his smithwork. She had been 'twice twenty years with him, blowing the bellows and helping him in all his work'. We can take 'twice twenty' as meaning a lifetime, an established *status quo* of identification on the part of the shamed female, with her male patriarchal protector.

This seeming identifying by the abused, youthful *cailleach* with the smith-magician, has the nature of a pathological over-identification in it. It is an attempt to escape the shame of her primal abuse and the guilt that arises from her vengeful murder of the young man and his wife (who is an archetypal equivalent of her own, feminine self). Dressed in man's clothes, and unrecognizable (as a daughter *and* as a woman) to even her own father and mother, she lives a deception that turns her personality into that of a destructive, hostile agency, in 'human' form; she becomes a wealthy landowner (i.e. territorial sovereign) who outlives the succession of male labourers/champions whose death she causes.

When, in the aftermath of her defeat by Donnchadh she sickens and begins to die, 'the old women of the place' are said to come to minister to her, as if she is the focal point for a local concentration of feminine consciousness and feminine concern. The old women learn from her that her (their own?) enduring longevity has been a function of a balanced relationship between the feminine and the world of nature, a balance encapsulated in the gnomic explanations that she provides. The denial of this primal balance and the wisdom it represents is sharply expressed in the narrator's direct comment: 'But we know that this was a lie in her mouth when she was dying.' In the order that has prevailed since the dislodging of the hag-goddess from her place in the web of psychic, social and cosmic relationships within and between individuals, and between the social order and the natural environment, knowledge of the proper harmonies – in psyche, in society and in cosmos – is devalued and denied. Stories such as this one, however, purporting to recount the ousting of an enemy of human wellbeing, actually bear witness to an enduring apprehension – in the traditional cosmology to which legends of the *cailleach*, and her overthrow, give creative, narrative expression – of the crucially disordered state which the denial of autonomous female agency entails. In such disordered state, the relationship of masculine and feminine is based on destructive deception and betrayal rather than on a nurturative complementarity that pays due respect to the harmony principle in culture as well as in nature, in the domestic as well as in the wild, in society as well as in the cosmos. Stories such as this draw their listeners – and their readers – back to the fundamental acknowledgement of this harmony principle, an acknowledgement that runs through the transmission in narrative performance of the legends that express centrally important aspects of the ancestral worldview of the communities from whom these tales were recorded.

Displacement of the feminine in a male-centred symbolic order

10. **The *Cailleach Bhéarthach* (*Carna: Áird Thoir*)**[44]

    As everyone knows this *cailleach* is supposed to have thousands of years of life. She was there thousands of years before the time of St Patrick and when St Patrick was travelling about the country he happened to meet up with her, himself and his servant. He enquired of the *cailleach* and how old she was and she told him like this:

    'I buried nine times nine people on nine occasions in nine graves in Tralee'.

    'What gave you that length of life?' said Patrick

    'I didn't ever carry the muddy dirt of one place beyond that of another place without washing my feet'.

    'Have you any other ideas, *cailleach*, about your age?'

    'No seven years of my life ever passed that I didn't toss the bones of a slaughtered bullock up onto that loft there and if you like you can go up there and count them.'

    Patrick sent up the servant onto the loft and he started to throw down bones for Patrick to count. It wasn't long before the floor was covered and Patrick asked up to his servant if there was any prospect of their coming to an end. What the servant answered was that he was beginning to make a start on them and that was all. 'Oh, throw them back up again out of my sight', said Patrick. The servant did as he was told.

    When that much was done, Patrick walked over to the *cailleach* and told her that she wouldn't toss up another bone there ever again. He caused her to disappear in a red flash and that was the end of her.

This short text, from *Carna* in Connemara combines several motifs that express the longevity of the *cailleach* in the landscape and in traditional cosmology. They are uttered by the *cailleach* herself in response to questions about her great age put by St Patrick who has – like the travelling friar of the Ballycastle text below – encountered her on his missionary travels. This great age is presented at the very beginning of the piece as a matter of common communal knowledge: 'As everyone knows ...' We are told she was there thousands of years before St Patrick, though her own formulation of this is far more tightly poetic, with its cumulative repetition of the 'nine times' motif, as applied to lifetimes and the 'life' of a graveyard. Her explanation is couched in terms similar to those used by the *Cailleach Bhéarrach* of the *Donnchadh Mór Mac Mánais* story and represents the conception of the hag-goddess as being at one with the landscape, its features and its processes, interacting with it in ways that we would speak of today as being environmentally appropriate and in harmony with nature.

The *cailleach's* poetic formulation of the extent of her great age and its basis in intimate relationship with landscape and nature, stand in contrast to the narrator's initial prosaic expression of her age in the linear terms of 'thousands of years', and to the attempt of St Patrick and his servant to reckon it by prosaically counting the bullock bones tossed onto the loft every seven years. This attempt to account scientifically for and understand the *cailleach's* existence fails and we can take from the story that insofar as credence can be given to the concept of the hag-goddess as the intimate personification of landscape and nature, that credence must be in terms of imagination rather than calculation, poetic utterance rather than numerical reckoning, affective as much as cognitive knowledge.

St Patrick and the 'new' Christian order is shown as unsympathetic, to say the least, to the figure and the significance of the *cailleach* in ancestral tradition. Patrick is portrayed as immediately pronouncing the demise of the *cailleach* and all she represents. He causes her to disappear 'in a red flash' and that, we are told, was 'the end of her'. We can again however, point to the continued transmission and performance of this narrative itself as a continuing afterlife for the *cailleach* and for the perception of ancestral cosmology in a worldview that is officially Christian and in the modern era, increasingly rational. In this, as in other texts that purport to show the displacement and expulsion of the *cailleach,* we can sense the abiding allure of the older wisdom and the poetically privileged way in which it continues to find expression even in accounts of its supplanting. Such accounts serve to renew the ambiguity of cosmological allegiance that marks the Irish repertoire of legend regarding landscape, as both domain of the hag-goddess and God's creation. As is the case with the present text, the legends recounted can appear to make short shrift of the claims of the *cailleach*. Nevertheless, we still get a sense of the way in which vernacular tradition preserves the potential for significance of that which it portrays as being lost.

11. **The *Cailleach Bhéarra* and *Saint Caitiairn*[45]**

There was a *cailleach* in *Béarra* in the otherlife that they used to call the *Cailleach Bhéarra*. She was a thieving, scoundrelly hag, without religion or without conscience, the butt of everyone's anger and everyone's malicious gossip. And that's how things continued at that time. What she didn't make off with, she spoiled and destroyed, and everyone vented their anger on her. Some of them fled from home in mortal fear of their life, because of her. And it was in that way that she was there at that time.

She used to go north inland into the glens and south to Whiddy Island and she used to gather up all before her in her domination of the whole territory. She heard tell one time that there was a certain salmon above in the glen that no one could catch. She went after it and she brought it back with her to *Béarra*.

And after that she went to Whiddy Island gathering sea-shore food, as was her wont, and her preference. And, on her return home to Ballycrovane she came upon *Naomh Caitiairn* asleep on a bare hillock, without shelter or protection from rain or wind or from the business of the day. And the name that people call that place ever since is *an ola ae* (?) because of the little sleep the saint made there which the *cailleach* disturbed. It was her wont to search and rifle the pockets of anyone she could get an advantage of. And when she got the chance, since *Naomh Caitiairin* was asleep, she went through his garments and whatever she found she put into her bag. She put it into her bag and she took his magic staff that was beside him.

There was a cripple living in that place. He saw the thieving that the *cailleach* was at and he shouted at *Naomh Caitiairin*. The cripple's shout and the noise the *cailleach* was making woke *Naomh Caitiairin* and he saw what had happened. He called after the *cailleach* and the more he called, the more she ran. He followed after her and he caught up with her in a place called *Ard na Caillí* in Kilcatherine/ *Cill Chaitiairn*. He turned her into a bare, grey pillar-stone: her back to the hill; her face to the sea and she is there from then until the Last Day.

The *cailleach* of this story was, we are told, 'in the otherlife' in Beara, thus attributing to her an existence at once remote in time from the human present and situated in a cosmological order encompassing a co-existence of the ancestral otherworld with the human domain. She is presented as an agency inimical to human life and human welfare, the subject of everyone's anger and hostility. In particular she is said to have been 'without religion or without conscience' and is thus portrayed as a figure of opposition to the morality of that Christian community life that is the *status quo* prevailing in the aftermath of her displacement by the representative of Christianity, Saint *Caitiairn*. Her dominance of the landscape of the natural world is seen in her drawing of her sustenance from the furthest reaches of her territory, whose natural resources she exploited for herself. Human resources too fell prey to her, whenever she had the opportunity of taking them away from people. *Caitiairn*, though no ordinary person – he is a saint, with the authority and powers that Christian sainthood implies – presents her with an opportunity to take advantage of him too, when she comes on him 'asleep on a bare hillock, without shelter or protection'. Along with his human possessions, she helps herself to his 'magic staff' – the crozier-like symbol of his Christian priestly or episcopal authority – an act that represents both the grossest affront to the new religion and an incompatibility of cosmological dimensions; the placing of the symbol of power of the male Christian God, or his representative, into the possession of the pagan, irreligious otherworld female.

The witness to this act of transgression is said to have been a cripple who lived locally. We have already been told that humans fled 'in mortal fear of their life' out of the path of the *cailleach*. Now a cripple (incapable of fleeing and representing the weak and the downtrodden whom Christian ideology especially embraces), acts to oppose the mighty agency of the ancestral otherworld, in shouting out his warning to the saint, and his own opposition to her activity. Awakened and alerted by the cripple's call, the saint rouses himself, rises up and takes up the call in the official voice, as it were, of the Christian vision, the Christian moral order, the Christian cosmos from which, in turn, the hag-goddess flees. Given her superhuman stature and ability to move – implicit in her food-gathering travels across her huge domain – we can take the catching up with her by the saint as proof of his superior powers. He does so in Kilcatherine/*Cill Chaitiairn*, the place of his church, the centrepoint of his Christian jurisdiction, at a particular spot called *Ard na Caillí*/Hag's Rise, the prominent centre of the *cailleach*'s ancestral landscape jurisdiction. At this place, named for them both, the two orders face each other in showdown fashion. It transpires that it is really no contest: the saint's Christian powers, the 'magic' symbolized by his 'magic staff', the new dispensation of the male divinity of the world religion that is establishing itself in the land, petrify her. She is turned 'into a bare, grey, pillar-stone'. She stands there yet, we are told – her back to the hill, to the land, to the homeplace that is now a site of the temples of the Christian Lord, a location of the City of God – facing out to the wilderness of the sea, the primal, watery chaos out of which, in Christian myth, God formed the dry land and the Christian order that is commanded by him to prevail upon it. And there, we are told, she will remain 'until the Last Day' that point when the natural physical order, out of which the hag-goddess was formed from time immemorial, will be no more and the kingdom of the Christian God will be all that is.

Short as this story from Beara is, it renders a powerful and dramatic account of the aggressive conquest and displacement of the representative of ancestral cosmology in Irish tradition. An account such as this, seen already in the poem of a thousand years earlier (also with strong Beara connections), gives pause for thought in regard to the ability of Irish venacular tradition to entertain an imaginative allegiance to both the Christian and ancestral cosmologies after a fashion that exemplifies the constantly creative tension of local–global, vernacular–cosmopolitan, subaltern–hegemonic cultural relations, that is the hallmark, everywhere, of cultural process.

12. Meelick Round Tower[46]

It is believed by the older people in this locality that the Round Towers were built by a witch called the *Cailleach Bhéarra* who figures prominently in the folklore of Connaught. It was this same *cailleach* who is supposed to have built Meelick Round Tower outside Swinford which was never finished. To add to the labour of building it 'she carried the stones up in her pocket' (according to my mother).

Judging by my mother's version of the story she intended, like those who undertook the erection of the Tower of Babel, to build the tower to the sky, if unmolested. When the erection was well under way a boy passed who made the underquoted remark. She became highly indignant and jumped down to her doom, leaving the impression of her two knees on a stone in the ground below.

> When the *Cailleach Bhéarra* was at the top of the tower, working away at it with all her might, a boy came along the way. He looked up and he said:
>
> '*Cailleach Bhéarra*, I spy your arse.' Great anger came over her then and she said:
>
> 'But for that I would have put it up to the sky.'
>
> She jumped down and the mark of her two knees are in the rock below, to this day.

It was my mother who gave me this version of the story. She heard it from her own grandmother. I've heard the story from other people too but it isn't always told the same way.

The sense of the displacement of the *cailleach,* the shift in cosmological consciousness, that this story expresses is communicated at the very outset of the text when the narrator states that it is 'the older people in the locality' who believe that the Round Towers were built by *Cailleach Bhéarra.* She figures prominently in tradition all over Connaught, we are told, but she never finished building the Meelick Round Tower that stands, incomplete, near Swinford. The comparison which the narrator makes between her work on the Meelick Round Tower and the work that the descendants of Noah proposed to carry out in the Biblical account of their determination to build the Tower of Babel, suggests that it is the power of the Judaeo-Christian divinity that is at work in the frustration of the activities of *Cailleach Bhéarra* and her apparent demise, in the worldview of the younger contemporaries of the narrator.

The incident that brings about the apparent demise of the hag-goddess is one that contains an echo of the treatment of her that was commented on at some length above in respect of the inset-tale and frame-tale motifs of the story of *Cailleach Bhéarra* and *Donnchadh Mór Mac Mánais.* It is revealing that the word the narrator uses in the English introduction he provides here to the actual Irish text, when he speaks of the *cailleach*'s intention to build her tower to the sky is the word 'unmolested'. If she had not been 'molested' she would have continued building the tower; the geotectonic work of landscape formation on the part of the hag-goddess and, thus, the cosmology – or cosmogony – of ancestral worldview would have remained, narratively, in place. However, she was molested (i.e. suffered abuse of a sexual nature), 'at the hands' of a young male who, though unnamed here and featuring only fleetingly in the text, can nevertheless be taken as the equivalent of the young male in the *Donnchadh Mór* inset-tale who abuses the young *Cailleach Bhéarra* and, indeed, the equivalent of *Donnchadh* himself who abuses and abandons the *cailleach*'s daughter at that tale's conclusion. The male gaze and the male utterance here bring about a similar ravishing and destruction of their female recipient, as do the actions and words of the male abusers of the *cailleach* and her daughter in the earlier story.

It appears as if nothing remains of the hag-goddess but the imprint of her two knees, where she hit the ground on being dislodged from her position on high, a position that is metaphorically 'high' in both the sense of 'visibility', and also, the sense of importance accorded her in the cosmological scheme of things. And yet, we learn the *cailleach* is remembered, together with her high and cosmically mighty role, from generation to generation: 'It was my mother who gave me this version of the story. She heard it from her own grandmother.' Moreover, it is not as some fixed, empty, post-closure item of a receding tradition that she is remembered, as varying versions exist in the contemporary narrative repertoire of 'the people' for whom the work and the mark of *Cailleach Bhéarra* are a narratively ever-renewed feature of landscape and of world-view.

13. **'Don't Believe a Woman's Words'**[47]

Cailleach Bhéarra had a servant boy one time. He went out this day to shake out the hay without the *cailleach*'s permission. Out with her after him and she was furious at the hay being shaken out that day. 'You stupid fool', said she, 'what reason have you to shake out the hay when it is going to rain today?' 'How do you know that it's going to rain?' said the servant boy.

'Because', said the *cailleach*, 'the scald-crow screamed it and the deer spoke it.'

The boy then said:

> Heed not the scald-crow nor the deer
> And heed not a woman's words
> Whether it's early or late the sun rises
> The day will be as God wills it.

My father told me this. The old fellows used to be telling it long ago, he said, when he was a youngster.

Certainly significant here are the two sources from which the *cailleach* claims to have knowledge of the weather, which we can take to mean the whole natural order: the scald-crow and the deer. The crow we can take as a form of the *Badhbh*/sovereignty goddess (see p. 54), while the deer is a representative of the horned, animal life-forms of the natural world, whose personification the *cailleach* is, as in the story about her and the Black Bull (see p. 120). Having delivered the quatrain in which the pre-eminence of the Christian divinity is proclaimed – over not only the goddess and the natural world with its ancestral female personification, but over the feminine in general – in a somewhat dismissive fashion, the narrator tells us that it was his own father who told him this and that he has it from his father too that in his own youth 'the old fellows used to be telling it long ago'. In such narrative fashion does the *cailleach* and the feminine endure and survive their alleged supplanting at the hands of Christian patriarchy.

14. *Ana ní Áine*[48]

I suppose that it is ever so long ago now since a certain rich and prominent man of the MacCarthy people lived in Kenmare; he was a man of great wealth. He was married and he had but one only daughter whose name was *Ana McCarthy* – though *Ana Ní Áine* only is what is given in the story. She was a very beautiful girl and many were the young men who desired to marry her, but she didn't marry until she was quite mature. A young gentleman came from Ulster and she fell in love with him and he is the man that she married. She was married only about a dozen years or so when this travelling man went into the house to her one evening. She set him to a meal and then she began to question him. It appears that the travelling man had second sight. Anyhow, in the course of their talking he told her that she would never die until Friar *Seán Ó C'nuchúir* would prepare her for death. 'Do you know', she asked, 'who that man is?' 'I don't know that', said the travelling man. He departed from her and left her there.

Life was going on and, if it was, she was becoming no older. Her children and her children's children were settled and she was still living. It is how it finished up that she was so very old altogether that the daughter of her daughter's daughter was rocking her in a cradle. That is how things remained.

A young priest had come to her parish and he was only a couple of months there. He liked to be moving about since he was a stranger in the place. On a fine summer's evening when he was returning to his house he was seized with thirst. He was unable to see any watering place round about but he saw a house of good appearance a little distance from him. He went to the house and, on going in, he found no-one inside except a middle-aged woman. She was sitting in a corner and she was rocking a cradle. She gave a welcome to the priest. 'I am thirsty, good woman of the house', said the priest. 'Would you have a drink that you would give me?' 'Indeed I have, Father', said she. She got up and went to get the drink for him. While she was away he moved in by the cradle as if to rock it, as it were. She who was in the cradle spoke. 'Well, indeed,' she said, 'there is no need for you to have any of the trouble of me.' The priest very nearly dropped on the spot, because he had imagined that it was a little child that was in the cradle.

'What sort of person are you?' asked the priest. 'Well, 'tis easy to reckon me now', she said, 'but there was a time when I wasn't like that. But who are you that is talking to me?' 'I am a priest', he said, 'What is it that causes you to be like that?' 'It was prophesied of me that I wouldn't ever die until *Friar Seán Ó C'nuchúir* would prepare me for death. I don't know if any such as he ever existed or every will exist, but I am waiting for him, it seems, because I'm so old that the third generation is rocking me in the cradle, as you can see.' 'Most excellent', said the priest, 'that man is sitting here beside you today; I am myself that very man now.' *Áine* became happy and it's little wonder that she did. The woman of the house came and she had the drink for him. When his thirst was slaked he began to ask questions of the old woman.

'I suppose it's many the wonder you saw ever in the course of your life', he said.

'Indeed it is many', she said 'but there is one thing that I marvelled more at than anything else I ever saw, and I'll tell it to you, Father. When I was a young woman, lots of strangers used to come to our house. My father had a pleasure boat and they would often sail in her to one place or another. One fine autumn day myself and another girl got ourselves ready to go with them. There was a young priest in the boat along with us. We had a try at sailing to the Skellig but before we made a landfall there was a terrible darkness gathered in the west. My father said it would be best to turn the boat around, but the others wouldn't be satisfied. This dark black cloud was heading for us together with a gust of wind. The priest looked towards it "There is some sort of opening in that cloud", he said. It was heading for us until it was very close to the boat. As soon as it had come alongside the boat what was [to be seen] in the cloud only a woman! The priest stood up quickly, put the stole around his neck and reached for his missal. Then he spoke and he asked her what had made an evil spirit of her. "I killed someone", she said. "That is not what caused your damnation", said the priest. "I killed two people'. 'Nor that neither' said the priest. 'I killed a child that wasn't baptised in my desire to become a priest's spouse." "That is precisely what damned you," said the priest. Then he began to read his missal and after a short time she rose up out of the water in a flash of matter and she left our sight. We didn't go to the Skellig that day. We returned home; and that is the greatest wonder that I ever saw during my life.'

'But you won't have any more of life, now', said Friar *Seán*. 'I'll come to you early tomorrow morning and I will prepare you for eternity.' He came the following morning, as he had promised, and he annointed *Áine Nic Chartha*. As soon as ever he was finished with her, her soul departed and there was an end to her then. Ever since when someone lives to a great age it is a saying of people, 'She is as old as *Ana Ní Áine.*'

This text comes from an anthology of stories recorded in Irish by Kenneth Jackson from *Peig Sayers* in the Great Blasket Island in the early 1930s.

Despite its brevity it covers a great deal of cultural ground and lends itself very well to a reading strategy that attempts both to expand the contractions and condensations of meaning in the surface story-line and to bring out the concealed meanings of a symbolic and mythological character that underlie the surface plot. As with this type of material in general, the reading strategy employed here seeks to distinguish the operation of the narrator's creativity in respect of three levels of performance.

At the surface level of the text it appears easy to say what the plot or storyline is and who the characters or *dramatis personae* are. We have, however, a cast of characters who seem to merge or to transform into each other in ways that cannot be explained at the level of surface storyline alone. The young curate of the surface plot becomes for us (and understands himself to become) the medieval cleric prophesied by the travelling man with second sight. The woman in the cloud encountered by the young MacCarthy woman becomes a kind of prevision of herself in her age-old dealings with the representative male Christian cleric and takes on the archetypal identity of the eternal female. The skill of the narrator, *Peig Sayers*, in developing and progressing the story and its manifold meanings at all levels within so small a compass is extraordinary by any measure.

It must be emphasized that the written text as discussed here is a very non-dynamic record, in translation, of the verbal performance of a narrator whose artistic creativity in speech gave rise, on the occasion of the Jackson transcription, to a story that is laden with cultural richness for the discernment of the native ear or – in terms of written text – the native eye. A close reading of the text, even in translation, can hope to reveal something of that cultural richness by drawing attention to the worlds of significance that lie behind and beneath the nuances of the written word and that were available, as cultural knowledge, to the native audiences among whom legend material like this circulated in the haphazard narrations of daily life and in the specific locations of verbal art performance.

In a sense, this text is itself a kind of cultural gloss on an everyday item of narration in the Irish-speaking *Corca Dhuibhne* of the 1930s. At the very end of her story, *Peig Sayers* tells us 'when someone lives to a great age, it is a saying of people, "She is as old as *Ana Ní Áine*".' A 'saying of people', a proverb, and its explanation is here the ostensible reason for telling the story of *Ana Ní Áine* and that story's ostensible meaning. Working through the text of the story, even in translation, with a sensitivity to the nuances of traditional narrative and with a reading strategy of the sort mentioned earlier, it is possible to discover or, at least to suggest a good deal of the cultural depth and richness of significance which the story offers and to which it bears witness in the various tellings that sustained it in the narrative repertoire of Irish legend.

The narrator's opening and closing statements constitute a kind of framing within which the 'story' takes place. The opening words, 'I suppose that it is ever so long ago now since ...' hint at that mixture of the credible and the fantastic that is a characteristic of the genre of mythological legend of which this text is an example. This is not, however, the complete fantasy world of the wonder tale, with its 'Once upon a time ...', or its 'Long, long ago ...', openings that signal the distancing of the narrative location to outside of the human order proper; to that realm of magical happenings and fantastic characters, that for all their brilliance and capacity to enthrall, have no interior life-world with which we can humanly identify. Here we are introduced to an account of what happened – and what happens – to real people in an existence that is not restricted to the bright and quick surfaces of fantasy life, but engages with the symbolic and archetypal depths that underlie the plot. If the international wonder tale is entertaining and clever in a cerebral fashion often associated with masculine intelligence, then the mythological legend is instructive and wise in a way that operates in the heart and the soul as much as in the mind, and that has been regarded as being characteristic of the 'feminine repertoire' of traditional narrative.

In our text the female narrator supposes that it is a very long time now since a particular rich man lived in Kenmare. The 'I suppose' signals the 'as if' nature of this as of all other legend. Legends tell 'true' stories in a sense that has to be distinguished from the truth of history, in the strict and narrow sense of the term. Legends are told *as if* they are true and the relationship between legend and belief is a complex and dynamic one that recognizes the creative mixture of memory and imagination that operates in all human accounts of the experience of human life. The account that follows here remains true to that experience, or at least to a historic and mythic Irish version of it. The story of *Ana Ní Áine* is set in the world of modern times, invokes symbols and motifs of an earlier medieval world and conveys an apprehension of the eternal, or timeless, or ever-present truths of human existence, caught up in gendered and contested ways in the context of a cultural landscape and a historical horizon that are grounded both in the physical universe of the senses and in history and are, at the same time, open to the limitless and creative reaches of the imagination.

The story's closure is effected in the narrator's performance and in the textual product of that performance, by reference to 'a saying of people', a kind of proverb that is held to be part of the traditional knowledge and the ordinary speech of the community; a proverb that condenses and encapsulates in common parlance, all that our text articulates – at its various levels – of the nature of human life and its contested and competing elements. The apparant reason implied by the ending of our text for its narration in the first instance – as the explanation of a proverbial saying – is a narrative device of a kind very well known in a characteristic form of Gaelic narrative tradition. This is the tradition of *dindsenchus* or placename lore which consists of a huge body of narrative purporting to explain the legendary, quasi-historical origins of the names of places, the features of landscape and the legendary characters whose names are associated with them. The most prominent corpus of *dindsenchus* is the twelfth-century compilation called *Acallam na Senorach*[26] in which St Patrick and his monks are supplied with a seemingly endless commentary on the legendary origins of topographic features of the Irish landscape during a series of journeys throughout Ireland. The sources and narrators of this traditional legendary in the *Acallamh* narrative are *Caoilte* and *Oisín*, two members of the Warrior Band of *Fionn Mac Cumhaill* himself, who have, through a combination of narratively convenient circumstances, survived into the earliest Christian Irish century in order, as it were, to bear witness in the 'modern' world to the verities and the quasi-history of the old order of 'tradition'. *Ana Ní Áine*, as a text narrated in the twentieth century, can be seen to bear like witness to a concern to remember an older order and to memorialize in discourse the same process of displacement in respect of the local, native, ancestral ideology that the establishment of institutional Christianity effected in Irish culture and in Irish history as reflected in the narrative materials of a thousand years ago. *Ana Ní Áine* is presented as the daughter of 'a certain rich and prominent man of the MacCarthy people' who lived in Kenmare. He has one daughter whose name is *Ana* – an uncommon female first name form – readily taken as a version of the name *Áine*/Ann. At this point we are told by the narrator that while the daughter's name is *Ana Nic Chartha*/McCarthy, '*Ana Ní Áine* only is what is given in the story'. In fact, the form *Ana Ní Áine* does not otherwise occur in this text of the story at all, apart from the final sentence in which the proverb featuring the name *Ana Ní Áine* is referred to. The forms of the daughter's name that do occur in the text: *Ana Nic Chartha, Áine, Áine Nic Chartha* have in common that they are recognizably ordinary names for 'ordinary' people (allowing for *Ana* as a variant of *Áine*). However, the form *Ana Ní Áine* cannot be recognized as the ordinary name of an ordinary human; rather it suggests a reduplication of the name *Áine* (a prominent local goddess and 'fairy queen'), or a reduplication of the name *Anu* (the paramount ancient goddess especially associated with Munster, and the forms and fertility of its landscape). Both *Áine* and *Anu* are thus invoked in this reduplication in a way that alerts the audience and readers that the story operates within symbolic and mythological dimensions. Indeed the narrator's assertion that '*Ana Ní Áine* only is what is given in the story' should make it clear to us that it is at those symbolic and mythological levels that the legend delivers its chief significance, rather than in terms of any surface plot in which a mortal woman, Anne McCarthy, has a role. It is also true that the supernatural or otherworld association of *Ana Nic Chartha* and of the form *Ana Ní Áine* are accentuated by the accommodation of the name – and to some extent the figure – of Ana/*Áine* – to the Christian St Ann. The Christian Ann is both the virgin saint, whose feastday is 18 January, and the St Ann, mother of the virgin Mother of God. Thus the names *Ana/Áine*/Ann incorporate into its otherworld female the Hebrew name and the Christian holy persons who bear it. All of these *Áine*-like forms carry with them associations of an eternal, divine or otherworld order of things and the native Ann/*Áine* form specifically attests to the female personification of the cosmic forces and forms of the landscape and territory of Ireland, and especially of Munster, in the figure of a landscape goddess and sovereignty queen of the territory of the royal dynasties who ruled Munster in medieval times.

The *Ana/Áine* of our story is the only daughter of a rich and prominent man of the McCarthy people who lived in Kenmare. In terms of surface plot, grounded in the social realities of early modern Ireland, towns like Kenmare would indeed have featured some rich and prominent merchants of Gaelic stock and McCarthy is a very common name in south Munster. However, the narrator 'supposes' that it is 'ever so long ago now' since McCarthy lived in Kenmare as 'a man of great wealth' and what is really being invoked here is the hegemony in south Munster in pre-modern times of the McCarthy branch of the *Eoganacht* dynasty, who claimed descent from the Kings of Cashel, with the McCarthy Earl of Desmond as their leader and head. In the early eighteenth century *Aogán Ó Rathaille* had, in his poetry, conveyed powerfully an apocalyptic sense of the destruction of the native Irish world order in terms of the downfall of McCarthy rule. McCarthy of Kenmare, in this legend text, is an allegorical representation of that same traditional McCarthy and *Eoganacht* hegemony and McCarthy's daughter *Ana/Áine* is invested – even as daughter, rather than wife – with something of the significance of the supernatural or divine spouse who personifies the sovereignty of hereditary royal rule over ancestral territory. The tradition of the sovereignty queen/spouse of early medieval Irish culture was transformed, in Ó Rathaille's era into the *spéirbhean* apparition of the *aisling* (vision) poetry, and *Ana Ní Áine* is capable of being understood as possessing characteristic qualities of both types of personification. She is both beautiful young woman and shrivelled hag. She has had many suitors in the course of a lengthy period when, as McCarthy of Kenmare's eligible only daughter, she offered the prospect to many young men of access by marriage and succession, to the hereditary authority and wealth of the ancestral kingdom.

We can understand the succession of serial suitors as a transform of the serial mortal royals who, in medieval literature, were married in turn to the everlasting sovereignty queen who endures in her otherworld divinity when her human spouses pass away. *Ana* here endures, not in royal and divine splendour but, in these later days and in the context of the narrative traditions of the vernacular or folk culture rather than those of élite literature, as a *cailleach* or hag figure.

The turning point of her life as quasi-sovereignty queen was her marriage – when she was quite mature – to the young gentleman from Ulster with whom she fell in love. He is young, he is noble, he is from Ulster (a faraway land of mysterious status in the eyes and ears of a west-Munster audience), and he has himself something of a mysterious charisma in that she falls in love with him despite having withstood the allure of succeeding generations of suitors who were eager to marry her in her youthful splendour. 'He is the man that she married', we are told, and then we hear not another word of him. Having travelled from Ulster he is somehow displaced in the story by the travelling man who comes into her house and into her life when she had been married for what in human, domestic terms is a significant length of time. In the narrator's words, however, the length of time, after which the man arrives with exotic knowledge of her destiny (surely a metaphor for some kind of recognition or awakening in herself), is 'only about a dozen years'. One has again here a sense of the huge spans of time that the plot and significance of this story cover. The notion that the travelling man with second sight might possibly be equated with that of the Ulster husband is heightened by the domesticity of the setting in which her destiny is revealed to her. Having set the travelling man to a meal she then sits with him (as quasi-married couple), and it is in the course of their talking together, in a sense that can be understood as a kind of commensality or communion, that she learns that she is to live on until one Friar *Seán Ó C'nuchúir* prepares her for death. The travelling man (alias Ulster spouse), has no knowledge of who this Friar *Seán Ó C'nuchúir* might be and we can glimpse here the cultural distance between the ancient native order of things (represented by the royal marriage of the sovereignty queen *Ana* to her noble spouse), and the world of medieval Christendom to which the native order yielded in accommodation and displacement. Friar *Seán Ó C'nuchúir* is, in Irish oral narrative tradition, a representative figure of that accommodation to the larger, European and Christianized world into which the figure of the sovereignty queen/*cailleach* survives and, with his introduction into the story we move towards the central significance which this legend articulates and witnesses. This is the displacement of the cosmology of the native ancestral order by the cosmology of the Christian faith which had been established in

Ireland for well over a thousand years before our narrative was recited in the early twentieth century. This theme had been notably dealt with in the ninth century poem 'The Lament of the Old Woman of Beare', regarded as one of the greatest in early Irish; in that work a shrivelled, elderly female is portrayed as awaiting her liberation out of an eternity of existence in this world and into the Christian afterlife. That vernacular folk narrative tradition in the twentieth century should still carry versions of this victory of Christianity over the native religious system, suggests that the victory and displacement were not, perhaps, as total or as final as might be imagined. The continued allegiance of native tradition in Ireland – and throughout Gaelic Scotland – to a narrative repertoire of legend featuring the sovereignty queen/*cailleach* figure is testimony to the continued sensibility of the tradition to the conception of the female personification of landscape, territory and cosmic power and to the cultural resource which such a conception offers in terms of the interpretation and memorialization of life experience and the articulation of the knowledge and the values of an ancestral worldview.

Friar *Seán Ó C'nuchúir*, having been mentioned as the one for whom, in a sense, *Ana Ní Áine* is waiting, disappears from the story again for a while. In fact, at the time she first hears his name, it could be said that the married daughter of McCarthy is not yet *Ana Ní Áine* in any full sense, either in her own recognition or in ours, as audience of the legend. While the narrator has told us that '*Ana Ní Áine,* only is, what is given in the story', meaning, surely, that it is still as *Ana/Áine* McCarthy, an actual young woman in the town of Kenmare, that she encounters the travelling man and his prophecy. Her full awakening to and embracing of her mythological, symbolic, and archetypal identity comes later in the narrative, as we shall see.

The figure of Friar *Seán Ó C'nuchúir*, in tradition, is that of an Irish representative of the sort of medieval Christendom Ireland shared with other parts of the European world, rather than of the insular monastic Christianity of the early Middle Ages. He is a Friar (*Bráthair*), a cleric of one of the mendicant monastic orders that established Irish foundations in the high Middle Ages rather than being a Monk (*Cléireach/Manach*) of the earlier monastic order of pre-Norman Ireland. As such, however, he is perceived to retain something of the dual identity of *Colm Cille*, in being a product, culturally and cosmologically, of both a native, secular and a Christian, monastic formation. The tension of the dual allegiance on Friar *Seán*'s part is illustrated in the traditional account of how, while in Rome, he succumbed one day to the 'pagan' superstition that in native Irish tradition made any kind of shearing a taboo activity on Mondays. It is said that while shaving himself in Rome on a Monday morning, he remembered the secular pagan injunction against so doing, and yielded to it, to the extent of leaving half his face unshaven. Straight away, so the story goes, the bells of Rome rang out to give warning that a sinner was at large in the holy centre of Christendom. The sinner is discovered, brought before the Pope, confesses and recants and has imposed on him the penitential task of returning to Ireland to found a church in a location that he has to seek out because it is unknown to him. Having thus, as it were, fallen from Christian grace and having been restored again, he has, henceforth, a kind of redoubled identity and status as a representative of Christianity. As the one prophesied to prepare *Ana Ní Áine* for death and the Christian afterlife, we can view him as a most appropriate oppositional figure to that of the native Irish female personification of the ancestral otherworld that *Ana Ní Áine* – alias Ana McCarthy – represents. However, it is as an ordinary clerical figure of modern, Catholic, Irish Christianity that Friar *Seán* makes his first appearance in our story.

Following the travelling man's prophecy to Ana McCarthy, life, we are told, went on. Despite the passage of time and of the generations, *Ana* becomes no older, her life continues beyond any human span. She ends up (in the surface plot of our text), being rocked in a cradle by the daughter of her daughter's daughter, in a sort of inverted nativity image (not that of the son of God) but of an incarnate female principal. This, we are told, is how things remained. The reckoning of how very old she is in terms of the daughter's daughter's daughter's ministrations, can be taken to represent the attempt, in traditional terms, to communicate the great cultural as well as temporal, span that has elapsed since *Ana* was the beautiful young sovereignty queen of the native ancestral order ruled over by the *Eoganacht* royals. In the patriarchal kinship reckoning of the Irish and Christian worlds, descent traced through the female line can be thought of as becoming quickly obscured or forgotten, and *Ana*'s latest pedigree, so to speak, stretching back from her cradle, is consonant with her archaic identity and the obscurity into which her former powerful autonomy as sovereignty queen has fallen in the Christian patriarchy of early modern and modern Ireland.

In that modern world, the young priest, we are told, had come to Ana's parish and had wished to become acquainted with his flock. We are shown him being seized with thirst while abroad on a fine summer's evening, and resorting to a house, for refreshment, which he discovers near at hand. A native audience will respond here to the echo of so many stories – in both literary and vernacular/folk Irish tradition – in which a hero (e.g. *Fionn MacCumhaill*) is similarly induced to visit a strange dwelling at evening and is presented there with an otherworld encounter. Such an experience also awaits our curate who unwittingly enters the house where a middle-aged woman rocks a cradle. The fact that the woman tending the 'child' is, in this instance, middle aged, while of no apparent, immediate significance to the curate in the story, signals to the audience and readers that this is no ordinary mother–child dyad, but is a manifestation of an enduring female order or cosmology that persists in the midst of a masculinized world. While this middle-aged woman (representing all females rather than just mothers), is away getting the young priest something to drink (and here the native tradition echoes loudly in the image of the sovereignty queen's provision to the hero/king-to-be of the libation of sovereignty) he, again all unwittingly and in moral and cosmological innocence, 'moved in to the cradle as if to rock it'. At this juncture the deepest levels of significance erupt into the consciousness of the participant characters and of the listening and reading audiences. The narrative device that brings about this explosion of mythological and archetypal significance is the image or trope of the Christian cleric rocking a cradle; a conjunction of symbolic forces that are, for different compelling reasons, historically and cosmologically anathema.

Historically, there has been the misogynist strain within Christianity which has seen it, in Ireland as elsewhere, give rise to ideas and practices that have tended to devalue and to displace the woman, the female, as a source of danger to spiritual, and indeed civil, well-being, in terms of her essential emotionality rather than rationality and her capacity for destructive, licentious sexuality and its frequent illegitimate fruit: the child in the cradle. In terms of cosmology there is a profound antipathy between Christian and ancestral conceptions of the universe and of the personification of its cosmic forces, in terms of male and female divinities. In moving in by the cradle, 'as if to rock it', the young priest is bringing together elements which, in terms of the institutionalized Christian religion, are so profoundly incompatible as to be necessarily explosively unstable – in the story, in history, and at the level of mythology. In the priest/cradle trope scene the ground of the story yawns open, as in an earthquake, to reveal chasms of significance of a historical and symbolic order that have, hitherto, only been hinted at in the consciousness of characters and audiences alike.

And yet, in this great confrontation between rival cosmologies, the personification of the native ancestral side, the figure of the *cailleach,* is shown as without aggression and not really a threat to the Christian hegemony that has, through the medieval, early modern and modern eras in Ireland, accommodated an element of traditional heterodox allegiance, in popular culture, to the conception of a supernatural female personification of the natural world. In her words, spoken from the cradle, the ancient but eternal feminine articulates the condition to which history and social process has reduced her:' 'tis easy to reckon me now'. On his part, the young priest is also the least aggressive or triumphalist of Christian, patriarchal opponents. Perhaps his transformational shift in narrative terms to being Friar *Seán O C'nuchúir,* helps to contain and diffuse the dominant, masculine, belligerence; Friar *Seán* is too well acquainted with the mingling of the native ancestral worldview with the Christian in Irish vernacular culture, to be a bitter, implacable and unrelenting enemy of the *cailleach* in the form of *Ana* McCarthy or *Ana Ní Áine*. There is a recognition that, since the 'time when it wasn't like that' is long passed, it is mercifully appropriate to bring matters to a head, and to a conclusion, in terms of the continuing life of *Ana* McCarthy. We can glimpse her own acquiescence in this conclusion in the provision, to the curate/Friar, of a drink by the woman of the house (alter ego of *Ana's*) after the mythological *dénouement* has taken place. This drink operates in the present story just as the sovereignty libation does in the early Irish stories of the hero/king encountering the *cailleach*/queen and being confirmed by her as the rightful wielder of power. This is how *Áine*, we are told (noting the use here of the name-form for the goddess which is the most widespread in terms of both personal appellation and the toponymies of place-lore), 'became happy'. Our narrator adds a metacomment at this point, signalling her own 'belief' (not forgetting the 'as if' factor in respect of all legendary), that all is turning out for the best. In terms of the surface plot – and we need not require of the narrators to comment on other than the surface plot – it is merciful for the ancient creature to be released into the joys of Christian heaven from the misery of such an incapacitated, and seemingly unending existence in this life. Her last day on earth has finally come and, in its anointed state, 'her soul departs and there was an end to her then'.

But is there an end to her then? Is the priest ever 'finished with her' as the curate/Friar is said to be with *Ana/Áine Nic Chartha*? In respect of this text, there are three grounds for believing that the end of *Ana* – the goddess, the autonomous, archetypal feminine – has not yet been procured in Irish tradition, no more in the twentieth than in the ninth century when the Old Woman of Beare so regretfully forsook the pleasures of her former identity as sovereignty queen in favour of the, for her, somewhat dubious delights of the Christian afterlife-in-prospect. In the first place we are told by the narrator that *Ana Ní Áine* is remembered constantly in the daily discourse of people who frequently quote the proverb that attests to her longevity. Secondly, the import of her name and the non-finality, as it were, of the displacement of her and what she represents, is provided in the constant narration and transmission of her story through time, as in the present instance. Thirdly, the timeless, archetypal nature of an opposing femininity and masculinity, expressed in a narrative creativity that is grounded in the life-experiences of the contemporary community, is exemplified here in the content of the inset tale of *Ana's* account of the greatest wonder she has seen in the course of a long life. The motif of 'the greatest wonder seen' is an international one, occurring in the oral narrative traditions of many cultures. Here it is put to use to both confirm, in condensed form, the message of the frame-tale – the victory of Christianity over the forces of the ancestral cosmology – and by the very form of its condensation and re-iteration to question the finality of that victory and to suggest the constructed and artificial nature of its continual assertion.

What *Ana Ní Áine* relates, as the greatest wonder she has marvelled at in the course of her seemingly eternal existence is, literally, her own story, embedded paradigmatically in the context of her childhood as *Áine McCarthy*, the daughter to whom we are introduced at the start, at the top, at the surface of the legend. As *Áine* she witnesses a much more dramatic and dismissive encounter between female fertility and clerical male authority than is involved in the frame-tale encounter of the ancient *Ana/Áine* with Friar *Seán*/the young curate. Such patriarchal, judgmental dismissal as is meted out to the woman in the cloud is the official line, so-to-speak, of both celibate, medieval Christian orthodoxy and the celibate, Catholic Christianity of the early twentieth century Ireland whence our legend narrative derives. Repeated baldly here, as the point of the inset-tale, the story of the dominance of the male, celibate and clerical order is, by comparison, rendered in a softer and more diffuse manner in the frame-tale with its greater expanses of time and cultural space. The truth is that however often and however baldly asserted, the victory of the Christian clerical patriarchy and its male divinity over the ancestral allegiance to a conception of a female otherworld agency, is forever less than complete. Oral narrative tradition, in minor forms such as that of the proverb and in major forms such as the mythological legend – as represented by our text, *Ana Ní Áine* – carries forward in a quiet, but enduring way the name, the story and the significance of the *cailleach*; the otherworld, female elder who personifies, in Irish tradition a cosmology alternative to, yet not unreconcilably incompatible with, the practice of the Christian faith. That alternative cosmology (which allows the feminine a central and dynamic role in the universe, in society and in the human psyche), constitutes an imaginative resource the cultural creativity of which carries implications for certain questions regarding both the cultural representation of the feminine and the application (or relevance) of traditional materials to the field of contemporary therapeutic provision. These are considerations which the present work seeks continually to address.

Retention of the feminine in a vernacular accommodation

15. The *Cailleach Bhéarthach (Carna: Cill Chiaráin)*[49]
There was a woman here long ago that they used call *An Chailleach Bhéarthach* and she never shed a tear and she never drank or ate anything, hot or cold, only cow's milk, always. She was always on the go, moving around. I'd say she used never get tired. She never wore a stocking or a shoe but went barefoot all the time. When she was walking, if she came across a soft boggy place with mud and mire in it she would go on immediately to the nearest pool of water and wash the mire down off herself from the knees to her foot for fear that she would carry any of it on with her. She never brought mud or mire on farther, from the place where she dirtied her feet or where she washed them clean again in water; that was her way of doing things, always.

And from the first day she was able to attend Mass, she never neglected to go to Mass on a Sunday. When she would be coming home from Mass she would take up a small stone in her hand and she would bring it home with her. She had a great big storage chest – bigger than any coffin – and she would throw her stone into the chest, every Sunday.

One day when she was greatly ageing, she was inside when a woman came in and asked her: 'Is it there you are?' she said to the *Cailleach Bhéarthach*. 'It is', said *Cailleach Bhéarrach*. 'Why do you ask?'

'Isn't it a wonder', said the woman, 'that you didn't hear that one of the daughters of your line of daughers has had a child – a little daughter.'

'I didn't hear it', said *Cailleach Bhéarthach,* 'but it won't be long till I know all about it.' She got up and she went out, with a mantle around her neck and shoulders, and went to where her own daughter was. She saw her daughter there before her. 'Is this where you are?' said she. 'It is', said her daughter.

'Wisha, get up daughter', said *Cailleach Bhéarthach*, 'and go to your own daughter's house. Your daughter's daughter gave birth to a young daughter last night.' So the daughter went off and *Cailleach Bhéarthach* came back home to her own house.

Almost a hundred years later on, after that, she was still alive, sitting down at the fireside in her own house, fine and strong. She heard footsteps coming to the house and an old man came in. He was very grey and he had a beard, too, down to his waist and a cane in his hand. He sat down and the two of them sat there, talking, and she had never seen him before. He said to her that, surely, it had to be that she was a big age now. She said she thought that she must be a good age indeed by this but that she would have an indication shortly of what age she was – and what age he was, too.

'There was never a Sunday', she said, 'from the time I was able to go to Mass until today, that I didn't go. And there was never a Sunday when I was coming home from Mass that I wouldn't pick up a stone in my hand and throw it into that chest over there.'

'Very well', said the old man, 'and how did you conduct yourself from the start of your life until today?'

'I never shed a tear', she said. 'The second thing, I never ate food, hot or cold, and the third thing is if my foot went into a muddy place, I didn't ever bring that mud with me to the next muddy place but washed my feet in the first pool I came to.'

'Wisha', said the old man, said he, 'it's best for us to look into the chest. By rights, it should be full up.'

'Well, it couldn't be far from it', said *Cailleach Bhéarthach*.

'Do you mind if I look in?' asked the old man. 'Wisha, indeed I don't mind', said *Cailleach Bhéarthach*.

The old man got up and he lifted the top-board off the chest and there were only two stones inside it.

'Wisha, *by dad*', said the old man, said he, 'there's only two stones here.'

'Wisha, I'm very amazed at that', said *Cailleach Bhéarthach*. 'I thought myself that it was full up.'

'Well, you only ever heard Mass twice during your life and that's the reason for it.'

She was left with nothing whatsoever to say in reply.

'You are a good woman', the old man said, picking up his cane and walking out. And it's how the old man was really a messenger from the God of All Grace to tell her that she never properly heard any Mass during her life – except two Masses.

The tears fell from her eyes, with the heartbreak and the regret she had, for the way she had been so negligent of all the other Masses she had had throughout her life.

No man living or no woman, either, knew what the *Cailleach Béarthach*'s name was. It was her destiny never to die until she was called three times by her name. A magician was passing by outside her house, one day, and he heard the *Cailleach Bhéarthach* singing a song.

'Wisha, short life to you', said the magician, 'oh *Sibléal, Sibléal, Sibléal*, if you haven't got the sweet voice!'

Cailleach Béarthach knew that it was all up with her and she was dead by the following morning.

That's what I heard about the *Cailleach Bhéarthach*.

The story ends with the narrator's words, 'That's what I heard about the *Cailleach Bhéarthach*', having begun with his statement that, 'There was a woman here long ago that they used call *An Chailleach Bhéarthach*'. One can deduce a communal tradition concerning her, not fixed in permanent form but which issues in narrative varying according as it is recounted in occasional verbal performance. She is part of the imaginative and narrative landscape which the community inhabits, just as it inhabits a natural landscape of whom she is the personification.

The non-human nature of the *cailleach* is signalled immediately the story opens in the assertion that, in all her life, she never shed a tear. We are told also that her diet consisted entirely of cow's milk, linking her in intimate fashion with animal life and the natural produce of the landscape. We see in other stories, how the diet of the *cailleach* is sometimes said to be exclusively cereal or exclusively marine, indicating in every case, an emphasis on the closeness and directness of her links with landscape and the natural forces of the cosmos. Her never having 'hot' food excludes from her diet the products of cooking – cooking being emblematic of the cultural order – and reinforces the sense of her identification with nature.

The beginning of the story also establishes her ubiquity in the landscape, a barefoot ubiquity, that again emphasises her direct, non-culturally mediated, relationship to the natural world (shoes and stockings being, of course, examples of such human cultural mediation). 'She was always on the go', we are told, 'moving around'. She cannot be considered as being confined to any one territory, any one terrain, and she carefully frees herself, in her washing of her feet, from the physical associations that would restrict her symbolic identification with the landscape and the natural world as a whole.

Notwithstanding her establishment at the tale's outset as a figure and an agency predominantly associated with the world of nature and ancestral tradition, we learn that she is, apparently, also a Mass-goer; that, in fact, she never neglects her Sunday obligation to attend Christian service and marks off her attendance at Mass by means of bringing back a small stone to be added to the store of such marker-stones that she keeps in the house. We are reminded here of the attempt to count up the *cailleach*'s age in other legends by means of counting ox-bones, attempts that fail because of the inability of human reckoning to measure the eternity of her existence; she is symbolic personification of a cosmos that has been in place since time immemorial, certainly since before human society, not to mention Christianity, came on the cultural scene.

In this story, the mention of how the *cailleach* attempts to register her Mass-attendance by way of a Christian calendar, is followed by an incident that emphasizes the eternity of her feminine existence before and beyond any Christian, or human, calendar or reckoning. A woman comes to her with news of the birth of a daughter to one of her line of daughters, news which she, in turn, conveys to her own daughter who hurries off to another in the line of daughters descended from the *cailleach*. The passage of immense amounts of human time is suggested in this invocation of the recurrent generations of descent in the female line of the otherworld Female herself.

The incommensurability of the cultural calendar and cosmic cycles of the Christian and ancestral worlds is spelled out in the account of how the grey, bearded old man, who, we are later told, is 'really a messanger from God of all Grace' reveals to her that despite her own attempts to count her attendance at Mass (i.e. to reckon herself as a Christian), she has, in imaginative and cosmological reality, an external or oppositional relationship to Christianity, represented by there being only two stones in her stonechest. We can understand that two stones are appropriate to the circumstances of the *cailleach* and her Christian visitor, in that one stone represents her presence at the establishment of Christianity here, while the other represents the continuity of the accommodation which that ancestral cosmology and tradition achieved with Christiantiy, the contemporary accommodation within the story and within the worldview of the community in which this story is still being narrated and transmitted on through time. In a sense there have been but two Sundays: the original 'Sunday' (i.e. *Domhnach,* 'Day of the Lord,' meaning the time of the establishment of Christianity here, 'the [first] time when I was able to go to Mass'); and the 'Sunday' of today when Christianity and ancestral otherworld tradition co-exist in vernacular narrative tradition. That it is an accommodation between two different orders of worldview and cosmology is emphasized by the *cailleach's* reiteration, along with the account of her Mass-going, of the three characteristics that have established her ancestral otherworld female significance: no human tears, no cooked food, no human territorial constraint. The superiority of the Christian worldview, its supremacy over the figure and the self-knowledge of the female representative of ancestral tradition, is communicated to her – and to us (listeners and readers) – in a way that leaves no doubt as to where the balance of authority lies: 'I'm very amazed', she says and later 'She was left with nothing whatsoever to say in reply.' Unlike, however, St Patrick and other Christian authorities in other legends we have considered, there is no aggressive displacement of the ancestral *cailleach* here. On leaving her, the old man/messenger from God actually praises her: 'You are a good woman', he says.

The effect of this revelation on the *cailleach* (gentle and all as is the treatment she receives here at the hands of Christianity), is to reduce her to the state of a human penitent, conscious at last of her neglect of her Christian duties and filled with remorse for this. Tears, we learn, fell from her eyes with the heartbreak she experienced, and clearly her reign as autonomous, otherworld female is at an end. This 'end' is envisaged in the story as a further reduction of her from her powerful, suprahuman, Christianly-unknowable identity (which has been so reduced already in the encounter with the messenger of God). Her secret name is the sign of that ancestral alterity which Christianity opposes but it is not a direct representative of Christianity who names her three times in final deflation of her image and her power. A 'magician', we are told, a wise man, who overheard her singing to herself, as he passed by her house, recognized her and, in both praising her voice while wishing her 'short life' complies with the requirements of her death-destiny by naming her three times with her secret name *Sibléal*. She knows, herself, that this is the end and 'was dead by the following morning'; not so much killed by Christianity as by the revelation of her situation *vis à vis* Christianity which the encounter with God's messenger and her subsequent state of mind represents. We are not told what song she was singing when her destiny arrived to her in the magician's triple invocation of her secret name. We can surmise that it may well have been some rehearsing to herself of the form of that destiny, as was the case with the *cailleach* of each of the two Scottish texts seen earlier (see pp. 112–114). In this case too, the account of her demise is seen as a part of communal knowledge that endures in narrative tradition and keeps her alive in performance and in imagination. 'That's what I heard about the *Cailleach Bhéarthach*' has the implication of a certain duty of retelling and thereby recreating and re-energizing the legend and the significance in tradition of the hag-goddess.

16. **The *Cailleach Bhéarach* (Ballycastle)**[50]

There was an old woman in it, and long ago it was, and if we had been there that time we would not be here now; we would have a new story or an old story, and that would not be more likely than to be without any story at all.

The hag was very old, and she herself did not know her own age, nor did anybody else. There was a friar and his boy journeying one day, and they came in to the house of the Old Woman of Beare.

'God save you', said the friar.

'The same man save yourself', said the hag; 'You're welcome, sit down at the fire and warm yourself.'

The friar sat down, and when he had well finished warming himself he began to talk and discourse with the old hag.

'If it's no harm of me to ask it of you, I'd like to know your age, because I know you are very old' [said the friar].

'It is no harm at all to ask me,' said the hag; 'I'll answer you as well as I can. There is never a year since I came to age that I used not to kill a beef, and throw the bones of the beef up on the loft which is above your head. If you wish to know my age you can send your boy up on the loft and count the bones.'

True was the tale. The friar sent the boy up on the loft and the boy began counting the bones, and with all the bones that were on the loft he had no room on the loft itself to count them, and he told the friar that he would have to throw the bones down on the floor – that there was no room on the loft.

'Down with them', said the friar, 'and I'll keep count of them from below.'

The boy began throwing them down from above and the friar began writing down [the number], until he was about tired out, and he asked the boy had he them nearly counted, and the boy answered the friar down from the loft that he had not even one corner of the loft emptied yet.

'If that's the way of it, come down out of the loft and throw the bones up again', said the friar.

The boy came down, and he threw up the bones, and [so] the friar was [just] as wise coming in as he was going out.

'Though I don't know your age', said the friar to the hag, 'I know that you haven't lived up to this time without seeing marvellous things in the course of your life, and the greatest marvel that you ever saw – tell it to me, if you please.'

'I saw one marvel which made me wonder greatly', said the hag.

'Recount it to me', said the Friar, 'if you please.'

'I myself and my girl were out one day, milking the cows, and it was a fine, lovely day, and I was just after milking one of the cows, and when I raised my head I looked round towards my left hand, and I saw a great blackness coming over my head in the air. "Make haste", says myself to the girl, "until we milk the cows smartly, or we'll be wet and drowned before we reach home, with the rain." I was on the pinch of my life [literally, 'the boiling of the angles-between-the-fingers was on me'] and so was my girl, to have the cows milked before we'd get the shower, for I thought myself that it was a shower that was coming, but on raising my head again I looked around me and beheld a woman coming as white as the swan that is on the brink of the waves. She went past me like a blast of wind, and the wind that was before her, she was overtaking it, and the wind that was behind her, it could not come up with her. It was not long till I saw after the woman two mastiffs, and two yards of their tongue twisted round their necks, and balls of fire out of their mouths, and I wondered greatly at that. And after the dogs I beheld a black coach and a team of horses drawing it, and there were balls of fire on every side out of the coach, and as the coach was going past me the beasts stood and something that was in the coach uttered from it an unmeaning sound, and I was terrified, and faintness came over me, and when I came back out of the faint I heard the voice in the coach again, asking me had I seen anything going past me since I came there; and I told him as I am telling you, and I asked him who he was himself, or what was the meaning of the woman and the mastiffs which went by me.

"I am the Devil, and those are two mastiffs which I sent after that soul."

"And is it any harm for me to ask", says I, "what is the crime the woman did when she was in the world?"

"That is a woman", said the Devil, "who brought scandal upon a priest, and she died in a state of deadly sin, and she did not repent of it, and unless the mastiffs came up with her before she comes to the gates of Heaven the glorious Virgin will come and will ask a request of her only Son to grant the woman forgiveness for her sins, and the Virgin will obtain pardon for her, and I'll be out of her. But if the mastiffs come up with her before she goes to Heaven she is mine."

The great Devil drove on his beasts, and went out of my sight, and myself and my girl came home, and I was heavy, and tired and sad at remembering the vision which I saw, and I was greatly astonished at that wonder, and I lay in my bed for three days, and the fourth day I arose very done up and feeble, and not without cause, since any woman who would see the wonder that I saw, she would be grey a hundred years before her term of life was expired.'

'Did you ever see any other marvel in your time?' says the friar to the hag.

'A week after leaving my bed I got a letter telling me that one of my friends was dead, and that I would have to go to the funeral. I proceeded to the funeral, and on my going into the corpse-house the body was in the coffin, and the coffin was laid down on the bier, and four men went under the bier that they might carry the coffin, and they weren't able to even stir the bier off the ground. And another four men came, and they were not able to move it off the ground. They were coming, man after man, until twelve came, and went under the bier, and they weren't able to lift it.

I spoke myself, and I asked the people who were at the funeral what sort of trade had this man when he was in the world, and it was told me that it was a herd he was. And I asked of the people who were there was there any other herd at the funeral. Then there came four men that nobody at all who was at the funeral had any knowledge or recognition of, and they told me that they were four herds, and they went under the bier and they lifted it as you would lift a handful of chaff, and off they went as quick and sharp as ever they could lift a foot. Good powers of walking they had, and a fine long step I had myself, and I cut out after them, and not a mother's son knew what the place was to which they were departing with the body, and we were going and ever going until the night and the day were parting from one another, until the night was coming black dark dreadful, until the grey horse was going under the shadow of the docking and until the docking was going fleeing before him.

> The roots going under the ground,
> The leaves going into the air,
> The grey horse a-fleeing apace,
> And I left lonely there.

On looking round me, there wasn't one of all the funeral behind me, except two others. The other people were done up, and they were not able to come half way, some of them fainted and some of them died. Going forward two steps more in front of me I was within in a dark wood wet and cold, and the ground opened, and I was swallowed down into a black dark hole without a mother's son or a father's daughter next nor near me, without a man to be had to keen me or to lay me out; so that I threw myself on my two knees, and I was there throughout four days sending my prayer up to God to take me out of that speedily and quickly. And with the fourth day there came a little hole like the eye of a needle on one corner of the abode where I was; and I was a-praying always and the hole was a-growing in size day by day, and on the seventh day it increased to such a size that I got out through it. I took to my heels then when I got my feet with me on the outside [of the hole] going home. The distance which I walked in one single day following the coffin, I spent five weeks coming back the same road, and don't you see yourself now that I got cause to be withered, old, aged, grey, and my life to be shortening through those two perils in which I was.'

'You're a fine, hardy old woman all the time', said the friar.

The story begins with the simple presentation of the figure of an old woman, long ago. Where the Scottish texts used the Biblical reference to indicate her antiquity, this text has a formulaic passage, 'and if we had been there that time ...' to distance her from the 'present' order. This device is more commonly used in Irish traditional narrations of international tales but is here applied to indicate the legendary timelessness of the hag-goddess — an application which is paralleled by the similar use of another non-legend narrative device which we will note later in the text. It supports the storyteller's contention that no-one knew, or could know, in human terms, the age of the *cailleach*. Into this seemingly timeless, feminine dispensation comes 'the friar and his boy', journeying about like Patrick and his missionary retinue, in the medieval legends of the Christianizing of Ireland. The invocation of the male Christian divinity is on his lips as he greets the *cailleach*. Her reply can be taken to subtly indicate further the cultural or cosmological distance between her world and that of the Christian cleric, in that her reference to 'the same man' (i.e. God) in her response, seems to convey her incomprehension of the nature of the one in whose name the friar greets her. Her invitation to him to warm himself at her fireside and his ready acceptance of this until 'he had well finished warming himself' indicates the absence of any enmity between them as cosmologically representative figures, something which is not always the case.

When the friar enquires of her regarding her great age we get an account of the well-known motif of the counting of the bones, which leaves the friar none the wiser. He then asks her twice about the greatest marvel that she ever saw in the course of her immensely long life; the resulting two marvel stories doubly reinforce the sense of her being present at cosmologically transformative moments in consciousness and in history. Both marvel motifs are known, unrelated to hag-goddess legend, in Irish and in European traditional narrative. Their use here brings the medieval sense of the mysterious forces that operate in the cosmos and their Christian personification in the persons of the Devil and the Virgin Mother of God, to bear on the figure of the Irish ancestral otherworld female. The woman who brought scandal upon a priest and is fleeing to the protection of the 'glorious Virgin' from the retribution of eternal damnation (that in the eyes of the Christian order she merits), is, of course, another expression of the stigmatized feminine that we saw in the inset tale of the *Ana Ní Áine* text (see p. 150). It is to be noted how both texts reserve the expression of medieval Christian enmity towards the feminine – in the projected person of the fallen woman, the source of clerical temptation and scandal – to inset motifs, while the frame tales in both instances portray a much more benign relationship between the *cailleach* and the Irish cleric who encounters her. We have here an indication of a degree of accommodatory co-existence of the alternative Christian and ancestral cosmologies in the vernacular culture and worldview of Irish tradition. In this present text, the story ends without the ultimate displacement of the *cailleach* from her quasi-eternity of life on/in earth into the Christian next life. Though she herself admits to being brought nearer to the end of her life by virtue of witnessing 'those two perils in which I was', the friar leaves her be, remarking on her hardiness. This is in marked contrast to the way the *cailleach* is treated on p. 150 which tells of an encounter with a local Saint, narrated as a short legend narrative with none of the rhetorical devices that give this present tale its flavour of recreational storytelling. I have mentioned the formulaic opening of the present tale; also to be noted are the descriptions of travel, in both inset motifs, in that again, each draws on the narrative rhetorics of the storyteller in a fashion not always characteristic of the recounting of legends. The woman-in-the-cloud is said to have passed the witnessing *cailleach* like a blast of wind and we are given a description of her speed that is reminiscent of the way the travels of the chief protagonists of the hero tales are conveyed to us: 'and the wind that was before her, she was overtaking it, and the wind that was behind her, it could not come up with her'. When the *cailleach* relates how she had travelled with the funeral of the herd, we find her using a formula that is narratively associated with the description of the hero's travels in the storyteller's repertoire: 'we were going and ever going until the night and the day were parting from one another, until the night was coming black dark dreadful, until the grey horse was going under the shadow of the docking and until the docking was going fleeing before him'. These differences in narrative style in the recouning of legend material relating to the *cailleach* may be taken as reflecting the narrative performance characteristics of the individuals from whom the stories are recorded. They also reflect the way in which knowledge of the hag-goddess is part of the common worldview shared by the narrators of an Irish storytelling tradition encompassing both ancestral Irish legends and tales of a common, European story provenance.

STORIES OF THE WISE-WOMAN

Accommodating female knowledge and power

17   **The Woman who used to see the Fairies**[51]
An old woman lived in *Gleann Fhreastail*, one time, whose name was *P. Ní L.* She was married to *M. C.* and she was aged and wise. It was said that she used to see the fairies. I don't know, myself. Any wake she used attend, she frequently went off into a weakness during it. She would be a long time in the swoon before she would come out of it. It was out of those fainting fits that she used to bring her prophetic knowledge, so they said.

This report presents us with a named and identified married woman; with a pattern of actual behaviour on her part and with an interpretation of that behaviour on the part of at least some members of her community. That she was both aged and wise is emphasized; she was an old woman, we are told, and she is described as *críona* (see discussion of *críona* on p. 233). This term here means old, mature but has connotations also of wisdom, sagacity and a degree of shrewdness. The belief existed, we are told, that she used to 'see the fairies'. In ancestral, narrative tradition this is code for 'acts strangely', 'does mysterious or at least unusual things', 'has hidden depths to her', 'knows more than the rest of us'. *P. Ní L.* was certainly believed by some to know more than the rest of them. It was said that she had access to prophetic knowledge though we are not told of what kind; how she made it available to her community or whether people actually consulted her after the manner of the wise healer. We are told, however, of one way in which this shrewd, elderly woman was purported to make contact with and enter into the ancestral otherworld realm. We do not hear that she herself gave any explanation or interpretation of her behaviour pattern at the wakes she attended, where she frequently swooned and stayed in that state for 'a long time'. We do not hear whether there were any other gatherings of the community at which she was wont to faint, in similar fashion, or whether she was subject to such faintings when at home in her own house. Certainly, the laconic account of her fainting, regularly, at the wakes she attended gives the impression that, for her, fainting away in a swoon like this is a kind of performance, engaged in in full public view. Though somewhat unusual, it is not at all implausible that some individuals are able to exercise control over their states of consciousness and produce the kind of alteration of consciousness that would manifest itself as the fainting swoon that P. Ní L. regularly produced at the wakes in *Gleann Fhreastail*.

The deciphering of this pattern of behaviour – as evidence of otherworld contact and of access to prophetic knowledge – comes, here, not from the performer of the behaviour, but from the community of interpretation that is familiar with a repertoire of ancestral narrative telling of the otherworld realm and contact with it as reported of a variety of individuals who are frequently the possessors of unusual skills or talents – musical, athletic, quasi-surgical, therapeutic, poetic. As someone believed to be frequently in contact with the ancestral otherworld and acquiring from these contacts the prophetic knowledge she is believed to possess, P. Ní L. obviously has a public reputation in her community that sets her apart. As mentioned already, we do not hear anything of how, if at all, that reputation was utilized by P herself or by her community in terms of the uses to which such knowledge could be put. This little narrative concerning her does serve, however, to draw attention to an ancestral cosmology featuring the native otherworld as a realm in which feminine consciousness and female agency is especially prominent and from which individual flesh-and-blood female humans are able to draw powerful autonomy for themselves in respect of their performance of a variety of therapeutic social roles at times of stress and danger, when something of the figure of the *cailleach*-goddess can be seen to underlie and even to underwrite – mythologically – the social roles in question.

18. *Máire ní Mhurchú* and the Carters[52]

There was a wise woman here long ago that they used to call *Máire Ní Mhurchú*. She lived in Eyeries Beg. She lived in many other places too, along with that, and she was no sooner in one place than in another. It used to be said, and I suppose it was a true saying, that she used to go along with the fairies and the people of the night. This night, anyway, she was back west with some women who were stripping flax; at a place they call *Cathair Caim*.

Some of them . . . they were great women for the tobacco, even though they had no tobacco because it wasn't to be had. Hardly any shop sold it – the tobacco trade was in the hands of the hucksters who used to sell it from home, illegally, because those times weren't too honest and were not law-abiding. It was the law of the wild that was there then, anything they wanted to do, they did, and anything they didn't like, they didn't do it at all. But that is not how it is nowadays, thanks be to God. There is law and the rule of law and justice available to all and penalties for those who deserve them. It was at night, especially, that they used to be stripping flax, talking away to each other and passing the time. And when it was getting on for midnight, footsteps came to the door. The rest of them heard the sound of the walking up to the door and there was a knock at the door. *Máire Ní Mhurchú* gave over stripping the flax, the poor woman, and, she took her cloak, that was hanging as a screen until morning, so as to go home, and she bade them a good night and she went out the door.

When the day broke – and no one knew where she was gone, and neither did they ask her where she went – when the day broke she came back home and she came in drowned wet and prostrate with exhaustion after the course of the night's activities. They put her up to the fire, put dry clothes on her and were trying to revive her since she was almost dead. Some of them gave her milk, as there was no tea to be had – even though they had plenty of coffee, as I'm told. They didn't know anything at all about tea at that time.

The carters were gone to Cork with two or three days before that and they were expected home that night. But they hadn't arrived yet and many people were at the want of tobacco, which didn't please them at all because they were troubled by the absence of it. The women, too, used to smoke tobacco and were mad for it. When they would be together of a night, stripping flax, that is when they really wanted to have the tobacco, to smoke in their clay pipes.

When she came to – and she was very satisfied that they had made so much of her and cared for her so well – she told them that the carters weren't far away from home at all and to be patient – that they would have plenty of tobacco tomorrow. She said she had passed them on her way home: that they were coming down *Barr Iarthach* now, on their way home, and the rest of them coming down *Loch 'á Bhonn*.

Hardly any of them, the women that were there, believed her – that she could be back from *Loch 'á Bhonn* so fast – except for a small few that knew about how she used to go journeying. And it was true for her. The carters were back home the next day, as she had said, and then everyone believed her.

The affliction featured in this story is a non-grevious one (the lack of tobacco) and is experienced as a group by the community and especially, in the focus of the story itself, by a company of women engaged during a long night in the work of drawing linen thread from the flax plant. Despite being concerned with such slight distress as, in comparative terms, this affliction constitutes, this story states clearly several emphatic features of the wise-woman tradition.

There is, firstly, the confident assertion that *Máire Ní Mhurchú* lived, as a flesh-and-blood female, at the definite location of Eyeries Beg. This assertion is accompanied immediately by a narratively characteristic qualification that recasts the figure of the wise-woman into something of a landscape figure, with associations of the *cailleach* goddess and the sovereignty queen, personification and guardian of the territory over which she reigns as wise and powerful otherworld agency: 'She lived in many other places, too'; 'she was no sooner in one place than in another'. As a further association of her with such agency, our narrator tells us that he supposes the truth of what used to be said concerning *Máire Ní Mhurchú*, that she used travel with the fairies and 'the people of the night'. That he mentions this allegation underlies for us again the provisional, constructed nature of individual and communal belief in the truth of tradition regarding the existence, and operation in human affairs, of those ancestral otherworld forces that are acknowledged as a traditional component of worldview in Ireland, along with the components of popular Christianity and secular rationalism. The latter can be seen hinted at in the reference to 'law and the rule of law and justice available to all'.

The 'taken as given' truth of the wise-woman's journeying with the otherworld forces is caught convincingly in the account of how she was called for, out of the group of humans, by the mysterious footsteps and the knock on the door when it was 'getting on for midnight'. We notice that the narrator has sympathy for *Máire Ní Mhurchú* in her role/obligation to go off with the midnight callers – he refers to her as 'the poor woman' – and we can see the knocking itself as marking the otherness of the dimension into which the wise-woman is summoned, in that a human caller, even at midnight, would not need to knock in order to gain access to a house where a communal work party was gathered together. *Máire Ní Mhurchú* is shown as taking her cloak as if to go home, and a kind of conventional ignorance of the 'real' significance of her going is registered in the declaration that 'no one knew where she was gone, and neither did they ask her where she went'. When she comes back to them at daybreak, they have the evidence of their eyes as to the explanation of her going: she is soaking wet and 'prostrate with exhaustion'. As a matter of course and without questioning (it seems), they set about reviving and restoring her.

Neither her female work companions nor ourselves are made any the wiser as to where she has been, or what she has been doing. However, to reward them, as it were, for the care she is shown and for the credence in her wise-woman function which resides in at least a few of the women, she reveals the closeness to home of the men from the district who had gone to Cork city (more than a hundred miles distant) some days ago, and who are now, in her account, nearing the end of their return journey, bearing supplies that include the longed-for tobacco.

The majority of the women present are said to have disbelieved *Máire Ní Mhurchú's* claim to know how close the men were to home, finding it difficult to accept that she passed them by on her own return journey in the fleet company of her otherworld partners. The truth of her words are borne out in the accurately predicted arrival of the men and the tobacco, and 'then everyone believed her'. This, again, can be taken to illustrate the shifting, dynamic basis of belief in the wise-woman and her powers to which a kind of differential credence is given in the community. Such credence waxes and wanes, we can understand, in accordance with times of want and affliction, of various degrees of severity, on the part of different individuals, at different times, and is attested to, here, as an enduring feature of popular worldview and vernacular cultural process that is embodied in the recounting and transmission, in the community, of stories regarding the ability of the wise-woman to diagnose and alleviate such affliction. The present narrative reinforces such credence as an element of tradition, even though the lack of tobacco is not, by any means, a matter of tragic or mortal import. In this, however, our narrator underlines in an unconscious way, how normal and ordinary as well as how important a part of the cultural process of the creatively imaginative representation, remembering, interpretation and transmission of human life-experience, is the figure of *Máire Ní Mhurchú* and the oral narrative tradition of wise-woman legend.

19. **Incident recounted of a healing woman from *Baile Bhoithín*–I**[53]

It happened that the same priest was saying mass, north at *Carraig,* a while after that. It was always a saddle-horse he had to go north. This Sunday he was coming back south across the strand from *Muiríoch* and the minute the horse put her foot into the rill near *Baile an Rannaigh,* she became lame. She was only barely able to walk back up to *Baile an Rannaigh.* Some man there told the priest to take her over to *Eibhlín Ní Ghuinníola.* He didn't say 'yes' or 'no' or 'take' or 'leave' to that, because he was self-conscious about how he used preach about her every Sunday – and he wouldn't give it to say that he'd go looking for a cure from her. However, a messenger went off and went to *Baile Bhoithín,* to *Éibhlín Ní Ghuinníola.* He told *Eibhlín* what brought him, that the priest's horse was lame. 'I know that,' said *Eibhlín,* 'and it would be better for the priest to let me be, every Sunday, since I'm not interfering with him in any way.' 'Now that he has been shown that I have knowledge and healing, let you say when you are coming to the house, that his horse is getting better. Tell him that it was when his horse put her right foot into the rill that is next to *Baile an Rannaigh* that she was struck lame. Then he will know that *Eibhlín Ní Ghuinníola* has knowledge.' From that day out, the priest never mentioned her again, in English or in Irish, on any Sunday or on any church holiday.

This is the middle one of a series of three stories about a woman named *Eibhlín Ní Ghuinníola* who lived in *Baile Bhoithín* 'long ago'. Throughout the narrative she is referred to as a healing woman, a *bean leighis* rather than a wise-woman or *bean feasa*. There is no definitive distinction to be drawn between the application of these two terms to females whose activities range across the provision of herbal cures, the location of missing objects and creatures, the diagnosis of the cause of misfortune or affliction, the divination of hidden knowledge. Some healers practice nothing other than herbal curing. Nevertheless, the knowledge of which herbs to gather, where, when and in what condition to gather them is, in many instances, still somewhat mysterious and inaccessible to outsiders. Also one might point to the combination of the application of the herbal substance with ritual formulas of behaviour and speech – sometimes Christian, like making the sign of the cross and saying the Hail Mary, sometimes not – as suggesting that more than vernacular herbal pharmaceutics is involved. It is clear in these stories about *Eibhlín Ní Ghuinníola* that she is regarded as having the diagnostic and divinatory powers of the wise-woman as well as the knowledge and the skill of the herbalist.

Many accounts exist of the tension between wise/healing women and Christian clergymen who regarded the activities of the former as constituting a threat both to their own moral authority and to the spiritual well-being of their flocks. In some cases the clergy are reported as regarding the wise healers as witches of the Christian-demonic variety, in league with the powers of Satan. In other cases, their perception of the wise healer is said to be that such women are somewhat deranged, prone to pagan superstition and disruptive of good social order and clerical authority. In almost all cases, wise healers constitute an antagonist for the priest and this antagonism is portrayed as being expressed routinely in sermon and denouncement from the altar. The non-clerical view portrayed of the wise healer is that of a woman who offers valuable services to individuals afflicted by life crisis or misfortune. In this 'lay' perception, the wise healer is morally neutral, or perhaps we might say, theologically neutral; the source of her knowledge and power is believed to come, not from Satan, but from the native ancestral otherworld of the *sí*. Demonstration of the equal, if not superior powers available to the wise healer from this source – compared to the powers of the Christian cleric – are commonplace in the tradition, as indeed this text exemplifies.

The incident related here features *Eibhlín* as the wise-woman healer who diagnoses and alleviates a misfortune suffered by the priest himself; his horse – which symbolizes his status and his authority, as well as providing his transport – is mysteriously disabled. Having ridden to say mass at *Carraig*, the priest is returning across a strand when misfortune strikes. In traditional narrative a strand is often associated with the otherworld: something that derives from its liminal position as a margin between land and sea, a margin on which the two elements seem to alternate back and forth in a ceaseless, cosmic rhythm. There is a streamlet or rill running down across this strand which the priests' horse steps into and immediately goes lame. We understand the rill, in its mediation, physically, between land and sea, as symbolically analogous to the mediation roles of both priest and wise-woman in respect of the relationship of human life to Christian and ancestral otherworlds. Dismounted, and thus himself symbolically disabled also, the priest takes his horse up into *Baile an Rannaigh* and off the liminal stage of the strand, with considerable difficulty. The community is portrayed as immediately suggesting he resort to *Eibhlín Ní Ghuinníola*; the voicing of the suggestion, and thereby of that part of the community's cultural understanding and cultural resources, is put in the mouth of a male – 'some man there'. The priest is now in a quandary. Having seen the previous demonstration of her powers (see pp. 184–5), he is still loath to yield to the 'alternative' therapeutic prescription of the ancestral tradition, especially as it has been his practice 'to preach about her every Sunday' as someone to be doubted and avoided, if not shunned.

In this situation, the community takes the initiative, sending a messenger to *Eibhlín,* and demonstrating the existence of an allegiance on their part to the alternative worldview that is not finally subordinated to the authority, or the pronouncement, of the Christian cleric. *Eibhlín*'s declaration of foreknowledge of the laming of the horse is a kind of confirmation and justification of the cultural reliance of the community on her powers and, in her declaration that the horse will now recover without any further treatment, it is as if her revealing her power of foreknowledge is, in itself, sufficient therapy. Crucially, she does not say why the incident occured. In the context of this narrative sequence one could say that it happened in order to provide the opportunity for *Eibhlín* to demonstrate her knowledge and authority. Therefore it is this text – and its narrator – who are the actual creators of the context for this demonstration and we may thus regard the story here as first-hand evidence of a lively and continually productive allegiance on the part of its 'community of interpretation' to the figure and the significance of the wise healer. The consolidation of this allegiance and its reinforcement within the worldview of the community from whence our text comes (and, thereby, the reinforcement of that worldview itself), is reflected in the assertion that *Eibhlín Ní Ghuinníola* was never again mentioned by the priest – not only in theory (the theological and moral levels) but also in the practicalities of Sunday and holyday homilies and in the historical practicalities of his catering, pastorally, to a congregation experiencing and embracing the realities of a language/culture shift from Irish to English. The implication is of course, that something of the figure and the significance of the wise healer and her mythological, *cailleach*-goddess matrix is capable of crossing over the linguistic divide occasioned by the flow of a language shift which was still in full spate at the time when these anecdotes about *Eibhlín Ní Ghuinníola* were recorded, as it had been two generations previously when those anecdotes had their genesis in the narration of our informant's maternal grandfather.

20. **Máire Ní Mhurchú and the priest**[54]

That's how it used to be with poor *Máire Ní Mhurchú* and it was a bad and a hard purgatory she had, the poor creature, in this life. With God's help, I hope that there is no purgatory on her at all, in the otherworld. Because it was true about *Máire Ní Mhurchú;* it's not a case of gossip or hearsay, as I can tell you myself, since there is further evidence of her doings. It was the truth.

It was true, because I heard that a priest said it was: that the hat was taken off his own head one time when he was coming from Ardgroom, making for Eyeries, where he was living. The hat was taken off his head twice over in a place that they call *Droichead na mBarr.* He saw no one but his hat was put back onto his head and *Máire Ní Mhurchú* said it to him afterwards that it was she herself who put his hat on his head. He hadn't ever said anything to her about the hat. Instead, he used to be talking against her and trying to stop her from doing the things she used to be at, and that was the time then that he gave in to her. From that day on, until the day she died, the same priest never again said anything against her, only praised her and gave her as much as he was able to put in her way, by means of help, in her living.

This legend of *Máire Ní Mhurchú* that we have from *Pádraig Ó Murchú* of *Gort Broc* is one that he narrated for the Folklore Commission collector immediately after the recounting of the incidents related above in the tale of the wise-woman and the flax-strippers (see pp. 175–6). It is almost an addendum to the previous legend and both a commentary on it and a defence of its truth (and the truth of other such wise-woman legends), in that it appeals to the highest authority that can witness to the veracity of our narrator's, or his community's, testimony: the priest.

'It was the truth', he says of such accounts of the knowledge and the power of the likes of *Máire Ní Mhurchú;* 'It was true, because I heard that a priest said it was'. He then proceeds to tell of an incident involving an actual parish priest of Eyeries in the third quarter of the nineteenth century; an incident that is known to us also from another local informant, who also recounted it to the Folklore Commission collector. In fact there is a large repertoire of such legends in oral narrative tradition, showing how 'the priest' was taught a lesson by the wise-woman regarding the reality of her powers (see the *Eibhlín Ní Ghuinníola* stories here, pp. 178–9, 184–5). The most common motif in this repertoire involves an injury to or disablement of the priests' horse, which the local wise-woman is able to diagnose and cure. The motif of the priest's hat being knocked off/restored to his head, is also frequent. In almost all cases, the priest is portrayed as having hitherto opposed the wise-woman by preaching against her and attempting to prevent people from resorting to her in their afflictions. Following the personal demonstration of her knowledge and her power, the priest inevitably ceases his opposition to the wise-woman; this story is unusual in going so far as to say that, ever after, the priest went out of his way to praise her and to assist her, materially, 'in her living'. We can take it, perhaps, that *Pádraig Ó Murchú*, in this, as it were, crowning account and assertion of the validity of wise-woman tradition in vernacular worldview, imaginatively enlists the services of the priest in both the work of positively evaluating the function of the wise-woman in cultural process *and* in the work of nurturing the life of the wise-woman as she lives in narrative tradition. *Máire Ní Mhurchú*, as other wise-women of legend, lived in the words and in the imaginations of those who both recited and received the narratives that recount her wisdom and her prowess. Her status, as rhetorical embodiment in human form, of the mother-goddess *cailleach* figure of ancestral cosmology, was opposed by forces of modernity as well as by the forces of religious orthodoxy, in the era in which *Pádraig Ó Murchú* told his *Máire Ní Mhurchú* legends for the benefit of the Folklore Commission collector. Knowing his own marginalization in that modern, rational, respectable, English-speaking world – as a representative of a subaltern, Irish-speaking world-view encompassing an ancestral cosmology that contrasted in fundamental ways with the cosmologies of both science and Christianity – *Pádraig Ó Murchú* appeals to the witness of the three strongest and most powerful voices he can invoke regarding the truth (in cultural and imaginative terms), of what he knows and narrates about *Máire Ní Mhurchú*: his mother, his father and his priest (c.f. 188, 191). These three are guaranteed not to tell him lies or lead him astray. They are portrayed as lively, energetic intelligences, participating in the modern world that has left the *cailleach*-goddess behind, apparently, but who nevertheless experience the presence and the power of her representative, who lives on as a powerful symbol of an ancestral hermeneutic that has the potential for adapting to, and surviving, in the circumstances and contexts of the modern – and indeed postmodern – world and as a powerful source of imaginative therapeutic renewal.

Ordinary troubles remedied through resort to wise-woman

21. **The stolen colt and the wise woman**[55]

A colt was stolen from my grandfather, in *Baile an Chóta*. He was searched for, east and west and up and down, and there wasn't a trace of him to be found, nor any account of him. They had him given up. Then my grandfather was advised to go to a wise-woman who lived on the old Chapel Road, at the holy stone there. She was an elderly woman who used to travel about on foot. She used to be selling sieves and bowls. The sieves used to be bought for sieving wheat.

He went to visit her, anyway, and as soon as ever he said that he wanted her she said to him, 'A four-footed animal went missing from you.' 'It did', he said 'and I've come to you to see if you could find out for me where is he.' She concentrated on the bowls then, mixing and tossing them. 'The colt', she said, 'is at *Cam Bhaile Uí Shéaghdha* and he's fettered there.' And t'was true for her. Whatever scoundrel had stolen him had put him there. My grandfather went to *Cam Bhaile Uí Shéaghdha* and he found the colt there fettered.

This item of lore was recorded in 1931 from a man of eighty-two years, whose date of birth is, accordingly, 1849. Since the anecdote concerns this man's grandfather, who is likely to have been born around 1790, we can take it that the incident of the loss and recovery of the colt and the visit to the wise-woman in Dingle is envisaged as having occurred in the early part of the nineteenth century, a time when the population of West Kerry, as of Ireland as a whole, was at its greatest. It is in the context of this high population density that the stealing of the animal by an unknown local 'scoundrel' and the occupation of the wise-woman as a travelling saleswoman or pedlar – walking with her wares from place to place, from her residence on the outskirts of the town of Dingle – can be understood as plausible aspects of ordinary life.

This account of two aspects of ordinary life contains a considerable density of signification and has layers of complexity attaching to its interpretation. In two short paragraphs of text, we have recorded here an example of the operation of a cultural system and a social order that centred on male wealth and authority and power but was, nevertheless, vulnerable to loss. The experience of this type of loss occasioned a turning to female authority and power, and indeed female wealth of knowledge, that would otherwise be incomprehensible.

The grandfather and the wise-woman are representative figures in this story. The grandfather represents a male world of farmwork, the wealth it produces and the authority it creates, a world fixed and regular and rational. Having searched east and west and up and down, 'they' had 'given up' on the lost colt. Who are 'they'? We can take it that the owner's family and neighbours are meant, a whole little social world, symbolized in the figures of the male animal and its male owner. Since no trace of the missing colt or no account of him is to be had in this masculine world of work and reason, the owner is, we are told, 'advised' to go to the wise-woman. We are not told the source of the advice but what is important is that such advise should exist in context of the male order of things.

The wise-woman represents here an order of things very different to the 'ordinary' world of the farmer. We are told that she is an elderly woman and that, while she has a fixed residence, she is constantly on the move, travelling on foot throughout the region in nomadic fashion, present everywhere but not permanently. Her residence is said to be located near the holy stone in Dingle. This stone bears cup marks that attest to what is taken to be its ancient mysterious significance, and cohere with the cup-tossing technique used by the wise-woman to obtain hidden knowledge. She is said to supply goods such as bowls and sieves to the population of the district in the course of her travels. The sieves, we are told, 'used to be bought for sieving wheat', and the bowls too, no doubt, can be associated with flour and with bread-making. Thus, in contrast to the farmer, who is associated with the animal order through the colt, the wise-woman is associated with the plant order and the corn harvest. As an elderly, nomadic female practising divination and connected to the corn harvest, she attracts identification as a figure carrying at least echoes of the *cailleach*-goddess. The farmer, who suffers a mysterious loss (as if the animal had gone into an otherworld), has in him something of the hero figure who is frequently portrayed in the older literature as having mysterious encounters with otherworld powers. The hero-goddess paradigm permeates both oral and literary narrative tradition in Ireland and what we see here is how its impression is found on a narrative of the *seanchas* or legend genre. Our story purports to be an account, at no more than second hand, of an actual historical incident. Accepting it as being just that does not, however, preclude our being able to apprehend it as part of the expression of larger or deeper cultural messages regarding the nature of reality and the mysteries of ordinary life.

The narrator makes no judgement of the events about which he tells us. Neither does he express any surprise, nor indicate in any way that what he tells us about is unusual. His story, then, and its presumed circulation as an item of the local repertoire of *seanchas* in West Kerry, serves to bear witness to and recreate in narrative performance, an allegiance to a worldview, or a cosmology, in which female autonomy and female power are a necessary adjunct to the male order of things. The wise-woman and the grandfather-farmer in this story, are respectful equals, counterbalancing each other in the business of life and its interpretation. For as long as similar accounts of the resort to the wise-woman remained as active elements in the narrative repertoire of a district, their narration served to recreate and energize the allegiance to the *cailleach*-goddess that lies behind them in a paradigmatic and, perhaps, even archetypal way. It also served to energize and embolden individual females to occupy social roles associated with a certain dynamic of identification between human actors and a mythological mentor. The wise-woman, the handy-woman or country midwife and the keening-woman at the wake are examples of the filling of such social roles at times of life-crisis and affliction. The powerful females who are portrayed as acting with female authority in such situations, were drawing their legitimation and their autonomy from the cultural resources of a social order that recognized imaginative dimensions of reality beyond the everyday in a way that allowed for their representation and articulation as part of ordinary life, as happens in this West Kerry story.

22. *Máire Ní Chearbhaill* and the Heifer[56]

> 'Twas said that *Máire Ní Chearbhaill* used to go with the good people. She lived somewhere up about Castle Donovan and she had power to find things that were lost.

My mother's aunt was serving in a certain house up in Gallans, and *Máire* used to come in there every day. Anyway the man of the house had lost a heifer and he had been searching for her, everywhere, for three weeks before that. This day, he was inside before *Máire*, when she came in, and he asked her in Irish if she could tell him anything about the heifer.

She said nothing but began to examine the cups in the dresser and mix them up here and there. Then she replied:

'Wisha, in truth, she is'nt dead yet, but it won't be long 'till she is. You passed by her three times this morning.'

The man began to think and think what place he had crossed three times that morning. At last he remembered a place where there was an underground hole, and he went there. When he looked down there he saw his heifer, buried beneath the ground. She had all the *cortha* (bogsoil) eaten around her and this had kept her alive for three weeks.

In the short anecdotes featuring a wise-woman called *Máire Ní Chearbhaill*, we see again the two chief characteristics of the females to whom the term wise-woman is commonly applied. The first of these is the ability to go into the spirit world or ancestral otherworld of the *sí* for periods outside of human time. The second is the possession, as a consequence of such otherworld visitation and travel, of kinds of knowledge not otherwise available to humans. This may be knowledge of the whereabouts of people or things that have gone missing from the daily life of the individual, the family group, the community. It may also be knowledge – circulated as prophecy – of events yet to take place in the future. It can also be knowledge of the true causes of situations that otherwise lack any explanation, either by the wider community or by those who are themselves involved in the situation in question. These hidden causes are generally revealed as being due to the unwitting transgression of otherworld sensibilities and unadmitted enmity in the field of social relationships, both within the family and in the wider society.

In this *Máire Ní Chearbhaill* anecdote she is able to locate the whereabouts of a heifer that has been missing for a period of three weeks. The animal had become trapped in an 'underground hole' that was out of sight of passers-by, including the farmer who had been searching for the heifer every day and had himself passed her by on three occasions the day he asks for the wise-woman's help. We can understand that the place where the heifer was hidden from normal eyes and from normal knowledge was quite near to the farmhouse and not remote from the comings and goings of the farmer and his neighbours. There, in the midst of daily life, a secret resides, incapable of being known by other than the gifted woman who 'used to go with the good people'.

This imaginative and symbolic transcendence of the layer of ordinary consciousness is a resource available to the farmer and to the community in the course of their daily lives in an insecure and unpredictable universe. The wise-woman and her divinatory technique, involving the homely artefacts of delph and dresser, gently expand and extend the community's consciousness so as to encompass glimpses of a wider, deeper, higher order of life. These glimpses, as fleeting and occasional as the wise-woman's otherworld visits, provide answers to otherwise unanswerable questions, and thereby provide the basis of healing to the afflicted, in a tradition where affliction is the consequence of unwitting or unadmitted transgression of the cosmic and psychic principles governing human life. In the present story, we are told that, having been prompted by *Máire's* diagnostic intimation of the whereabouts of the lost animal, 'the man began to think and think' and eventually brought to his conscious mind the location where he was to find his heifer. She had been sustained in the course of her three week sojourn in her secret location, by the organic resources of the landscape; a landscape on which the technology and economics of farming and husbandry have overlaid, in a sense, the cosmology of ancestral tradition with *its* knowledge of the mythic and the psychic as well as the organic resources of landscape.

We can note, too, that the Irish language is regarded in this text as the appropriate medium for communication with the wise-woman regarding the solution of the mystery of the lost beast. The man asks, in Irish, we are told, if Máire can tell him anything about the heifer. Her reply to him is rendered in the text here in Irish, 'Whisha, indeed and she is not dead yet, but it won't be long now. You have passed by her yourself three times this morning' indicating the bilingual situation of the community in which this story of the wise-woman and her powers is being transmitted. Her name in this story is given in its correct Irish form and it is the Irish word *cortha* that is used of the bog-soil that the heifer ate during her time 'in hiding'. In the nineteenth century, when this incident is alleged to have happened while the narrator's mother's aunt was in service 'in a certain house up in Gallans', the majority of the population of that area (the County Cork barony of West Carbery) would have been Irish speakers and familiar with an Irish narrative repertoire commonly featuring the wise-woman.

23. **Incident recounted of a healing woman from *Baile Bhoithín*–II**[57]
There was a healing woman in *Baile Bhoithín* long ago, who was called *Eibhlín Ní Ghuinníola*. The sermon the priest had every Sunday used

to be directed at how she was practising healing. It happened that there was a person sick in *Baile Bhoithín,* in her own townland, and the priest was sent for. The priest came and *Eibhlín Ní Ghuinníola* was inside before him, when he arrived. He looked at *Eibhlín* and he said: 'It shouldn't have been necessary to send for me when the healing woman was there to cure him.' 'Nobody has asked me to do that', said *Eibhlín*. 'I'm asking you to do it', said the priest. 'Very well', said *Eibhlín*. 'Wait a while so', said she, going out. She wasn't long outside when she came back in, with this plant. She put the plant down to boil in a saucepan. When she had it on the fire for a while she took it off and poured it out into a cup. She said to the sick man to take three drinks of it. He did and he got up as good as ever he was. 'Now then', she said to the priest, 'there it is for you.' The priest went away home without saying another word.

The local priest's Sunday sermon, we are told, used to feature *Eibhlín Ní Ghuinníola* on a regular basis, presumably warning people away from resort to her (in his view), dubious, certainly fraudulent and possibly demonic activities. In the incident related in our text, we see demonstrated to the Christian cleric the therapeutic efficacy of the wise healer in the provision to a man of a cure that is wholly herbal. When, having been sent for, the priest arrives at the sick man's side he finds that *Eibhlín Ní Ghuinníola* is already there. His remark about the sending for the priest not having been necessary, since *she* is available, combines complaint, patronization and challenge. 'Nobody has asked me to do that', she says, indicating that she possesses therapeutic powers, on the lines of his own, which she can operate on request and which make her, therefore, his rival as mediator in matters spiritual. His challenge emerges fully when the priest responds 'I'm asking you to do it', to the disavowal by *Eibhlín* of any determination on her part to exercise her powers. The collected and immediate response to his challenge underlines her status as his rival in this respect. She is an autonomous female, sure of her role and the legitimacy of that role in the eyes of her community. Her authority derives from the acknowledgement, in ancestral tradition, of the power and authority of cosmic and natural forces that are gendered and personified in the figure of the *cailleach*-goddess. The performance, in narrative, of stories of the *cailleach*-goddess and also of stories about the practitioners of a range of female roles in society – of which the wise healer is one – served to transmit and to renew the cultural perception of a relationship between the activities of such as the wise healer and the mythological figure. The story of how *Eibhlín Ní Ghuinníola* – despite the cynical, hostile, and no doubt ordinarily intimidating gaze of the Christian cleric – immediately proceeds to gather, prepare and administer her cure (and to such positive and immediate effect), is both a memorialization of and a kind of communal rededication to a cosmology and a worldview that privileges the feminine in important ways with regard to the cultural derivation of meaning from everyday experience. The priest – the male representative of official and hegemonic Christianity that offers its own cosmology, mythology and morality to the community that *Eibhlín Ní Ghuinníola* also serves – 'went away home' on this occasion, we are told, 'without saying another word'.

24. **Incident recounted of a healing woman from *Baile Bhoithín*–III**[58]
    Another time, a sister of *Eibhlín Ní Ghuinníola*'s was putting the potatoes on the fire. *Eibhlín* told her to put more potatoes into the pot 'because', said she, 'maybe there might be a stranger who is far from home there to eat them, when they are boiled'. Just when they were boiled, strangers from east of Dingle came looking for a cure from her. When they had finished eating the meal, she enquired of them what had brought them. One of them said that it was looking for a cure they were, for their sister who was sick. He was given the cure – the plant – whichever one was called for. 'Close your fist on that plant', she said to the young man to whom she handed it, 'and put it drawing on the boil as soon as you get home. Give her three drinks off the top of it and she will be as good as ever she was. Don't look behind you now', said she, 'until you have gone down across *Mám na Gaoithe* – or, if you do, you won't have the plant at all.' 'Very well, so', said the stranger.

    When the stranger was making for *Mám na Gaoithe* he heard an uproar behind him. He looked back but didn't see anyone. When he opened his hand there wasn't even a scrap of the plant in it. He returned back again. 'You looked back, to be sure', said *Eibhlín*. 'By God, I did', said the stranger, 'because I heard uproar behind me.' 'Well you'll get this chance now', said she, 'but if you look behind you till you've passed the *Mám* – do without!' He got the plant and he went off. He heard the same uproar the second time, but didn't, however, look behind him. He brought the plant home and he gave three drinks from the top of the boiling broth to his sister and she got up as well as ever she was.

    It was my father who related these incidents to me. He said that it was often he heard *Séamas Ó Mainnín* (my mother's father) talking about her. He used to say that there was a fairy lover along with *Eibhlín Ní Ghuinníola* when she used to gather the plants; that he was often seen.

This futher story involving *Eibhlín Ní Ghuinníola* suggests that knowledge of the power of this wise healer was widespread in West Kerry, far beyond the confines of her own place. Strangers from east of Dingle came to her for a cure for their sister. In having foreknowledge of the arrival of these strangers and in her concern that they will have enough to eat when they come, we see *Eibhlín Ní Ghuinníola* herself signalling that her knowledge and the range of her powers extend far and wide, drawing strangers to her who have to be provided for. In none of these incidents about the wise healer and her activities is there any sign of her being paid for her services or receiving any recompense for them in kind. Her hospitality, in this story, in providing her visitors with food, is of a piece with the generosity with which she dispenses her healing services to individual clients and to the community in general. Her wisdom and her healing powers have the nature of a gift, which she in turn, as intermediary between human experience and the ancestral otherworld, is obliged to dispense as generously as the landscape itself dispenses its abundant herbal favours. She requires only to have her services requested of her by those who share an allegiance to the cosmological perspective in which the figures of the *cailleach*-goddess and the wise healer personify the gendered, ancestral understanding of how the forces of the cosmos interact with human life and with the human imagination as it later expresses itself in cultural construction. In all of this, *Eibhlín Ní Ghuinníola* is shown as understanding her gift and her application of it, as not being in conflict with, or in opposition to, the work of the priest; in another text she says, 'I'm not interfering with him in any way' (see p. 179).

The otherworld and the mysterious nature of even the seemingly straightforward procedure of boiling up the herbal remedy and giving it as a drink to the sick person, is indicated clearly in this story in the instructions that the wise healer gives along with the herb itself. The young man to whom she hands it is told to 'close your fist on that plant' as if it is not to be gazed on by other eyes or, perhaps, because it is 'alive' – charged with the vitality of a cosmic energy that is normally not apparent to people but that is ready for release at the wise healer's direction and has to be contained carefully in its passage to the sick person's drink.

A further instruction to the young man is not to look behind him until he has passed a certain point on his journey across the landscape. In this and in his loss of the plant when he does look back, we have again a sense of the immense energies and force-flows that lie beyond our normal perception of the universe. Having been brought into close contact with these energies (in the form of the plant given to him by *Eibhlín*), the client-stranger is required to demonstrate his trust, or faith, in her and her powers, by doing as she requests and not looking back at the final manifestation of closeness to hidden levels of cosmic energy which occurs as he draws away from her through the mountain pass, on his way home. When he fails to do as she has asked, he loses his ability to bring back with him the benefits of contact with these cosmic energies, and thus, when he opens his hand (compounding his transgression of her instructions), he finds it empty of 'even a scrap of the plant'. The power to cure has vanished.

On his return to the wise healer she already knows what has happened, what he has done wrong. But she is merciful, as the plant is mercifully abundant, and he is again given his herbal cure and sent off. In giving him this second chance she says that if he fails again to carry the cure home safely with him, then he must 'do without'. Faithfulness and obedience are required of those who would benefit from the knowledge and power of the wise healer and there is a recognition here that not everyone is able to have that faith and that obedience, which are not given, or automatic, but are creative cultural constructions of an ancestral tradition that is transmitted and renewed in the narration of stories of the wise healer such as the one under consideration here. In this story the young man does succeed in bringing the herb home safely, at the second attempt, and his sister is indeed cured when she has three drinks of the broth made with the herb.

Finally this text confirms the otherworldly nature of the business of the gathering of plants by the wise healer. We are told that a 'fairy lover', a *leannán sí*, was often seen with *Eibhlín Ní Ghuinníola* as she gathered plants. The *saol sí*, the fairy realm, is the ancestral cultural embodiment of that imaginative mythological and spiritual otherworld lying beyond the 'normal' ranges of human perception. It can, on occasion, manifest itself in figures like the *leannán sí*, as well as the *cailleach*-goddess, or in the activities – and in the narrative of the activities – of those women who filled the social roles of wise healer, keening-woman or country midwife. Such women, acting decisively in the face of affliction and life crisis, draw their autonomy and legitimacy from the traditions and the traditional narratives of the *cailleach*-goddess and from the narratives about former occupiers of their own roles such as *Eibhlín Ní Ghuinníola*.

Wise-woman reveals deeper significance of life events

25. *Máire Ní Mhurchú* and my own mother[59]

As regards *Máire Ní Mhurchú*, I am going to say to you again that the people of the township where I was had good testimony about *Máire Ní Mhurchú*, such that my own mother could recognize her as well as she could recognize any other woman of the place. And its often she was in company with her and talking with her because *Máire Ní Mhurchú* was – as I've heard the storytellers of the place itself say – a pleasant, affable, companionable, kindly little woman. She would do anything she could for anyone around her. Moreover, my mother told me that the stories about *Máire Ní Mhurchú* were true stories, that they were not just tittle-tattle and gossip.

One night she herself [mother] was spinning thread by the hearth – something she did very often and it was very late. It was twelve o'clock in the night, she said, at least that, if not later. Her husband's mother was there with her – that would be my own grandmother, may God be gracious to them all. My grandmother started to get apprehensive about something – she heard this whistling, whining noise going around about the house outside, but my mother didn't hear it at all, at the time. She was working the spinning wheel and I suppose maybe that stopped her hearing: she was listening to the spinning wheel. But my grandmother told her to leave the hearth, and to go to bed, because there was a young child in the house, who was only a month or two old.

My mother didn't make anything of it. She took her time and went off to bed some time later. She was about another hour at least at the hearth after my grandmother had gone to bed. My grandmother wasn't at all pleased about that, the following day. She said to my mother that she had stayed too long at the hearth after herself – and asked her did she hear anything going on around the house, as she herself had heard. And my mother said she heard nothing but that maybe it was a horse that was outside the house.

'I didn't hear a thing worth mentioning', my mother said, 'maybe it was a stray horse, nosing around outside the house, that you heard. I cleaned and swept the hearth in the way I usually manage since I wasn't a bit nervous.'

'Well, I was very anxious', said my grandmother, 'because I did hear noise, and there was more than a horse there; it was no horse there at all. If it was a horse that was there there had to be a dozen of them there, because a horse on his own wouldn't make anything like the racket that was made around the house. It was a big assembly of people and horses that came about the house because I heard all the noise and the clatter.'

My mother didn't give it too much credence. She said that it was how, 'Maybe you are right, but that, maybe, you are wrong, too, – that, maybe, you were dreaming' – this said sarcastically to my grandmother.

That didn't go down well at all with my grandmother, because she knew she was right in what she said herself. But my mother didn't like to give in since she used to be up and about – she was a great worker – as often in the dark as in the daylight.

The Sunday following, she went to Mass to Eyeries. There was a church in Ardgroom too but that's now where she used to go to Mass. She used always go along with her own people – she was from just west of Eyeries originally. And *Máire Ní Mhurchú* came up to her after Mass, as *Máire Ní Mhurchú* often did before. And she said to my mother:

'*Máire*' – my mother was *Máire* too, *Máire Ní Urdail*, – '*Máire*, wasn't it behindhand you were on Saturday night, that you didn't have the hearth swept in time. When you got the warning you went sweeping it then, but don't ever do that again. Whatever it is you still have to do, whenever you hear something, when you are late at the hearth, leave everything as it is and go to sleep for yourself, or at least go to bed. Don't ever again do what you did.'

'What are you on about?', said my mother, 'sure I wasn't at home at all on Saturday; I was west at *Cluain*.'

'Oh! 'tis well I know you were, indeed, because I was there when you were sweeping the hearth, sitting next to you at the head of the settle-bed.'

Pádraig Ó Murchú, the narrator of the seven legends presented here regarding the wise-woman of Beara, *Máire Ní Mhurchú*, emphasizes the truth of what he relates in terms of having heard it from his own mother, who, herself knew *Máire Ní Mhurchú* and who assured her son that the stories about the wise-woman and her powers were true stories and 'not just tittle-tattle and gossip'. *Pádraig Ó Murchú*'s mother who was often, he claims, in company with and in conversation with the 'pleasant, affable companionable, kindly little woman' who would 'do anything she could for anyone around her', had no occasion, herself, apparently, to resort to the knowledge and powers of the wise-woman. Nevertheless she had personal experience of that knowledge, as is recounted in this tale.

Pádraig's mother is presented in this tale as a confident, independent-minded woman not given to the kind of fairy-superstition that causes her mother-in-law to fear for the safety of the young infant of the house when she believes she hears mysterious noises about the place, in the dead of night. Such superstition operated in Irish tradition as a form of social control, dictating the organization of domestic tasks and, as in this story, providing a basis whereby the female family elder was able to impose a form of authority on her in-marrying daughter-in-law. When *Pádraig*'s mother reports to have heard no mysterious noises – something that he justifies in terms of her attention being focused on the spinning wheel she is operating so late into the night – it gives rise to a confrontation with her mother-in-law who claims, in the aftermath of her solemn advice having been disregarded, that a big assembly of otherworld forces was gathered about the house, with a consequent increased degree of danger. Because *Pádraig*'s mother suggests to her mother-in-law 'that, maybe, you were dreaming', the daughter-in-law appear to us, in her son's account of the incident, to be a most unlikely direct source of, or witness to, 'proof' of the intervention of otherworld forces in human affairs, or of the mediatory role of the wise-woman between the two worlds.

Yet this is just what the story goes on to do; to present us with vivid evidence, in the presumed self-reportage of *Pádraig Ó Murchú*'s mother, of how otherworld forces were, indeed, close at hand when she defied her mother-in-law's wishes – and fears – and swept the hearth in the small hours. *Máire Ní Mhurchú*, wise-woman of the district, traveller with the otherworld host and mediator for her people in their dealings with that host – tells her, when they meet after Mass, in the narrator's mother's home village, how she herself was present in the distant house when the woman defied her mother-in-law and traditional fairy superstition. 'I was there when you were sweeping the hearth', the wise-woman says, 'sitting next to you at the head of the settle-bed'. The story breaks off here without further comment or elaboration, with the truth of stories about the wise-woman, her knowledge and her powers, having achieved a notable endorsement, in the reported experience of the narrator's clear-headed, sceptical and, above all, trustworthy, mother. The caution of the mother-in-law is vindicated in the warning the wise-woman gives regarding the appropriate response to intimations of the otherworld. And yet, we are left with the impression that individual and community life is lived ambiguously, yielding to and yet defying the conservatism of tradition in the narrow sense.

What is revealed in general, in the repertoire of legend concerning the *cailleach* and the wise-woman alike, is that these stories present us with an interpretative frame for experience; that they comment and explain *after the event*. They tell how the community claimed to understand what happened in the course of its experience of life. That claim is creatively embodied in the legend narratives whose performance and re-creation in transmission serve to keep alive and to renew in memory and in imagination, the figures and the exploits that form a central part of a traditional cosmology that – along with the cosmology of a popular Christianity – represented foundational aspects of the worldview of Irish communities until comparatively recently. That worldview, in its totality, also contained ideas and values, explanations of experience and accounts of people's lives that, in espousing a kind of early modernity, gave no place to the goddess and the wise-woman. *Pádraig Ó Murchú* presents his mother as registering in her actions and in her words an awareness of the duality – or better, perhaps, the multifariousness – of cultural process, whereby meaning is constructed out of experience, in a crucible that consists of both the inherited pathways, modalities and materials of memory and the original creative energies and configurations of imagination. Apparent, too, I believe, is a humorous element in the narration of the legends, especially in those that present the approximate, ambiguous, contingent, relativist, partial nature of the interpretative grasp which – individually or communally – human beings are capable of, in respect of understanding the meaning of the ultimately mysterious experience of their, and our, life. *Pádraig Ó Murchú*'s stories of the wise-woman of Beara combine a rational presentation of the mundane realities of Beara life with an acknowledgement of the possibilities of numinous significance, in a manner that succeeds in incorporating such humorous twinkle as a constant feature of rhetorical performance.

26. *Máire Ní Mhurchú* and the miner[60]

Here is another story about *Máire Ní Mhurchú* that I am going to tell for anyone who would like to hear it.

My father was working in the mines, one time; he was a miner, even though he was a tailor, too, making clothes. And he was abroad in foreign parts for another part of his life. He was a miner and one time he was working in the Beara mine – the old Beara mine they call it, you will understand it better, like that. The place that he was at work was Allihies North. I know that place well enough myself, loath and all as I am to mention it, since it's many the fine man who lost his health there and many of whose death it was the cause.

When the holes were put in that were to be blown in the drilling – the holes that my father and two other men opposite him made – they got the ladders to escape from the danger. Ladders they had, at that time, to escape. They had no other way of getting free, in the Beara mine, only ladders.

When they came out on top, the holes blew and three of them failed to blow. They went wrong or something happened them that they didn't go off. This other miner who was working across on the other side, he said that it was the holes that my father had put down that had failed to blow. My father said those holes had blown; that he himself had fired them; that he had tested the fuse and that it was good that there was no danger they hadn't gone off.

'Still and all', he said, 'to satisfy you, I'll go back down, and you stay where you are.' My father was a level-headed, easy-going man and everyone liked him and besides that, the two of them were good neighbours.

My father went down the ladder and when he got near the holes below, where they were loaded and charged, the three holes blew around him and he was unscathed. He came up the ladder and when he got above ground everyone who saw him was terrified and amazed. They thought he was blown to pieces down at the holes. He told them that everything was in bits below, when they blew, but that he came to no harm.

The following Saturday, when he was coming home, *Máire Ní Mhurchú* met him in Eyeries, and she called him over to her and she spoke to him as I am going to tell you.

'*Seán*, wasn't that the foolish thing you did on such and such an evening?'

'What's that, *Máire*?', he said, not letting on at all that he understood her.

'When you went down for *Séamas Ó Sé*, to look after the holes that didn't blow for him, and you knowing full well that they weren't any of your business. You went down and you told him to stay where he was. *Seán*, don't ever again do such a thing, she said. You will never be killed in any mine – it wasn't you they wanted – but he will be taken, *O'Sé* will, sooner or later.

At the end of two years after that, my father went to America. He went to the Lakes and *Séamas Ó Sé* was at home in Ireland at that time. He went out a year after him and when he went out, to the same mine – the Red Jacket they call it – *Séamas Ó Sé* went to work there. He went to work in the same mine where my father went and the first day he went to work there he told my father of a strange experience he had: that he saw something in the shape of a white hare that had crossed the road as he was coming to the mine. They used to go to the mine on foot. There were no wagons going from mine to mine that time; it is since then that all the machinery was put in.

The first shift he worked after going to America, he was blown up and brought up dead to the surface. And *Máire Ní Mhurchú* said that that is what they had wanted, back in Beara mine.

In this story it is the narrator's father who serves as the witness to the knowledge of the wise-woman as to the true causes and meanings of things that happen. Again here there is a combination of the tragic reality of human loss and suffering with a colourful and even slightly comic sense of the way in which unpredictability and uncertainty accompanies human action. We are also given the opportunity of seeing the foreknowledge attributed to the wise-woman as being signalled as a communal back-projection of meaning, in the light of subsequent events. The narrative skilfully carries, and marries, a sense of both of these readings.

When our narrator's father had his seemingly miraculous escape from the delayed explosion in the Beara mine after he had, in patently foolhardy fashion, re-entered the mine to investigate the failure of some holes to blow, the terror and amazement that his ordeal and survival occasioned in his companion workers would have ensured that news of the incident would have been communicated to everyone in the community. Everyone would surely have wondered how this could have happened, how he could have come to no harm in what was clearly a fatal situation, in the normal course of events. The explanation is constructed in terms of otherworld forces having been involved in what happened and the power of those forces to override the usual human consequences of being caught up in such a situation, when it was the wrong human who was involved. This is directly expressed in the recounting by the narrator of how his father was called aside by *Máire Ní Mhurchú* a few days after the incident and upbraided for his foolhardiness. This foolhardiness consists, at one level, of his willingness to re-enter the mine in the knowledge that there were unexploded charges in it, and, at another and more significant level – in terms of the interpretation by the community of the meaning of what transpired – of his substituting himself, *Seán Ó Murchú*, for his workmate and good neighbour, *Séamas Ó Sé*, in the mysterious liminality of that threshold between life and death, above ground and under ground, onto which the protraction of the explosion (in a kind of stoppage of normal time), has placed them. *Máire Ní Mhurchú*'s words are succinct in their encapsulation of the meaning of it all: 'it wasn't you they wanted'. If *Seán* – in a show of unconcern or a registering of dubiousness in respect of the 'traditional' interpretation of the mysterious or the unexpected – feigns non-understanding of the wise-woman's approach, she assures him that, in her view and that of communal tradition, what he did in examining the unblown holes should not have been his concern: 'and you knowing full well that they weren't any of your business'.

Here we can see our narrator presenting his father – as he had presented his mother in the previous legend – as someone not in thrall to what might, from the outside, be regarded as traditional superstition. Nevertheless, here again, it is the 'level-headed, easy-going' individual who becomes the guarantor of the truth of the wise-woman's diagnosis and prophecy: 'he will be taken, Ó Sé', she had told him, 'sooner or later'. Three years later, in fact, when the unfortunate *Séamas Ó Sé* is killed in the blast in the Red Jacket mine in America (in which *Seán O' Murchú* has already worked for a year), it seems as if not only her words, but her presence is realized in the mention by the man destined to die that very day, that he saw something like a white hare crossing his path on the way to work, and to his fate. The motif of the *cailleach* in the guise of a hare is a well-known one, in the repertoire of traditional narrative. Its use here suggests the accompanying, mediating presence of the wise-woman at the places and times when the otherworld forces of ancestral tradition are understood to intervene in human affairs. *Pádraig Ó Murchú* recounts, in these two consecutive narrations, how each of his parents was admonished by *Máire Ní Mhurchú* for not conforming to the cautionary standards of action that would ensue from a lively adherence to the dictates of tradition. In doing so, he shows us that traditional belief in the powers of the otherworld forces, and the role of the wise-woman in regard to them, was one modality among others in the community's worldview and cultural process of constructing meaning from experience.

At the time that *Pádraig Ó Murchú* narrated these legends to the Folklore Commission it was a fact of history that his father's neighbour and work companion in mining – in Beara and in America (in the vicinity of Butte, Montana) – had actually lost his life in the Red Jacket mine accident in the States. *Pádraig* tells us that part of the wise-woman's 'message' – her diagnosis and prophecy at the time of the Beara mine incident – had been that his father would come safely through his mining career but that *Séamas Ó Sé* would die in a mine. The question arises as to whether such dire – and accurate – prediction was known and narrated in the community prior to the Red Jacket fatality. Did our narrator's father recount it publicly in the immediate aftermath of his own Beara mine escape and did *Séamas Ó Sé* knowingly disregard it in maintaining his mining activities? Was the prediction kept a secret in the *Ó Murchú* family? Far more likely is the addition of the prediction of *Ó Sé*'s death – in the aftermath of its unfortunate coming about – to the story of the admonition attributed to *Máire Ní Mhurchú* at the time of the Beara mine incident. This would illustrate how oral narrative tradition is itself an ongoing process, adapted and shaped in performance, to the historical and social contexts of narration. Thus we can appreciate how wise-woman and *cailleach* legends serve to carry forward, in a dynamic and creative fashion, the representations and interpretations of experience – individual and communal – that draw on the figures and functions that go to make up the worldview of ancestral tradition as a component of vernacular culture.

27. St Fanahan's Well and *Máire Liam*[61]

St Fanahan's Well was at first in a place called *Brí Gabhann*. But the people of the place around Mulberry used to wash clothes and dirty the well, so it moved out of that place to the place it is at present, about two miles away from it. There was a man who would always make a round at the well on St Fanahan's Night, 25 November. On this St Fanahan's night he came to the well as usual but he found that the well was gone. He stood there, wondering what had become of the well and t'wasn't long until a woman, all dressed in white came up and asked him what he was looking for. He told her. She told him the well had moved about two miles south-east from the place on account of the people washing clothes and dirtying the water of it, and she showed him where to find it.

There were two young lads from Mulberry went for a bucket of water to the well after that. They were bringing the bucket of water, between them, with a long pole and the bucket hanging on it. Just as they were coming from the well with the water a rabbit jumped up in front of them. They left down the water and ran after the rabbit. One of them got a very sore leg after that. It was sore with him for a long time and worse it was getting, every day. There was an old woman living down near Lismore at the time. She was great to cure sore legs or hands and people used come from all parts to her, to get cured. She used never take any money for curing, only you'd have to bring her a little present, anything you liked to give. Anyway they brought this boy down to the old woman. Her name was *Máire Liam*. When they were coming near the old woman's house she was at the door before them and she says to them:

'Don't tell me what happened because I know. Why didn't you bring on the water that day and not mind the rabbit. Go home now again. I've nothing to do for him. He'll be dead in a few days.' And so he was.

The opening incident of this story relates how a holy well, dedicated now to a Christian saint, but the site of pre-Christian ancestral sacredness also, moved, by its own agency, from its original location to another place about two miles distant. The reason why the well moved is, we are told, in response to the disrespect shown to it a – and to the otherworld realms it symbolizes and makes manifest – through the washing of dirty clothes in its water. The agency by means of which the well moved is not clear but we can take it that the cosmic power that operates in the otherworld – and in this – and that ultimately rules our lives, is the agency in question. The presence of such cosmic power in the world, the sacred vitality of the universe itself, is, in general, hidden from us. It is symbolized in such things as holy wells and in the mythological figures such as the *slua sí* (fairy host) and the various figures of the *cailleach*-goddess that are associated, in narrative tradition, with prominent features of the landscape.

In our story, it is a mysterious female figure who reveals to the man who wishes to make his respectful round at the holy well, where it is now located. 'She showed him', we are told 'where to find it', as if knowledge of it was now hidden and the offices of a mediatrix was required in order to discover its location. The woman is dressed all in white and we can take it that she is come from the otherworld to help the man in his perplexity as he 'stood there, wondering what had become of the well'. The other mediatrix in our story, the old woman healer named *Máire Liam,* is a human woman, but she too, has the ability to know hidden things and to see the cosmological significance, in ancestral cultural terms, of various life experiences.

The two young lads who go for the bucket of water to the holy well are from Mulberry and belong, therefore, to the people who had previously treated the well with disrespect. We are not told why the two boys wish to obtain a bucketful of the holy well water but it becomes clear that they, too, lack any full sense of its sacred value, as they are willing to discard it in favour of chasing a rabbit that crosses their path. The traditional audience for this story would be familiar with the narrative motif of the hare who is really a shape-shifted female, and who makes mischief at May eve, including interfering magically with wells on farmlands. Whether or not one should hear some echo of the hare/*cailleach* in the present tale, it is certainly the case that the encounter the two lads have with the animal leads to mysterious affliction of the gravest kind. This affliction affects one of them only, prompting such explanations as that their youth and innocence saves them (or one of them) from the imposition of a full, double affliction involving both of them, or that the affliction which befalls them is of an exemplary nature, intended to teach the other lad and all other Mulberry people (and all hearers of the tale), a lesson regarding the danger involved in carelessness with respect to the ancestral otherworld.

When the afflicted boy is brought to *Máire Liam* she has foreknowledge of what has happened him, but is without the ability to save him or cure the affliction. Her words are devastatingly direct and unsoftened with any expression of regret for the suffering and the death foretold: 'Go home now again. I've nothing to do for him. He'll be dead in a few days.' And yet the wise healer is a human woman, capable of being a channel of sacred assistance on occasion, but subject too, to the greater authority and power of the forces for whom she can mediate. The reality seems to be that the people of Mulberry have learned nothing from their experience of having their holy well withdrawn from them and are culpable in respect of allowing the two lads to, as it were, tamper further with the well by allowing the youthful frivolity of the rabbit-chase to again cause the well water to be treated without proper respect.

That *Máire Liam* is not hard-hearted or calculating in the performance of her mediatory role as wise healer is shown clearly by the emphasis placed in the text on her 'never tak[ing] any money for curing' even though 'people used come from all parts to her, to get cured'. The inability of such a generous and helpful woman to do anything to save the afflicted boy is, in this instance, an extra demonstration of the need for mindfulness of the ancestral cosmological perspective to which this story – and its narration in the present text – attests.

28.   The girl who was struck dumb[62]

There was this only girl in Sherkin Island and she lost her speech. She went to bed in her health and in the morning she was unable to speak. There was a woman east in *Béal Átha an Fhíona* who used to be giving out knowledge – she used to be going with the good people. The girl was brought to visit her to see if she could cure her. When she saw her, she couldn't do anything for her and she told her to come back again after a fortnight.

She came back and the woman asked her father why he built his house so close to a *port* and said that while they would never thrive there, neither would they ever want for anything there. She took a basin off the dresser and she asked the girl did she recognize it. She said she did and that she had missed it. 'I was at your house since', said the woman, 'and I took this basin.' 'Weren't you', she said, 'driving a horse down the hillside when you met with an angry, red-haired woman of the Harnedys and she had a woollen cloak around her and she struck you a blow on each side of you and the third blow down on top of your head? There was poison in that.'

She cured the girl then, but the loss of speech used to return, at the same time, regularly, until the day she died.

In this short text from the narrative repertoire of Cape Clear, we hear of resort, in the face of sudden affliction, to a woman said to have those two chief characteristics associated with the actual *P Ní L* who was known to go into fainting fits at wakes in *Gleann Fhreastail* (see p. 174). These two characteristics are the ability to have access to the otherworld (i.e. 'to be going with the good people',' to see the fairies') and the ability 'to be giving out knowledge', to bring knowledge from the otherworld. The victim of the affliction in this case is a young girl who was an only child, living in Sherkin island, who lost her power of speech overnight. She went to bed, we are told, 'in her health' and was unable to speak 'in the morning'. It is unclear, initially, whether the affliction she suffered happened during her sleep or if she was involved in some waking incident in the course of the night that resulted in her speechless condition. The way the story progresses, however, and especially the way it ends, lead us to believe that it was in the course of her sleep that the young girl experienced the crisis that caused the affliction, which is diagnosed and 'cured' by the wise healer to whom the girl is brought, presumably by her parents or other family. Certainly, on the occasion of the second visit to the wise-woman, the girl is accompanied by her father. The second visit is required because of the wise-woman's pronouncement, on the first occasion that the girl was brought to her, that she could do nothing for her and that she should come back again after a fortnight.

This reaction by the wise-woman is consistent with the notion that it was in the course of occasional visits to the otherworld realm, along with 'the fairies' or the 'good people', that the *Béal Átha an Fhíona* wise-woman acquired her knowledge – in the same way that we saw imputed to *P Ní L* of *Gleann Fhreastail*. By the time of the second visit, the wise-woman of this story has indeed acquired 'knowledge' relevant to the affliction that has befallen the girl. She gives her visitors to understand that she has since paid a visit – via the other world – to their homeplace, and she proceeds to prove the reality of this in terms of producing the basin from the dresser which she claims she took from their house and which the girl now identifies and says she had noticed to be missing from her home. The text here establishes the competence and authority of the wise-woman at the same time as it establishes a possible suggestibility on the part of the young girl in acquiescing in the wise-woman's demonstration of her powers.

The question the wise-woman asks of the girl's father, however, on the occasion of the second visit, requires no sense of suggestibility on the part of any individual. It picks ups, instead, on the general community belief that the choice of a location for a house is a matter entailing the possibility of intrusion on the otherworld realm of 'the good people', in an unwarranted (even if unintentional) way that can have misfortunate consequences for human lives.

Why, the wise-woman wants to know, has the father built his house so close to a *port*. The term *port*, in Irish, has the senses of being both a physical location, as a landing place in a harbour or on the bank of a river, and also a social and symbolic centre, occupied and even fortified, as the seat of some group or agency. It is less definitive, as a location or centre of the ancestral otherworld realm, than a *lios* or a *ráth* (ringfort), but it has, nevertheless, connotations that should not be deliberately ignored in the matter of housebuilding. No one would dream of deliberately building a house in a *lios* or a *ráth* or on a trackway that was known, traditionally, as being frequented by otherworld beings. Precautions were taken to ensure that one did not, unwittingly, build on such an inappropriate site; twigs were put standing overnight at the four corners of the proposed dwelling place and inspected later for possible signs of disturbance that would indicate the displeasure of the otherworld powers at the prospect of the erection of the house in that location.

In our story, the afflicted girl's father has built, not actually on, but very close to such a location, and, perhaps also, a disputed civil boundary. This, it transpires, is something that brings both advantages and disadvantages to the man and to his family. They will never want for anything there but they are to be prone, in other ways, to misfortune. The particular misfortune with which this man's only daughter has now been afflicted has arisen as the result of an encounter she had – whether in a dream or at some other time is not specified – with an angry, red-haired woman wrapped in a woollen cloak. Such a figure can be interpreted, in the context of tradition, as that of an ancestral otherworld figure, or a human neighbour (a deceased ancestor of the Harnedys, who resents, it appears, human intrusion into the otherworld domain, localized in the vicinity of the *port* in question). The driving of a horse downhill by the girl had constituted, on some former occasion, or in the dream, such an intrusion and a transgression of cosmological and social boundaries. The blows administered to the girl by the angry red-haired woman are a manifestation of the enmity that can arise between human neighbours and between the otherworld and human realms when the latter intrudes, even unwittingly, on the former. They are a consequence of the inappropriate location of a human dwelling, in this world and in relation to the otherworld. This enmity is the 'poison' which has rendered the girl dumb, according to the wise-woman, who has acquired recent knowledge of what really happened.

Having diagnosed, as it were, by means of her access to the otherworld realm, in 'going with the good people', the true cause of the girl's affliction, the wise-woman then effects a 'cure'. We are not told of what this cure consisted but we can understand that the identification of both the source and the occasion of the affliction is, in itself, therapeutic for the victim. The cure, however, is not complete since the loss of speech used to return, regularly, throughout the remainder of the unfortunate girl's life. Two levels of significance would appear to be involved in this final statement of the text. In one sense the affliction cannot be totally removed since, we can assume, the girl and her family continue dwelling at the ambiguous location at which the father had built their house – a location at which their fortune is destined to be forever mixed, in the pronouncement of the wise woman. The continued, intermittent affliction of the girl 'until the day she died' is a vivid, cautionary manifestation of that mixed fortune and serves to remind the community of the day and the community of interpretation, of the social and cosmological implications of human action, even of a seemingly mundane sort, and the specific cosmological hazards of neglecting due deference to the realities of an ancestral worldview in which landscape is shared with personalized otherworld forces whose agency is never to be taken for granted.

At another level, this story presents the situation of an individual who was afflicted in the course of a dream in which her psyche dealt symbolically with troubling issues, whether arising from 'real-life' (i.e. waking) experiences or the imagination. We are not told of any troubles the girl or her family were experiencing in their community, yet the identification of the angry, red-haired woman in the woollen cloak as a woman 'of the Harnedys', suggests some basis in social relationships for the terror (perhaps guilt?) that initiated the affliction of loss-of-speech and that gave rise to the lasting psychic wound that manifests itself in the regular recurrence of the affliction thereafter.

The story ends with an ambiguity that mirrors that of the family's destiny as residents at a location too near the *port* for their own social, cosmic or psychic security. We are told, in the same breath, that the wise-woman 'cured' the girl but that the affliction remained with her 'until the day she died'. In these circumstances, 'cure' must be more a matter of interpretation, of 'knowing' rather than of somatic 'healing'. This suggests that affliction is essentially a lack of knowledge – causing an inability to interpret experience – rather than some specific condition of a perceived pathological nature. The wise-woman is the traditional source of help to whom the community has resort in the face of affliction when the nature, onset, or course of the affliction seems to evade an interpretation that looks only to the surface of life and landscape for its 'facts'. Stories such as the present one, both in their content and in their transmission-in-performance, attest to a 'traditional' understanding of and allegiance to a worldview that in characteristic ancestral and creative fashion goes far beyond the superficial.

29. *Carn Tighearna*[63]

Carn Tighearna is about two miles to the south of Fermoy. It is a very high hill – the end of the mountain ranges that run from west to east in that district. There is a large cairn at the top of the hill and it is called *Carn Tighearna*.

A great lord or chief lived at Fermoy at one time, long ago. He had a great big mansion beside the Blackwater. He was married and all he had in family was an only son. He was, needless to say, terribly fond of the child; why would he not be?

One day a wise-woman came into the house to them and she asked them to give her some help, but they refused her. She then said that the child wouldn't live to be grown up, because he would be drowned. Even though the lord took no notice of this at the start, he never forgot it and used to think about it and ponder on it until, in the end, he made up his mind to leave the mansion, since it was too near the river. He decided to go instead, to some place that was not near water.

He decided to build a new house at the top of this hill that is two miles south of Fermoy. He set his labourers working at it and they had it partly built; it was to be another splendid mansion. The view from the hill is very fine indeed. You would see the countryside around for miles in every direction. You would see Cork to the south, Tipperary and Limerick to the north, and the Blackwater, flowing slowly west to east, as far as Lismore.

Well, one day the lord went up to the hilltop to find out for himself how the work was progressing. He was impatient for the house to be ready for living in, because his fears for his son and the death that was prophesied for him were growing every day. He brought his son with him, that day, to the top of the hill; a little boy of about six years of age. Everyone was working to the best of their ability, on the hilltop, building the house. The Lord stayed talking to the man in charge of the work and he let the little boy to run about the place.

They had barrels of water there and the little boy came to one of them on the western side of the building. He leant in over the barrel and, God save the hearers, didn't he fall in and drown. He was drowned before anybody noticed anything. The Lord was distraught then. It broke his heart and he didn't live very long after. The house was left just as it was at that time, without ever being finished. That's the cairn that is on the top of *Carn Tighearna* to this day.

This story features an unnamed and, apparently, nomadic or travelling wise-woman who comes to the house and asks for charity. When she is refused she prophesies the death by drowning of the child of the house. At first glance, it might appear that the prophecy is some kind of retaliatory act because of the refusal of the help the woman asked for. If that were the case, the prophecy would in fact constitute a kind of curse and the wise-woman would be put in the role of the agent from whom – or, at least, by whom – this great evil is inflicted. Such a reading, however, would be at variance with the established interpretation of the wise-woman and her function in society. In that interpretation the wise-woman was a source of knowledge and help to her community in times of affliction and misfortune. She is portrayed as morally neutral in respect of the hidden knowledge to which her contact with the ancestral otherworld gives her privileged access. While traditional narrative portrays the Christian cleric's view of the wise-woman as being a kind of witch-figure, and likely to be malevolent in intention and in action, the traditional narratives portray this as a mistaken view; there are many accounts of the priest being forced to learn by experience the power of the wise-woman in operation and that she was not his enemy (theologically or morally) even if she was his rival in respect of her role as mediator to the community of the knowledge and the power of the ancestral otherworld that was part of the alternative cosmology to that of Christianity, in ancestral narrative tradition.

The prophecy that the travelling wise-woman makes, in the great mansion beside the Blackwater, is the revelation of something that arises in tandem with the refusal to her of the help she has requested, but these two things are not to be seen as causally related, with the death as the consequence of the prophecy. The death is of course, related to the refusal, but not as a consequence, rather, I would say, as a concomitant. The great lord of the Fermoy district, with his huge mansion on the banks of the great river, wealthy and powerful as he is, has had to recognize a limit to his power and ambition and to his dynastic identity in that he has had only a single child. He has an only son, of whom, we are told he was 'terribly fond', with the textual apposition of the question 'why would he not be?' His circumstances make plain to him the powerlessness and the limitation of the human being, in the face of the inscrutable and unyielding cosmic forces that rule our human lives. He has it demonstrated directly and, catastrophically, painfully to him, that the tenderness and the affection he feels for his own only child is due also to all human children of the cosmos.

In this context and in the context of his great material wealth, his refusal, and the refusal by his household, of charity to a travelling female beggar is incomprehensible except as a mark of some kind of impairment of his sense of humanity and human community. This is reinforced by hearing that, at first, he took no notice of the prophecy. When it does impress itself upon him, his response is to its literal rather than its symbolic meaning. He wants to take his child away from the waters of the river when, in a tragic sense, it is the depths of the materially well-off, social and cultural incomprehension, in which he and his household are sunk, that constitute the drowning threat to the boy. In deciding to build his new house at the top of a hill, he compounds his difficulties. The top of a high hill, and one giving the view over three counties and over the great river that is described for us, is a location not really fit for human habitation. This is because it is a place charged with the nearness, and, indeed, the presence of that ancestral otherworld that is portrayed in mythology as being an ultimately female realm. Landscape features such as hills and rivers, traditionally manifest that otherworld and its divine personages: *Cnoc Áine*/ Knockaney, *Carraig Chlíodhna*/Clíodhna's Rock, *An Bhóinn*/The River Boyne etc. We have been told at the beginning of our text that the mountain ranges of which this high hill, *Carn Tighearna*, is the end, run from west to east and we have been shown, in the view from the hill's summit, the sacred river also flowing out of the west across the landscape. In tradition, the west is the direction most associated with the ancestral otherworld and it was regarded as unlucky to extend one's house to the west, since this could represent a symbolic, human encroachment on the territory of the otherworld and its forces. In building his huge mansion on the hilltop, the lord of Fermoy is intruding foolishly, negligently and tragically into that otherworld realm and there is something shockingly simple and fitting, in hearing that it was into a barrel of water, on the western side of the intrusive structure, that the little boy is drawn – as much as falls – and is drowned. He was drowned, we are told, 'before anybody noticed anything'. Everybody, here, we can say, has failed to 'notice anything', to be open to the cultural and cosmic significance of their life experience for far too long and there is an inevitability about the little boy's death that is a great sadness in the story and in its recounting in the community repertoire. Note the interjection 'God save the hearers' that is uttered, as it were, between the little boy's leaning over the rim of the barrel and his falling into the water. That rim is, in many respects, the boundary edge, the margin of the otherworld from where in ancestral perspective, the gift of fertility, like all other gifts, comes. In falling so far short of the lordly requirements of generosity in this life and respect for the presence and power of the ancestral otherworld, the lord of Fermoy forfeits even the one child that had been granted to him, and suffers the loss of that child into the otherworld as prophesied that fateful day by the wise-woman who was refused hospitality and who read the signs aright.

More than the child goes into the otherworld at the end of this story. Distraught, the lord soon dies of a broken heart. The house is left unfinished, to be transformed in the community's perspective into the cairn that sits on top of the hill 'to this day'. As such, it is a conventional marker of the sacred presence of the otherworld – the neglect of whose existence has been the grievous cause of the great affliction told of in this story – that serves in its recounting, to bear witness to and to renew the sense of otherworld in those who hear it.

30. **Máire Ní Chearbhaill and the blow from the Red-haired woman**[64]
I remember hearing another story about *Máire Ní Chearbhaill* from D. M.'s grandfather who lived over there in Moulnagerra, in the parish of Leap. His wife's people were living over beyond Reenascreena, near Rosscarbery, and *Máire* used to come in visiting them every day.

One night one of his brothers-in-law went conveying a neighbour home from scorauíochting (social visiting) and when he was coming back home, he got sick. Next day he was almost dying and the priest or doctor could not do anything to cure him. About the middle of the day they saw *Máire* coming in and she having a bottle in her hand.

She asked where was Jack and they told her how he got sick last night and that he was very bad.

'Ah', she said 'it was a good job for him that I was by his side when he was struck the blow, or he would be here with you now as a corpse. It was a red-haired woman from *Poll na Piseoige* who struck him and I knocked the stick she had out of her hand before she was able to do him any more damage. Rub this bottle to him, now, and he will be alright again.'

They rubbed the bottle to him and he was cured.

This anecdote has the wise-woman, *Máire Ní Chearbhaill,* as a daily visitor to a household in Reenascreena, near Rosscarbery, even though the earlier story, from the same narrator, had her similarly visiting a house in Gallans [sic], near Drimoleague, some twenty miles from Reenascreena. The suggestion is that we are hearing about a woman who exists more surely in the repertoire of the narrative tradition than she does in historical record. The narrator's references, in the case of both stories, to specific relations and neighbours of his own whose lives and experiences validate the existence and the operations of *Máire Ní Chearbhaill,* are examples of the way in which traditional narratives about the wise-woman bridge social and symbolic realities, so that an ancestral cosmological allegiance to the figure and significance of the *cailleach*-goddess and her partly legendary, partly flesh-and-blood cultural transforms are articulated anew in the contemporary historical world.

In this particular story, the affliction for which only the wise-woman has an explanation and a cure, when priest and doctor fail, is the sudden taking sick of a man who was walking home alone in the night, having accompanied a neighbour home to his house after an evening's socializing in the locality. The term *scoraíochting* is used to characterize the social activities of the evening in question and is one of a number of terms, from different regions of Ireland, that all refer to the same kind of assembly of neighbours, most often males. They gather into the kitchen of a local house on winter evenings and, seated around the hearth and along the walls, spend the hours, until around midnight, exchanging news, gossip and reminiscences, perhaps card-playing, perhaps listening to the reading out of a newspaper or listening to some local, accomplished storyteller narrating hero- or wonder-tales, the recreational function of which was somewhat akin to that of the major soap serials and other dramatic entertainments of the television age. Another part of the repertoire of traditional narrative that found expression in the performances at *scoraíocht*-type assemblies was the stock of stories about encounters with otherworld figures by people of the district. Such encounters were often connected to certain places having known otherworld associations and such a place is indicated in our story by the placename *Poll na Piseoige*, for some local landscape feature of the pit or ground-hole type that was associated in local tradition with superstitious belief.

One of the central characteristics of wise-women is their possession of fore-knowledge and knowledge of hidden causes. Both kinds of knowledge are displayed by *Máire Ní Chearbhaill* here, when she arrives at the victim's house already bearing a bottle containing a cure for his affliction, before hearing from his family of the misfortune that has befallen him. On being told how sick he is, she proceeds to describe and explain what happened to him the previous night, as he returned home alone from the *scoraíocht*. *Máire* can relate these matters to his family because, she says, she was there at his side when he was attacked by a red-haired woman from *Poll na Piseoige*. The red-haired woman has, in traditional perspective, the air of an otherworld figure and, in claiming to have been at the man's side at the time, the wise-woman is presented in the story as equally otherworldly.

Máire Ní Chearbhaill's apparent ability to be 'present' in both Gallans and in Reenascreena, on a daily basis, is complemented by her 'presence' at the time and place of affliction in the case of the victim in this story. Overall, the tradition articulated in these stories about her, present her as an abiding, wise, autonomous, female agency who is easily resorted to in affliction since she, as it were, regularly presents herself to the community as a ubiquitous household visitor. In the present instance her ubiquitousness is doubly displayed by her claim to have been present on the road when the victim encountered his misfortune. Like other wise-women such as *Máire Ní Mhurchú* and *Biddy Early*, *Máire Ní Chearbhaill* is presented to us – and to her interpretative community – in the corpus of stories regarding her and her exploits, as a figure to be situated towards the flesh-and-blood end of that list of female figures, ranging from the mythological to the historical, who give expression to the allegiance which is found in Irish oral narrative tradition to an ancestral cosmology in which the *cailleach*-goddess is the personification of an essentially female conception of the universe and its cosmic forces.

Wise-woman remedies extraordinary affliction

31. **Máire Ní Mhurchú and the woman who was 'swept'**[65]
    From the time I was a child I have heard a great deal about the fairies; many people asserting that they didn't exist at all. But if they weren't there, isn't it the great amount that is talked about them.

    But my own mother told me many times about the woman who lived in Eyeries who was called *Máire Ní Mhurchú*. And the place she had her house – and some of the old ruin is still standing – was at what is called *Baile na nAoraí*, within a quarter mile of the village; so that now, at the end of my life, since I'm old now too, I'm living myself within a quarter mile of that place. The outline of the ruin is there still today, so that there is good evidence that she was there. It was said that she was ...

    A woman fell sick in Ardgroom and she was very ill indeed – a woman of the O'Sheas she was – and there was no expectation that she would pull out of it. And the priest came and the doctor came and everyone came, asking for her and trying to cure her and no cure could be found for her. As a last resort her husband went to visit *Máire Ní Mhurchú*. He would never have believed, before, that *Máire* had any special knowledge – rather was he one of those who used to mock her sarcastically and jeer at her. And he asked her if she had any knowledge of any cure that she could work for him, or did she understand what was involved here, was it that his wife was (magically) 'changed' or was it a proper illness?

    Máire laughed and she said – 'It was about time for you to come', she said. 'She has been "swept" [abducted] from you for a long while now and there are times when she is very near-at-hand and it's very

negligently you are minding the one you have in her place. And I haven't much mind to do anything for you or for herself now because it's always very bitter and insulting you were about me – that I knew nothing – and it's many dangers and much blame I have had from lots of you.'

She told him then that his wife was across in Kerry, with the fairy host, in a place called *Dóinn* and if he were to go across with a boat-crew on the Tuesday night coming, that she would go with him herself; that his wife would be up on the second horse from the front in the crowd coming west from Kenmare; that she herself – that is *Máire* – would give him water in a bottle and that he should sprinkle this water in a circle with his fingers on the road; that he should catch at his wife and drag her into the circle of water and that he would have her back then.

He agreed to it and he asked some of the neighbours around the place that he felt wouldn't refuse him – even though they themselves judged it to be hard work and dangerous work, crossing over the sea in pursuit of the woman. And it was true for them and they were slow to agree but they went anyway. They didn't like to refuse him since he was such a good man himself.

They went over there on Tuesday night and he did what *Máire Ní Mhurchú* had told him to do and *Máire* herself was with them in the boat. And the horses came and the riders and those riding pillion and he tried to take his wife down off the horse and it failed him to do so and they had to come home without her.

A week on from that day they got ready again and they went there and at midnight the horses were again coming west the road and he did the same business again as *Máire Ní Mhurchú* had instructed him to do. And he brought her down off the horse and into the circle that he had made on the road with the water and they brought her with them back down to the boat. They didn't have far to go to get to the boat as the road is very near the sea there.

She [i.e. *Máire Ní Mhurchú*], told them then to row the boat away as fast and as hard as ever they could, with all the strength and endurance they could call on, that they would be pursued straight away. There were great seas behind them and great seas all around them, swells and breakers, only that they weren't swamped, and they came across halfway. She told them to take it easy then, and the sea was quieter now, and they brought the woman home to *Puillín* strand. And when they arrived back to the house, the woman that had been in the bed was gone away: there was nothing in the bed only the bedclothes.

> And the woman lived on for twenty years after she was brought down from the horse and brought from Kerry and she had a large family. But for ten or twelve years after that the husband couldn't keep a cow or a calf; all his stock used to die on him and he was set back very much in his affairs.
>
> That was no word of a lie, whatever lies there are about the fairies, nor no lying concoction. That was as true as the sun shining in the sky.

The plot of this story is embedded in a kind of commentary or cultural context that the narrator himself – *Pádraig Ó Murchú* of *Gort Broc* – provides. The commentary embodies, in a striking fashion, the complex and dynamic nature of the relationship between legend and belief. The narrator makes it clear that communal belief in the existence of the fairies is ambiguous with 'many people asserting that they didn't exist at all'. His questioning of the great amount that was talked about the fairies 'if they weren't there', applies, equally, to the 'talk' about the wise-woman, in this case *Máire Ní Mhurchú*. He says that his own mother told him many times about her; how she lived in the village of Eyeries and where she had her house, a house which as a ruin, 'is still standing'. He takes this, he claims, as 'good evidence that she was there', but adds, 'It was said that she was.'

Máirtín Verling, the editor of the anthology of the *Pádraig Ó Murchadha* material in which these stories of *Máire Ní Mhurchú* are reproduced states that, despite detailed research, no documentary historical evidence can be adduced for the claim that a *Máire Ní Mhurchú* lived at Eyeries during the period in question. The truth of her presence there and of her activities as wise-woman would appear to be the imaginative truth of creative and therapeutic fiction, akin to the imaginative truth of the existence of the fairy realm into which the human female in our story is 'swept' or abducted, and out of which she is rescued with the advice and assistance of *Máire Ní Mhurchú*. At the end of the story, the narrator attests that what he has told is no word of a lie, 'whatever lies [imaginative fictions?] there are about the fairies', but 'as true as the sun shining in the sky'. The overall effect of the story testifies to and re-inforces, the sense of a native otherworld realm with which humans and human life are obliged to have an ongoing relationship that is mediated by the figure and the activities of the wise-woman, among others.

The role of *Máire Ní Mhurchú* in this story is that of the wise-woman legend pattern in general, even though in this instance, the stages of the affliction, the resort, the diagnosis, the treatment, the aftermath are all elaborated to a degree that is unusually specific in its detail and in the way that it is embedded in the physical and social reality of the community in which the story is both set and narrated. In that community life, we are given to understand, there are those who are normally scornful of the figure and the stories of the wise-woman and her powers, as well as those who 'believe' in her, as our narrator ostensibly does, in protesting the 'truth' of his story and the 'evidence' of the 'real' existence, in the village, of the *Máire Ní Mhurchú* of whom his own mother told him so much.

The story makes it clear that it is when all else has failed that the sick woman's husband – a non-believer in the powers of the wise-woman – resorts to *Máire Ní Mhurchú*. Her reaction is reported as one of compassion, despite her resentment at the insult and danger that have resulted for her from the lack of faith on the part of the husband and his like. Her diagnosis of the affliction – the abduction or 'sweeping' of the man's wife and the substitution of a 'changeling' in her place – is accompanied by a listing of the disadvantages that follow from the blindness to, or lack of belief in, the involvement of the native otherworld in human affairs – a corollary of the lack of belief in the wise-woman, in *Máire Ní Mhurchú* herself, in this instance.

This belief in the operation of the fairies in human life and in the mediating function of the wise-woman in respect of them, is activated and brought into play – however reluctantly, or dubiously, on the husband's part – in a way that suggests its functional availability in the cultural resources of the community. In order to carry out the activities prescribed as treatment by *Máire Ní Mhurchú* – crossing the bay with a boatcrew and forcibly reclaiming his wife from her otherworld captors – the husband, we are told, 'asked some of the neighbours round the place that he felt wouldn't refuse him'. Though slow to undertake such a hard and dangerous task, they oblige him out of human and social solidarity in the face of affliction: 'They didn't like to refuse him since he was such a good man himself.' This consent to the course of action called for (and the implied consent to the knowledge and authority of the wise-woman) results, in the story as recounted – and as *experienced* by both its protagonists and its hearers – in the tangible presence of *Máire* herself, in the boat, along with the husband and the rescue party: 'And *Máire* herself was with them in the boat'.

At the first attempt at rescue, the husband's nerve (or belief?) fails him: 'he tried to take his wife down off the horse and it failed him to do so and they had to come home without her'. A week later, another attempt is made: 'he did the same business again as *Máire Ní Mhurchú* had instructed him to do'. This time his efforts at rescue are successful, to the extent that he is able to bring his wife out of the otherworld and 'into the circle that he had made on the road with the water' given to him by the wise-woman. From there he brings her to the boat in which he has crossed over from the other side of the bay – a crossing easily seen as metaphorical – and he and his crew row away back across the bay as hard and as fast as possible to escape from the pursuing forces. *Máire Ní Mhurchú* is again represented as being with them, in the boat, encouraging their flight back and telling them, when half-way across, to take it easy now, that they are 'free', safe, home again, in cosmic as well as in topographical terms.

When they arrived back to the house, we are told, 'the woman that had been in the bed (i.e. the otherworld changeling, substitute wife) was gone away: there was nothing in the bed only the bedclothes'. We can envisage a cultural and narrative relationship between the three women of the story – the human wife, her otherworld replacement and the wise-woman who mediates between human life and the otherworld realm, and we can further envisage that the impact of this relationship is 'understood' not only by the legendary protagonists and by ourselves, as analytic commentators, but also by the interpretative community among whom this story and other legends of the wise-woman circulated. For that community, the figure and the stories of resort to the wise-woman in times of otherworld affliction were both an explanation of misfortune and a promise of the restoration of cosmic and social harmony through the activation in narrative performance (i.e. in story), of the therapeutic function of imagination (c.f. n. 65).

Recent feminist scholarship seeks to decode the later, nineteenth-century repertoire of Irish fairy legends as a discourse in which forms of social control, gender inequalities, psychosomatic illness and sexual abuse, were symbolically articulated, in displaced ways, in a patriarchal society overtly committed to the values of a modernizing, Victorian, Catholic, Irish respectability. In the case of the story under consideration here, such a reading would imply that the wife's illness, her 'being away with the fairies' is a metaphor for some condition or other of marital disharmony or dysfunction in the relationship between her husband and herself. The wise-woman's diagnosis that 'she has been "swept" from you for a long while now' implies that the affliction from which the wife – and the marriage – is suffering has been developing over a considerable period of time. The assertions that 'there are times when she is very near-at-hand' and that 'it's very negligently you are minding the one you have in her place', speak of the failure of the husband to register and/or to comprehend his wife's trouble or the opportunities he has had to do something about it.

It can be held to be of some significance that, in this story as told by *Pádraig Ó Murchú*, the wife is stated to be, herself, an O'Shea. In West Munster coastal tradition the O'Sheas are held to be the descendants of a seal-woman who was married, for a while, to a human husband and who bore him children before returning to the sea. Similar beliefs are attached by coastal tradition to other families, for example the Conneelys. It has been argued that this motif is a vestigial, maritime adaptation of the early medieval

Celtic and Irish theme of the sacred marriage between male human ruler and otherworld sovereignty goddess in which the harmony, and, indeed the continued existence of the relationship, is dependent on the proper behaviour of the male partner. In terms of the present story from Beara, we can see how it can be understood as showing the wife being 'returned' or translated to the native otherworld realm in the face of some unstated (but implied) neglect or abuse on the husband's part. That the condition afflicting the woman and the relationship, could have presented – directly or indirectly – as infertility, is hinted at by the narrator's statement, towards the end of the story, when the woman has been restored to her husband, that 'the woman lived on for twenty years ... and she had a large family'. Twenty years would not seem a great span of married life and one can sense something of the return of the seal-woman/sovereignty goddess to the otherworld that has traditionally marked the breach of marital and cosmic harmony between man and wife, king and sovereignty goddess, the human order and the cosmos. The continuity of rupture in the relationship is, in the present story, conveyed in the telling by the narrator of how 'for ten or twelve years after' (i.e. continually, as an ongoing state of affairs) 'the husband couldn't keep a cow or a calf; all his stock used to die on him and he was set back very much in his affairs'. Such a failure to thrive in nature is, in the earlier medieval tradition, a mark of the rupture of harmony between king and sovereignty goddess. In later vernacular, or folk tradition, it is a condition inviting interpretation as 'fairy' (i.e. native otherworld), trouble or affliction, just the kind of affliction calling for the proper diagnosis and relief which recourse to the knowledge and power of the wise-woman gives access.

In the non-linear, oral narrative discourse of legends such as this, there is a recurrent circularity of significance in the last and first states of the marriage relationship at the heart of the story (the wife for whom no cure could be found and the husband whose stock is constantly blighted). The explanation of this state of affairs and the result of it, it appears, is the same: the going into the otherworld (abduction/death) of the female partner in a way that is consistent with ancient and continuing native traditions of otherworld female agency, and the mediating role played by the figure of the wise-woman.

And all this – the story and its manifold significance – is, we are assured by the narrator at the end, 'no word of a lie ... nor no lying concoction'. Rather, he claims, it is 'as true as the sun shining in the sky'; it is true-to-life and true-to-life-in-nature, the life of the body *and* the imagination.

32. *Máire ní Mhurchú* and the young man who was 'swept'-I[66]
    There was this man in our parish, at a place that people know as *Cathair Caim*. This man's name was *Mícheál Ó Gúgáin*. He was the only

son that his father had and, even though he had sisters too, his father was solely dependent on him. His father married him off very young so as to keep him at home, since he himself was for going to America, if he could. His father thought that the only way he had of holding on to him was to hand over the place to him and get him married in time.

A year or two after the son married, he fell sick. Even though he was a strong, durable man, he took sick very quickly and his health failed. And everyone wondered at what could have come against him, a man as strong and powerful as he was. When none of the doctors, nor the priest, could tell what was happening to him, they went to *Máire Ní Mhurchú* about him. And, of course, *Máire Ní Mhurchú* said to them that it was time for them to come to her; that it was well they knew that he wasn't sick at all and that it wasn't he himself was with them for a good while. She said that if they wanted to cure him the place they would get his cure was *Cill Macallóg* graveyard and that if they didn't go about it and get it that they would be at the loss of him before very long.

They had no way of going there without herself along with them and they asked her would she go there along with them. And she said she would and to get two more men – *Tadhg Caobach* from the place and *Diarmuid Ó Murchú* – who would go with them also; who wouldn't refuse them. They were asked and they [all] went there that same night.

And when they came to the gate of the graveyard at *Cill Macallóg* she said to them to stay at the gate and that she herself would go in to the graveyard. And she went to the back of the graveyard and she picked this herb that she required and she came to the gate to them. She got up as pillion behind *Tadhg Caobach* and she told him to get off home – that he would be pursued at once – and to drive on the horse as fast as he was able until they came east to the Kerry border at *Glaise*, in the place that is known as *Glaise na Naíonán*. She used to be dragged off the horse constantly in the course of the journey – only that *Tadhg Caobach* held on to her with his arm back around her – until they came to *Glaise na Naíonán* – and she told him he could take it easy then; that they weren't able to go any further.

They came back home to *Cathair Caim* and the sick man was inside in the bed and she gave him the herb. Nobody knew how she gave it to him, only herself, because she allowed no one into the room with her for a few minutes. And it wasn't long before the man in the bed spoke. He sat up in the bed and spoke out directly to them and told them about the fairies and proved the good truth of *Máire Ní Mhurchú*'s story.

He told them that *Máire Ní Mhurchú* was right; that he himself had been west in a place known as *Tráigh an Phéarla,* for a year, in a fairy court there. That he was inside in it for most of the time and that he had no way of ever getting back. That there was a relation of his inside there – a female relative – and she told him not to eat even a morsel of their food – or that if he did, that he'd never, ever get back again.

The only food that he had, all the time he was away from home, was the food left over after the supper at night in the houses that he went into along with them in the course of their journeying about to entertain themselves.

There was a red-haired young woman in the court, he said, and she often quarrelled with him trying to get him to eat of their supper or their breakfast because she would have dearly loved to have him for herself. And this woman who was related to him, always told him to have nothing to do with it and that if he did that he would never come out. She said she hoped all the time that maybe those at home would get a cure for him. And when he gave back the food, one time, the red-haired young woman hit him a blow on the face with the palm of her hand and caused him to lose his sight.

And I myself was at that man's wake and at his funeral, and I saw for myself, with my own eyes, that he was without sight from the time he got sick until the day he was buried.

This story, together with the one following it, tells of how the wise-woman actively participates in the rescue and cure of a hitherto strong, healthy man who falls prey to a mysterious wasting sickness. In both cases the cure is effected in terms of the administration to the afflicted victim – or rather to the victim's changeling substitute – of a herbal drink made from a herb brought with great difficulty and danger by the wise-woman herself from the graveyard of the next parish. On being restored to his family, the victim, in each of these stories, tells of how he resisted attempts to get him to marry into the fairies while in the otherworld. Though rescued now, in each case the man who was swept carries with him to the grave a severe disablement arising from his experience of abduction and rescue. These stories are two versions of a single tale-pattern. We know that they were recounted three years apart by *Pádraig Ó Murchú* to two different collectors. The differences between the two versions offer clues not only to the social world of the narrator's experience in which the stories are grounded, but also to the central cultural knowledge which the narrator is, in both instances, attempting to represent and to communicate, both in the plot of his tale and in the metacomments with which – on occasion – he accompanies its narration.

The present story features as victim an only son of a farmer who thwarts the young man's ambition to get away to America by pressurizing him into marrying locally at a young age and by handing over to him the family holding and full adult responsibilities. We can note the implied 'peasant-patriarchal' relations between father and son and, of course, between father and daughter, in the account of how the father was solely dependent on his boy – despite having a family of daughters, also – and of how the father successfully held on to him by marrying him off very young without, one presumes, much care for the son's independence or happiness.

The social and imaginative capture of the son by the father, and his imprisonment in a domestic arrangement not of his own making or liking, is not consciously presented to us in the story as the likely cause of the sickness that befalls *Mícheál Ó Gúgáin*. Rather, we are told, when his health fails, 'everyone wondered at what could have come against him', as he seemed very strong and durable. Surely we can surmize here that, in the narrative life of such a story in community performance, this alleged naive bafflement of the neighbours as to the origin of *Mícheál's* affliction, would not be lost on the tale's audience as a kind of negative emphasis on the proper valuation and recognition of individual liberty and worth. In the story, neither doctors nor priests are able to divine the cause of the malady, an inability which results in the resort of the family to the wise-woman. Thus, in the deeper cultural significance of the tale, we are shown the wise-woman – *Máire Ní Mhurchú* – as the one who maintains and proclaims the values of imagination and the sensitivities of the individual psyche, in the face of what could be seen as the connivance and compliance of the medical and clerical professions, along with the neighbours, in the furtherance of the calculating father's wishes.

That such an appeal to the wisdom and vision of the wise-woman is an established part of the narrative repertoire of the storyteller, and his community, is conveyed in the first words attributed to *Máire Ní Mhurchú* here, that '*of course,* it was time for them to come to her'. Very interestingly, she claims that his family and neighbours 'know well' that it is not sick *Mícheál Ó Gúgáin* is at all, but 'swept'. Such a claim by her is an acknowledgement, on the part of the interpretative community of such stories, of the layered nature of consciousness, motivation and understanding. In resorting to the wise-woman, *Mícheál's* family have put themselves in the way of, at least symbolically, understanding his affliction and its therapy. For a limited time they are given – or provide themselves with – the opportunity of rescuing him from his predicament. The 'cure', we are told, consists of a herb that is to be obtained from a graveyard and is, therefore, charged with otherworld associations and otherworld power.

They are, themselves, unable to acquire this cure and must rely on the good offices of the wise-woman, as otherworld intermediary, to act on their behalf and to obtain it for them. This is a difficult and dangerous task, even for the wise-woman intermediary, and the story proceeds by means of the setpiece account of how, having brought the wise-woman to the graveyard in question – across the boundary of the next county and symbolic of the threshold of the otherworld – they have to flee from otherworld pursuers who would prevent their acquiring the cure and who would physically detain the intruding mediator if they could drag her from her pillion seat before the rescue party crosses back – over water – to the safe and human territory of the home county.

It is one of the neighbours whose specific assistance she had requested for the rescue attempt who is most instrumental in bringing the wise-woman safely back from the visit to the graveyard/otherworld wherein she provides herself with the imaginative curative power symbolized in herbal form. This can be taken to represent a communal understanding that *Tadhg Caobach,* the neighbour in question, who holds on to her and to whom she clings during the mounted pursuit and escape, represents symbolically both the generous general imagination of the community, with its feminine as well as its masculine psychic aspects, and the imaginatively alive individual male corresponding to the abused *Mícheál Ó Gúgáin* himself. There is also, of course, a contrasting correspondence with *Mícheál's* imaginatively (and psychically?) moribund father, doctor and priest who fail to address the necessity of imaginative transcendence over the exigencies of property, gender and social standing.

The story that the stricken man relates, on his 'return' from the otherworld, includes the well-known motif of his being warned by a deceased relative whom he encounters there, that if he consumes any fairy food he will be forever trapped in the otherworld. Only by surviving on the scraps that he comes upon during the course of his enforced nightly house visitings with the fairy host – an echo of the journeys with the otherworld host that are attributed to the wise-woman herself – is he able to maintain himself in the face of pressure from the red-haired fairy woman to succumb to her entreaties and eat of the otherworld fare. Were he to do so, we are told, this red-haired fairy woman would have had him entirely for herself. When he persists in resisting her ministration, this female subjects him to physical violence that renders him sightless. In terms of the tale itself, as narrative, and in terms of the significance of the tale for its interpretative community (both in Beara and in its subsequent and contemporary reception), the red-haired woman can be taken to represent the repressed and distorted feminine of the father's psyche as well as being an image of the unwanted and unloved female with whom *Mícheál* is supplied, against his will, by his father. Thus there is symbolic convergence between the illnesses that befall the victim both in his 'real' life and in his 'otherworld' life, a convergence which is, of course, really in the interpretation with which the listeners and readers of *Pádraig Ó Murchú*'s story respond to the incidents that he relates.

The narrator tells us that the male character at the heart of this wise-woman tale – the stricken farmer – attested to the truth of the wise-woman's diagnosis on his release from the otherworld realm. This is an attestation on the narrator's behalf, too, but put into the words of his characters. *Pádraig Ó Murchú* further attests to the veracity of this account of *Máire Ní Mhurchú* in claiming that he was, himself, present at the wake and funeral of *Mícheál Ó Gúgáin*, the chief male protagonist of his story. The establishment of *Ó Gugáin* as an actual flesh-and-blood neighbour of the narrator, provides *Pádraig Ó Murchú* with the opportunity to witness for himself (and on our behalf), the reality of the form of affliction that remained with *Ó Gúgáin* throughout his life and attests, too, to the presence and powers of *Máire Ní Mhurchú* , whose historical, flesh-and-blood existence is, as it were, taken for granted. The community of the narrator's experience did indeed include *Máire Ní Mhurchú*, wise woman, but we can take it that it was in creative imagination and in the therapeutic embodiment of that imaginative energy in narrative performance that she had – and continues to have – her primary existence.

33. **Máire Ní Mhurchú and the young man who was 'swept'-II**[67]

Seán Rua was a farmer and a fisherman – a strong vigorous man. It happened that he fell sick and it was a strange kind of sickness that not one of the doctors was able to cure. He was lying in bed for a long time and he wasn't recovering at all.

One day then, *Máire Ní Mhurchú* came into them and enquired after the man who was sick. They told her how it was with him. Then Máire spoke and she said:

> It's a poor state of affairs with him, the unfortunate. He is quite bad, and he will be too. There is only one thing that would do good for him and that would make him healthy again. That thing is a herb that is growing in *Cill Macallóg* graveyard and it cannot be had except in the dead hour of the night. I am able to get it for him. Now, my friends, if you are satisfied to give it to him, I will bring it here to him – but I will have to get assistance from you.

The family agreed to her request and the assistance she asked for was two horsemen to be ready for her, on horseback, at eleven o'clock the following night. She also wanted the other horsemen of the locality to come along with them because, she said, there was danger and high risk in the work that lay before them.

The following night the horsemen were all ready and waiting for *Máire*. She had no horse but she settled herself as a pillion rider up behind one of them. They set off on the journey at about half past eleven o'clock. When they came to the graveyard *Máire* left them and ordered them to stay where they were until she would come back again to them. She spent quite a long time inside in the graveyard and it was after one o'clock when she returned back to them. She was in a great hurry but the men were ready for her and they moved off on the road without delay. *Máire* ordered them to go as fast as ever their horses' legs would carry them since there was grave danger that they would never get safely to their destination. They went at full gallop but, believe you me, they were followed and those that were following them were going as fast, if not faster, than they were themselves. It is many the attempt that was made between there and back west as far as the border between County Cork and Kerry to capture *Máire* but they all failed. When they had gone across the border *Máire* said that they weren't in any danger any more.

When they arrived at *Seán's* house, *Máire* gave him a kind of drink. After a while he improved a great deal and his speech came back and it is the strange tale that he had to tell to his family. He told them how he had been living in a fairy-dwelling on a wild strand in *Alaithe Thiar* for the past year. It was a beautiful mansion and he had plenty there to eat and to drink. There were living there also, along with him, he said, his own friends and relations who were long dead. Also there, he said, was a young woman – the young woman of the yellow hair he called her – who was all the time urging him to marry her but he wouldn't give in to her entreaties. The food that was there, it is how they used to gather it up for themselves in houses where they would have forgotten to clear off the table after the evening meal. The young woman had come to him that night, he said, when he had finished his supper, and she had gone very hard on him to marry her and, in the end, when he wouldn't give in to her, she had slapped him in the eye with the palm of her hand. From that day out, until the day he died, the unfortunate man was blind in one eye. God save us from the likes of it.

In this second version of the 'young man swept' story we are given no clues, from his social context, as to why the young man should be subject to the 'strange kind of sickness' to which he falls victim and which no doctor is able to cure. In this instance, it is *Máire Ní Mhurchú* who herself comes, one day, to visit the house of the sick man rather than, as in the other version, and in so many other tales of the wise-woman, being sent for. We can see a way of distinguishing, in terms of these two stories, between the sort of affliction which is, in some ways, related to social relationship and to the transactions of social life, and the sort of affliction which appears to be unrelated to human, social action and to arise solely from the operation of otherworld agencies that are the symbolic and mythic representations of the structure and dynamic of the individual psyche. To that extent this version of the story of the 'young man swept' can be compared with the following text recounting how the king's son, *Seán 'ac Séamais,* was abducted by the *cailleach-*goddess *Clíodhna.* In both cases the affliction of abduction appears to arise from a kind of primal imbalance, in the individual character in question, of the gender harmony that is required for human happiness and for harmonious human relationship with that ancestral otherworld (which impinges on human life in ways that are attested to, as here, in legends of the *cailleach* and legends of the wise-woman).

Seán Rua, the sturdy, vigorous farmer cum fisherman, is not seen in this story as having contact with any female partner before his abduction, or after his restoration to his family. While he was in the otherworld – a year he spent in the fairy-mansion on the wild strand (i.e. liminal margin, twilight zone, borderline psychotic state) – he resisted the attentions and the enticements of 'the young woman of the yellow hair' who had consistently attempted to form a relationship with him. His rejection of her – the symbolic refusal of partnership with the feminine in his psychic and imaginative life, as in, evidently, his social life – leads to his going through the remainder of his life as a one-eyed man – an external manifestation of his psychic lopsidedness.

Máire Ní Mhurchú is represented as taking the initiative herself – out of human sympathy and a concern for the well-being of her community – in doing what is required to try and rescue *Seán Rua* from his affliction. The wise-woman is seen in this story as having the awareness – the sensitivity, the psychodynamic insight without active resort to her by the victim's family, of the presence of disharmony and its invaliding consequence. The help which *Máire Ní Mhurchú* proffers to *Seán Rua*'s family to 'do good for him' is the same service which she has in the other 'young man swept' story, performed for the victim of patriarchal abuse in the form of the forced early marriage. In neither instance is her diagnosis, her difficult dangerous journey to the borders of the otherworld and her administration of a sacred therapeutic potion, sufficient to effect a complete 'cure'. In each case the victim is left disabled for life by impairment of sight; the symbolic equivalent of impaired self-knowledge and impaired psychic function. We could surmise that in the case of *Mícheál Ó Gúgáin,* in the first story of the pair, this impairment is the unfortunate consequence of the injurious forcing, by the father, of the son's marriage. In the second story it is the continuing presence of a disorder of psychic harmony in the personality of *Seán Rua*. In both cases, the victim's damaged condition persists despite the intervention of the wise-woman, whose knowledge and powers serve, ultimately, to elucidate and interpret the meaning of human social and psychic experience, rather than provide individual or communal immunity from, or redemptive antidote against, the vicissitudes of the human condition, in either its somatic or symbolic reaches.

It is worth mentioning that *Pádraig Ó Murchú,* the narrator of these two 'young man swept stories', that feature the impairment of vision, was himself, in the aftermath of measles infection, blind. He was in receipt of a blind person's pension, but had sufficient sight to engage to a limited extent in both farming and fishing as means of livelihood. He remained unmarried and cared for by his mother; in turn caring for her, in her old age, when his siblings had all emigrated. In recounting such stories containing the motifs of bachelorhood and blindness, *Pádraig Ó Murchú* did not appear to see them as necessarily relating directly to his own circumstances, if we are to judge by his final utterance in the second version of the story. When he tells us: 'From that day out, until the day he died, the unfortunate man was blind in one eye', he follows it immediately with the comment 'God save us from the likes of it.' We can take it, I would maintain, that the knowledge, performance and transmission of the repertoire of legend – whether of the *cailleach* or of the wise-woman – operated in tradition at an aesthetic and rhetorical level that was at an imaginative remove from the personal and that it was primarily from, and to, communal processes of cultural consciousness that such legends speak. What they say is that experience always has meaning and that that meaning is given, and carried forward, in communally validated and communally accessible ways, in the public performance of oral narrative tradition. The individual lessons to be learned, the application of patterns of communal cultural knowledge to individual cases and individual situations remains unspoken, perhaps unspeakable, in the public domain. Such lessons and such applicability, however, at the individual and private level, can be envisaged as forming the unconscious foundation connecting and bonding the individual imagination with communal cultural knowledge. Modern psychotherapy attempts, among other aims, to stimulate and energize the individual imagination at just this foundational level so that some relief may be obtained, in transaction, from the emotional afflictions that have given rise to the resort to the psychotherapist in the first instance. It would appear that pre-modern vernacular culture in Ireland, shows a grasp of the psychodynamic of therapy, making it available, however, in the public domain of oral narrative performance rather than in the private domain of the professional individual consultation.

34. **Seán 'ac Séamais**[68]

There was a king of Ireland long ago whose name was *Séamas*. He had a son who was known by the name of *Seán Mac Séamais*. There wasn't anywhere, during his time, a finer or a more beautiful prince. One Sunday he was in a crowd who were assembled for dancing. In the course of the day this striking-looking woman went to the king's son and held out an apple to him. He took the apple but his nobility wouldn't allow him to eat it in front of the people's eyes. When she saw that he didn't eat the apple she gave him a small slice of another one. He was too shy to put this into his pocket. He ate it and he was obliged to go along with her because she was an otherworld woman. She brought him off with her and on and on until they were arrived down at *Carraig Chlíodhna*. The woman's name was *Clíodhna* and *Carraig Chlíodhna* was the name given to the place where she lived, down in Cork. She kept *Seán Mac Séamais* there with her under enchantment and his people didn't know what had happened to him or where he was. He himself was deeply troubled and upset and he didn't know what he should do. He wasn't taking any food that was in the place. Instead he ate sorrel and watercress and anything else he could come by. The rock/*Carraig* offered no opportunity of escape at any time from when the sun rose in the morning to when it set in the evening time. One fine evening when the sun had set, the king's son stepped outside with a letter that he had written in blood. He let it off in the wind to see if anyone would come across it and bring news to his father as to where he was. And didn't a cow-herd of his father's find it. When he had read it he went to the king with the letter. The king was greatly astonished to learn where his son was and to know that any one of three women would be able to get him back, namely *Déidbhean*, *Rós Chaoldubh* or *Máirín Dubh* who lived in Dunquin. The call went out to her to come and rescue the king's son. She was sick at the time and she couldn't go along. She had a young daughter, however, who said that she would go instead of her mother.

'It's no good for you to go there', said her mother, 'because you wouldn't be able to do the business.' 'I will make an attempt at it, anyway', said the daughter. 'Very well so', said the mother, 'since you are going to go I will tell you what it is right for you to do.' She brought out a dress of the sort called baft and she put it on her daughter. Then she said to her, 'Go on off now to such and such a place where he is being kept under enchantment. There is no morning of the year when *Clíodhna* isn't outside of that *Carraig* before sunrise, combing her hair. And you must be able to come up to her without her noticing you and catch a twistful of her hair so that she's not able to turn her head one way or the other; because if she lays her eyes on you, you're finished.'

Then when her mother had said her goodbyes and given her blessing, the daughter went off. She never paused in her journey until she came to the right place. And there, sure enough, was *Clíodhna*, outside the *Carraig*, with her tresses of hair undone. *Máirín*'s daughter came at her without her noticing and twisted a handful of her hair and spoke to her like this.

Máirín's daughter:
    '*Clíodhna, Clíodhna,* dear gentle and lady-like woman
    Christ's blessing on you and that of all the saints
    How goes it with *Séan Mac Séamais* here
    Has he married yet or is he still without spouse
    And do you know of any young maiden who makes free with him?'

Clíodhna:
    'Who are you that demands to know
    Are you the *Déidbhean* or *Rós Chaoldubh*
    Or are you *Máirín Dubh* from the far west of Ireland?'

Máirín's daughter:
    'I'm not any one of those at all,
    But the King of Greece's beloved daughter:
    The golden bauble on the warrior's table
    That used renew youth in those grown aged.'

Clíodhna:
    'If you were a king's daughter – and indeed you're not,
    Your hair would be in ringlets to the ground
    Your delicate cheek would be the colour of the red berries
    And golden rings on every one of your fingers.'

Máirín's daughter:
    'If you gave seven years in the dripping grey rock
    With only sorrel and watercress and the green grass to nourish you;
    And, of a grand sunny day, with only the badger up out of the valley
    And the wolf-cub for company,
    You would be more concerned about that

Than about all the rings in Ireland.
Or if that's not the case
Then give him his dowry
Give him seven hundred cows with their seven hundred calves
Seven hundred sheep with their white fleeces bright
And seven hundred horses all of one hue.
Seven hundred perfect, brown, hornless goats
Seven hundred whitebacked long-loined cows
Seven hundred bullocks, their horned heads erect,
Seven hundred barrels of bright, shining silver
Give him seven hundred acres of the holy heavens
And, for my own part, I'd prefer him dead
than to see him married to any otherworld wife.'

Clíodhna:
'If you had kept away from me until it was midday outside
Until my troop could gather themselves together
I would break up the hills and shatter the mountains
I would tear apart the bodies of a great many,
I would pour down blood in bitter streams –
The whole world would hear the dint of it
Or I should have for myself your *Seán Mac Séamais*.'

Clíodhna had to give in and let *Seán* go along with *Máirín*'s daughter back to his father. When they got to the house *Seán*'s father gave him as husband to *Máirín*'s daughter, he was so grateful. *Clíodhna* had to let him be and have nothing to do with him from then on – even though she made up every last bit of the dowry on the spot – except for the seven hundred barrels of shining silver and the seven hundred acres of the holy heavens because she wasn't able to have anything to do with those things.

Some features of this text may be pointed out as suggesting the way in which the figure and the significance of the otherworld female is carried forward by narrative performance into the consciousness of the early twentieth century in a rural, indeed island, community that is still Irish-speaking. The story operates on three levels. Beneath the surface plot that reflects a version of the contemporary world of everyday local life, there exists an older, symbolic world, medieval in character. Deeper again in the text, the performance, and the significance of this legend there is a level of imagination that is archetypal in its touching on the fundamental and primal relationships of humans to each other and to the landscape in which they exist as conscious beings.

Clíodhna is an archetypal female otherworld presence in both the learned literature of early medieval Ireland and the vernacular narrative traditions of the early modern and modern eras. Cross and Slover[69] have a translation by Whitley Stokes of a text featuring her that was copied into the Book of Leinster in the twelfth century. In this text we read that *Clíodhna*, having fallen in love with *Aonghus* of *Brú na Bóinne* at Newgrange, leaves her otherworld dwelling to sail to her beloved in a boat of bronze. Put into a magic sleep by a musician and cast up in the boat on the shore at *Cuan Dor* (Glandore), she is drowned there when a great wave floods the harbour. From her, we are told, *Tonn Clíodhna*/'Chlíodhna's Wave' – one of the three great flood-waves of Ireland – is named.

In another medieval story[70] she is wooed out of the otherworld by the human *Ciabhán* who brings her to Glandore harbour in his boat and leaves her sleeping there while he goes inland to hunt. While she lies sleeping in the boat, the great flood-wave rises and drowns her and, again, she gives her name ever after to the surge-flood that occurs in that place. In both tales we are told how this otherworld female paragon of beauty arrives at the liminal edge of the human world in the cause of love, and is overwhelmed there, in sleep, so as to remain forever embedded into ancestral knowledge of physical landscape.

In later vernacular culture, *Clíodhna* is very prominent as the chief otherworld female of County Cork tradition. She is associated with prominent landscape features and with two prominent Cork lineages. The landscape features are two rocks – each called *Carraig Chlíodhna* – one near the shore at Rosscarbery, the other, inland, to the south of Mallow. The two lineages with whom *Clíodhna* is associated in tradition are those of the MacCarthys and the O'Keeffes and for both of whom she represents the sovereignty principle. A widespread legend[71] that connects her to one of the Fitzgeralds – a Norman rather than a Gaelic lineage – shows renewal at work in the application of the otherworld female lover theme to an actual historical event of the eighteenth century: the real-life sudden death of John Fitzgerald, Knight of Glin, who was taken mysteriously ill at Youghal during a celebration of his engagement to Isabel Butler. Tradition holds that this death was an instance of abduction.

The legend presented here tells of the abduction into *Carraig Chlíodhna* of a *Seán Mac Séamais* and his restoration to the human realm through the good offices of a wise-woman and her daughter, who engages in poetic contest with *Clíodhna* and thereby wins him back from the otherworld. In this version *Seán Mac Séamais*, while present at a dancing assembly, does not appear to be attached yet to any woman in particular. His beauty and his excellence render him attractive to all and, no doubt, vulnerable, to the attention of the supernatural female who is identified for us in the story itself as *Clíodhna* of *Carraig Chlíodhna* in County Cork. (This is most likely the *Carraig Chlíodhna* of the parish of Kilshannig near Mallow although the location of the *Carraig* is not, in the case of this text, germane to the significance of the story.) As in the other versions of this legend, it is the young daughter of a wise-woman or traditional healer, who actually goes to confront the otherworld female and wins back *Seán Mac Séamais* from her.

In terms of plot we have the following *dramatis personae* presented to us: a king; his son; a young woman from the otherworld; a cowherd; a wise-woman; the daughter of the wise-woman. We can pair the king and his son with the wise-woman and her daughter, and can produce another intergenerational pair from the figure of *Clíodhna* in that she is presented to us both as an ancient and mature presence in the *Carraig* landscape while appearing at the dance-assembly, from which she steals the young man, as a young and attractive female. This kind of splitting metaphor can be extended to the wider circle of the plot that includes both the father and the spouse of the man *Seán Mac Séamais*. The story opens with the presentation to us of the king, *Séamas,* and his male offspring, without any mention of a wife or mother relationship for either of them. The absence of the feminine in their lives is thus very pointed and pronounced and, in the symbolic and archetypal scale of things, invites or attracts the encounter with the supreme or otherworld feminine in a sort of cosmic compensation. This encounter takes place on the site of the usually innocent coming together of the sexes in the dancing assembly. When word arrives to the king via the cow-herd – who can be taken to represent a source of experiential knowledge of the sacred female aspect of cosmic power as located in the animal kingdom – the king himself seems to grasp that the source of a restoration or healing of the affliction that masculinity has suffered (in the persons of his son and himself), lies in resort to the type of wise, independent, human female that *Máirín Dubh* represents. *Máirín Dubh* and the other two females mentioned are human women who, by virtue of their independence are able to 'bring home' (i.e. to restore to the proper human order of things), the representative male who has been enchanted – out of life and into the landscape – as a consequence of the unbalanced relationship of male and female in the life of the king, where the feminine is not so much absent as absorbed to the point of disappearance in an overweening masculinity.

Máirín Dubh is unwell when word reaches her that she is wanted for the task of winning back the king's son. We may interpret this unwellness in at least two ways. Firstly, it is a mark of injury to the feminine which flows in the human kingdom from the condition of the king and his son and their excessive masculinity. The other two named, wise and independent women who could help are in fact rendered unavailable, while the one remaining to whom the king has access is damaged or handicapped and unable to spring fully into action, sending her unadorned and plainly dressed daughter in her stead. Alternatively, it is possible to understand the unwellness of *Máirín Dubh* as being related to her as a mother, as being a special female connected related to child-bearing, a weakness which is, in reality, a source of the extra strength and extra power of the feminine. The splitting of the feminine in the case of *Máirín Dubh* and her daughter, because it is somehow more in the order of things (biologically, archetypally), can have the successful outcome of the restoration of the king's son to the human world and the human household (*tigh*) where he is joined in marriage to the female equivalent of himself as offspring. In his first existence as unprotected male offspring of a solipsistic masculinity, the king's son was vulnerable to the attentions of *Clíodhna* whose carrying him off to the otherworld realm where the feminine is sovereign, is a kind of cosmic retribution for the absence, or absorption to absence, of the feminine in the human world represented by the king, *Séamas,* and his alter ego son, *Seán*. In this, our last story, the figures of the sovereignty goddess and the human wise-woman combine to bear joint witness to the importance in Irish oral tradition of the articulation, in narrative form and performance, of the presence in Irish vernacular cultural heritage of autonomous feminine authority and wisdom.

PART THREE

Scéalta i dtaobh Cailleach Bhéarra agus i dtaobh Mná Feasa

Preface

This Part contains the Irish-language texts of the stories presented and translated in Part Two. It includes, for completeness sake, the texts of stories that are are only partially in Irish or that contain no more Irish than the personal names of the characters involved. The order in which the stories are presented is the same in each section. Information regarding the sources of the texts will be found in the notes to Part Two as the various stories make their appearance there, in translation.

It will be obvious below that the texts in Part Three that are taken from the manuscript archive of *Coimisiún Béaloideasa Éireann*, The Irish Folklore Commission, vary in details of spelling and orthography in accordance with diversity of dialect and the individual conventions of transcription adopted by the field collectors. While some small number of silent editorial emendations have been made, in places, to aid comprehension, no attempt has been made to standardize either the text or the editorial practice of its presentation. These texts are, after all, representatives of *oral* narrative tradition and, in any case, a translation has been provided for readers whose command of Irish might not extend to coping with divergences from today's written standard Irish in terms of the regional dialect features and the personal ideolects of the Irish speakers from whom these stories were obtained in the first place.

An example of the kind of editorial problem that has been left unresolved in these Irish texts is to be seen in the case of the story of '*The Woman who used to see the "fairies"* (story 17 of Parts Two and Three). It will be noted that P Ní L is described in the translation as being 'aged and wise'. Here I am attempting to render the meaning of two separate Irish words – the adjectives *críon*, 'old', 'withered' and *críonna*, 'wise' 'shrewd' – in a situation where the manuscript has *críona*. The orthographic and semantic ambiguity that remains should not, I believe, detract from the reader's ability to comprehend the significance which the story accords P Ní L.

These texts as presented here, are offered in the first place, as valuable witness in their own right, of the presence of the *cailleach* and the *bean feasa* in the creativity of oral narrative and of imaginative life within Irish folklore and tradition.

Scéalta I dTaobh Cailleach Bhéarra

Comharthaí soirt ar an mbaineannacht a bheith i gcroílár na cruinne

1. An Chailleach Bhéarthach agus fuacht luan Bhealtaine
Bhí bean fadó ánn a dtugaidís a' Chailleach Béarrthach uirthe. Bhí sí an-tsean agus shiúil sí go leór d'Éirinn. Bíot sí a' coinneál i gcúnaí stoc mór beithíoch, agus bhíot gabhairaicí amanntaí agus is dóichí go ru caora' aici. Ach bíot sí ag imeacht ó áit go h-áit leis na beithí, agus ó chúndae go cúndae eile; agus ní ru sí 'fanacht mórán achair i n-áit ar bith áithrid ach ag imeacht a' siúl roímpi i gcúnaí. An áit a dtagach na beithí ina chéile ins an oíche, chuile thráthnúna a ndianaidís aon chárnán amháin leis a' trathnúna i dteannta chéile, ní fhanat sí mórán achair a' bith ins an áit sin ná ar a' gcroc sin. Ach bhí sí a'siúl léithí nú go dtáinic sí faoi dheire i n-áit a dtugann siad Croc Néifinn air, i gCúndae Fuigheó, agus sheol sí amach a cuid beithíoch ar maidin agus nuair a tháinic a' trathnúna ní ru an dárna ceann go na beithí i n-éineacht: bíodar sgaipithe anúnn agus análl, agus an áit a rudar, chaon cheann acab, ar feadh a' lae níor chorruíodar as ins an oíche. Bhí an oiread rite acab agus nár mhath leóthab níos mo siúil a dhiana an tráthnúna sin ná 'thíocht i dteánnta 'chéile. Agus d'fhan an chailleach ag bun Chnoc Néifinn blianta fada, agus í fhéin agus na beithí i ndiaidh an lae sin. Ach bhí fear ins an áit agus ba mhaith leis sgéalta nuai agus tuairisgíochaí fháil ar níthe go leór ón gcailleach, mar bhí 'fhios aige go ru seanachas aici ar chuile shórt agus go ru sí chó sean agus go bhfaca sí agus go gcuala sí agus go ru fios aici céard a bhain go chuile ní mórán gá ru ann leis na céadta bliain. D'fiarthaí sé dhí a'raibh sí i n-ánn tuairisg a thóirt dó cé an fuacht a bhí i lá tháinic na céadta bliain roimhe sin a bhí an- fhuar. Agus ba dh'é an t-am gon bhliain a dtáinic a' lá sin Luan Lae Bheáltainne, an chéad lá gon tSamhra. Dúirt a' chailleach na'raibh aon tuairisg aici le tóirt dó faoin bhfuacht a bhí ann Luan Lae Bheáltaine, ach é dhol go dtí an t-Iolrach a bhí ina leithide seo g'áit i sean-teach ceártan agus go mb'fhéidir go ru fhios aige sin cén fuacht a bhí

ann; go ru an t-olrach, go ru sé trí chéad bliain ní ba sine ná í fhéin, agus go ru fhios ag an Iolrach go leór thar mar bhí fhios aici fhéin.

D'imigh leis agus níor stop sé aríú go ndeacha sé go dtí an sean-teach ceártan, agus bhí an t-Iolrach ann roimhe. Labhair sé leis an Iolrach agus d'fhiarthuí sé dhe an ru sé i n-ann innseacht dó cén fuacht bhí ann Luan Lae Bheáltaine nach dtáinic aon lá aríú ó shoin bhí chó fuar leis, agus bhi sé na céadta bliain ó bhí an lá sin ann.

'Tá mise annseo', dúirt a' t-Iolrach, 'le seacht gcéad bliain', adeir sé, 'Bhí an inniún seo ins a' gceárta,' adeir sé, 'nua, agus bhí an adhairc bhí ar an inniún', adeir sé, 'bhí sí chó ramhar le aon adharc bhí ar aon inniún cheártan aríú ... Nuair a d'ithinn mo bhéilí,' adeir a' t-Iolrach, 'chuimlínn mo ghob gon adharc – na h-inniún – ar achan taobh anúnn's análl, a'glanadh mo ghoib, agus tá sí anois chó caol, chó caithte á'm a' cuimilt mo ghoib dhi th'réis mo bhéilí ó shoin agus go bhfuil sí chó caol le biorán beag. Níl aon tuairisg agam cén fuacht a bhí ánn,' adúirt a' t-Iolrach. 'Bhí sé na céadta bliain ánn rúm. Ach téirigh' adúirt an t-Iolrach, 'go dtí Mada Uisce na Carraige agus b'fhéidir go n-innseót sé sin duit nú go mbeadh tuairisg aige cén fuacht a bhí i Luan Lae Bheáltaine.

D'imigh leis agus chuaidh sé go dtí Mada Uisge na Carraige agus bhí Mada Uisge na Carraige roimhe. D'fhiathraí sé gon Mhada Uisge 'raibh sé i n-ánn innseacht do cén fuacht a bhí i Luan Lae Bheáltaine thainic fadó.

'Tá mise 'luighe ar an gcarraig seo', adúirt a' Mada Uisge, 'le cúig céad bliain, agus tá an charraig caithte agam síos chomh domhain agus nach bhfuil aon bhlas dhíom le feiceáil aníos ar aon taobh gon charraig 'bhfuil mé 'mo luighe uirthe tá sí chomh caithte sin agam. Agus níl aon tuairisg agam le tóirt duit air. Ach téirigh go dtí Bradán Caoch an Easa Rua agus mara bhfuil aon tuairisg aige sin le tóirt duit faoi fhuacht Luan Lae Bheáltaine, ní mheasaim go bhfuil aon tuairisg le fáil agat air.

D'imigh leis agus níor stop sé aríú go ndeacha sé go dtí an t-Eas Rua, agus bhí an Bradán ann. Ghlaoí sé ar an mBradán agus tháinic an Bradán chuige agus d'fhiathraí sé dhe an ru sé i n-ann innseacht dó cén fuacht a bhí i Luan Lae Bheáltaine.

'Tá mé in n-ánn é sin innseacht duit', adeir an Bradán. 'Bhí mise annseo', adúirt a' Bradán, 'san áit chéanna a bhfuil mé anois, san Eas Rua, agus d'éirí mé go léim as an abhainn annseo a' breith ar chuileog. Agus idir m'éirí agus shul a dtáinic mé anuas aríst, bhí leic oidhre chomh láidir ar an abhainn annseo agus gur choinní sí suas mé nuair a thit mé, agus d'fhan mé titithe annsin ar an leic oidhre nú gur tháinic faoilleán agus gur bhain sé an tsúil asam agus gur thosaigh fuil a' tíocht as mo chloigeann ar áit na súlach, gur leágh an fhuil a' leic oidhre agus go ndeacha mé síos aríst ins an uisge. Agus sin é an fuacht a bhí i Luan Lae Bheáltaine.

2. Cioth cloch na Caillighe Béarra

Tá dá chnocáin thuas sa bPoll, tamhnach sléibhe i n-íochtar pharóiste Magh-Culainn. Tá carnán mór clocha leath mhór ar bárr leathcheann acab. San tsean aimsir nuair a bhí an Chailleach Béarra 'na mhaith, thárla clampar idir í féin agus cailleach oil-bhéasach eile a bhí inann urchar cloiche a chur abhaile chó maith lé fear a' bith sa'n aimsir sin.

Ar chuma a' bith tharrnuigheadar cárnán clocha ar bhárr chaon chnocán acab seo tráthnóna amháin agus bhí siad lé tosuigh a speireadh a chéile lá'r na bhárach.

Le breacadh an laé d'eirigheadar agus thosuígheadar a chaochadh a chéile i ngan fhios go mhuintir a'bhaile a bhí na gcodhladh dóib héin. Bhíodar a gabháil dhá chéile gan fhios cé aige a mbheadh an buadh nó gur thosuigh an Chailleach Bhéarra a chur a cuid clocha fhéin i bfad taobh thiar go'n chailleach eile. Bhí an chailleach eile a gcomhnidhe, ag iarradh an Chailleach Bhéarra a dhonúghadh agus a bhualadh 'chaon lindéar uirra a bhí a' baint osnáighíl ó chroídhe aiste. Bhí an oiread sin cúthach uirra nach dthug sí faoi deara go raibh a cuid clocha go léir caithte aici agus iad thall ar chnocán na Caillighi Bhéarra. Nior thuig sí an cleas a bhí ag an gCailleach Bhéarra nuair a bhí sí a' caitheadh a cuid clocha féin siar thart'se agus iad a' tuitim síos as a sroicheachtáil lé fánadh an ghleanna. Sé an cleas a bhí ag an gCailleach Bhéarra ná ag iarradh cnocán na caillíghe eile a fhágáil bán gan aon chloch.

Nuair a fuair sí an sgéal mar sin d'ionnsuigh sí an chailleach eile agus bhí sí dhá dalladh nó go ndearna sí cuailin-cnámh dí ar bhárr an chuic. Nuair a d'éirigh muintir an bhaile ar maidin chonnaiceadar an Chailleach Bhéarra sínte ar bharr a' chnuic agas í a'tabhairt fhola go tiugh. Bhí an chailleach eile curtha aice faoi an gcarnán cloch ar bhárr a' chnuic.

Duine a' bith a thiucfadh tart faoi na bólaíbh sin fós, tá an carnán cloch sin socruigh ar bhárr an chnuic agus níl aon chloch eile i bfoisgheacht tamall maith dhó thar a bhfuil clocha a' dtalamh ann. Níl na clocha a chaith an Chailleach Béarra le fánáidh an chnuic lé feiceál mura sluigthe a tá siad mar is riasg atá ann. Sin é an fáth a bhfuil na clocha ar bhárr an chnuic go dtí an lá atá inniu ann.

Is ó Phádhraic Ó Céidigh, Poll, Magh-Culainn, Co. na Gaillimhe a chuala mé an sgéal seo. 'Sbáin sé dhom iad agus mé in éindigh leis a seoladh a chuid seasgachaí amach ar an gcreathrach.

3. An Chailleach Bhéarthach agus an coisí

Bhí fear fadó ann, le linn an Chailleach Bhéarthach a bheith ina cónaí ag bun Chroc Néifin i gCúndae Mhuigheo agus bhí an fear a' ceapadh go ru sé fhéin ina choisí cho maith agus bhí in Éirinn. Ach bhí fhios aige go ru an Chailleach Bhéarthach, go ru sí rud éin ní b'fheárr ná é, agus rinne sé íntinn a dhul chun cainte leis an gCailleach go dtugat sé ag siúl í go bhfeiceat sé cén siúl a bhí sí i n-ann a dhéana thairis fhéin. Agus tháinic sé faoi n-a déin agus dúirt sé go ro gnótha go Gaillimh aige agus d'fhiartha' sé dhon Chailleach an dtiocat sí i éineacht leis, go mb'fhéidir go dteastóch rud éigin uaithe a cheannacht sa mbaile mór. Dúirt sí go ngabhfadh sí in éineacht leis go Gaillimh, gur thasta' péire cártaí uaithe le haghaidh a cuid olla a chárdáil, agus ó bhí seisean a dhul ann go mbeidíst in éineacht agus go mba mhór an cumhlódar beirt a bheith ag siúl in éineacht thar aon nduine amháin a bheith ag imeacht leis fhéin.

Réitíodar amach iad féin is chuadar an siúl, agus ní achar an-fhada a thóig sé orthab go rabhadar istigh i nGaillimh. D'itheadar a ndínnéar agus cheanna' an Chailleach, cheanna' sí na cártaí. Agus nuair a bhí chuile shórt gur thasta' uathab – rudaí beaga – ceannaith' acab, thrialladar ar ais abhaile arís. Bhíodar ag siúl go tréan sgaithtí, sgaithtí ag rith agus sgaithtí ina sodair, ach ní achar fada go rabhadar annan, 's a bheith ag bun Néifin. Ach tháinic abhainn mhór rompu ar an mbealach. Ní ru na bóithrí ann an t-am sin mar tá ó shoin. Agus casú fear eile dhóib a bhí [ag dul] sa mbealach céanna a rabhadar fhéin ag dul, cuid dhon bhealach. Ach nuair a bhíodar a'teanna leis an abhainn, rith an Chailleach rása agus chroch sí léithi an fear a bhí ina chúmrádaí aici i gcatha an lae faoi 'na h-asgail, agus chua' sí dho léim thar an abhainn. Nuair a bhí an fear a bhí in éineacht léithi i gcatha an lae tagtha thar an abhainn aici faoi 'na hasgail, ní ru an fear eile, ní ru sé i n-ánn a dhul thar an abhainn dho léim chor ar bith, ná leathbhealach. Agus bhí an áit go ru an easa le dhoil thar an abhainn, bhí sé b'fhéidir naoi nó deich go mhílte uatha. Ach bhí an-aithghiorra déanta ag an gCailleach agus ag an bhfear a chroch sí léithe faoi 'na hasgail thar an abhainn.

'Cé an t-olc a rinne mise ort', adúirt an fear a d'fhág sí ina diaidh, 'nach dtiúrthá' mé fhéin thar an abhainn chomth maith leis a' bhfear eile?'

'Ní dhearna tú olc ar bith orm', adúirt sí, 'ach bíodh sin agus siúd i n-aghaidh a chéile.' D'fhág sí ansin é th'réis nach ndearna sé tada ariamh a chur as di, ach cheap sí ná raibh sé ceart aici a bheith ag déana maith ar chuile dhuine.

Ach nuair a bhí sí ag sgara leis an bhfear a bhí ina chomrádaí aici i gcatha an lae roimhe sin, bhí an Chailleach a goil achar níos fuide ná mar bhí le dul ag an bhfear a bhí in éineacht léithe. Agus bhí fhios aici go math go ru sé buailte suas dhe bharr an tsiúil. D'fhiartha sí dhe:

'B'fhuil mórán ime ag do bhean', adeir sí, 'ins a' mbaile romhat anois?'

'Tá', adeir sé, 'roínt aici; tá cupla croc' ime aici', adúirt sé.

'[Bheul], nuair a ghabhas tú abhaile anocht', adúirt an Chailleach, 'abair le do bhean croc' ime'thóirt léithi agus íoc[h]tar an chroc' a ionntú leis an tine agus béal an chroc' a ionntú ón tine, agus tusa leagan buínn do dhá chois,' adúirt sí, 'ar an ím i mbéal an chroc' agus fanacht mar sin', adeir sí, 'go dí amáireach. Mara ndiana tú sín', adeir si, 'beidh tú cáillte roimhe mhaidean amáireach'.

Rinne sé mar a dúirt a' Chailleach leis. Dúirt sé lena bhean, nuair a tháinic sé isteach, croc' ime a leagan ar an teallach agus béal an chroc' ionntú suas ón tine. Agus bhain sé dhe a bhróga agus a stocaí. Leag sé buínn a dhá chois leis an im i mbéal an chroc'. Agus ar maidin lá arna mhárach ní ru aon bhlas ime dá ru sa gcroc' ná raibh suaithaite ag bunnuíochaí a chos. Agus marat sin, bhí sé caillte go bharr cho trean agus shiúil sé leis an gCailligh i gcaitha an lae roimhe sin.

Tar éis an Chailleach a thíocht abhaile, thug sí léithi canna agus bhlí sí a chuid gabhar agus bhíodar blite, réitithe aici sula ndeacha an ghrian i dtala' ag bun Néifin i gCundae Mhuigheo.

4. Rian na Caillí Béaraighe

Nach iongantach an chaoi nach bhfuil páiste indán siubhal chomh luath agus béurthaidhtear é mar tá an óg go chuile chineál feithide eile. Ní a' cur páiste i gcomórtas le gamhain ná le uan, ach níl ceachtar acu an uair an chluig beirthí nuair atá siad indán siubhal agus tá an páiste dhá bhliadhain – roimh a gcuirfe sé aon chos faoi. Deir siad gur b'í an Chailleach Bhéarra is cionntaigh leis sin. San am gur rugadh páiste éicint, ach níl fhios ámhsa cén páiste é, ach nuair a rugadh é, leag sí a láimh ar chaol a dhroma agus d'fhág san na páistí gan a bheith indán siubhal go luath i ndiaidh iad a theacht ar an saol ó shoin. D'fhág an Chailleach Bhéarra an méid sin orthu.

5. Cailleach Bhéara (Dun Chaoin)

Tá lán trácht ar an gcailligh seo ó Bhéara i mbéaloideas na sean-daoine sa Ghaédhaltacht. Deirtear gur mhair sí ar mullach Chnoc an t-Sídhe. Más fíor gur annsúd a bhí an bothán aici, is a rádh nár séideadh chun súibhail amach go Carraig na n-Ingheanach i n-Inbhear Scéine í, le gaoith agus droch-uain

Bhíodh lé n-ithe aici:

> 'An madhbhán fior-ghlan firinneach ó Fhaoide
> An duileasg ó chuanta Chléire
> An t-iasg ón Leamhain adtuaidh
> Is an chneamh ó Bhealach Bhéimis'

Ní h-iongadh gur mhair si chómh fada, más fíor iad na sgéalta.

Bhí cáil an airgid uirthi leis agus b' fhada leis na daoine ná rabhthas ad'iarraidh é ghoid uaithe, mar bhí daoine ann an uair sin ná beadh abhfad á dhéanamh.

Thuig sí féin é sin cómh maith le h-aoinne, agus cad a dhein sí lá acht dul síos go Scéic i gCuan Leitid agus gleamach a ghoid as pota a bhí ann. Thug sí abhaile 'na h-aprún é agus é 'na bheathaidh agus chuir sí isteach sa bhosca 'na raibh an t-airgead é.

Lá'r na máireach nuair a bhí sí ag cnúsach ar fuaid láithrigh ghaib gaduidhe suas leaca an chnoic agus d'éalaigh sé isteach tríd an bhfuinnéoig i dtig na Caillíghe. Ní fheadfadh sé na pinginí d'aimsiú thíos ná thuas go dtí go bfeacaidh sé an bosca fe'n t-sean leabaidh. Tharraing sé amach é, ní raibh sé ró-mhór acht bhí ana mhéadhchaint ínnti.

'Lán d'ór atá sé, ní foláir,' arsa an gaduidhe. Thug sé fé ndeara go raibh poll cuibheasach mór 'na chliathán.

'Mo thruagh thú, a chaillichín shúghaigh' ar seisean. 'nár chuimhníghis ar an bpoll san a dheisiú acht is olc an ghaoth ná séideann do dhuine éigin.'

Leis sin rop sé a láimh isteach sa pholl, agus thosnaigh sé ag cuardach istigh sa bhosca a'lorg an óir. Cad a dhein an gleamach ach bheir sé ar a láimh idir a dhá chrúibh agus d'fáisc go daingean air.

Ba chuma chonas a iompuigheadh sé n'dfeadfadh sé an greim a baint ná í tarraingt amach. Nuair a bhí an ghrian ag dul fé chas an Chailleach abhaile.

'Tán tú go maith a ghleamaig', arsa sí, 'agus mhairbh sí an gadaidhe lé tuaigh.'

Bua na Fireannachta sa tSaol Sóisialta

6.   A' Chailleach Bheur agus Loch Bà–I

Anns na linntean a dh'aom anns an Ros Mhuileach, bha bean a' còmhnuidh ris an abradh daoine, 'A' Chailleach Bheur'. Cha b'ann do dhaoine an t-saoghail so a bhuineadh i, oir tha e air innseadh dhuinn gu'n robh A' Chailleach Bheur 'na nighinn óig an uair a bha Eubha agus Adamh fhathast a'mealtuinn 'na sìthe anns a' ghàradh, oir 'na facail fhéin, ' 'Nuair a bha muir 'na coille 's 'na críonach, bha mise sin 'nam nìoghnaig òig. Bitheadh sin mar a bhitheas e agus fada uainn bitheadh e teagamh a chur ann, tha e do réir coltais gu'n do sheachainn am bàs A'Chailleach Bheur mar nach do sheachainn e duine riamh roimhpe no as a déidh.

Air an taobh an iar de Mhuil tha lochan bòidheach a'foillseachadh 'uisgeachan gorma do na nèamhan o'n a dh'éireas an ear a'ghrian gus an laigh i an iar 'sa' chuan. Mar is trice tha uisgeachan an locha 'nan laigh gù sèimh, ciùin, gun aon luasgan orra o'n a chuir a'chailleach eòlas air an eilean

Mhuileach an toiseach. Ach, tha an sgeul ag aithris gu'n robh nì aonraichte a'tachair aig Loch Bà a h-uile ceud bliadhna

Mar a ruigeadh a 'Chailleach mu dhà bhliadhna de'n cheud, bha atharrachadh mór a' tighinn air a cruth. Bha i a' fàs sean, liath, glas, crom mar a tha seann daoine eile, ach, eu- coltach ri seann daoine eile, bha e 'na comas i-fhéin a' dhèanadh 'na nighinn oig a rithis gun mhóran dragha dhith féin. 'Se sin nan tumadh i i- fhéin ann an uisgeachan Loch Bà mu'n dèanadh beothach no eun fàilte a chur air éirigh na gréine. An uair a bha ceud bliadhna gu bhith seachad thilgeadh i dhith cruth na h-aoise agus bhitheadh i aon uair eile 'na maighdin mhaisich.

Latha de na làithean, an uair a bha ceud bliadhna ach gann air dol seachad agus a bha a' Chailleach a' mothachdainn gu'n robh i gu math feumach air tumadh 'nan uisgeachan, bha i a'tèarnadh gu math socarach ri taobh Loch Bà agus a'ghrian ag éirigh le a' gathan òr – bhuidhe anns an àird an ear. 'N uair a bha i 'na seasaimh air bruaich an locha agus i-fhein a' dèanamh deas gus i fhéin a thumadh, dé chuala i fad air astor ach tabhann coin, agus mar gura b'ann seadh 's nach seachainneadh am fuaim a' Chailleach, thog mac-talla an gleadhar, agus cho-fhreagair na creagan mu'n cuairt Loch Bà gu h-ard iollagach. Sheas a' Chailleach mar gum b'ann ag éisdeach ris an fhuaim, agus air ball,'n uair a bha an anail 'g a fàgail ghlaodh i gu h-ard ghabh i ceum no dhà o thaobh gu taobh agus a null 's a nall agus thuit i le glag air an làr. 'N uair a bha an anail 'ga fàgail, ghlaodh i gu h-àrd -

'S moch ghoir orm an cù

Orm an cù, orm an cù

'S moch ghoir orm an cù

Maduinn chiùin os cionn Loch Bà

7. A' Chailleach Bheurr agus Loch Bà-II

Nis, creidibh e no na creidibh; ach bha foimhirean ann ans an t-seann shaoghal. Tha'm Biobull ag innse sin dhuinn. Ma sheallas sibh anns an t-siathamh caibideal do Ghenesis, chì sibh ann a sin gu robh foimhirean ann. 's an t-seann shaoghal.

Ach bha aon fhoimhir, cha chreid mi nach e an té ma dheireadh a bh'ann am Muile, do na foimhirean sin, b'e 'Chailleach Bheurr a bha fuireach ann an eilean Earraid ... ris an abair ... 's e eilean Earraid a their sinn ris an diugh. Tha'n t-eilean sin ainmeil gu leòr ann a'leabhraichean Beurla 'nis, ach 's an àm ud cha robh 'fuireach ann ach a' Chailleach Bheurr agus na trì mairt a bh'aice, a bhiodh i ... 'g ionaltradh a chuile madainn. Nis, feumaidh gu robh i fiadhaich mór. Agus tha iad ag radh rinn – thàinig e 'nuas ann am beul-aithris – nach robh ach an aon sùil agus ... nach robh aic' ach an aon sùil agus gu robh i an clàr a h-aodainn.

Ach bha uair a siod agus bh i a' sealltainn a-mach ris an iar, agus thuirt i, 'Nuair a bha 'mhuir na coill 's na craobhaich, bha mise sin 'am nighneig òg'. Nis, nuair a labhradh am boireannach ud – agus 's ann glé ainneamh a labhradh i idir – ach nuair a labhradh i, chluinneadh a chuile duine 's a cheann dùthcha i, agus dh'fhaoite ann an àiteannan eile.

Nis, bi sibh a' smaointinn gu bheil e faoin a' radh ... gu robh 'chailleach fhaoite 'g innse bhriag, gu robh 'mhuir na coill 's na craobhaich dar a bha ise na h-ighneig òig. Ach carson nach creideamaid e? Nach eil e còltach gu leòr? Mur a facaic a chuile h-aon agaibh na sgeirean Torranach, chuala sihb iomradh orra. A' sealltainn a-mach bho eilean Earraid gu rath? na Dubh h-Irtich, tha sgeirean cunnartach a-mach ann a sin, tha sìneadh a-mach seachd mìle deug. Agus anns an t-seann shaoghal, nach fhaodadh na sgeirean a tha sin a bhith 'nam barran chnocan. Monaichean a shìolaicheadh sìos le criththalmhainn na rud air choireigin mar sin. 'S chan urrainn dhuinn a' radh nach robh 'Chailleach Bheurr ceart nuair a thuirt i, 'Nuair a bha 'mhuir na coill 's na craobhaich, bha mise sin 'am neighneig òg'.

Ach bha aon rud crochta ris a' Chailleach Bheurr. An ceann a chuile ceud bliadhna, dh'fheumadh i i fhéin fhailceadh ann an Loch Bà, shuas aig ceann eile Mhuile. Chuala sibh air fad iomradh air Loch Bà. 'S e loch bhòdhach a th'ann, agus i glé fhad agus domhain. Agus dar a gheibheadh i 'failceadh, daonnan anns a Chéitean – cho luath 's a gheibheadh i 'failceadh – dh'ath-shnuadhachadh a h-óige, agus bha i na h-ighneig òg a' rithist. Nis dh'fhaoite gu bheil sibh 'cuir teagamh ann a sin, ach bheil fhios agaibh-se, 's iomadh rud neònach a tha tachairt anns an t-saoghal agus a thachair ann o shean aig nach eil fios sam bith againn idir ach mar thig e 'nuas ann am beul-aithris.

Bha na trì boin aice agus bhiodh i 'falbh a eilean Earraid 's ga saodachadh troimh Mhuile, a-sìos gus a' ruigeadh i Maol Chinn-tìre, chuile latha. Nis feumaich gur e ceumannan fiadhaich fada bhiodh aig a' chrodh a' rachadh a-síos gu Maol Chinn-tìre agus sin thòisicheadh iad air ionaltradh gus am biodh iad air an rathad dhachaidh. Ach cha robh e cho neonach idir, nuair a smaointeachas sibh a seòrsa boirionnaich a bha 's a' Chailleach Bheurr; chionn bha i gearain ma Chrùlachan. 'S aithne dhuibh Crùlachan, chan eil i fada o'n Ghleann Mhóir ann am Muile.

> Crùlachan dubh domhain
> A' loch as doimhne 's an domhain
> Ruigeadh Caol Muile mo ghlùinean
> Ach ruigeadh Crùlachan mo shléisdean.

Sin a' rud a bha i fhéin ag radh. Agus carson nach creid sinn e? Dé fios a th'againne nach robh i fìor?

Nis cha robh ach an aon àite anns am biodh an crodh aig a' Chailleach

Bheurr ag òl uisge nuair bha i air falbh a Muile fhéin. 'S e sin tobar a bha shìos leth a' rathaid gu Maol Chinn-tìre. Chan eil cuimhn 'am gu d'ainm a bh'air, ach co dhiùbh, bha leithid de thobair ann. Agus bha brod mor de chloich . . . de chloich air an tobar agus cho luath 's a ruigeadh i 's a mhadainn, thogadh i'm brod seo airson gu faigheadh an crodh òl nuair a bhiodh am padhadh orra. Ach na fàgadh i am brod far an tobar gus a' rachadh a' ghrian fodha, thigeadh an t-uisge aiste agus chuireadh e tuil thar . . . na domhain air fad. Thaomadh e as an . . . tobar a bha seo, gus an cuireadh e tuil air an domhain air fad. Bha i seo ma tà, aon uair, agus i fàs car sean, 's ì fàs lag, coltach ri boirionnach sean eile. Agus thòisich i air . . . an cadal a' tighinn oirre 's i na suidhe faisg air an tobar. Ach dhùisg i le froineadh. Thàinig ràic uisge searbh as an tobar, agus bha 'ghrian dìreach a' dol . . . sìos, cha robh ach crioman beag dheth 'n uachdar. Ach leum i agus phut i sìos . . . am brod, agus shàbhail i 'saoghal fo thuil. Ach ged a shàbhail i 'saoghal air fad, tha pàirt dheth ann a siod fhathast, agus 's e Loch Obha th'ac' air.

Sin agad . . . sin agaibh a nis mar a bha 'Chailleach Bheurr. Ach an truaghan, thàinig i air a h-aghaidh an uair seo, agus thug i'n crodh do dh'eilean Earraid. Ach bha samhradh a' tighinn; bha'n Céitean ri teachd, agus bha'n t-àm aice tighinn dlùth a' dhol a dh'fhaotainn a failceadh. Nis, dh'fheumadh i bhith air a failceadh mar cluinneadh i comhairt coin agus mu'n cluinneadh i'n t-eun beag a' beagail a's na preaslaichean. Na'n cluinneadh i 'h-aon dhiubh sin, bha i réidh. Dh'fholbh i latha seo agus i 'dol a-sìos a' bhruthaich gu taobh . . . na loch, 's i folbh air a socair fhéi 's bat aice, a' dol 'g a failceadh fhéin. Agus dìreach nuair a bha i aig cois na tuinne, bha cìobair nach robh fad air folbh agus thug an cù aige comhairt. Cha bu luaithe chualaig i 'chomhairt na thuit i 'na cùl-chnàmh. Nis bha fhios aig a'chìobair glé mhath gu robh 'n t-àm aig a' chailleach a bhith 'tighinn a nann agus bhiodh e daonnan a' fiachainn ris a chù 'chumail a-staigh gus a' faigheadh i 'bhith air a failceadh. Ach an oidhche seo bha an cù a-mach agus 's ann leis a sin a chomhairt e nuair a chunnaic e 'chailleach a' dol a-sìos. Agus thuit i na cùl-chnamhach. Ruith an cìobair 'g a . . . 'uice cho luath 's a b'urra' dha, fiach an déanadh e dad air a son. Cha robh i . . . uile gu léir marbh agus bha i 'seinn rithe fhéin oran tiamhaidh, muladach. Agus chan aithne dhomhsa seinn, ach seo car mar a bha e 'dol:

> 'S moch an diugh a ghoir an cù
> Ghoir an cù, ghoir an cù
> 'S moch an diugh a ghoir an cù
> Madainn chiùin os cionn Loch Bà.

Sin mar a bha'n oran a' dol. Bha móran earrannan ann ach b'e sin . . . an ceòl a bh'air.

Nis, duine sam bith nach eil a' creidsinn na sgeulachd sin, chan eil aige ach 'dhol a-suas gu na Barrachan – 's aithne dhuibh air fad na Barrachan – agus iomradh a-suas troimh Abhainn na Slat, agus chì sibh air a' laimh chlì, an staighre bh'aig a' Chailleach Bheurr a' dhol a-suas gu'n àite 's a robh i 'fuireachd. Agus their iad Tobhta na Cailleach Bheurr ris gus an latha 'n diugh.

Nis fhiù 's a tha sibh creidsinn sin na nach eil, chan eil fhios agamsa; ach 's ann mar sin a chuala mi e, agus ma's briag 'uam e, 's briag 'ugam e.

8. Cailleach Ghleanna-na-mBiorach, agus an tarbh dubh

Ann san tsean-aimsir, do bhí cailleach na cómhnuidhe i nGleann-na-mBiorach, i gcondae Chiarraighe. Ní raibh teach ná árus aici, acht poll do bhí faoi bhún carraige móire, ar thaoibh an ghleanna. Bhí sí ann san áit sin le linn an duine is sine ann san gcómharsanacht, agus níor athruigh sí pioc, ar feadh an ama sin. Ní raibh aon tslighe bheatha aici d'á bfacaidh aon neach, agus ní facthas í ariamh péirse ó bheul an phuill, agus ní fhacaidh na daoine biadh ná deoch ag dul chuici, acht bhí tuairim ag gach uile dhuine 'san áit gur cailleach draoidheachta do bhí innti; agus ní rachadh duine ar bith, sean nó óg, dá bhfághadh siad ór agus airgiod, tré Ghleann-na-mBiorach tar éis dorchadais na hoidhche. Ní raibh oidhche 'san mbliadhain nach gcluineadh na daoine tafan mór ann san ngleann, amhail agus dá mbeadh na ceudta madadh ag troid innti.

Aon lá amháin, roimh éirghe na gréine, chuaidh sean-fhear dar bh'ainm Murchadh Ruadh Ó Conchubhair, tré Ghleann-na-mBiorach le punnann choirce do thabhairt do tharbh dubh do bhí aige ar feurach 'san ngleann. Nuair d'fheuch sé ar bheul poill na caillighe, agus é ag gabhail thart, chonnaic sé corr-ghlas agus eascon mhór fhada ann a gob; leig sí do'n eascoin tuitim ag beul an phoill, agus níor bhfada go dtáinig madadh bán amach agus thug an eascon isteach leis. Bhreathnuigh Murchadh Ruadh go raibh ocht gcosa faoi an madadh bán, agus chuir sin iongantas agus eagla mhór air. Dar m'anam', ar sé, 'tá tuairim na ndaoine ceart, is cailleach draoidheachta atá ann san bpoll úd thall.'

Bhí an tarbh dubh ag éisteacht le Murchadh Ruadh ag rádh na bhfocal sin, agus chuir sé a chluasa i n-áirde, rinne géim bheag, agus dubhairt: 'A Mhurchaidh Ruaidh, ná bíodh iongantas ná eagla ort, acht éist le mo bhriathraibh mar tá siad fior. Tá an chailleach liath ann san bpoll sin ó aimsir na bhFear Bolgach [= Bolg], agus is í do chuir an slad mór ar bha [bhuaibh] na tíre; b'éidir nach gcualaidh tú an slad mór do rinne an phláigh cheudna. Níor fhág an phláigh sin tarbh, bó, ná biorach ann san tír, acht mise agus biorach óg do bhí 'san ngleann so, agus is uainn do tháinig an chuid is mó de bha na tíre. Níl acht aon chaoi amháin leis an gcailleach agus a mac, sé sin madadh na n-ocht gcos, do chlaoi. Fágh an oiread de mo bhualtrach-sa agus dheunfas teine mhór, agus nuair bhéas sé tirm agad, deun carnán dé i mbeul puill na caillighe, agus cuir splanc faoi. Beurfaidh sin í féin amach, agus a mac, madadh na n-ocht gcos, léithe. Máthair na caillighe an chorr-ghlas. Seachain thú féin uirri, nó ní fhágfaidh sí súil ann do cheann. Tabhair súiste leat, ná buail an chailleach, acht tabhair faoi an madadh agus faoi an gcorr-ghlas má thagann siad i n-aice leat, agus troidfidh mé féin an chailleach.'

'Mise mo bhannaidhe go ndeunfaidh mé mar deir tú,' ar sa Murchadh Ruadh, 'acht cogair! An innseóchaidh mé do na buachaillibh gur labhair tú liom?' ar seisean.

'Go deimhin is cuma liom', ar san tarbh dubh, 'mar nuair mharbhóchas mé an chailleach liath, a mac agus a máthair, béidh mo theurma saoghalta caithte, acht b'fhearr dhuit féin gan labhairt air.'

Bhí imnidhe mhór ar Mhurchadh Ruadh ag imtheacht abhaile dhó. Ar maidin, an lá ar na mhárach, ghair sé ar a mhnaoi agus dubhairt léithe iasacht súiste d'fhághail dó.

'Cia an graithe [gnó] atá agad le súiste?' ar san bhean, 'níl coirce ná cruithneacht agad le bualadh.'

'Nach cuma dhuit cia an graithe atá 'gam leis, acht fágh dham é.'

D'ith Murchadh a bhéile ann sin, agus 'na dhiaigh sin d'imthigh leis go Gleann-na-mBiorach, agus chruinnigh sé roinn mhór de bhualtrach an tairbh dhuibh, agus chuir sé ar bhárr cloiche móire é le tirmiughadh. Tháinig sé abhaile arís, ann sin, agus d'fhiafruigh de'n mhnaoi an bhfuair sí an súiste. 'Fuaireas,' ar sí, 'tá sé ann san gcoirneul, agus tá mé le na thabhairt ar ais amárach, má bhím beó.' 'Seadh!' ar seisean, 'muna mbéidh sé briste.'

Lá ar na mhárach, chuaidh sé go Gleann-na-mBiorach, agus rinne sé cárnán de'n bhualtrach tirm i mbeul puill na caillighe, agus chuir splanc faoi, agus níor bhfada go raibh sé 'na lasair, agus bhí an deatach ag dul isteach 'san bpoll.

Fuair Murchadh greim ar a shúiste, agus dhruid sé amach ó bheul an phuill, 'san ngleann; agus níor bhfada gur chualaidh sé tafan agus casachta 'san bpoll. Níor bhfada ann sin go dtáinig an chailleach agus an madadh bán amach. Bhí fhios ag an tarbh dubh go rabhadar ag teacht. Tháinig sé ann a láin-rith agus d'ionnsuigh sé madadh na n-ocht gcos. Ghread an chailleach a bosa agus ghlaodh sí: 'Fágh greim air, a choileáin, fágh greim air, nó béidh tú sguabtha, agus mise leat; an tarbh sin atá ann do láthair is [é] Domblas Mór é, námhad láidir, do chongbhuigh mé faoi gheur-chrádh ó aimsir phláighe na mbó.'

'Seadh! a chailleach ghránna, mharbh tú na mílte bó, agus d'fhág tú na ceudta agus na mílte daoine i n-easbhuidh, gan bainne, gan feóil', ar san tarbh dubh.

Rinne an madadh léim ann sin, agus shaoil sé greim sróna d'fághail ar an tarbh, acht chuir an tarbh a dhá adhairc faoi, do chaith sé suas 'san aer é mar do chaithfea meuróg laimhe, agus nuair bhí sé teacht anuas, tharraing Murchadh an súiste agus bhuail sé buille air idir an dá shúil, agus sgoilt sé a chloigionn. Acht ní raibh madadh na n-ocht gcos marbh. D'ionnsuigh sé an tarbh an dara uair gus shaoil sé a thabhairt go bruach an phuill, acht bhí an tarbh ró ghlic dó, thug sé árdughadh eile 'san aer dó, níos áirde 'ná an cheud cheann, agus nuair bhí sé teacht anuas bhí Murchadh réidh le buille eile do thabhairt dó, acht mar bhí sé ag tarraingt na buille tháinig an chorr-ghlas agus shaoil sí gob 'san tsúil do thabhairt dó, acht ní ann san tsúil bhuail sí é, acht ar a chlár-eudain, agus chuir sí ar a thárr-anáirde é. Rith an chailleach agus fuair greim air, agus bhí d'á chrathadh agus d'á thachtadh, gur shaoil sé go rachadh an t-anam as. Bhéadh sé marbh aici acht go dtáinig an tarbh dubh, agus thug sé buille coise do'n chailligh, do chuir go dtí an taobh eile den ghleann í. D'fhill sí arís go tapa, agus dubhairt leis an tarbh dubh, 'Fág an cath idir mé féin agus Murchadh.'

'Tá mise sásta', ar sa Murchadh, 'acht fuair tú buntáiste orm, nuair bhí mé ar lár le buille ghuib ó do mháthair draoidheachta.' Leis sin tharraing sé an súiste agus bhuail í ann san gclár-eudain, gur chuir sí sgread aiste gur cluineadh seacht míle ó'n ngleann í. Bhí madadh na n-ocht gcos sínte, amhail mar bheadh sé marbh, acht nuair chualaidh sé sgread na caillighe d'éirigh sé, agus thug léim, agus fuair greim sgórnaighe ar Mhurchadh, agus bhí 'gá thachtadh, go dtáinig an tarbh dubh le na bheul fosgailte, fuair greim ar an madadh, agus rinne minmhidirlíni(?) de gach uile chnámh ann a chorp. 'Bheirim buaidh agus mo sheacht míle mallacht leis, duit', ar san chailleach, agus thuit sí marbh ós cionn madaidh na n-ocht gcos. Tháinig an chorr-ghlas ag screuch' go hárd, agus thug sí iarraidh ar Mhurchadh, acht bhí sé ar a choimhéad, agus bhris sé a muinéal le buille de'n tsúiste, agus thuit sí marbh ar mhullach na beirte eile.

'Dar m'fhocal is maith an laoch thú,' ar san tarbh, 'lean mise agus taisbéanfaidh mé ciste óir agus airgid duit'.

Lean Murchadh é isteach i bpoll na caillighe, agus a leitheid d'amarc ní fhacaidh súil ariamh roimhe. Bhí bord mór de'n ór buidhe i lár an tseomra, agus carnán de phíosaibh óir agus airgid air. 'Anois,' ar san tarbh dubh, 'beir leat an oiread de'n ór agus de'n airgiod agus bhéas ag teastáil uait féin ar feadh do bheatha, agus má chuireann aon duine ceist ort d'á thaoibh, abair gur dhíol tú mise ar luach mór, óir ní fheicfidh aon duine mé ó'n lá so amach.'

'Go deimhin tá brón orm faoi sin, ba mhaith an caraid thú, acht ó tharla nach bhfuil neart air, bheirim mo mhíle beannacht duit', ar sa Murchadh.

'Tá sporán leathair faoi an mbord, líon é go tapa, agus bí 'g imtheacht,' ar san tarbh dubh.

Rinne Murchadh amhlaidh, agus nuair tháinig sé amach, thuit carnán ithire síos i mbeul an phuill agus[do] dúnadh é.

Bhí sé mall 'san lá nuair tháinig Murchadh abhaile. Bhí buailtín an tsúiste briste. 'Cia an áit a raibh tú, nó cia an chaoi ar bhris tú buailtín Pháidín Sheumais?' ar san bhean.

'Bhris mé an buailtín ag bualadh mo thairbh dhána: tháinig tighearna as Connacht, agus dhíol mé mo tharbh leis tá mé ró shean agus ró lag le smacht do chur air.'

'Cia an luach fuair tú air?' ar sise.

Tharraing sé amach an sporán mór, agus dubhairt. 'Féach, tá an sporán so líonta le ór agus le airgiod. Sin an luach is mó fuair fear ar tharbh ariamh.'

'Grádh mo chroidhe thú', ar sise, 'támaoid saidhbhir go bráth.'

Chaith Murchadh agus a bhean beatha shona 'na dhiaigh sin, acht nuair bhí fhios aige go raibh an bás i bhfogus dó, chuir sé fios ar charaid, agus d'innis an sgeul dó ó thús go deireadh. Chuaidh an sgeul ó bheul go beul, go bhfuair mo mháthair mhór é, agus is uaithe fuair mise é.

9. An Chailleach Bhéarach agus Donnchadh Mór Mac Mánais

Ann san tsean-aimsir tháinig cailleach agus a hinghean léi go Gleann-na-Madadh [i gconndae na Gaillimhe].

Ní raibh fhios ag duine ar bith cia an áit a dtáncadar as, agus níor cuireadh aon tuairisg orra.

Bhí go leór saidhbhris ag an gcailligh, agus níor bhfada gur thaisbeán sí sin. Cheannuigh sí teach mór, gabháltas talmhan, capaill, ba agus caoirigh, agus thosuigh sí ag feilméaracht. Ní ghlacfadh sí aon bhuachaill aimsire acht an té do shocróchadh léi ar feadh leith-bhliadhna, agus ní raibh aon pháidhe aige le fághail ag deireadh na leith-bhliadhna muna mbeadh sé i ndan congbháil suas leis an gcailligh anns gach obair dá mbeadh i láimh aici, agus ní raibh aon bhiadh le fághail aige acht arán min-choirce, brochán, agus leite.

Anois ba chailleach draoidheachta an chailleach Bhéarach, agus níor fheud aon bhuachaill aimsire congbháil suas léi ag obair, agus is iomdha buachaill breágh do mharbh sí. Níor fheud aon bhuachaill fanacht l'ei an dara seachtmhain, théigheadh siad abhaile agus gheibheadh siad bás.

Aon lá amháin chualaidh Donnchadh Mór Mac Mánais trácht mór ar an gcailligh, – nach raibh aon fhear san tír i ndan congbháil suas léi ag obair, agus dubhairt sé go mba shuarach na fir do bhí ann san tír, nuair nár fheud siad congbháil suas le sean-chailligh ag obair. 'Rachaidh mise chuici amárach', ar seisean, 'agus muna mbuailead í báithfead mé féin.' Anois bhí an Donnchadh so chomh láidir le stail agus chomh luath-chosach le fiadh, agus ní raibh margadh ná aonach nach nglanfadh sé le plannda fuinnseóige dá mbeadh fearg air, agus is annamh théigheadh sé i n-áit ar bith gan an plannda.

Ar maidin, lá ar n-a mhárach, chuaidh Donnchadh mór go tigh na caillighe agus dubhairt sé léi go gcualaidh sé go raibh sí ag tóraidheacht buachaill-aimsire.

'Tá easbhaidh buachall' orm', ar sí, 'acht níl aon mhaith ann sna buachaillibh atá ann san áit seo, ní fiú a gcuid salainn iad; bhí go leór aca do shocruigh liom ar feadh leith-bhliadhna, acht níor fhan aon fhear amháin aca liom an dara seachtmhain.'

'Cuirfidh mise mo bheatha leat anaghaidh caora ramhair' go bhfanfaidh mé leat leith-bhliadhain má thugann tú páidhe mhaith dham, agus mo sháith le n'ithe', ar seisean.

'Deunfaidh mé an margadh céadna leat-sa do rinne mé leis na buachaillibh eile,' ar san chailleach.

'Cad é sin?' ar sa Donnchadh Mór.

'Trí fichid píosa deich bpighne, agus an oiread céadna mí an fhóghmhair, agus caora ramhar lá Samhna, má tá tú i ndan a caitheamh thar balla na páirce an lá sin; acht muna dtig leat congbháil suas liom ag obair, ní bhéidh aon pháidhe agad le fághail.'

'Saoilim gur ag magadh fúm i dtaoibh na caorach ramhair' atá tú,' ar sa Donnchadh, 'acht ó thárla gur magadh é, deun magadh maith dhe, abair scór caora, agus deunfad an margadh leat.'

Cidh gur cailleach draidheachta bhí innti, níor shaoil sí go bhfeudfadh aon fhear san domhan caora ramhar chaitheamh thar balla cloiche do bhí fiche troigh ar áirde; ar an ádhbhar sin dubhairt sí, 'Bíodh sé' na scór, agus rud eile', ar sise, 'bhfuil fhios agad an biadh gheobhfas tú le n'ithe ann mo thigh-se?'

'Go deimhin níl fhios', ar seisean, 'níl mo ghoile mór, ní deacair mo shásughadh'.

'Gheobhaidh tú leite min-choirce, arán agus brochán, agus feóil mhuice Dómhnach Cásga.'

'Tá mé sásta leis an margadh sin', ar seisean, 'agus tiucfad chugad ar maidin amárach má bhím beó'.

Chuaidh Donnchadh abhaile agus d'innis sé d'á mháthair an margadh do rinne sé leis an gcailligh. 'A chuisle mo chroidhe,' ar san mháthair, 'is mí-adhamhail an chailleach í sin, ní dheachaidh aon bhuachaill ar aimsir chuici nach bhfuil san uaigh anois.'

'Feicfidh tú féin a mháthair go gcuirfidh mise síos í roimh mí o'n lá so. Chualaidh mé go minic gur fearr stuaim 'ná neart, agus tá neart agus stuaim agam-sa.'

Ar maidin, lá ar n-a mhárach, chuaidh Donnchadh go tigh na caillighe. Nuair bheannaigh sé isteach bhí mias leite ar an mbord, agus dubhairt sí leis, 'Suidh síos agus ith, ní thig le bolg folamh obair chruaidh a dhéanamh.'

Shuidh Donnchadh, acht níor ith mórán. Tháinig inghean na cailighe i láthair, agus bhí gnúis uirri chomh gránna leis an mbás. Acht thosuigh Donnchadh d'á moladh, agus dubhairt go raibh an t-ádh air seirbhís d'fhághail san tigh a raibh cailín deas mar í ann!

'Bí do thost,' ar sise, 'b'éidir go bhfuil mo mháthair ag éisteacht.'

'Dá mbeadh an poball ag éisteacht, mholfainn cailín deas,' ar seisean.

Níor bhfada go dtáinig an chailleach, agus dubairt,

'Teanam, rachamaoid ag rómhar conlaigh indiú.' Chuadar amach 'san bpáirc, agus thosuigheadar ag rómhar. Thug an chailleach leath-iomaire i dtosach, agus Donnchadh leath-iomaire 'na diaigh. Níor bhfada go raibh an t-allus ag rith as Donnchadh Mór. Chongbhuigh sé suas léi fad an lae, acht níor oibrigh sé aon lá ariamh chomh cruaidh, agus bhí sé beag-nach marbh tráthnóna.

Bhí sé ag brath ar éalódh abhaile an oidhche sin, agus d'imtheóchadh, muna mbeadh inghean na cailighe. Nuair fuair sise faill ar a máthair, d'fhiafruigh sí de Dhonnchadh cia an caoi chuaidh sé ar aghaidh ar feadh an lae. D'innis sé dhí nach bhfanfadh sé fad lae eile, acht go raibh sé i ngrádh léi féin. Dubhairt sise má bhí seisean i ngrádh léi go raibh sise i ngrádh leisean, agus dubhairt sí dá bhfanfadh sé nach mbeadh aon obair chruaidh air níos mó, agus go ndéanfadh sí é chomh láidir le leómhan.

Bhí cú dubh ag an gcailligh, agus cia bé d'ólfadh bainne an chú[na con] bheadh sé chomh láidir le trí fichid fear. Ar maidin, lá ar n-a mhárach, do fhliuch an inghean arán Dhonnchaidh le bainne an chú, agus nuair chuaidh sé ag rómhar leis an gcailligh an lá sin d'fheud sé congbháil suas léi go réidh. An dara lá bhí sé níos láidre, agus an tríomhadh lá d'fheud sé an chailleach do bhualadh, gan dochar ar bith do chur air féin. Bhíodh sé ag éirghe níos láidre ó lá go lá agus bhíodh iomaire faid na páirce rómhartha aige sul do bheadh an chailleach leath bealaigh. Bhíodh sise ar mire agus ag fághail lochd ar a láidhe chuile lá.

Chuaidh sí go gabha draoidheachta agus dubhairt leis láidhe úr do dheunamh dí. Rinne sé sin, acht níor fheud sí Donnchadh do bhualadh le láidhe ar bith, mar bhí an inghean ag fliuchadh a chuid aráin le bainne an chú dhuibh, agus bhí sé ag éirghe níos láidre chuile lá.

Aon uair amháin bhíodar ag rómhar le chéile ann san bpáirc agus chuaidh Donnchadh amach roimh an gcailligh, agus chuir sin fearg uirri. 'Congbhuigh taobh shiar díom', ar sise.

'Ní chongbhóchad', ar seisean, 'muna bhfuil tú i ndan congbháil rómham tabhair tosach dam'.

'Níor thug mé tosach d'aon fhear ariamh, agus níl tusa dul d'á fhághail uaim', ar sise.

'Fan mo dhiaigh,' ar sa Donnchadh

Leis sin tháinig lasadh feirge uirri, agus thug sí iarraidh ar bhuille de'n láidhe do thabhairt dó, acht fuair seisean greim ar chois an láidhe, tharraing uaithe é, agus chaith sé seacht bpéirse taobh amuigh de'n pháirc é. Ann sin fuair sí greim sgórnaigh air, agus thug iarraidh le na thachtadh. Chuir seisean í faoi, acht níor fheud sé an greim do bhí aici ar a sgórnach do sgaoileadh, agus bhí sé tachttha aici go cinnte, acht go dtáinig an inghean go díreach i n-am le na shábháil, agus sgaoil sise greim na caillighe. Rinne sí síothcháin idir an mbeirt, agus thug sí an mháthair abhaile léi.

'Na dhiaigh sin chuadar ar aghaidh go maith go dtáinig aimsir bainte an fhéir. Ghleus an chailleach speal dí féin, agus ghleus Donnchadh ceann eile. Tráthnóna Dia Dómhnaigh dubhairt an chailleach 'Béimid ag spealadóireacht amárach'. 'Maith go leór', ar sa Donnchadh, 'táim réidh.'

An oidhche sin dubhairt inghean na caillighe le Donnchadh, 'Táir [tá tú] dul ag spealadóireacht amárach, agus tabhair aire dhuit féin. Cuirfead spící cliath [cléithe] síos san talamh i mbouta [lorg] mo mháthar, agus ní bheidh trioblóid ar bith ort ag congbháil suas léi.'

'Go raibh maith agad, a chuisle mo chroidhe,' ar sa Donnchadh, 'tig liom congbháil suas léi go réidh.'

'Ní thig leat,' ar sise, 'tá speal ag mo mháthair agus congbhuigheann sí an faobhar ar feadh an ama bhéas an féar d'á bhaint, go mbéidh deireadh an fhéir gearrtha, acht má chailleann sí an faobhar aon uair amháin, ní bhéidh sí níos fearr 'ná aon speal eile. Is faobhar iongantach atá ar speil mo mháthar. Chuile shéasúr sul thosuigheann sí ag baint léi tugann sí go srothán uisge í. Cuireann sí an lann ann san uisge. Ann sin sgaoileann sí ribeacha d'olainn anuas ag snámh leis an sruth agus níl sí sásta muna ngearrtar chuile ribe aca bhaineas le lann na speile nuair thiucfas siad chomh fada leis.'

Ar maidin Dia Luain chuaidh an chailleach agus Donnchadh chum an mhóinfhéir ag baint. Thosuigh an chailleach ar an mbouta tosaigh, an áit a raibh na spící sáidhte ann san talamh ag an inghin. Níor bhfada gur casadh ceann aca léi. Ghearr sí í, acht bhain sí an faobhar de'n speil. 'Cupóg chruaidh,' ar sise. 'Seadh' ar sa Donnchadh. Casadh ceann eile léi agus rinne sí an rud céadna leis. 'Dar m'anam,' ar sise, 'is cruaidh na cupóga atá ann san móinfheur i mbliadhna.' 'Is cruaidh go deimhin,' ar sa Donnchadh.

Chuaidh sí píosa eile, acht ní raibh an speal ag gearradh go maith dhí, agus ghlaodh sí 'Faobhar, a Dhonnchaidh.' Chuir sí suas faobhar, acht ní dheachaidh sí cúig slata gur gháir sí amach arís. 'Faobhar, a Dhonnchaidh'. Thug sé am dí an dara faobhar do chur suas, acht faoi cheann cúpla móimid ghlaodh sí arís 'Faobhar, a Dhonnchaidh, le faobhar gearrtar féar.'

'Ní headh, a chailleach,' ar seisean, 'acht le fear maith agus le sean-speil ghéir. Agus muna bhfágann tú mo bhealach bainfidh mé na loirgne dhíot.'

'Tabhair am dam leis an bhfaobhar do chur suas an uair seo, agus má chliseann mo speal orm arís go mbeidh an cúsra so críochnuighthe deunfaidh mé dá leith de'n lann.'

Chuir sí suas faobhar eile agus thosuigh sí ag baint, acht ní dheachaidh sí fiche troigh go raibh an faobhar imthighthe arís. Bhí sí ar mire, agus thug sí iarraidh le lann na speile do bhriseadh ar a glúin, acht thionntuigh an lann agus ghearr sé an ghlún go doimhin, agus b'éigin dí fios do chur ar a hinghin le na hiomchar abhaile; agus ní tháinig sí anaice le Donnchadh, go raibh an móinfhéar gearrtha.

Chuaidh Donnchadh ar aghaidh go maith ann sin, go raibh an coirce apuidh. Bhí glún na caillighe cneasuighthe an uair sin, agus í i ndan obair do dheunamh.

Tráthnóna Dia Dómhnaigh dubhairt sí le Donnchadh, 'Bí réidh, ar maidin amárach, béimid ag baint choirce.'

'Tá mé réidh am ar bith,' ar seisean.

Dubhairt an inghean, an oidhche sin, le Donnchadh, 'Tá tú dul ag baint choirce amárach. Tabhair aire mhaith dhuit féin, nó buailfidh mo mháthair thú ag an obair sin.'

'Níl baoghal orm,' ar seisean, 'thig liom dá oiread léi 'bhaint.'

'Muna mbeadh aon nídh amháin, d'fheudfá,' ar sise, 'acht níl fhios agad go bhfuil dardaol i lámh chorráin mo mháthar, agus chomh fad agus béidh sé ann ní bhéidh sé ar chumas aon duine san domhan congbháil suas léi.

'A stóir mo chroidhe,' ar sa Donnchadh, 'bhéinn marbh abhfad ó shoin muna mbeadh go bhfuil tusa ag cuidiughadh liom, acht béidh laethanta maithe againn go fóill, nuair bhéas do mháthair ann san gcré.'

Ar maidin Dia Luain chuaidh an bheirt chum an ghuirt agus thosuigheadar ag baint choirce. Do ghlac an chailleach an chéad bouta agus bhí Donnchadh ar a cúl ag baint 'na diaigh. Níor bhfada gur imthigh sí amach uaidh, agus níor fheud sé congbháil suas léi ar aon chor. Nuair bhí sí timchioll fiche troigh amach roimhe gháir sí: 'A Dhonnchaidh, saoilim go bhfuil fallsacht éigin ort indiú.'

'Creud deir tú, a chailleach?' ar sa Donnchadh, agus 'san am ceudna rith sé chuici agus sgiob sé an corrán uaithi, tharraing an lámh as, agus thuit an dardaol ar an talamh. 'Ha ha! a chailleach bhradach, tá tú gabhtha anois, acht cuirfidh mise deireadh le do chleasaibh draoidheachta, is iomdha fear óg do mharbh tú leó, acht ní mharbhóchaidh tú mise.'

Thug an chailleach iarraidh greim d'fhághail ar an dardaol, acht leag Donnchadh a chos air, gur chuir sé a phutóga amach as a bheul. 'Anois, a chailleach,' ar seisean, 'téigh ar d'aghaidh leis an mbaint.'

'Ní bhainfidh mé níos mó,' ar sise, 'acht ceanglóchaidh mé do dhiaigh, suidh síos agus leig do sgíth.'

'Níl easbhaidh sgíth orm,' ar sa Donnchadh, 'dá luaithe thagann lá Samhna is é is fearr liom.'

'Tig leat imtheacht amárach agus gheobhaidh tú an oiread agus dá bhfanfá go lá Samhna. Má thugann tú d'fhocal dam go gcongbhóchaidh tú mo rún go bhfágh' mé bás – agus níl an t-am sin abhfad uaim, mar tá mé an-aosta – bheurfaidh mé do pháidhe dhuit amárach agus leigfidh mé dhuit imtheacht.'

'Cad é an aois thú?' ar sa Donnchadh.

'Tá mé níos mó 'ná naoi bhfichid bliadhan d'aois,' ar sise, 'agus má gheallann tú dham nach n-innseóchaidh tú mo rún inneseochaidh mé dhuit sgeul mo bheatha.'

'Dar m'fhocal,' ar sa Donnchadh 'ní chluinfidh cluas aon duine beó do rún uaim-se, chomh fad agus bhéas tú beó.'

Ann sin thosuigh an chailleach, agus dubhairt mar so.

'Nuair bhí mé mo chailín óg thuit mé i ngrádh le mac cómharsan, agus gheall sé mo phósadh, acht ann san deireadh thréig sé mé, agus phós sé cailín eile. Aon oidhche amháin d'éaluigh mé as tigh m'athar, agus chuaidh mé go tigh gabha draoidheachta, agus d'fhiafruigh mé dhe an bhfeudfadh sé cúmhachta draoidheachta do thabhairt dam. "Bheurfad agus fáilte," ar seisean. "Seó dhuit casarán(?) agus biombol(?): tabhair leat iad go bun crainn úbhall atá i ngáirdín d'athar. Caith iad ann san tobar atá ag bun an chrainn, agus tiucfaidh cúmhacht na draoidheachta chugad." D'imthigh mé agus chaith mé na neithe sin san tobar, agus ar an mball tháinig cú dubh agus dardaol amach as an tobar. Tá an cú[chú] agam fós, acht mo bhrón! mharbh tú an dardaol orm. Tá brígh mhór i mbainne an chú [na con], aon neach d'ólfadh é bheadh sé chomh láidir le leómhan, agus duine ar bith a mbeadh an dardaol ar iomchar leis ní fheudfá a bhualadh ag obair. Ní raibh mé abhfad ag ól bainne an chú go raibh mé an-láidir. Chuaidh mé san oidhche go tigh an bhuachall' do thréig mé agus mharbh mé é féin agus a bhean, agus ní raibh amhras ag duine an bith gur mise do rinne an choir sin. D'fhan mé i dtigh m'athar go raibh mé mór le cloinn, gan fhios dóibh. Ann sin d'fhag mé teach agus baile le náire. Lean mo chú dubh mé, agus chuir mé fúm an oidhche sin i dtigh an ghabha draoidheachta, agus is ann do rugadh m'inghean. Ar maidin, lá ar n-a mhárach, d'fhiafruigh an gabha dhíom cia an áit rachainn. "Áit ar bith le mo náire chur i bhfolach," ar sa mise. Ann sin thug sé eudach fir dham, le cur orm, agus d'athruigh sé mé i riocht nach n-aithneóchadh m'athair nó mo mháthair féin mé. Chaith mé dá fhichid bliadhan aige ag séideadh na mbolg agus ag cuidiughadh leis anns gach uile obair. Aon lá amháin do bhí mé ag bualadh an uird thruim dó, agus bhuail mé ar an ordóig é: Chuir sin fearg air, agus bhuail sé mé le slaitín draoidheachta gus rinne cráin mhuice dhíom, agus chuir sé go Cnoc-Meadha ar feadh ceud bliadhan mé. Nuair sgaoileadh as an áit sin mé, cuireadh ar ais chuig an sean-ghabha mé, agus tugadh dham sporán líonta le ór agus le airgiod. Fuair mé m'inghean mo chú agus mo dhardaol rómham gan athrughadh ar bith orra nó orm féin. Thug mé iad liom go dtí an áit seo. Cheannuigh mé í, agus chuir mé fúm inntí. Sin chugad mo sgeul anois, agus agraim ort gan a leigean amach as do bheul chomh fad agus bhéas mise beó.'

'Ní leigfead go deimhin,' ar sa Donnchadh.

D'imthigh an fóghmhar agus tháinig an tSamhain. Ar maidin, lá Samhna, thug an chailleach a phíosaí airgid do Dhonnchadh, agus dubhairt leis teacht léi go páirc na gcaorach leis na caoirigh do chaitheamh thar an mballa.

Nuair thángadar isteach ann san bpáirc rug sé grreim ar an gcaora ba thruime do bhí ann sin, agus chaith sé í thar an mballa mar chaithfeadh sé meuróg. Bhí sé d'á gcaitheamh thar an mballa go raibh scór aige.

'Dar m'fhocal ní holc é do pháidhe leith-bhliadhna,' ar san chailleach.

'Ní fearr 'ná shaothruigh mé,' ar sa Donnchadh, agus leis sin do thiomáin sé a fhiche caora amach roimhe, agus chuaidh sé abhaile leó.

Níor bhfada 'na dhiaigh sin go dtáinig tinneas ar ar gcailligh. Tháinig sean-mhná an bhaile le freastal uirri.

'Cad é an aois thú?' arsa bean de na mnáibh.

'Níos mó ná naoi bfichid bliadhan,' ar sise.

'Agus cia an fáth thusa bheith chomh buan?'

'Ní dheachaidh gaoth na maidne ann mo bholg folamh ariamh; níor fhluich drúcht roimh ghréin mo chos; chaith mé te agus chaith mé fuar, agus sin é an fáth mise bheith chomh buan sin.' Acht tá fhios againn go raibh breug ann a beul agus í ag fághail bháis.

An oidche sin tháinig stoirm mhór, agus toirneach agus teintreach, agus leagadh teach na caillighe go talamh. Marbhuigheadh an chailleach, an inghean agus an cú. Ar maidin, lá ar na mhárach, bhí na ceudta madadh timchioll an tighe, agus ó'n lá sin go dtí an lá so níl aon ainm ar an áit sin acht Gleann-na-Madadh

Díspeagadh na baineannachta laistigh den réimse siombalach fireannach

10. An Chailleach Bhéarthach (Carna: Áird Thoir)

Mar [a] tá fhios ag chuile duine fuair an chailleach seo na mílte bliadhain d'aois más [fíor]. Bhí sí ann na mílte bliadhain roimh aimsir Naomh Pádhraic agus nuair a bhí Pádhraic ag dul ar fud na tíre casadh isteach é go dtí í é féin agus[a] ghiolla. D'fiarradh sé den chailleach cé an aois [a] bhí agus dubhairt leis mar leanas.

'Chuir mé naoi naonmhar naoi n-uaire i naoi uaighe i dTráigh Lí.'

Céard [a] thug an aois sin duit arsa Pádhraic.

'Níor thug mé salachar na lathighe i bhfus thar an lathach thall ariamh gan mo chosa i níochán.'

'B'fhuil aon tuairim eile agad le t'aois [a] chaillighe.'

'Tá' [a] deir sí.

'Níl aon tseacht – mbliadhana de mo shaoghal ariamh nár chaith mé cnáimh mart suas ar an loca sin agus más maith leat é gabh suas agus comhair iad.' 'Chuir sé suas an giolla agus chuaidh sé ag caitheamh anuas agus Pádhraic ag comhairadh agus is gearr go raibh an t-urlár lán, agus d'fhiafraigh Pádhraic den ghiolla[a] raibh aon bhaol ortha [a] bheith [a] bhus, agus séard dubhairt an giolla go raibh éadan ar éigin aige ortha agus gur b'in é an méad, 'Ó chaith suas aríst iad' arsa Pádhraic, 'as mo radharc'. Rinne an giolla amhlaidh.

Nuair a bhí sin déanta aige shiubhail Pádhraic anonn go dtí an chailleach agus dubhairt léithe nach gcaithfeadh sí aon chnáimh aríst choidhche ann ar chaoi ar bith.

Rinne sé splainc dhearg dhi agus sin é an deireadh a bhí aici.

11. An Chailleach Bhéarra agus Naomh Caitiairn

Bhí cailleach i mBéarra san eile-shaol go nglaoidís an Chailleach Bhéarra uirthi. Cailleach bhradach ab ea í, cailleach gan chreideamh, gan choinsias, go raibh mí-fheirg agus mí-ghreann nach aoinne uirthi. Agus mar sin do bhí sí ann. Méid ná goideadh sí do laiteadh sí é agus bhí mí-fheirg gach aoinne uirthi. Do theith cuid acu le heagla báis as an mbaile. Agus mar sin do bhí sí ann.

Théadh sí sa ghleann ó thuaidh agus go [h]Oileán Faoide ó dheas, agus do thugadh sí an dá thráigh léi. Agus do chuala sí uair go raibh bradán sa ghleann gur chuaigh de gach nduine breith air, ach chuaigh sí féna dhéin, agus do thug sí léi é go Béarra.

Chuaigh sí ina dhiaidh sin go hOileán Faoide a d'iarraidh cnósach, mar b'é ba mhó ba thathach léi, a thaithneadh léi, leis. Agus ar a casadh abhaile i mBaile an Chorra Bháin, do bhuail Naomh Caitiairn uimpi ina chodladh ar chnocán lom lomnochta, gan foithin gan fascadh ón ngréin n'a ón bhfearthain, ó chúrsa an lae. Agus sé an ainm a ghlaonn siad ar an áit ó shoin, an ola ae(?), i dtaobh an codladh beag a dhein sé, mar do dhúisigh an chaille é. Ba thathach léi dul trí phócaí agus cuardach nach aoinne d'fhaigheadh sí faillí. Agus nuair a fuair sí faillí, gafa age codladh, Naomh Caitiairn, do chuaigh sí thrína chuid éadaigh, agus pé ní do fuair sí do chuir ina mála é. Do chuir sí ina mála é agus do thóg sí a shlat draíochta a bhí ina aice.

Bhí mairtíneach ina chónaí san áit. Do chonaic sé an ghadaíocht do dhein an chailleach, agus do liúigh sé ar Naomh Caitiairn. Liú an mhairtínigh agus fuaim na caillí do dhúisigh Naomh Caitiairn, agus chonaic sé cad a bhí déanta. Do ghlaoigh sé ar an gcailleach, agus dá mhéid a ghlaoigh is ea 'mhó a rith sí. Do lean sé ina diaidh agus do tháinig sé suas léi in áit go nglaonn siad Ard na Caillí i gCill Chaitiairn air. Do dhein sé gallán lom glas di; a cúl ar an gcnoc; a hgahaidh ar an muir; agus tá sí ann ón lá san go dtí Lá Deireadh an tSaoil.

12. *Meelick Round Tower*
[*It is believed by the older people in this locality that the Round Towers were built by a witch called the Cailleach Bhéara who figures prominently in the folklore of Connaught. It was this same cailleach who is supposed to have built Meelick Round Tower outside Swinford which was never finished. To add to the labour of building it 'she carried the stones up in her pocket' (according to my mother).*

Judging by my mother's version of the story she intended, like those who undertook the erection of the Tower of Babel, to build the tower to the sky, if unmolested. When the erection was well under way a boy passed who made the underquoted remark. She became highly indignant and jumped down to her doom, leaving the impression of her two knees on a stone in the ground below.]

'Nuair a bhí an Chailleach Bhéara ar bárr an túir ag obair a ndícheall tháinic buachaill an bealach. Dearc sé suas is dúbhairt sé. 'Feicim do thón a Chailleach Bhéarrach' Tháinic fearg uirthi annsan is dubhairt sí 'Ach beag sin chuirfinn go spéir í' Léim sí anuas agus tá lorga a dá ghlún sa cloch go dtí an lá seo.'

Sí mo mháthair a thug an leagan seo shuas dhom. A sean-mháthair a thug an scéal di. Do chualas an scéal ó daoine eile ach ní mar a gcéadhna a ghabhann sé.

13. 'Ná creid briathra mná'
Bhí buachaill aimsire ag an gCailleach Bhéarra aon uair amhain.

Chuaidh sé amach lá a craitheadh an fhéir gan an chailleach a cheadú. Amach leithe 'na dhiaidh agus í lé buile agus lé báinídhe faoí an féar a chraitheadh amach. 'Ara, phleóca', ar sise 'cén'n fáth dhuit an fear a craitheadh amach agus báisteach ar an lá iniu'?. 'Cabh 'ios a'dsa a bhfuil' ars' an buachaill aimsire. 'Mar', arsa an chailleach, 'sgread an fhinneóg agus labhair an fiadh'. 'Á, 'arsa an buachaill.

> 'Ná creid finneóg 's ná creid fiadh
> 's ná creid briathra mná,
> más moch máll eirigheas an ghrian
> is mar is toil le Dia a bheas an lá'.

14. Ana ní Áine

Is dócha gur fadó riamh anis ó bhí fear múr saibhir do mhuíntir Mhac Cártha 'n-a chónuí a gCeann Mara; fear anashaibhir a b'ea é. Bhí sé pósta, is ní raibh aige ach aon iníon amháin, gur'b ainim di Ana nic Chártha, ach ní tugtar 'sa scéal ach Ana ní Áine. Cailín anabhreá a b'ea í, agus is mú ógánach a bhí tnú le h-í phósa, ach níor phós sí nú go raibh sí críona cruaig go math. Do tháinig fear óg uasal ó Chúig' Ola, agus do thit sí a ngrá leis; sin é an fear a phós sí. Ní raibh sí ach pósta dosaen blian nú mar sin, nuair a ghaibh fear siúil isteach chúihe tránhúna. Do chuir sí chuin bíg é; ansan do thosanaig sí er a bheith dá cheistiúil. Is deárhach go raibh fios ag an bhfear siúil; 'sa chainnt dóibh, pé scéal é, dúirt sé lé ná faigheach sí bás go deó nú go dí go n-olóch Seán Bráthir Ó Cnuchúir chuin báis í. " A' bhfuil fhios agut,", ar sise, "ce hé an fear san?" "Níl a' t-eólas san agum," ers' an fear siúil. D'imig sé bhuaithe agus d'fhág sé ansan í.

Bhí an saol ag imeacht, agus má bhí, ní raibh aon chríne a' dol uirthi. Bhí clann agus clann a cluine curth' a gcrí, agus í féin beó fós. 'Sé crí agus deire na mbeart e, go raibh sí có críona san go raibh sí á luasca a gclíobhán aige h-iníon iníon a h'níne. Bhí san go math agus ní raibh go h-olc. Bhi sagart óg tacaithe 'sa ph'róiste go raibh sí, ní raibh sé ann ach cúpala mí. Ba mhath leis a bheith a' siúl tímpal, tuisc é bheith 'n-a stróinséir 'san áit. Tránhúna breá samhraig agus é a' file chuin a' tí, do bhuail tort é. Níorbh' fhéidir leis aon uisge fhisgint 'n-a thímpal, ach do ch'nuic sé tig math deárhatach tamailín uaig. Chuai' sé go dí an tig, is er dhol isteach do, ní raibh ruimis ach bean mheán-aosta. Bhí sí suite 'sa chúine agus í luasca clíobháin. Do chuir sí fáilte ruimis an sagart. "Tá tort oram, a bhean mhath a' tí," ers' an sagart, "a mbéach deoch agut a thurfá dhom?" "Tá go deimhin, athir," ar sise. D'eighri' sí 'n-a suí, agus chuaig a' trial er dheoch chuige. An fhaid a bhí sí 'muh do dhrid suas leis an gclíobhán chuin é luasca mar dhe. Do labhair an té bhí ansa' chlíobhán. "Mhuise go deimhin," er sise, "ní gá duit múran do m' dhua a dh' fháilt." Ní múr ná gur thit an sagart mar a raibh sé, mar do shaoil sé gur leanabh beog a bhí 'sa chlíobhán. "Cad é mar shórt duine thu?" ers' an sagart. "Mhuise, is f'rist' me mheas anis," er sise, "ach ní rabhas mar sin tamal; ach ce h-é tusa tá cainnt lium?" "Sagart isea me," er seisean; "cad a bheir duit a bheith mar sin?" er seisean. "Do bhí sé 'sa tairigireacht agum ná faighin bás go deó nú go dí go n-olóch Seán Bráthir Ó C'nuchúir chuin báis mé. Níl fhios agum an raibh a lethéid ann riamh, nú mbeig a lethéid ann go deó; ach táim a' fithamh leis, is deárhach, mar táim có críona agus go bhfuil an tríú glún a m'luasca 'sa chlíobhán, féin mar chíon tu." "Tair slán," ers' an sagart, "tá 'n fear san suite anseo le t'ais aniubh; is mise an fear céana san anis." Tháinig áthas er Áine, ní nach úna. Do tháinig bean a' tí agus an deoch aici chuige. Nuair a bhí thort múchta, do thosanaig sé er a bheith a' ceistiúchán na seanamhná.

"Is dócha gur mú úna a ch'nuicís riamh a rith do bheatha," ar seisean. "Is mú go deimhin," er sise, "ach n' fheaca aení riamh is mú gur dhineas úntas do ná aení 'mháin, agus neósfai' mé duit é, athir. Nuair a bhíos a m' bean óg, bhíoch a lán stróinséirí a' teacht go dí n-ár dtig. Bhí bád pléisiúir aige m'athir, agus is minic a bhídís ag imeacht ó áit go háit lé. Lá breá fôir do dhineas féin agus cailín eile suas sin féin chuin dol a n-aonacht leó. Bhí sagart óg 'sa bhád le n-ár gcuis. Do thugamair fé dhol 'on Sceilig, ach sula shroihamair an talamh do tháinig duiriheacht úfásach thiar. Dúirt m'athir gur mb' fheár an bád a chasa, ach ní bhéach an chuid eile sásta. Do bhí an scamal dubh doracha a' déanamh orain agus séideán gaoithe. D'fhéach an sagart 'n-a threó. "Tá úntráil éigint 'sa scamal san," er seisean . . . Bhí sé a' déanamh orain nú go raibh sé anachûngarach don mbád. Có lua agus do tháini' sé a n-aic' an bháid cad a bhí 'sa scamal ach bean. D'eighrig an sagart go tapuig, agus do chuir sé an stoil er a mhineál is do tharaig sé chuige a leabhar. Ansan do labhair sé agus d'fhiarhuig di cad a dhin díol di. "Mharuíos duine," er sise. "Ní h-é sin a dhamanuig tu," ers' an sagart. "Mharuíos beirt." "Ní h-é sin leis," ers' an sagart. "Mharuíos leanabh gan baiste a d'fhonn is a bheith a m'chéile sagairt." "Sin é díreach a dhamanuig tu," ers' an sagart. Ansan do thosanaig sé er a leabhar a léumh, agus a gceann tamail bhig d'eighri' sí 'n-a splannc ní as an uisge agus d'imi' sí ar ár radharc. Níor chuamair 'on Sceilig an lá san. D' fhileamair abhaile; is sin é an t-iúna is mú ch'nuc riamh er fheag mo bheatha."

"Ach ní bheig a theile sael agut anis," ersa Seán Bráthair. "Tucfai' me chút go much er maidin amáireach, agus olói' me a gcóir na síoruíochta tu." Do tháinig sé er maidin amáireach, féin mar gheall se, agus chuir sé an ola dhéanach er Áine nic Chártha. Có lua agus bhí sé olamh lé, do dh'imig an t-anam aiste agus bhí crí lé ansan. Nuair a mhairean duine anachríona ó shin, tá sé mar fhocal a mbéal na ndaoine, "Tá sí có críona le h-Ana ní Áine.

Buanú na baineannachta i gcomhoiriúntas an choitinn

15. An Chailleach Bhéarthach (Carna: Cill Chiaráin)
Bean a bhí anseo fadó, a dtugaidís An Chailleach Bhéarthach uirthi agus níor chaoin sí aon deor ariamh agus níor chaith sí deoch na greim, te ná fuar, ón lá ar rugadh í go dtí an lá a bhfuair sí bás, ach í i dtaobh le bainne na bó. Bhíodh sí ag siúlóid i gcónaí. Ní bhíodh aon tuirse uirthi, is doigh liom. Níor chaith sí bróg ná stoca ariamh, ach [í] cosnochtaithe. Nuair a théadh sí amach ag siúl, dá gcastaí áit bhog léithi, a mbeadh puiteach, ar an bpointe boise agus thiocfadh sí ins an áit a mbeadh lochán uisce – an lochán ba ghaire dhi – chromadh sí ar an lochán agus níodh sí síos óna glúna a dá cois, le faitíos go mbeadh salachar ar bith uirthi. Níor thug sí riamh ón áit a salaíodh sí a cosa [anonn] go dtí an áit a bhfaigheadh sí uisce arís, gan a cosa a níochán ann – sin é an bealach a bhí léithe riamh. Agus ón lá bhí sí i n-ann dul ar Aifreann, níor fhailligh sí aon Domhnach ariamh gan dul ar an Aifreann. Agus ag teacht ón Aifreann di thogadh sí cloch bheag ina láimh agus tabharadh sí léithí í go dtiocfadh sí abhaile. Agus bhí arg mór, millteach aici – bá mhó an t-arg ná cónra – agus caitheadh sí san arg é, an chloch, gach uile Dhomhnach.

Bhí sí, lá, istigh ansin, agus í ag dul in aois, agus tháinig bean isteach go dtí í agus d'fhiarrthaigh sí: 'an ansin atá tusa?' adeir sí leis an gCailleach Bhéarthach.

'Seadh', adeir an Chailleach Bhéarthach, 'Cad chuige'.

'Nach iontach', adeir sí, 'nár chuala tú go raibh páiste óg – iníon óg – ag duine den chlann iníon tháinig uait?'

'Níor chuala mé é', adeir an Chailleach Bhéarthach 'ach is gearr go mbeidh fhios agam é.'

D'éirigh sí agus ghabh sí amach agus brat ar a bráid, agus ghabh sí go dtí ára[s] a hiníon féin. Chonnaic sí go raibh an iníon roimpi.

'Mar sin atá tu?' adeir sí

'Sea', adeir an iníon

'Muise, éirigh suas, a iníon', adeir an Chailleach Bhéarthach, 'agus téir go dtí teach iníne: rug iníon d'iníne iníon óg aréir.'

Ach ghaibh an iníon ann agus tháinig an Chailleach Bhéarthach abhaile go dtí a teach fhéin. Agus suas le céad bliain ina dhiaidh bhí sí beo agus í ina suí síos cois na tine i dteach léithi fhéin agus í láidir. D'airigh sí siúl ag teacht chun an tí agus tháinig seanfhear isteach, liath agus liath go maith. Agus é faoi fhéasóg liath go dtí n-a bhásta agus cána ina láimh. Shuigh sé fhéin agus í fhein síos ag caint, agus ní fhaca sí fhéin ariamh é. Dúirt sé leithi go gcaithfeadh sé go raibh aois mhaith anois aici. Dúirt sí go raibh sí ag ceapadh go raibh aois mhaith aici ach go mbeadh barúil aici ar ball cén aois a bhí aici agus aige fhéin.

'Níl aon Domhnach ón lá', a dúirt sí, 'go raibh mé i n-ann a dhul um an Aifrinn nach ndeacha mé ann go dtí an lá atá inniu ann agus níl aon Domhnach agus mé ag teacht abhaile ón Aifreann nach dtabharfainn cloch bheag i mo láimh liom agus nach gcaithfinn san arg sin thuas é.'

An-mhaith', adeir an seanfhear, 'ach cén bealach a bhí leat ó thús do shaoil go dtí inniu?'

'Níor chaoin mé aon deor, ariamh', a deir sí. 'An dara ní, níor chaith mé te nó fuar ariamh. An triú ní, dá dteigheach mo chos sa lathach, níor thug mé an lathach seo go dtí an chéad lathach eile ariamh gan mo chosa a nigheachán sa gcéad lochán a casfaí dhom.'

'Muise,' adeir an seanfhear, adeir sé, 'is fearr dhúinn breathnú san arg. Ba cheart dó a bheith lán suas'.

'*Well*, ní fhéadfadh sé bheith i bhfad uaidh', adeir an Chailleach Bhéarthach.

'An miste dom breathnú ann?' adeir an seanfhear

'Muise, go deimhin, ní miste', adeir an Chailleach Bhéarthach.

D'éirigh an seanfhear agus chroch sé an clár den arg agus ní raibh san arg ach dhá chloch.

'Muise, *by dad*,' adeir an seanfhear, adeir sé, 'níl anseo ach dhá chloch.'

'Muise, tá mé an-iontach ansin', adeir an Chailleach Bhéarthach, 'cheap mé féin go raibh sé lán'.

'*Well*, isé a ndearna tú feadh do shaoil, dhá Aifreann a éisteacht, agus sin é an t-údar atá leis.'

Ní raibh aon bhlas le rá aici.

'Bean mhaith thú', adeir an seanfhear, ag breith ar a chána agus ag dul amach. Mar ba dhea céard a bhí ann teachtaire ó Dhia na nGrást le hinnseacht di nár éist sí aon Aifreann feadh a saoil ceart ach dhá Aifreann.

Thit na deora óna súile le briseadh croí agus le haiféala, an faillí a bhí déanta aici ar an gcuid eile de na hAifrinn trína chéile ar feadh a saoil.

Ní raibh fhios ag aon fhear beo ar an talamh, ná ag bean, cén t-ainm a bhí ar an gCailleach Bhéarthach. Ní raibh i n-ann bás di go nglaotuí trí h-uaire ina hainm uirthi. Bhí druítheadóir ag dul thar an teach lá agus chuala sé an Chailleach Bhéarthach ag gabháil fhoinn.

'Muise, giorrashaoil chugat', adeir an druítheadóir, 'a Sibléal, a Sibléal, a Sibléal! mara binn é do ghlór cinn'.

Bhí fhios ag an gCailleach Bhéarthach go raibh sí fhéin reidh agus bhí sí caillte ar maidin.

Sin é mar chuala mise faoi 'n gCailleach Bhéarthach.

16. An Chailleach Bhéarach (Baile an Chaisleáin)

Bhí cailleach ann, agus is fad ó bhí, agus dá mbeadh, sinne an uair sin ann, ní bheadh sinn ann anois; bheadh sgeul úr nó sean-sgeul againn, agus níor dhóighe sin 'ná bheith gan aon sgeul!

Bhí an chailleach an-tsean, agus ní raibh fios a haois' aici féin ná ag duine ar bith eile. Bhí bráthair agus a bhuachaill ag siubhalóideacht aon lá amháin, agus tháinig siad isteach go teach na caillighe Béaraighe.

'Go mbeannuighidh Dia ann so', ar san bráthair.

'Go mbeannuighidh an fear ceudna dhuit,' ar san chailleach, 'sé do bheatha, suidh síos ag an teine agus deun do ghoradh'.

Shuidh an bráthair síos agus nuair bhí a ghoradh deunta go maith aige, thosuigh sé ag caint 's ag cómhradh leis an tseannchailligh.

'Muna bhfuil dochar dam fiafruighe dhíot budh mhaith liom fios fhághail ar d'aois, mar tá 's agam go bhfuil tú an-tsean.'

'Ní dochar ar bith dhuit fiafruighe dhíom', ar san chailleach, 'freagróchaidh mé thú chomh maith agus thig liom. Níl aon bhliadhain ó tháinig mise ann [chum] aois nach marbhuighinn mart, agus nach gcaithfinn cnámha an mhairt suas ar an lota tá ós do chionn, má's maith leat fios do beith agad ar m'aois-se, tig leat do bhuachaill do chur suas ar an lota agus na cnámha do cómhaireamh.'

B'fhíor an sgeul. Chuir an bráthair an buachaill suas ar an lota agus thosuigh sé ag cómhaireamh na gcnámh, agus leis an méid cnámh do bhí ar an lota ní raibh achar [áit go leór] aige ar an lota le n-a gcómhaireamh, agus dubhairt sé leis an mbráthair go gcaithfeadh sé na cnámha a chaitheamh anuas ar an urlár, nach raibh achar aige ar an lota.

' 'Nuas leó,' ar san bráthair, 'agus congbhóchaidh mise cuntas orra ann so ó íochtar'.

Thosuigh an buachaill ag caitheamh anuas, agus thosuigh an bráthair ag sgríobh síos, go raibh sé bunáite tuirseach, agus d'fiafruigh sé de'n bhuachaill an raibh siad i gionnsaighe [beagnach] cómhairthe aige; agus d'fhreagair an buachaill an bráthair anuas de'n lota nach raibh coirneul de'n lota folmhuighthe go fóill.

'Má's cúrsaí mar sin é, gabh anuas de'n lota agus caith na cnámha suas arís,' ar san bráthair.

Tháinig an buachaill anuas, agus chaith sé na cnámha suas, agus bhí an bráthair chomh críonna ag teacht isteach do, agus do bhí sé ag dul amach.

'Nuair nach bhfuil fios d' aois' agam,' ar san bráthair leis an gcailligh, 'tá 's agam nach bhfuil tú go dtí an tráth so gan iongantais fheiceál ar feadh do shaoghail, agus an t-iongantas is mó do chonnaic tú riamh innis damh-sa é, má sé do thoil é.'

'Chonnaic mé iongantas amháin do chuir iongnadh mór orm', adubhairt an chailleach.

'Aithris dam é,' ar san bráthair, 'má 's é do thoil é.'

'Bhí mé féin agus mo chailín, lá amháin, amuigh ag bleaghan na mbó, agus bhí sé 'na lá breagh aoibhinn agus bhí mé tar éis ceann de na ba [buaibh] do bleághan; agus nuair thóg mé mo cheann, dhearc mé tharm taobh mo láimhe cléithe dhíom, agus chonnaic mé duibheachán mór ag teacht ós mo chionn ann san spéir. "Deun deifir", arsa mé féin leis an gcailín, "go mblighfidh sinn na ba go haibéal [tapa] nó béidh sinn fliuch báidhte sul má shroichidh sinn abhaile, leis an bhfearthainn". Bhí bruith-a-ladhair[deifir áidhbheul] ormsa agus ar mo chailín leis na ba do bleághan, sul má bhfuigheadh sinn an cith, mar shaoil mé féin gur cith do bhí ag teacht, agus ar tógbháil mo chinn dam arís dhearc mé tharm, agus chonnaic mé bean ag tigheacht chomh geal le eala bruaich na toinne. Chuaidh sí tharm mar sinneán gaoithe, agus an ghaoth do bhí roimpi bhí sí ag breith uirri, agus an ghaoth do bhí 'na diagh níor fheud sí teacht suas léithe. Níor bhfada go bfacaidh mé, andiagh na mná, dá mhaistín agus dá shlait d'á dteangaidh casta timchioll a muinéil agus caor teinneadh as a mbeul; agus chuir mé iongnadh mór ann sin. Agus andiagh na madadh chonnaic mé cóiste dubh, agus cuingir capall 'gá tarraing, agus bhí caor teineadh gach aon taobh ar an gcóiste. Agus ag dul tharm do'n chóiste, sheas na beithigh, agus chuir rud éigin alugur [guth no fuaim gan chéill] as, ann san gcóiste. agus sgannruigh mé, agus tháinig laige-beó orm, agus nuair tháinig mé ar ais as an laige mhothuigh mé an glór ann san gcóiste arís, ag fiafruighe dhíom an bhfacaidh mé rud ar bith ag gabhail tharm ó tháinig mé ann sin; agus d'innis mé dhó mar tá mise ag innseacht duit-se, agus d'fhiafruigh mé cia é féin, nó creud is brigh do'n bhean agus do na maistínibh do chuaidh tharm.

"Mise an Diabhal, agus sin dá mhaistín do chuir mise andiagh an anam' sin."

"Agus bhfuil dochar dam fiafruighe," ar sa mise, "cad é an choir rinne an bhean sin nuair bhí sí ar an saoghal."

"Bean í sin," ar san diabhal, "thug sganna ar shagart, agus fuair sí bás i stáid pheacaidh mhairbh, agus ní dhearnaidh sí aithrighe ann, agus muna dtigeann na maistíní suas léithe sul má dtigeann sí go geataí flaithis tiucfaidh an Mhaighdean ghlórmhar agus iarrfaidh sí impidhe ar a haon-mhac maitheamhnas do thabhairt di, ann a cuid peacadh, agus gheobhaidh sí párdún di, agus béidh mise aiste [caillfidh mé í.] Acht má thigeann na maistíní suas léithe sul má dtéigheann sí go dtí an flaitheas, is liom-sa í."

Thiomáin an diabhal mór a bheithigh agus d'imthigh sé as m'anc [m'amharc] agus tháinig mé féin agus mo chailín abhaile, agus bhí mé trom tuirseach brónach ag cuimhniughadh ar an taisbéanadh do chonnaic mé, agus chuir mé iongnadh mór ann san iongantas sin, agus luigh mé ar mo leabuidh ar feadh trí lá, agus an ceathramhadh lá d'éirigh mé an-chlaoidhte lag, agus ní gan ádhbhar, mar bean ar bith d'fheicfeadh an taisbéanadh do chonnaic mise bheadh sí liath ceud bliadhain roimh a haois do bheith caithte.'

'An bhfacaidh tú aon iongantas eile ann d'am?' ar san bráthair leis an gcailligh.

'Seachtmhain 'réis mo leabuidh d'fágbháil fuair mé litir ag innseacht dam go raibh caraid liom marbh agus go gcaithfinn dul chum na sochraide. Ghluais mé féin chum na sochraide, agus ar dul dam go teach-an-chuirp bhí an corp ann san gcónra [cómhra] agus bhí an cónra leagtha síos ar an gcrócar, agus chuaidh ceathar fear faoi an gcrócar go n-iomchróchadh siad an cónra agus ní raibh siad i ndan gaeth do thabhairt do'n chrócar de'n talamh. Agus tháinig ceathrar eile agus níor fheud siad a chorrughadh de'n talamh. Bhí siad ag tigheachtt, duine ar dhuine, go dtáinig dáreug, agus go ndeachaidh siad faoi an gcrócar, agus níor fheud siad a thógbháil.

Labhair mé féin, agus d'fiafruigh mé de na daoinibh do bhí ar an sochraid cad é an sórt ceird' do bhí ag an bhfear so nuair bhí sé ar an tsaoghal, agus hinnseadh dham gur maor do bhí ann. Agus d'fhiafruigh mé de na daoinibh do bhí ann sin, raibh aon mhaor eile ar an sochraid. Tháinig ann sin ceathrar fear nach raibh aithne ná eólas ag duine ar bith do bhí ar an sochraid, orra, agus dubhairt siad liom gur ceathrar maor do bhí ionnta. Agus chuaidh siad faoi an gcrócar, agus thóg siad é mar thógfá greim lócháin agus d'imthigh siad leó, chomh tiugh, geur, agus d'fheud siad cos do thógbháil. Bhí siubhal maith fútha, agus bí coiscéim bhreágh fhada agam féin, agus bhain mé amach 'na ndiagh, agus ní raibh fios ag mac máthar cia an áit a raibh siad ag dul leis an gcónra, agus bhíomar ag imtheacht agus ag sír-imtheacht go raibh an oidhche agus an lá ag sgaramhaint ó chéile, go raibh an oidhche ag tigheacht dubh dorcha dannartha, go raibh an capall glas ag dul ar sgáth na cupóige, go raibh an chopóg ag imtheacht ar teitheamh roimhe,

> Go raibh na freumhacha dul faoi an talamh,
> Na duilleóga dul 'san spéir,
> An capall glas ag teitheadh,
> Agus mise liom féin.

Ar dearcadh tharm dom ní raibh aon ar an sochraid im' dhiaigh acht beirt eile. Do buaileadh síos an mhuinntir eile, agus ní raibh siad ábalta tigheacht leath bealaigh, cuid aca do thuit i laige agus cuid eile do fuair bás.

Ar dhul chum cinn dam dhá choiscéim eile ar m' aghaidh, bhí mé istigh i gcoill dhorcha fhliuch fhuair, agus d'fhosgail an talamh agus slugadh síos mé i bpoll dubh dorcha, gan mac máthar ná inghean fhir ann mo ghoire ná ann mo ghaobhar, gan fear mo chaointe ná mo shínte le fágháil, gur chaith mé mé féin ar mo dhá ghlúin, agus bhí mé ann sin ar feadh ceithre lá, ag guidhe suas go Dia mo thabhairt as sin go luath agus go tapa. Agus leis an gceathramhadh lá tháinig poll beag mar chró na snáthaide ar choirneul de'n áras a raibh mé ann; agus bhí mé ag guidhe i gcómhnuidhe, agus bhí an poll ag meudughadh lá ar lá. Ar an seachtmhadh lá mheuduigh sé chomh mór [agus] go bhfuair mé amach as.

Thug mé do na boinn annsin, nuair fuair mé mo chosa liom ar an taoibh amuigh ag dul abhaile. An méad do siubhail mé aon lá amháin ag leanamhaint na cónra, chaith mé cúig seachtmhainí ag tigheacht ar ais an bealach ceudna, agus nach bhfeiceann tú féin anois go bhfuair mé ádhbhar le bheith críon, sean, aosta, liath, agus mo shaoghal ag giorrachan, ar an dá ghábhadh sin a raibh mé ann.'

'Is maith cruaidh an chailleach thú i gcómhnuidhe,' ar san bráthair.

Scéalta i dTaobh Mná Feasa

Ag glacadh le fios agus le cumas na mná

17. An bhean a chíodh na fairies
Sean-bhean do bhí sa Ghleann Fhreastail uair gurbh ainm di P. Ní. L. Bhí sí pósta ag M. C. agus do bhí sí críona. Do bhí sé ráidhte go bfeiceadh sí na fairies. Ní fheadar-sa. Aon tórramh go mbíodh saí is minic a théigheadh saí I laigíochtaí ann. Thugadh saí tamall mór ionnta sar a dteagadh saí as. As na laigíochtaí sion a thugadh saí an fios, a deiridís.

18. Máire Ní Mhurchú agus na carréaraithe
Do bhí bean feasa anso fadó go nglaoidís Máire Ní Mhurchú uirthi. Chónaigh sí i mBaile na nAoraí mBeag. Chónaigh sí i mórán áit nách é, a leis, mar níor luaithe anso ná ansúd aici. Bhíodh sé ráite, agus is dócha gur ráiteachas fíor ab ea é, go mbiodh sí in aonacht le dream an uair (uabhair?) agus dream na hoíche. Ach an oíche seo bhí sí thiar in aonacht le mná a bhí ag tarrac lín, in áit go nglaonn siad Cathair Caim air.

Bhí cuid acu ... ana-mhná chun tobac ab ea iad, agus ní raibh aon tobac acu, mar ní raibh aon fháil air. Ní mór go raibh aon tigh á dhíol ... go dtugaidís leo go dtíos na hucstaerithe a bhíodh ag díol cois baile, an tobac, ag ganfhiosaíocht, mar ní raibh an aimsir sin ró-mhacánta ná aon dlí ann. B'é dlí na gCithearnach a bhí ann an uair chéanna ... pé ní ba mhaith leo a dhéanamh, do dhéanamh, agus an rud ná taithnfeadh leo, gan é a dhéanamh in aon chor. Ach ní mar sin athá sé anois, buíochas le Dia. Tá dlí agus ríocht agus ceart ages nach aoinne le fáil, agus pionós le fáil aige, d'réir mar a thuilfidh sé é. San oíche dhóibh go háirithe, bhíodar ag tarrac an lín, agus ag caint le chéile, agus ag caitheamh aimsire, agus amach i meán na hoíche do tháinig siúl go dtí an doras. D'airigh an chuid eile fuaim na gcoisithe ag teacht go dtí an doras, agus do buaileadh an doras. Agus d'éirigh Máire Ní Mhurchú ó tharrac an lín, an bhean bhocht, agus do bheir sí ar an clóca a bhí ag crochadh anuas – do bhí aici mar scáth ar theacht na maidean – chun dul abhaile, is thug sí oíche mhaith dóibh, agus do ghaibh sí an doras amach.

Ar teacht an lae – ní raibh a fhios ag aoinne cár chuaigh sí, ná níor fhiafraíodar di cár ghaibh sí, leis – ach ar theacht an lae do chas sí abhaile, agus tháinig sí isteach, fliuch, báite, tnáite, tuirseach, tabhartha, th'réis cúrsa na hóíche. Chuireadar chun na tine í, chuireadar éadach trim uirthi, agus do bhíodar a d'iarraidh í a thabhairt chun beo, mar bhí sí geall le bheith marbh. Cuid acu a chuir bainne uirthi, mar ní raibh aon té len fháil, ach bhíodh *coffee* coitianta acu, mar do chualag. Ní raibh a fhios acu in aon chor aon ní mar gheall ar an dté an uair chéanna.

Bhí na carréaraithe imithe go Corcaigh le dhá lá nó trí roime sin, agus bhí súil abhaile acu leo an oíche sin. Ach níor thánadar fós, agus bhí easpa tobac ar mhórchuid acu, agus níor thaithn san go ró-mhór leo, mar bhíodar go buartha 'cheal tobac. Thairigíodh na mná an tobac, leis, agus ba mhór é a ndúil ann, agus nuair a bhíodar i dteannta a chéile ag tarrac an lín, b'é ab fhearr leo an tobac a bheith acu, is a ndúidín.

Ach dúirt sí leo, nuair a tháinig sí chuichi féin – is bhí sí ana-shásta nuair a dheineadar an tsuim sin di – nach fada bhuathu na carréaraithe in aon chor; go mbeadh tobac go leor amáireach acu agus foidhne a bheith acu; gur ghaibh sí féinig thársa is í ag teacht abhaile; go rabhadar anuas Barr Iarthach anois, ag teacht abhaile, agus an chuid eile acu anuas Loch 'á Bhonn.

Ní chreid aoinne í – go mbeadh sí ó Loch 'á Bhonn comh tapaidh – dá raibh istigh, ach fíor-bheagán, iad so go raibh a fhios acu go mbíodh sí sa chúrsa. Agus b'fhior di: bhí na carréaraithe sa bhaile amáireach mar a dúirt sí, agus do chreid gach eile dhuine acu ansan í.

19. Eachtruighthe ar bhean leighis a bhí i mBaile Bhoithín–I

b) Ráinig leis an sagart céadna beith ag rádh Aifrinn thuaidh ar a' gCarrig, tamall 'na dhiaidh sin. Capall iallaite a bhíodh i gcómhnúidhe aige ag dul ó thuaidh. Domhnach áirighthe bhí sé ag teacht a dtuaidh a' tráig ón Muirígheadh agus chomh luath agus chuir a chapall a cois san tsrúil atá i n-aice Baile 'n Rannaigh buaileadh bacach í. Do réigin (is ar éigean) a shiúblaidh sí siar go Baile 'n Rannaigh. Dúbhairt fear éigin ansan leis a' sagart í thabhairt siar go Eibhlín Ní Ghuinníola. Ní dubhairt sé seadh ná ní h-eadh, ná tabhair nó fág, mar bhí náire air, mar bhíodh sé ag cur síos uirthi gach Domhnach, agus ní thabharfadh sé lé rádh é go raghadh sé ag lorg leighis uirthi. Pé sceal é, d'imthig teachtaire agus chuaidh sé go Baile Bhoithín, go dtí Eibhlín Ní Ghuinníola. D'innis sé d'Eibhlín cad a thug é – go raibh capall a' tsagairt bacach. 'Tá fhios agam go bhfuil,' arsa Eiblín, 'agus b'fhearra dhon sagart leigint domsa na' haon Domhnach, mar ná fuilimse ag cur aon chuisteach (cur isteach) air. Anois go gcuireadh in iúl do go bhfuil fios agus leigheas agam, abair-se nuair a bheir ag déanamh ar a dtigh go bhfuil a chapall ag dul i bhfeabhas. Abair leis gurb é an uair a buaileadh bacach an capall nó nuair a chuir sí a cois deas san tsrúil atá i n-aice le Baile 'n Rannaigh; Ansan beidh fhios aige go bhfuil fios ag Eibhlín Ní Ghuinníola. Ón lá san amach níor tharraing an sagart, i mBéarla ná i nGaodhluinn chuige, lá saoire nó Domhnach.

20. Máire Ní Mhurchú agus an sagart

B'in mar a bhíodh Máire Ní Mhurchú bhocht, mar b'olc agus ba chruaidh an phurgadóireacht, mo ghraidhin í, do bhí uirthi ar an saol so. Le cúnamh Dé, tá súil agam ná fuil aon phurgadóireacht, puinn, ar an saol eile uirthi. Mar b'fhíor é mar gheall ar Mháire Ní Mhurchú; ní scéal é gur 'nis bean dom gur 'nis bean di, ná go ndúirt bean léi é, mar neosfad féin díbh é, mar tá breis fianaise ar ghnó Mháire Ní Mhurchú. Bhí sé fíor.

Bhí sé fíor, mar chualag go ndúirt sagart go raibh sé fíor; gur tógadh an hata dhe féin uair, ag teacht ó Dhá Dhrom ag triall ar na hAoraíbh: is ann a bhí sé chun cónaithe. Tógadh an hata dhe dhá uair in áit go nglaonn siad Droichead na mBarr air. N'fheaca sé aoinne, ach cuireadh a hata ar a cheann, agus dúirt Máire Ní Mhurchú leis ina dhiaidh sin é go b'í féin a chuir an hata ar a cheann, agus níor 'nis sé riamh di aon ní mar gheall ar an hata, mar do bhíodh sé ag caint mar gheall uirthi agus a d'iarraidh í a stop ar na gnóthaí a bhíodh ar siúl aici agus sin é an uair a ghéill sé dhi. Ón lá san go dtí an lá a cailleadh í, ní dúirt an sagart céanna aon ní léi, ach í a mholadh, agus an méid a fhéadfadh sé de chabhair mhairiúna a thabhairt di, agus do thug sé dhi é.

An cruachás á riaradh trí dhul i muinín na mná feasa

21. An bramach a goideadh agus an bhean feasa

Goideadh bramach óm' athair chríonna a bhí i mBaile 'n Chóta. Cuarduigheadh soir is siar, síos is suas do is ní raibh aon phioc le fagháilt do ná aon tuairisc air. Bhí sé tugtha suas aca. Cómhairluigheadh ansan é dul go dtí bean feasa a bhí na comhnuidhe i mBóthar a' tSeana Saipéil ag an Hóilí Steón ansan. Seana bhean í seo a bhíodh a'siubhal roimpe. Bhíodh sí a' díol criathar is bodhlaí. Ceannuigheataí na créithre chun cuirneacht a chriathairt. Chuai'sé a 'triall uirthi pé'n Éirinn é is chómh luath is dubhairt sé go raibh cúram aige dhi dubhairt sí leis- 'D'imigh ainmhide ceathair-chosach uait.

'D'imigh' a dubhairt sé, 'is thánga chughat féachaint a bhfaigfeá amach dom cá'il sé'. D'fáisc sí chun na mbodhlaí ansan – á gcur trí chéile. Tá an bramach, a dubhairt sí, i gCam Bhail' Uí Shéaghdha is laincide fé. B'fhíor di. Pé bitheamhnach a ghoid é, chuir sé ansúd é. Chuaidh m'athair críonna go Cam Bhail' Uí Shéaghdha is fuair sé an bramach ann is laincide fé.

22. Maire Ní Chearbhaill *and the heifer*
'Twas said that Máire Ní Chearbhaill used to go with the good people. She lived somewhere up about Castle Donovan and she had power to find things that were lost.

My mother's aunt was sewing in a certain house up in Gallans, and Máire used to come in there every day. Anyway the man of the house had lost a heifer and he had been searching for her, everywhere, for three weeks before that. This day, he was inside before Máire, when she came in, and he asked her in Irish if she could tell him anything about the heifer.

She said nothing but began to examine the cups in the dresser and mix them up here and there. Then she replied:

'Muise, go deimhin, níl sí caillte fós, ach ní fada go mbeidh. D'imthighis thairsti trí uaire ar maidin indiu.

'The man began to think and think what place he had crossed three times that morning. At last he remembered a place where there was an underground hole, and he went there. When he looked down there he saw his heifer, buried beneath the ground. She had all the cortha *(bogsoil) eaten around her and this had kept her alive for three weeks.*

23. Eachtruighthe ar bhean leighis a bhí i mBaile Bhoithín–II
Bhí bean leighis i mBaile Bhoithín fadó go nglaodhtí Eibhlín Ní Ghuinníola uirthi. Sé an seana-móin a bhíodh ag an sagart gach Domhnach ná ag cur síos uirthi i dtaobh bheith ag deanamh leighis. Do ráinig duine breoidhte i mBaile Bhoithín, sa bhaile go raibh sí agus cuireadh fios ar shagart chuichí. Táinig an sagart chuichi, agus bhí Eibhlín Ní Ghuinníola istigh roimis ach a d'táinig sé. D'feach sé ar Eibhlín agus dubhairt sé: 'Ba chóir nár ghádh fios a chur ormsa chómh fada agus bhí bean a' leighis istigh chun í leigheas' ar seisean. 'Níor iarr aoinne orm é' arsa Eibhlín. 'Táimse ghá iarraidh ort' arsan sagart. '*Very well*, mar sin, fan go fóill', arsa Eibhlín ag imeacht amach. Ní fada bhí sí amuigh nuair a tháinig sí isteach agus thug sí léi luibh éigin. Bhuail sí síos a' beiriú i sáspan an luibh. Ach a raibh sé tamall ar a dteine aici thóg sí é agus sgaoil sí amach ar chupa é. Dúbairt sí leis an bhfear breóidhte trí deocha do san d'ól. Do dhein agus d'eirigh sé aniar chómh mhaith agus bhí sé riabh. 'Seadh anois' ar sise leis a' sagart 'sin é agat é. D'imthigh a' sagart abhaile gan aon fhocal eile á labhairt

24. Eachtraithe ar bhean leighis a bhi i mBaile Bhoithin–III

Uair eile bhí na prátaí gá chur ar a dteine aige drifiúr Eibhlín Ní Ghuinníola. Dubhairt sí lei a thuille prátaí a chur sa chorcán mar, 'b'fhéidir' ar sisean ' gur fada ó bhaile a beadh stróinséir chun iad san d'ithe, nuair a bheidís beirighthe.' Ach a rabhadar beirighthe, bí stróinséirí ó lastoir a' Daingean a lorg leighis uirthi. Nuair a bhí na prátaí ite acu d'fiafhruigh sí dhóibh cad a thug iad. Dúbhairt duine acu gur a d'iarraigh leighis dá drifeír a bhí breóite, a thánadar. Fuair sé an leigheas (an luibh) – pé rud a oir do. 'Dún do dhorn ar an luibh sin', ar sise leis an mbuachaill go dtug sí dho é, 'agus cuir a'tarrac (ag beiriú) é, ach a raghair abhaile. Tabhair trí deocha dá dhruim sin di agus beidh sí chómh maith agus bhí sí riabh. Ná féach id' dhiaidh anois', ar sise, 'go gcuirfir Mám na Gaoithe síos duit, nó má dheineann tú, ní bheidh an luibh agat'. 'Tá go maith' arsan stróinseir. Nuair a bhí an stróinséir ag deanamh ar Mhám na Gaoithe choimeád sé an gleó 'na dheoigh. D'féach sé siar ach ní fheacaidh sé aoinne. Ach a n-osgail sé a láimh, ní raibh briota don luibh ann. D'fill sé thar nais. 'Bi ceall (bíodh geall) go b'amhlaidh a fhéachais ad' dhiaidh' arsa Eibhlín. 'An diar go b'eadh' arsan stroinséir, 'mar chuala an gleó go léir am dhiaidh'. 'Bhuel geobhair an seans so anois', ar sisean, 'ach má fheachann tú ad' dhiaidh go dtí go gcuirfir an Mám díot, dein gan é!' Fuair sé an luibh, agus d'imthigh sé. Cualaidh sé an gleó céadhna an ath-uair ach, má 's seadh, níor fheach sí 'na dhiaidh: Thug sé an luibh abhaile agus thug sé trí deocha de dhruim an luibh dá dhriféir agus d'eirigh sí chómh maith agus bhí sí riabh:

M'athair d'eachtraigh iad so dhom. Dúbhairt sé gur bh'minic a chloiseadh sé Séamus Ó Mainín (athair mo mháthar) ag cur síos uirthi. Deireadh sé go mbíodh leanán sídhe i dteannta Eibhlín Ní Ghuinníola nuair a bhíodh sí ag baint na luibheanna, gur minic a connaictheas é.

Léiríonn an bhean feasa an bhrí cheart atá le cursaí an tsaoil

25. Máire Ní Mhurchú agus mo mháthair féin

I dtaobh Mháire Ní Mhurchú, táim chun insint díbh arís go raibh fianaise mhaith age an mhuintir a bhí ar an mbaile go rabhas-sa mar gheall ar Mháire Ní Mhurchú, mar d'aithn mo mháthair féin í comh maith is a d'aithn sí aon bhean eile do bhí ar an mbaile. Agus ba mhinic a bhíodh sí i gcomhluadar léi agus ag caint léi, mar beainín dheas, ghrámhar, mhuinteartha, chneasta ab ea Máire Ní Mhurchú, d'réir mar a chualag scéalthóirithe an bhaill féin á rá. Do dhéanfadh sí aon ní a d'fhéadfadh sí a dhéanamh d'aoinne in aon chor ina cóngar. Ach dúirt mo mháthair liom go b'fhíor (na scéalta mar gheall ar Mháire Ní Mhurchú; nár scéal dúirsé dáirsé ab ea iad in aon chor, ná scéal gur 'nis bean dom go ndúirt bean léi.

Bhí sí féin oíche ag sníomh ar an dtinteán – agus ba mhinic é sin aici – ana-dhéanach. Bhí sé a dódhéag san oíche, a dúirt sí, go háirithe dhe, nó níba dheireanaí. Bhí máthair a céile in aonacht léi, b'in í mo sheanamháthairse féin, go ndeine Dia grásta orthu go léir. Ach do tháinig faitíos éigin ar mo sheanamháthair: do chualaigh sí sians éigin timpeall an tí, agus níor chualaigh mo mháthair in aon chor é le linn na huaire sin. Mar bhí an turann aici á oibriú, agus is dócha mb'fhéidir gur bhain san an éistecht di; gur ag tabhairt aire don turann a bhí sí. Ach dúirt mo sheanamháthair léi an tinteán a fhágaint agus dul a chodladh, mar bhí leanbh óg ann ná raibh ach mí nó dhó.

Níor bhain mo mhathair aon tuairim as: thóg sí aimsir agus do chuaigh sí sa leabaidh ina dhiaidh sin. Uair a chloig a thug sí ar an dtinteán i ndiaidh mo sheanamháthair a dhul sa leabaidh go háirithe. Agus níor thaithn san lem sheanamháthair ró-mhór, amáireach, mar dúirt sí léi go raibh sí ró-fhada ar an dtinteán ina diaidh féin – nó ar chualaigh sí aon ní timpeall an tí, mar a chualaigh sí féin. Agus dúirt mo mháthair nár chualaigh, ach go mb'fhéidir gur capall éigin a bhí timpeall an tí.

'Níor chualasa aon ní,' a dúirt mo mháthair, 'gur bh'fhiú dhom a áireamh. B'fhé' gur capall éigin a tháining ag bradaíocht timpeall an tí a chualaís-se. Ghlanas agus do scuabas an tinteán, mar ba thábhach liom, mar nár tháinig aon fhaitíos orm.',

'Do tháinig faitíos go leor ormsa,' a dúirt mo sheanamháthair, 'mar do chualag (an glór), agus do bhí níos mó ná capall ann, mar ní capall a bhí ann: má bhí aon chapall amháin ann do bhí dosaen acu ann, mar ní dhéanfadh capall (aonair) in aon chor a leithéid do shians timpeall an tí agus do deineadh. Tháinig cóthalán mór daoine agus capaill timpeall an tí, mar do chualasa an fuaim go léir agus an fothram.'

Ní chreid mo mháthair ró-mhór é: dúirt sí go mb'fhéidir, 'go bhfuil an ceart agat, ach go mb'fhéidir go mbeadh an t-ancheart agat, leis; go mb'fhéidir gur ag taibhreamh a bhís,' – ag cnáid-mhaghadh fúithi – fém sheanamháthair.

Ach níor thaithn san lem sheanamháthair ró-mhór, mar bhí a fhios aici go raibh an ceart aici féinig á insint. Ach níor mhaith lem mháthair tabhairt isteach, mar bhíodh sí amuigh – ana-oibrí ab ea í – comh luath sholas ló is oíche aici.

Dé Domhnaigh a bhí chughainn, do chuaigh sí go dtí an tAifreann go dtíos na hAoraí: is ann a bhí an séipéal i nDá Dhrom, leis, ach ní ann a théadh sí: théadh sí sa chóthalán i gcónaí go b'as í féin – ón dtaobh thiar des na hAoraí ab ea í – agus do tháinig Máire Ní Mhurchú chuichi th'réis Aifrinn, mar ba mhinic san ag Máire Ní Mhurchú.

Agus dúirt sí lem mháthair:

'A Mháire, nach leathlámhach,' – Máire Ní Urdail ab ea mo mháthair, leis – 'a Mháire, nach leathlámhach a bhís istoíche Dé Sathairn, ná raibh an tinteán scuabtha in am agat. Nuair a cuireadh eagla ort, chuais á scuabadh, ach ná dein é sin go brách arís. An méid ná beidh déanta agat, nuair a chloisfir aon ní nuair a bheir déanach ar an dtinteán, fág nach aon ní mar a bheidh sé, is téir a chodladh dhuit féin nó téir sa leabaidh: ná dein a leithéid go brách arís.'

'Cad é sin agat á rá,' a dúirt mo mháthair, 'Ar ndóin, ní rabhas-sa sa bhaile in aon chor Dé Sathairn: bhíos siar go dtí an Chluain.'

'Á, is maith a bhís, mar bhíos-sa ansúd is tú ag scuabadh an tinteáin, im shuí ar cheann an racaidh taobh leat.'

26. Máire ní Mhurchú agus an Maidhnéir

Scéal eile mar gheall ar Mháire Ní Mhurchú atháim le hinsint d'aoinne gur mhaith leis é a chlos.

Bhí m'athair ag obair ar an mianach, uair: maidhnéir ab ea é, cé gur táilliúir ab ea, leis, é – éadaigh a dhéanamh. Do bhí sé ins na ballaibh iasachta tamall eile dá shaol. Maidhnéir ab ea é, agus lá bhí sé ag obair ann – ar Mhianach Bhéarra, ar Sheana-Mhianach Bhéarra a ghlaonn siad air: is fearr a thuigfidh sibh é. Sé an áit a bhí sé ná ar na hAlathaibh Thuaidh. Tá a fhios agamsa an áit, mé féin, maith go leor, cé gur oth liom é a insint, mar is mó fear maith do bhris a shláinte (ann), agus gurbh é an trúig báis a bhí aige é.

Nuair a cuireadh síos na poill seo a bhí le caitheamh sa druileáil a bhí déanta age mh'athair agus age beirt eile fhear a bhí ag obair ina choinnibh, do thógadar na dréimirí chun dul ó dhainséar, mar dréimirí a bhí acu san uair chéanna. Ní raibh aon tslí eile acu chun iad féin a shaoradh ach na dréimirí i Mianach Bhéarra.

Nuair a thánadar ar barra, do chaith na poill, agus bhí trí cinn acu gan caitheamh: do chuadar amú, nó go raibh rud éigin a bhain dóibh nár chuadar chun cinn. Bhí an maidhnéir eile do bhí sa taobh eile den obair ... dúirt sé gurb iad na poill seo a chuir mh'athair síos nár chaith. Dúirt mh'athair leis gur chaith na poill; gur thug sé féin tine dhóibh, mar gur thriail sé an *fuse*, agus go raibh an *fuse* go maith; nár baol ná gur chuadar chun cinn.

'Ach mar sin féin,' a dúirt sé, 'chun tusa a shásamh,' – mar bhí m'athair ana-réidh, agus ba mhaith leis nach aoinne é, agus comharsain mhaithe ab ea an bheirt, leis – 'raghadsa síos agus fainse mar atháinn tú,' a dúirt sé.

Chuaigh m'athair síos an dréimire, agus nuair a chuaigh sé i láthair na bpoll síos – an áit a bhíodar ládálta, agus tine tabhartha dhóibh – do chaith na trí poill mórtdtimpeall air agus níor bhain smáchail leis. Tháinig sé aníos sa dréimire, agus nuair a tháinig sé ar an dtalamh, do chuir sé ionadh agus uafhás ar gach nduine a chonaic é: shíleadar go raibh sé ina ghrean thíos ages na pollaibh. D'inis sé dhóibh go raibh sé ina ghrean thíos nuair a chaitheadar agus nár imigh aon mháchail air.

Ar an Satharn a bhí chughainn nuair a bhí sé ag teacht abhaile, do bhuail Máire Ní Mhurchú ar na hAoraí uimis, agus do ghlaoigh sé air, agus d'inis sí dho mar a neosfadsa dhíbh.

'A Sheáin, nach simplí an gnó do dheinis-se an oíche seo d'áirithe.'

'Cad é sin, a Mháire?' a dúirt sé: níor leog sé air in aon chor gur thuig sé í.

'Nár chuais-se síos do Shéamus Ó Sé, ag féachaint i ndiaidh na bpoll nár chaith dho, fios agat go maith nárbh é do ghnó féin iad. Chuais-se síos agus dúraís leis fanúint mar a raibh aige. A Sheáin, ná dein a leithéid do rud go brách arís,' a dúirt sí, 'ach ní marófar go brách in aon mhianach thú – ní thú a bhí bhuathu – ach béarfar air sin (Mac Uí Shé) luath nó déanach.'

I gceann dhá bhliain ina dhiaidh sin, do chuaigh mh'athair go Meirice – go dtíos na *Lakes* a chuaigh sé – agus bhí Séamus Ó Sé in Éirinn an uair sin. Chuaigh sé amach bliain ina dhiaidh, agus nuair a chuaigh sé amach, sa mhianaigh céanna – an *Red Jacket* a ghlaonn siad air – do chuaigh Séamus Ó Sé chun oibre. Chuaigh sé ag obair sa mhianaigh chéanna mar a chuaigh mh'athair, agus an chéad lá a chuaigh sé ag obair dúirt sé lem athair rud greannúr do bhuail uimis; gur chonaic sé mar a bheadh i bhfoirm giorré bán: tháinig sé treasna an bhóthair agus é ag teacht go dtí an mianach. Siúl cos a théidis go dtí an mianach. Ní raibh aon chairteanna ó mhianach go mianach an uair sin: ó shoin a deineadh na meaisíní go léir.

An chéad *shift* a d'oibrigh sé, do bleaisteáladh é, agus tugadh aníos marbh é, th'réis dul go Meiriceá. Agus b'in a bhí bhuathu i Mianach Bhéarra, a dúirt Máire Ní Mhurchú.

27. *St Fanahan's Well* and **Máire Liam**

St Fanahan's Well was at first in a place called Brí Gabhann. *But the people of the place around Mulberry used to wash clothes and dirty the well, so it moved out of that place to the place it is at present, about two miles away from it. There was a man who would always make a round at the well on St Fanahan's Night, 25th November. On this St Fanahan's night he came to the well as usual but he found that the well was gone. He stood there, wondering what had become of the well and twasn't long until a woman, all dressed in white came up and asked him what he was looking for. He told her. She told him the well had moved about two miles south-east from the place on account of the people washing clothes and dirtying the water of it, and she showed him where to find it.*

There were two young lads from Mulberry went for a bucket of water to the well after that. They were bringing the bucket of water, between them, with a long pole and the bucket hanging on it. Just as they were coming from the well with the water a rabbit jumped up in front of them. They left down the water and ran after the rabbit. One of them got a very sore leg after that. It was sore with him for a long time and worse it was getting, every day. There was an old woman living down near Lismore at the time. She was great to cure sore legs or hands and people used come from all parts to her, to get cured. She used never take any money for curing, only you'd have to bring her a little present, anything you liked to give. Anyway they brought this boy down to the old woman. Her name was Máire Liam. When they were coming near the old woman's house she was at the door before them and she says to them:

'Don't tell me what happened because I know. Why didn't you bring on the water that day and not mind the rabbit. Go home now again. I've nothing to do for him. He'll be dead in a few days'. And so he was.

28. An cailín ar baineadh a hurlabhra dhi

Bhí cailín aonair ann (Inis Arcán) agus do baineadh a h-urlabhru dhi. Chuaidh sí a chodladh slán agus ní raibh aon urlabhra ar maidin aici. Bhí bean thoir i mBéal Átha an Fhíona a bhíodh ag tabhairt feasa uaithi – bhíodh sí a' dul leis na daoine maithe. Do tugadh an cailín a' triall uirthi féach a'bféadfadh sí í leigheas. Nuair a chonaic sí í ní fhéadfadh sí aon nídh dhéanamh di agus dubhairt sí léi, teacht arís i gceann coicíse.

Tháinig, agus dubhairt sí len a h-athair cad 'na thaobh gur thóg sé a thigh ar cómhgar puirt, agus ná beadh aon ádhbhar (rath) go deó ann agus ná beadh aon uireasba go deó ortha ann. Do thóg sí báisín den dressúr agus d'fiafraigh sí den chailín ar aithin sí é sin. Dubhairt sise gur aithin agus gur airigh sí uaithi é.

'Bhíos ag do thig ó chuin agus do thógas an báisín seo' a dubhairt sí. 'Ná rabhais' ar sise, 'ag comáint capaill anuas an cnoc agus do bhuail bean ruadh cholgach de mhuintir Airnéidigh umat, agus do bhí falaing olna aniar uirthe agus thug sí clabhta ar gach taobh díot agus an tríomhadh ceann i mullach an chinn duit. Bhí nimh ansan. Do leigheas sí an cailín; ach thagadh an easba urlabhra uirthe timpeal an am céadna, go lá a báis.

29. Carn Tighearna

Tá Carn Tighearna timcheall dhá mhíle ar an dtaobh theas de Mhainstir Fhear Muighe (*Fermoy*). Cnoc an-árd iseadh é, deire na sliabh-raonta atá aniar siar san áit sin. Tá carn mór ar bhárr an chnuic agus glaodhtar Carn Tighearna air.

Bhí Tighearna mór, nú Taoiseach 'na chomhnuidhe i Mainstir Fhear Muighe uair amháin fadó. Bhí *mansion* bréagh mór aige cois na h-Abhann Móire. Bhí sé pósta agus ní raibh de chlainn aige ach an t-aon mhac amháin. Bhí an-chion aige ar an leanbh ní nach iongadh, cad 'na thaobh na béadh?

Lá amháin thainig bean feasa isteach 'dtí an tigh chucha agus d'iarr sí rud éigin ortha, ach thugadar an t-eiteachas dí. Dubhairt sí annsin, ná mairfeadh an leanbh críonna – mar go mbáithfí é. Cé nár chuir an tighearna puinn suime san mhéid sin i dtosach, níor dhearmhad sé riamh é agus bhiodh sé ag machnamh agus ag sior-mhachnamh air go dtí sa deire do shocraigh sé 'na aigne go bhfágadh sé an mansion, mar bhí sé ro-chomhgarach don abhainn, agus go raghadh sé go dtí áit éigin ná beadh aon uisce i ngar do.

Shocraigh sé ar tigh nua do thogáil ar bhárr an chnuic seo atá dhá mhíle ó dheas ó Mhainstir Fhear Muighe. Chuir sé a lucht oibre ag obair agus bhí cuid de tógtha acu; bhí sé le bheith 'na mhansion breágh. Is álainn ar fad an radhairc ón gcnoc san. Chídhfeá an tír ar feadh mílte ar gach taobh díot. Chídhfeá Corcaigh ó dheas uait, chídhfeá Co. Tiobraid Árann agus Co. Luiminigh ó thuaidh agus do chídhfeá an Abha Mhór ag snídhe go mall soir, síos chomh fada le Lios Mór. Bheul, lá amháin chuaidh an tighearna suas go barr a' chnuic go bhfeiceadh sé conas a bhí an obair ag dul ar aghaidh. B'fhada leis go mbeadh an tigh réidh chun comhnuidhe ann mar bhí ag méadú ar a eagla in aghaidh an lae i dtaobh a mhic agus an bás a tarraingeadh do. Thug sé an mac leis an lá so go dtí barr a' chnuic; buachaillín óg timcheall sé bliadhna d'aois do-beadh é. Bhíodar ag obair ar a ndícheall ar bhárr an chnuic ag tógaint an tighe. D'fan an tighearna ag cainnt leis an bhfear a bhí i mbun na h-oibre agus d'fhág sé an garsún ag rith timpeall.

Bhí barraillí uisce aca ann agus tháinig an garsún go dtí ceann acu, ar an dtaobh thiar den bhfoirgneamh, agus do chrom sé isteach thar an barraile, agus, slán mar a n-innstear é, thuit sé isteach agus báitheadh é. Báitheadh é sar ar thug aoinne fé ndeara é.

Bhí an-buairt ar an dtighearna annsin. Bhris sé a chroidhe agus ba ghearr a mhair sé 'na dhiaidh sin.

Fághadh an tigh mar a bhí, gan chriochnú riamh. Sin é an carn atá ar bhárr Charn Tighearna go dtí an lá indiu.

30. Máire Ní Chearbhaill *and the blow from the red-haired woman* (63)

I remember hearing another story about Máire Ní Chearbhaill from D. M.'s grandfather who lived over there in Moulnagerra, in the parish of Leap. His wife's people were living over beyond Reenascreena, near Rosscarbery, and Máire used to come in visiting them every day.

One night one of his brothers-in-law went conveying a neighbour home from scoruíochting (social visiting) and when he was coming back home, he got sick. Next day he was almost dying and the priest or doctor could not do anything to cure him. About the middle of the day they saw Máire coming in and she having a bottle in her hand.

She asked where was Jack and they told her how he got sick last night and that he was very bad.

'Ah', she said 'it was a good job for him that I was by his side when he was struck the blow, or he would be here with you now as a corpse. It was a red-haired woman from Poll na Piseoige who struck him and I knocked the stick she had out of her hand before she was able to do him any more damage. Rub this bottle to him, now, and he will be all right again.'

They rubbed the bottle to him and he was cured.

É ar chumas na mná feasa fóirithint ar an bhfuadach sí

31. Máire Ní Murchú agus an bhean a fuadaiodh

Ó bhíos im leanbh is mór atá cloiste agam mar gheall ar síóga; mórchuid ag áiteamh ná raibh a leithéidí in aon chor ann, nó mara rabhadar ann, is mór athá ráite mar gheall orthu.

Ach d'inis mo mháthair féin domhsa go minic mar gheall ar bhean a bhí ina cónaí ar na hAoraíbh go nglaoidís Máire Ní Mhurchú uirthi. Agus sé an áit a bhí an tigh aici, agus tá cuid den seana-áitreamh ann sa ló inniu, mar táimse im chónaí i ngiorracht ceathrú mhíle den áit anois i ndeireadh mo shaoil – táim fhéin chríonna, leis – in áit go nglaonn siad Baile na nAoraí air, i ngiorracht ceathrú mhíle den sráidín athá ann, in áit go nglaonn siad Draighneach air. Tá rian na cabhlaí ann fós sa ló inniu, sa tslí go bhfuil fianaise mhaith go raibhsí ann. Bhí sé ráite go mbíodh.

Do buaileadh bean breoite i nDá Dhrom Istigh – bean de Mhuintir Shé – agus bhí sí go dian, dochrach, breoite, gan aon súil le í a theacht thar n-ais. Agus tháinig dochtúir agus sagart agus gach duine á fiafraí, agus a d'iarraidh í a leigheas, agus ní raibh aon leigheas len fháilt di. Fé dheireadh do chuaigh a fear go dtí Máire Ní Mhurchú. Ní chreidfeadh sé riamh roime sin go raibh aon fhios age Máire: is ann a bhídís ag cnáid-mhagadh fúithi. Agus d'fhiafriagh sé dhi an raibh aon fhios in aon chor ar aon leigheas a dhéanamh di, nó an raibh a fhios aici aon ní mar gheall air, nó an raibh sí soinséaltha, nó ar bhreoiteacht cheart í.

Do gháirigh sí agus dúirt:

'Is mithid duit teacht,' a dúirt sí. 'Is fada dhi sin fuadaithe bhuaitse, agus is gearr ó bhaile bhuait í go minic, agus is olc an t-aoireacht athá agat a dhéanamh ar an té athá ina hionad agat. Agus ní mór gur maith liom aon ní a dhéanamh duit na d'ise anois, mar is ann a bhí searús agat ormsa riamh roime seo – ná raibh fios ar aon ní agam – agus is mó dainséar agus milleán atá fálta agamsa ó mórán agaibh.'

D'inis sí dho go raibh sí i gCiarraí thall in áit go nglaonn siad Dóinn air, ages na síoga, agus 'á raghadh sé ann le criú báid, treasna, istoíche Dé Máirt a bhí chughainn, go raghadh sí féin in aonacht leis, agus go mbeadh sí ar an dtarna capall tosaigh a bheadh ag teacht anoir ó Neidín, agus go dtabharfadh sí uisce dho i mbuidéal, agus bogha a dhéanamh timpeall lena mhéir leis an uisce ar an mbóthar, agus í a thógaint den chapall a bhí ar chúlaibh an fhir, agus í a thabhairt isteach sa bhogha is go mbeadh sí aige.

Do thoiligh sé leis, agus d'iarr sé ar chuid des na comharsain a bhí timpeall go raibh súil aige ná heiteoidis é, cé gur chruaidh an obair agus gur dhainséarach dul treasna na fairrge féna déin, dar leo féin. Agus bhí sé thíos go maith acu, leis: bhí faitíos ar mhórán acu ach gur chuadar ann. Níor mhaith leo é a eiteach, mar fear ana-mhaith do b'ea é féin.

Do chuadar ann istoíche Dé Máirt, agus do dhein sé an rud a dúirt Máire Ní Mhurchú leis a dhéanamh, agus bhí Maire Ní Mhurchú, leis, in aonacht leo sa bhád. Agus do tháinig na capaill agus na marcaigh agus na cúlóga, agus thug sé fé í a thabhairt den chapall leis, agus do mheath air: chaitheadar teacht abhaile á héamais.

Seachtain ón lá san, do fuaireadar iad féin ullamh arís agus do chuadar ann, agus ar uair a dódhéag san oíche bhí na capaill le teacht anoir an bóthar céanna arís, agus do dhein sé an cleas céanna arís, mar a dúirt Máire Ní Mhurchú leis. Agus do thug sé den chapall í isteach sa bhfáinne a bhí deanta aige leis an uisce ar an mbóthar, agus do thugadar leo go dtí an bád síos í. Ní raibh i bhfad le dul orthu go dtí an bád, mar tá an bóthar ana-chóngarach don fhairrge ann.

Dúirt sé leo an bád a iomradh chomh mear agus chomh láidir is d'fhéadfaidis é; comh acmhainneach is do bhí sé in acmhainn a dhéanamh – go leanfaí iad gan moill. Bhí fairrge ar a ndroim agus fairrge timpeall orthu, suaill agus calaithe – ach nár bádh iad – to dtí go dtánadar leathslí. Dúirt sí leo é a thógaint socair ansan – bhí an fhairrge ciúin – agus do thugadar leo abhaile go Tráigh an Phuillín an bhean an fhir bhreoite. Agus nuair a thánadar abhaile go dtí an tigh, an bhean a bhí sa leabaidh – ní raibh aon ní sa leabaidh rompu ach éadach na leapa – bhí sí imithe léi. Agus do mhair sí fiche bliain ina dhiaidh sin th'réis í a thabhairt ó Chiarraí den chapall, agus do bhí mórchuid clainne aici, ach go ceann deich mbliana nó dhá bhliain déag ina dhiaidh sin níor mhair bó ná gamhain aige: cailleadh a chuid stoic, agus cuireadh mórán chun deiridh é.

Ní raibh aon bhréag ansan – i dtaobh pé bréag athá mar gheall ar síoga –

ná suaite scéil ná bréaga. Bhí san comh fíor agus tá an ghrian ag taitneamh ar an aer.

32. Máire Ní Mhurchú agus an buachaill a fuadaíodh–I

Bhí fear inár bparóistene, áit go nglaonn siad Cathair Caim air – Cathair Caim. Mícheal Ó Gúgáin ab ea an fear. Ní raibh age a athair de mhac ach é – bhí sé i dtúrtaoibh leis, ach do bhí driféaracha aige – agus do phós sé ana-óg é, i dtreo é a chimeád sa bhaile, mar bhí sé chun dul go Meiriceá 'á bhféadfadh sé é, agus ní raibh aon tseans age a athair chun é a chimeád, dar leis féin, ach an áit a thabhairt do agus é a phósadh in am.

Bliain nó dhó th'réis é a phósadh do buaileadh breoite é. Fear acmhainneach láidir ab ea é, agus do tháinig sé breoite ana-thapaidh, agus do mheath a shláinte air. Agus do bhí ionadh ar mhórán cad a theangaigh do – fear comh tréan, comh láidir leis. Nuair a chuaigh de gach dochtúir a insint dóibh cad a bhí ag baint do, ná de shagart, chuadar go dtí Máire Ní Mhurchú. Agus dúirt Máire Ní Mhurchú leo, ar ndóin, gur mhithid dóibh teacht; gur mhaith a bhí a fhios acu nach aon easpa sláinte a bhí air, ach ná raibh sé acu le fada; agus 'á mhaith leo é a leigheas gurb é an áit a bhí a leigheas, i Roilig Chill Macallóg, agus mara raghfaí á iarraidh sin agus é a fháilt, go mbeidís ina éamaís gan moill.

Ní raibh aon tslí acu ar dul ann gan ise ina dteannta, agus d'iarradar di an raghadh sí ann lena gcois is dúirt sí go raghadh, is go bhfaigheadh sí beirt fhear do raghadh ... ná heiteodh iad, leis – Tadhg Caobaoch do bhí ar an mbaile agus Diarmaid Ó Murchú. Agus d'iarradh iad is chuadar ann an oíche chéanna. Agus nuair a chuadar go dtí geata na roilige i gCill Macallóg, dúirt sí leo fanúint age an ngeata agus go raghadh sí féin isteach sa roilig. Agus chuaigh sí sa taobh thiar den roilig, agus do bhain sí an luibh seo a d'oir di, agus tháinig sí go dtí an geata chuchu. Chuaigh sí ar chúlaibh Tadhg Chaobaigh, agus dúirt si leis an capall a thiomáint comh mear agus d'fhéadfadh sé agus breith leis – gur gearr go mbeithfí ina dhiaidh – go dtí go dtánadar go dtí (teora) Chiarraí anoir, sa Ghlaise, in áit go nglaonn siad Glaise na Naíonán air. Do stracathaí den capall í, ach do chimeádadh sé lena láimh féin oscail í, go minic agus ana-mhinic, go dtí go dtánadar go dtí an Glaise na Naionán, agus dúirt sí leis é a thógaint socair anois -ná féadfaidís dul níos sia.

Do tháinig sí abhaile go dtí Cathair Caim, agus do bhí an fear breoite sa leabaidh, agus do thug sí an luibh do. N'fheadair aoinne conas a thug sí dho é ach í féin, mar níor lamháil sí aoinne sa rúm go ceann neomataí éigin, ach í féin. Agus ba ghearr gur labhair fear na leapa: do shuigh sé suas sa leabaidh, agus dhírigh sé ar chaint leo, agus d'innis sé dhóibh mar gheall ar na sióga, agus dhein sé scéal ceart (fíor) de scéal Mháire Ní Mhurchú.

D'inis sé dhóibh gurbh fhíor scéal Mháire Ní Mhurchú; go raibh sé féin thiar in áit go nglaoid siad Tráigh an Phéarla (air) le bliain, i gcuirt sí a bhí ann; go b'é an áit is mó a bhíodh sé, agus ná raibh aon teacht thar n-ais aige go brách; ach go raibh duine muinteartha leis ann – bean mhuinteartha ab ea í – agus dúirt sí leis gan aon ní dá gcuid bídh a chaitheamh in aon chor, nó 'á gcaithfeadh ná tagfadh sé go brách thar n-ais.

Sé an bia a chaitheadh sé faid a bhí sé (amuigh) bhuathu, ná an bia a bhíodh fágtha ins na tithe th'réis suipéir san oíche, ar a ngabháilt timpeall agus ag caitheamh aimsire doibh féinig.

Bhí cailín rua, a dúirt sé, sa chúirt ann, agus do thit sí amach go minic leis a d'iarraidh go gcaithfeadh sé suipéar nó broicfeast do bhain leo féin, mar ba mhór ba mhaith léi í féin a bheith in aonacht leis. Agus dúirt an bhean mhuinteartha so leis gan bac leis, mar á mbacfadh ná tagfadh sé go brách; go raibh súil aici go mb'fhéidir go ndéanfaí leigheas éigin cois baile dho. Agus nuair a cuireadh thar n-ais é, do bhuail an cailín rua so clabhta air – baise – ar a aghaidh, agus do bhain sí radharc(na) súl de. Agus do bhíos-sa féin ina shochraid agus ina thórramh, agus chonac, le fianaise mo shúl, go raibh radharc (na) súl bainte dhe ón uair a bhí sé breoite go dtí an lá a cuireadh sa talamh é.

33. Máire Ní Mhurchú agus an buachaill a fuadaíodh-2

Feirmeoir agus iascaire ab ea Seán Rua – fear láidir groí. Thárla gur buaileadh breoite é, agus b'ait an saghas breoiteachta é mar do bhí sé teipithe glan ar dochtúiribh é a leigheas. Do bhí sé ar feadh i bhfad ina luí sa leabaidh agus ní raibh sé ag teacht chuige féin.

Lá, bhuail Máire Ni Mhurchú isteach chuchu is do chuir sí tuairisc an té a bhí breoite. D'inseadar di conas mar a bhí aige. Ansan do labhair Máire, agus dúirt sí:

'Is olc an scéal aige é, an fear bocht. Tá sé dona go leor, agus beidh go fóill, leis. Níl ach aon ní amháin a dhéanfadh maitheas do agus a dhéanfadh slán arís é, agus sé an ní é sin ná lus atá ag fás in Roilig Chill Macallóg, agus níl fáil uirthi ach in am mairbh na hoíche. Is féidir liomsa i d'fháil do. Agus anois, a dhaoine, má thánn sibh sásta í a thabhairt do, béarfaidh mise chuige í, ach ní mór liom cabhair d'fháil uaibh.'

Thoiltheanaigh muintír an tí dá [h]achaíní, agus sí an chabhair a d'iarr sí ná beirt mharcach agus iad a bheith ullamh roimpi ar a gcapaill timpeall a haondhéag a chlog an oíche ina dhia' san. Theastaigh uaithi, leis, na cinn a bhí sa gcomharsanacht, mar dúirt sí go raibh contúirt agus baol mór san obair a bhí rompu.

Istoíche amáireach, bhí na marcaigh ullamh roimh Máire. Ní raibh aon chapall ag Máire is do shocraigh sí í féin mar chúlóig taobh thiar de dhuine acu. D'imíodar leo chun bóthair timpeall leathuair t'réis a haondhéag a chlog.

Nuair do shroiseadar an roilig, d'imigh Máire uathu agus d'ordaigh dóibh fanúint mar a rabhadar go bhfillfeadh sí chuchu arís. Chaith sí tamall cuíosach fada istigh ins an roilig, agus do bhí sé taréis a haon a chlog nuair a d'fhill sí thar n-ais chuchu. Bhí dithneas an domhain uirthi, ach bhí na fir ullamh roimpi, is do ghluaiseadar chun bóthair gan mhoill. D'ordaigh Máire doibh dul comh tapaidh agus a bhí i gcosaibh na gcapall iad a bhreith, mar go raibh baol ana-mhór ann ná sroisfidís deireadh a gcúrsa slán. D'imíodar leo ar chos anairde, ach i mbéarsa, do leanadh iad, agus do bhí an slua a bhí á leanúint ag dul comh tapaidh agus b'fhéidir níos mire ná iad féin. Is mó iarracht a deineadh as san siar go teorainn Chondae Chorcaí agus Chiarraí ar Mháire do ghabháil ach do theip orthu. An tráth a d'imíodar treasna na teorann, dúirt ná raibh aon bhaol ann dóibh a thuilleadh.

Nuair do shrois siad tigh Sheáin, thug Máire saghas dí dho. I gceann tamaill tháinig biseach mór air, agus d'fhill a chaint chuige agus is ait an eachtra a d'aithris sé dá mhuintir. D'inis sé doibh conas mar a bhí sé ina chónaí i sí-bhrogha i dtrá fiáin ins na hAlaithe Thiar ar feadh bliana roime sin. Tigh fíor-álainn é, agus do bhí go leor le n-ithe agus le n-ól aige ann. Bhí, ina gcónaí ann, leis, a dúirt sé, a chairde agus a ghaolta féin a bhí le fada marbh. Do bhí ann, leis, cailín – cailín na gruaige buí a thug sé uirthi – agus do bhí sí i gcónaí ag tathant air í a phósadh, ach ní ghéilfeadh sé dá hachainí. An bia a bhí ann is amhlaidh a bhailidís chuchu é ós na tithibh ina ndéanfaí dearúd ar a mbordaibh do ghlanadh t'réis béile na hoíche. Tháinig an cailín chuige an oíche sin, a dúirt sé, nuair a bhí a shuipéar caite aige, agus chuaigh sí go dian air í a phósadh, agus i ndeireadh thiar thall, nuair ná géilfeadh sé di, thug sí clabhta baise sa tsúil do. Ón lá san amach go lá a bháis, bhí an fear bocht ar leathshúil, slán mar a n-instear é.

34. Seán 'ac Séamais

Bhí Rí ar Éirinn fadó gurbh ainm do Séamas. Bhí mac aige gurbh é an ainm a tugtaí air Seán ach Séamais. Ní raibh san áit le n-a linn aon phrionnsa ba bhreághtha ná ba dheise ná é. Do bhí sé lá Domhnaigh i gcómhthalán rinnce.

I gcaitheamh an lae dhóibh do ghaibh óigbhean bhreágh chuig mac an rí agus do shín sí ubhall chuige. Do thóg sé an t-ubhall ach ní leigfeadh an uaisleacht do é ithe os cómhair na ndaoine. Nuair a chonnaic sí nár ith sé an t-ubhall, do thug sí smut d'ubhall annsan do. Ní leigfeadh an náire dho é chur 'na phóca. D'ith sé é, agus do chaith sé i leannúint mar bean sidhe dob eadh í. Thug sí léithi é riamh is choidhche nó go ndeaghadar síos go Carraig Chlíodhna. Clíodhna b'ainm don mhnaoi agus Carraig Cliodhna tugtaí ar an áit go raibh sí 'na cómhnaidhe, thíos i gCorcaigh.

Bhí Shéan ach Séamais fé dhraoidheacht annsan aici agus ní raibh fhios aige n-a mhuinntir cá raibh sé imithe. Bhí sé buartha cráidhte agus ní fheadair sé cad do dhéanfadh sé. Ní raibh sé úsáid aon phioc den mbiadh a bhí ann. Bíodh sé ag ithe samhaidh, biolair agus gach aon ní go bhféadfadh sé aon úsaid a bhaint as. Ní bhíodh aon oscailt ag an gcarraig le déanamh ó éirghe gréine ar maidin nó go dtéigheadh sí fé tráthnóna. D'éirigh mac an rí amach tráthnóna breágh tar éis na gréine dhul fé agus litir scríbhte le fuil aige. Do scaoil sé leis an ngaoith í féachaint a bhfaghadh aenne í do thabharfad tuairisc don athair cá raibh sé. 'Om basa do fuair aodhaire bó a bhí age n'athair í. Nuair a léigh sé í, do chuaidh sé go dtí an rí agus an litir aige. Do ghlac iongnadh mór an rí nuair a chualaidh sé cá raibh a mhac, agus gurbh fhéidir le haon duine don dtriúr ban so é thabhairt abhaile, siad san an Déidbhean, Rós Chaoldubh, nó Máirín Dubh ó iarthar Éireann. Ní raibh aenna aca le faghail ach Máirín Dubh a bhí 'na comhnaidhe i nDún Chaoin. Tháinig an tuairisc chúichi chun dul ag fuascailt mac an rí. Bhí sí breoite agus ní fhéadfadh sí dul ann. Bhí cailín óg d'inghin aici agus dubhairt go raghadh sí féin ann.

"Ní haon mhaith duit dul ann," arsan mháthair, "mar ná féadfá-sa an gnó a dhéanamh." "Triallfad é ach go háirithe," arsan inghean. " Seadh anois," arsan mháthair, "an fhaid is go bhfuileann tú ag dul ann innseofad duit cad is maith dhuit a dhéanamh."

Do thug rí léithi gúna go dtugtaí beafaití air, agus chuir sí ar an inghin é. Dubhairt sí léithi, "Imthigh ort anois nó go raghaidh tú go dtí n-a leithéid seo d'áit go bhfuil sé fé dhraoidheacht ann. Níl aon mhaidean sa mbliain roim éirghe gréine ná go mbíonn Clíodhna ar an dtaobh amuigh den charraig ag cíoradh a cinn. Mara dtagaidh tusa uirthi i gan 'fhios di agus do lámh a chasadh 'na cuid gruaige agus gan leigint di iompú ar an taobh di, nó má fhéachann sí ort le n-a súile, tá deireadh leat."

Do leig an mháthair slán agus beannacht le n-a hinghin agus d'imthigh sí léi. Níor stad rí riamh ná choidche nó gur bain sí amach an áit cheart. Is amhlaidh a bhí Clíodhna i dtaobh amuigh den charraig agus a cuacha léi síos. Do tháinig inghean Mháirín i gan 'fios uirthi agus do chas a lámh 'na cuid gruaige agus seo mar dubhairt sí léi:

Inghean Mhairín:
"A Chlíodhna, 'Chlíodhna, a bhean mhín bhéasach,
Go mbeannuighidh Críost dúit agus na naoimh le' chéile;
Conus atá agat Seán ach Séamais,
Ar phós sé fós nó an bhfuil gan céile,
Nó an eol duit ar t'eolas aon óigbhean réidh leis?"

Cliodhna:
"Cé hé tu féin atá ar 'éileamh,
An tú an Déidbhean nó Rós Chaoldubh,
Nó Máirín Dubh ó iarthar Éireann."

Inghean Mhairín;
"Ní haenna aca san mise féinig,
Ach inghean dílis do Rí na Gréige;
An t-ubhallín óir a bhíodh ag an mbábán ar bórd na Féinne,
Go ndeineadh sé óg an té bíodh aosta."

Clíodhna:
"Dá mba inghean rí tu, agus ní headh i n-ao' chor,
Do bheadh do chuid gruaige 'na dualaibh go féar leat,
Do leacain dheas dhearg mar lasadh na gcaortha
Agus fáinní óir ar gach aon mhéir ded mhéaraibh."

Inghean Mháirín:
"Dá dtugthá-sa seacht mbliana fé shileadh na ré glas[?],
Agus gan de beatha 'gat ach samhad, biolar, agus féar glas,
Agus gan de chleachtadh' agat lá breágh gréine,
Ach broc ón ngleann agus coileán faolchon
Ba mheasa leat féin iad ná fáinní Éireann.
Nó munab é sin é tabhair-se spré dho
Seacht gcéad bó agus seacht gcéad laogh dho,
Seacht gcéad caora fí na lomraíbh gléigeal',
Agus seacht gcéad each ar dhath a chéile,
Seacht gcéad gabhar maol donn gan aon locht,
Seacht gcéad bó buineann druimionn bléineach,
Seacht gcéad bulán ceannárd péacach,
Seacht gcéad baraille den airgead réalach,
Nó seacht gcéad acra de fhlaitheas na Naomh do;
Is dob fhearr liom marbh é ar mo chuid féin do,
Ná é fheiscint pósta ag aon bhean sidhe i nÉirinn."

Clíodhna:
"Dá bhfantá-sa uam-sa go huair an mheánlae amuigh,
Go mbaileochadh m'fhuireann i bhfothain a chéile,
Do bhrisfinn cnuic agus réabfainn sléibhte,
Do chuirfinn cuirp go tiugh ó 'chéile,
Do dhoirtfinn fuil 'na caisí géara,
Do chloisfeadh an domhan mór fios fuaim mo scéil-se
Nó bheadh agam féinig Seán ach Séamais."

Do chaith Clíodhna tabhairt suas agus Seán a leigint i n-éinfheacht léi abhaile go dtí n-a athair. Nuair a shroicheadar an tigh do fuair sí le pósadh ó n-a athair é, agus fáilte; agus do chaith Clíodhna gan baint leis as san amach, cé gur dhein sí suas gach aon phioc den spré i n-aon neomat amháin ach na seacht gcéad baraille den airgead réalach agus na seacht gcéad acra de Fhlaitheas na Naomh, mar ná raibh neart aici baint leo san.

NOTES AND REFERENCES

A perspective on Irish oral tradition
1. W.G. Wood-Martin, *Traces of the Elder Faiths of Ireland*, vol. 1, p. vii (London, 1902).
2. See P. MacCana, *Learned Tales of Medieval Ireland* (Dublin, 1980).
3. A recent attempt to summarize and exemplify the aims of anthropology is that of P. Bohannan, *How Culture Works* (New York, 1995).
4. See especially Chapter 1, 'The Nature of Culture Today' in U. Hannerz, *Cultural Complexity* (New York, 1992).
5. W.D. O'Flaherty, *Other Peoples' Myths* (London, 1988) is a treatment of myth and legend that presents them in a light akin to my own treatment of the texts and functions of traditional Irish narratives in Parts Two and Three of this work.
6. Ibid., p. 156.
7. Ibid., p. 156.
8. Ibid., pp. 156–157
9. B. Malinowski, 'Myth in Primitive Psychology', p. 100.

Oral narrative as literature
1. See the discussions of the terms 'Performance' and 'Folktale' by R. Bauman, pp. 41–9 and D. Ben-Amos, pp. 101–118 in D. Ben-Amos (ed.), *Folklore, Cultural Performances and Popular Entertainments* (Oxford, 1992).
2. See the discussions of 'Consciousness', pp. 65–79 and 'Narrative', pp. 283–90 as key concepts in anthropology in N. Rapport and J. Overing, *Social and Cultural Anthropology* (London, 2000). Much of the remainder of this subsection is a reworking in English of a position presented in an earlier publication: *'Léann an Bhéaloidis agus Critic na Litríochta'*, M. Ní Annracháin agus B. Nic Dhiarmada (eag.), *Téacs agus Comhthéacs*, pp. 113–135.
3. Séamas Ó Duilearga, Honorary Director of the Irish Folklore Commission (*Coimisiún Béaloideasa Éireann*) and Professor of Irish Folklore in the National University of Ireland (UCD) published under both the Irish and English versions of his name. The English version is James H. Delargy and both versions appear in the bibliography to this book.
4. J. H. Delargy, 'The Gaelic Story-Teller', pp. 185–6.
5. M. H. Abrams, 'The Deconstructive Angel' in D. Lodge (ed.), *Modern Criticism and Theory* (London, 1988).
6. W. J. Ong, *Orality and Literacy* (London, 1982).
7. W. J. Ong, 'Text as Interpretation' in J. Foley (ed.), *Oral Tradition in Literature* (Columbia, 1986). Reprinted by permission of the University of Missouri Press. Copyright © 1986 by the Curators of the University of Missouri.
8. J. Foley (ed.), *Oral Tradition in Literature*, p. 16.

9. http://www.nobel.es/literature/laureates/1995/heaney-lecture.
10. W. J. Ong, *Orality and Literacy*, p. 8.
11. C. B. Harvey, *Contemporary Irish Traditional Narratives* (Berkeley, 1992).
12. S. Ó Duilearga, 'Irish Tales and Story Tellers' in H. Kuhn and K. Schier (eds.), *Märchen, Mythos, Dichtung* (München, 1963). I am grateful to Micheál Briody for locating the source of this reference.
13. Glassie's book, *Passing the Time* (Dublin, 1982) offers a holistic treatment of the traditions of a culturally polarised south-west County Fermanagh community that manages, as an ethnography, to be both intriguingly essentialist and reflective.
14. J. H. Delargy, 'The Gaelic Story-Teller', p. 184.
15. See the discussion of 'Technology' by P. Lemonnier, pp. 544–47, in A. Barnard and J. Spencer (eds.), *Encyclopedia of Social and Cultural Anthropology* (London, 1998).
16. See the seminal discussion and illustration of this contention by L. Dégh and A. Vázsonyi, 'Legend and Belief', pp. 93–124 in D. Ben-Amos (ed.), *Folklore Genres* (Austin, 1976).
17. D. Braid, 'Personal Narrative and Experiential Meaning', *Journal of American Folklore*, vol. 109, 1996, pp. 5–30.
18. J. Foley (ed.), *Oral Tradition in Literature*, p. 17.
19. M. Lüthi, *The European Folktale* (Philadelphia, 1982); *The Fairytale as Art Form* (Bloomington, 1984).

The representation of the feminine

1. See A. Baring and J. Cashford, *The Myth of the Goddess* (London, 1991); M. Gimbutas, *The Godesses and Gods of Old Europe* (Berkeley, 1982); M. Gimbutas, *The Language of the Goddess* (London, 1987); E. O. James, *The Cult of the Mother Goddess* (London, 1959).
2. See J. Puhvel, *Comparative Mythology* (Baltimore, 1987) pp. 151–2, 173–4, 183–4 etc. where Puhvel attempts to identify Celtic and Irish instances.
3. Ibid., p. 62.
4. See S. Billington and M. Green (eds.), *The Concept of the Goddess* (London, 1996) pp. 8–25.
5. Ibid.
6. L. Motz, *The Faces of the Goddess* (Oxford, 1997).
7. E. Neumann, *The Great Mother* (Princeton, 1963).
8. T. Moi (ed.), *The Kristeva Reader* (Oxford, 1986), pp. 187–213.
9. M. Nic Eoin, *B'Ait Leo Bean* (Baile Átha Cliath, 1998), pp. 33–78.
10. M. MacNeill, *The Festival of Lughnasa* (Oxford, 1962), pp. 42–3.
11. M-L Sjoestedt, *Gods and Heroes of the Celts* (Dublin, 1994), p. 31.
12. J. Kristeva, *About Chinese Women* (London, 1986), p. 35.
13. Máire Herbert convincingly argues and illustrates this assertion in her contribution, 'Goddess and King', pp. 264–75, to L. D. Fradenberg (ed.), *Women and Sovereignty* (Edinburgh, 1992).
14. The modern Irish term *sióg*, meaning 'fairy' is formed from the basic word *sí* (earlier *síd*) whose primary meaning is that of subterranean dwelling place of the denizens of the native otherworld realm and, by extension, the quality of life prevailing there. Such dwelling places and their entrances are located, by tradition, in the physical landscape–in such natural features as rock caverns and such human, artefactual features as ring-forts. The otherworld beings who inhabit these *sí/síd* are properly referred to as *aos sí, lucht sí, slua sí* ('otherworld people, folk, host'), terms that emphasize their cosmological make-up as personifications of the forces of a universe

that is perceived as both physical and spiritual. See 'The Semantics of *síd* by Tomás Ó Cathasaigh in *Éigse*, vol. 17, 1978, pp. 137–55.
15. See P. MacCana, 'Placenames and Mythology in Irish Tradition' in *Proceedings* (Ottawa, 1988) pp. 319–24.
16. M. R. Lieberman, *College English*, vol. 34, 1972, pp. 383–95.
17. A. Lurie, *New York Review of Books*, Dec. 1970, pp. 42–4.
18. See J. E. Heuscher, *A Psychiatric Study of Myths and Fairy Tales* (Springfield, 1974).
19. Such a reading of the international wondertale, the *märchen*, is propounded in the writings of the female Jungian analyst Von Franz. See M-L Von Franz, *An Introduction to the Interpretation of Fairytales* (New York, 1970) and *Problems of the Feminine in Fairytales* (New York, 1972).
20. B. Bettleheim, *The Uses of Enchantment* (New York, 1976), p. 226.
21. J. N. Radner (ed.) *Feminist Messages: Coding in Women's Folk Culture* (Urbana, 1993).
22. See p. 11 of J. N. Radner and S. Lanser, 'Strategies of Coding in Women's Cultures' in *Feminist Messages*, pp. 1–30.
23. E. Showalter, *The New Feminist Criticism* (London: Virago), p. 5.
24. J. Todd, *Feminist Literary History* (Cambridge, 1988), p. 63.
25. B. Nic Dhiarmada, '*An Bhean is an Bhaineann*' in M. Ní Annracháin and B. Nic Dhiarmada (eag.), *Téacs agus Comhthéacs* (Corcaigh, 1998).
26. D. Lodge (ed.), *Modern Criticism and Theory* (London: 1988).
27. M. Eagleton (ed.), *Feminist Literary Criticism* (London, 1991).
28. M. Nic Eoin, *B'Ait Leo Bean* (Baile Átha Cliath, 1998).

Historical displacement of the autonomous female
1. W. Stokes (ed.), 'The Rennes Dindshenchas: Second Supplement', *Revue Celtique*, vol. 16, 1895, pp. 279–81.
2. J. Kristeva, 'Women's Time' in T. Moi (ed.), *The Kristeva Reader* (Oxford, 1986), pp. 187–213.
3. W. Stokes (ed.), '*Echtra mac Echach Muigmedóin*', *Revue Celtique*, vol. 24, 1903, pp. 190–203.
4. W. Stokes (ed.), '*Aided Crimthann maic Fidaig*', *Revue Celtique*, vol. 24, 1903, pp. 170–89.
5. M-L. Sjoestedt, *Gods and Heroes of the Celts* (Dublin, 1994 reprint trans.), p. 31.
6. D. Ó hAodha (ed.), 'The Lament of the Old Woman of Beare', in D. Ó Corráin, L. Breatnach and K. McCone (eds.), *Sages, Saints and Storytellers* (Maynooth, 1989), pp. 308–31.
7. M. Ní Dhonnchadha, '*Caillech* and other terms for veiled women in medieval Irish texts', *Éigse*, Vol 28, 1994, pp. 71–96.

Retention/Reinterpretation of the autonomous female
1. P. Lysaght, *The Banshee* (Dublin, 1996).
2. Ibid., p. 191.
3. B. Ó Buachalla, *Aisling Ghéar* (Baile Átha Cliath, 1996).
4. Ibid., p. 557.
5. J. MacKillop (ed.), *Dictionary of Celtic Mythology* (Oxford, 1998), p. 288.
6. B. Ó Buachalla, *Aisling Ghéar*, pp. 552, 558.
7. R. Ó Foghludha (eag.), *Seán Clárach* (Baile Átha Cliath, 1934).
8. MN M 5: 127; B. Ó Buachalla, *Aisling Ghéar*, p. 558.
9. D. Crystal (ed.), *The Cambridge Encyclopedia* (Cambridge, 1990), p. 734.

10. B. Ó Buachalla, *Aisling Ghéar*, p. 719.
11. Ibid., p. 637.
12. RIA 23 D 42: 61; B. Ó Buachalla, *Aisling Ghéar*, pp. 637–38.
13. B. Ó Buachalla, *Aisling Ghéar*, p. 482; R. Ó Foghludha (eag.), *Liam Dall Ó hIfearnáin* (Baile Átha Cliath, 1939).
14. B. Ó Buachalla, *Aisling Ghéar*, p. 396.
15. Ibid., p. 542.
16. Ibid., pp. 541–42.
17. Ibid., pp. 630–31.
18. L. P. Ó Murchú (eag.), *Cúirt an Mheon-Oíche* (Baile Átha Cliath, 1982). While this spelling and style has been established for the title of the poem by its latest editor, I refer to it, throughout, in the form *Cúirt an Mheán Oíche*, by which title it is more generally known. The treatment of the poem by me draws heavily on a previous publication: 'The Vision of Liberation in *Cúirt an Mheán Oíche*' in P. de Brún, S. Ó Coileáin and P. Ó Riain (eds.), *Folia Gadelica* (Cork, 1983).
19. D. Corkery, *The Hidden Ireland* (Dublin, 1925), p. 133.
20. Quoted by R. Kearney, *Modern Movements, in European Philosophy* (Manchester, 1986) p. 91.
21. N. Schmitz, 'The Legend of an Irish Wise woman', *Journal of the Folklore Institute*, vol. 14, 1977, pp. 169–79. The attribution of a somewhat shamanic character to the figure of Biddy Early by Schmitz is taken up by Máirtín Verling (*Gort Broc*, pp. 297–300) in his discussion of the figure of *Máire Ní Mhurchú*, the *bean feasa*, 'wise-woman', of Beara tradition. Máirtín Verling also draws attention in this regard to the description of the wise-woman of *Gleann Fhreastail* who was wont to go into trance at wakes. I have myself also commented on this description and its significance in Part Two, p. 171.
22. c.f. Chap. 2, 'Fairies and Fairy Doctors' of A. Burke, *The Burning of Bridget Cleary* (Pimlico, 1999). pp. 24–38.
23. M. Verling, *Gort Broc*, pp. 297–98.
24. J. Dow, 'Universal Aspects of Symbolic Healing', *American Anthroplogist*, vol. 88, pp. 56–69.

Stories of the *Cailleach* and the Wise-Woman

1. M. Ní Dhonnchadha, '*Caillech* and other terms for veiled women in medieval Irish texts', *ÉIGSE*, vol. xxviii, 1994–5, pp. 71–96.
2. P. MacCana, *Celtic Mythology* (London, 1970).
3. J.G. MacKay, *More West Highland Tales*, vol. 1 (Edinburgh, 1940), p. xvii.
4. H. Wagner, 'The Origins of Pagan Irish Religion', p. 6.
5. A. Ross, *Pagan Celtic Britain* (London, 1967).
6. A. Ross, 'The Divine Hag of the Pagan Celts' published in the volume of essays edited by V. Newall under the somewhat unsatisfactory title of *The Witch Figure* (London, 1973). It is, of course, from the point of view of the student of Irish *cailleach* tradition that the witch figure of the title is unsatisfactory since, as should be obvious to the reader of the present work, the Celtic divine hag and the Irish *cailleach* figures differ very significantly, in many respects, from the European witch figure with which Venetia Newall's book is chiefly concerned.
7. E. Hull, 'Legends and Traditions of the *Cailleach Bhéarra*', *Folklore*, vol. 38, 1927, pp. 225–54.
8. A.H. Krappe, '*La Cailleach Bhéara*', *Études Celtiques*, vol. 1, pp. 292–302.
9. Ibid., p. 302.

10. D. De hÍde, *An Sgéulaidhe Gaedhealach* (Baile Átha Cliath, 1933).
11. G. Murphy, Review in *Éigse*, vol. 9, 1961, pp. 133–4. This comment and the one referred to in footnote 12, attributed to Jan Filip, are examples of a 'nativist' perspective on the materials of Irish tradition. This perspective is vigorously contested by some other scholars who would severely question the concept of such materials giving, as it were, direct glimpses into pre-Christian culture, since the materials themselves are the products of a thoroughly Christian era. In respect of the status of stories regarding the *cailleach* and the *bean feasa*, in this regard, I take the position that such traditional narrative as has come down to us is likely to represent, in highly transformed ways, traces of both the archaic and the psychodynamic sides of cultural reality.
12. J. Filip, *Celtic Civilization and its Heritage* (Prague, 1977).
13. T. F. O'Rahilly, *Early Irish History and Mythology* (Dublin, 1946).
14. T. Ó Cathasaigh, *The Heroic Biography of Cormac Mac Airt* (Dublin, 1977). This work, along with that of Marie-Louise Sjoestedt entitled *Gods and Heroes of the Celts*, helped to usher in a new era in the study and interpretation of medieval Irish literary tales. The comparative and structuralist cast of both scholars' perspective on their material is highly relevant to the kind of hermeneutic in respect of oral narrative tradition that this present work seeks to foster.
15. M. MacNeill, *The Festival of Lughnasa*, pp. 412–13.
16. G. Murphy, 'The Lament of the Old Woman of Beare', p. 84.
17. H. Wagner, 'The Origins of Pagan Irish Religion', p. 5.
18. G. Murphy, 'The Lament of the Old Woman of Beare', pp. 84–5.
19. P. MacCana, *Celtic Mythology*, p. 93.
20. P. Friedrich, *The Meaning of Aphrodite* (Chicago, 1978).
21. G. Broderick, 'Berrey Dhone – A Manx *Caillech Bérri*?', *Zeitschrift für celtische Philologie*, vol. 40, 1984, pp. 193–210.
22. G. Ó Crualaoich, 'Non-Sovereignty Queen Aspects of the Otherworld Female in Irish Hag Legends', *Béaloideas*, vol. 62–3, 1995, pp. 147–62. It should be noted that the Introduction as far as this, is, essentially, a reproduction of parts of an earlier publication, 'Continuity and Adaptation in Legends of *Cailleach Bhéarra*', *Béaloideas*, vol. 56, 1988, pp. 153–78.
23. T. Ó Cathasaigh, 'The Eponym of *Cnogba*', *Éigse*, vol. 23, p. 38.
24. P. Lysaght, *The Banshee* (Dublin, 1996), p. 191.
25. É. Sorlin, *Cris de vie, cris de mort* (Helsinki, 1991).
26. G. Ó Crualaoich, 'Contest in the Cosmology and Ritual of the Irish "Merry Wake"', *Cosmos*, vol. 6, 1990, pp. 145–60; 'The "Merry Wake"' in J.S. Donnelly and K.A. Miller (eds), *Irish Popular Culture* (Dublin, 1998), pp. 173–200.
27. Correll's paper was delivered to The American Folklore Society and is published on the Internet at http://www2.humnet.ucla.edu/folkmed/student/correll.html
28. A. Gregory, *Visions and Beliefs in the West of Ireland*, second edn. (Gerrard's Cross, 1970).
29. P. Ó Héalaí, 'Priest versus Healer', *Béaloideas*, vol. 62–3, pp. 171–88.
30. G. Ó Crualaoich, (1994–5) *Béaloideas* Vol. 62–3.
31. E. E. Evans-Pritchard, *Witchcraft, Oracles and Magic among the Azande* (Oxford, 1937).
32. N. Schmitz, 'An Irish Wise-Woman', *Journal of the Folklore Institute*, vol. 14, pp. 169–79.
33. M. Verling (eag.), *Gort Broc* (Baile Átha Cliath, 1996), pp. 297–300.
34. CBÉ, vol. 850, pp. 526–29.
35. CBÉ, vol. 74, pp. 22–24.

36. CBÉ, vol. 159, pp. 473–78.
37. CBÉ, vol. 788, pp. 130–1.
38. C. Lévi-Strauss, *Structural Anthropology*, vol. 1 (London, 1977), p. 215.
39. CBÉ, vol 11, pp. 103–5.
40. School of Scottish Studies Archives, University of Edinburgh Royal Celtic Society MSS: AM/35.8 Mull.
41. School of Scottish Studies Archives, University of Edinburgh. School of Scottish Studies MSS: SA 1953/49/B5.
42. D. De hÍde, *An Sgéulaidhe Gaedhealach*, pp. 132–36.
43. Ibid., pp. 227–36.
44. CBÉ, vol. 74, pp. 261–62.
45. M. Verling (eag.), *Gort Broc* (Baile Átha Cliath, 1996), p. 251. CBÉ, vol. 217, pp. 453–4.
46. CBÉ, vol. 17, pp. 12–13.
47. CBÉ, vol. 74, p. 14.
48. K. Jackson, *Scéalta ón mBlascaod* (Baile Átha Cliath, 1968 ath-chló) pp. 79–81.
49. CBÉ, vol. 850, pp. 346–50.
50. D. De hÍde, *An Sgéulaidhe Gaedhealach* pp. 145–49; D. Hyde, *Saints and Sinners* (Dublin, 1916), pp. 185–91.
51. CBÉ, vol. 30, p. 131. The text is already published in *Béaloideas*, vol. 4 (1933–4), p. 387.
52. CBÉ, vol. 623, pp. 117–21; M. Verling (eag.), *Gort Broc*, pp. 165–66. In the IFC manuscript this story is entitled *Eachtraidhthe eile i dtaobh Mháire Ní Mhurchú*. The title I use here is that used by Máirtín Verling.
53. CBÉ, vol. 22, pp. 306–8.
54. CBÉ, vol. 623, pp. 122–23; M. Verling (eag.), *Gort Broc*, p. 167.
55. CBÉ, vol. 4, pp. 262–63.
56. CBÉ, vol. 437, p. 392.
57. CBÉ, vol. 22, pp. 305–6.
58. CBÉ, vol. 22, pp. 308–10.
59. CBÉ, vol. 612, pp. 257–62; M. Verling (eag.), *Gort Broc*, pp. 163–64.
60. CBÉ, vol. 612, pp. 262–68; M. Verling (eag.), *Gort Broc*, pp. 164–65.
61. CBÉ, vol. 54, pp. 72–4.
62. CBÉ, vol. 49, pp. 143–44.
63. CBÉ, vol. 54, pp. 49–51.
64. CBÉ, vol. 437, p. 393.
65. CBÉ, vol. 612, pp. 60–3; In the IFC manuscripts this story is entitled *Eachtraidhthe i dtaobh Mháir' Ní Mhurchú*. The title I use here is that used by Máirtín Verling who has already published the story in *Gort Broc*. M. Verling (eag.), *Gort Broc*, pp. 157–59. In the Epilogue to her book, *The Burning of Bridget Cleary*, pp. 203–209, Angela Bourke maintains that fairy legends regarding the kind of 'sweeping'/abduction as is dealt with in this story are an art form with 'the potential to express profound truths and intense emotions', and can be 'resonant with awareness of mental and emotional turmoil'. She regards fairy-legends as 'well suited to the expression of ambivalence and ambiguity' and implies that a psychological theory of therapy might be built from them. In this book, I imply that just such a theory of therapy can be attributed, in respect of Irish legends of the wise-woman, not to any external psychologist, but to Irish vernacular culture itself and to its oral narrative traditions. My contention is that Irish legends of the resort to the wise-woman are – like fairy-legends – non-prescriptive articulations of a hermeneutic of the human experience

of affliction among whose functions was the provision of a communal therapeutic resource of archetypal dimensions and provenance. As such they constitute an important instance of how folklore and tradition can be regarded as a rich and creative repository of imaginative inspiration for the provision of cultural knowledge and cultural coping mechanisms that deserve – and even demand – to be acknowledged. In exploring them in relation to the figure and function of the *cailleach* and her cultural pedigree, this book attempts to further that acknowledgement.

66. CBÉ, vol. 612, pp. 251–57; M.Verling (eag.), *Gort Broc*, pp. 159–60.
67. CBÉ, vol. 842, pp. 60–3; M.Verling (eag.), *Gort Broc*, pp. 160–61.
68. P. Ó Siochfhradha (An Seabhac), *An Seanchaidhe Muimhneach* (Baile Átha Cliath, 1932), pp. 100–103. This version of the story comes from the Great Blasket.
69. T.P. Cross and C.H. Slover, 'Tonn Clidna' in *Ancient Irish Tales* (Dublin, 1969 rev. ed.), pp. 598–99.
70. Summarised by J. MacKillop, *Dictionary of Celtic Mythology* (Oxford, 1998), pp. 80–1.
71. D. Ó hÓgáin, *Myth, Legend and Romance* (London, 1990), p. 91.

BIBLIOGRAPHY

Abrams, M. H., 'The Deconstructive Angel', in D. Lodge (ed.), *Modern Criticism and Theory: A Reader* (London: Longman, 1988), pp. 264–76
Anderson, Benedict, *Imagined Communities: Reflections on the Origin and Spread of Nationalism* (London: Verso, 1983)
Ardener, Edwin, 'Belief and the Problem of Women', in J. S. La Fontaine (ed.), *The Interpretation of Ritual: Essays in Honour of A.I. Richards* (London: Tavistock, 1972), pp. 135–58
Baring, A. and J. Cashford, *The Myth of the Goddess: Evolution of an Image* (London: Viking Arkana, 1991)
Bauman, Richard, 'Performance' in R. Bauman (ed.), *Folklore, Cultural Performances and Popular Entertainments: A Communications-Centred Handbook* (Oxford University Press, 1992), pp. 41–9
Ben-Amos, Dan (ed.), *Folklore Genres* (Austin: University of Texas Press, 1976)
— 'Folktale' in R. Bauman (ed.), *Folklore, Cultural Performances and Popular Entertainments: A Communications-Centred Handbook* (Oxford University Press, 1992), pp. 101–18
Bettleheim, Bruno, *The Uses of Enchantment: The Meaning and Importance of Fairy Tales* (New York: Knopf, 1976)
Billington, Sandra and Miranda Green (eds.), *The Concept of the Goddess* (London: Routledge, 1996)
Bohannan, Paul, *How Culture Works* (New York: The Free Press, 1995)
Bourke, Angela, 'The Irish Traditional Lament and the Grieving Process', *Women's Studies International Forum*, vol. 11.4, 1988, pp. 287–91
— 'Caoineadh na Marbh: Síceoilfhilíocht', *Oghma*, vol. 4, pp. 3–12
— 'More in Anger than in Sorrow' in J. N. Radner (ed.), *Feminist Messages: Coding in Women's Folk Culture* (Urbana: University of Illinois Press, 1993), pp. 160–82
— *The Burning of Bridget Cleary* (London: Pimlico, 1999).
Braid, Donald, 'Personal Narrative and Experiential Meaning', *Journal of American Folklore*, vol. 109, 1996, pp. 5–30
Broderick, George, 'Berry Dhone–A Manx *Caillech Bérri*?', *Zeitschrift für Celtische Philologie*, vol. 40, 1984, pp. 193–210
Cixous, Hélène and Catherine Clément, *The Newly Born Woman* (Manchester: Manchester University Press, 1986)
Corkery, Daniel, *The Hidden Ireland* (Dublin: Gill, 1925)
Corrigan Correll, Timothy, 'Doctors, Priests and Fairy Healers: Folk Medicine, Conflict and Social Approbation in Lady Gregory's 'Visions and Beliefs from [sic] the West of Ireland', http://www2.humnet.ucla.edu/folkmed/student/correll.html)

Cross, Tom P. and C.H. Slover, 'Tonn Clidna' in *Ancient Irish Tales* (Dublin: Figgis, 1969 rev.), pp. 598–9
Crystal, David (ed.), 'Flora Macdonald', *The Cambridge Encylopedia* (Cambridge University Press, 1990), p. 734
Dégh, Linda and A.Vázsonyi, 'Legend and Belief', in D. Ben-Amos (ed.), *Folklore Genres* (Austin: University of Texas Press, 1976)
De hÍde, Dubhglas, *An Sgéulaidhe Gaedhealach* (Baile Átha Cliath: Institiút Béaloideasa Éireann, 1933)
Delargy, J.H., 'The Gaelic Story-Teller: With Some Notes on Gaelic Folktales', *Proceedings of the British Academy*, vol. 31, 1945, pp. 177–221
Dooley, Ann and Harry Roe, *Tales of the Elders of Ireland: Acallam na Senórach* (Oxford University Press, 1999 trans.)
Dow, James, 'Universal Aspects of Symbolic Healing', *American Anthropologist*, vol. 88, 1986, pp. 56–69
Eagleton, Mary (ed.), *Feminist Literary Criticism* (London: Longman, 1991)
Evans-Pritchard, E. E., *Witchcraft, Oracles and Magic among the Azande* (Oxford: Clarendon Press, 1937/1976 abridg.)
Filip, Jan, *Celtic Civilization and its Heritage* (Prague: Academia, 1977)
Foley, John M. (ed.), *Oral Tradition in Literature: Interpretation in Context* (Columbia: University of Missouri Press, 1986)
Friedrich, Paul, *The Meaning of Aphrodite* (Chicago University Press, 1978)
Geertz, Clifford, *The Religion of Java* (Glencoe, Ill: The Free Press 1960)
— *The Interpretation of Cultures* (New York: Basic Books, 1973)
Gimbutas, Marija, *The Goddesses and Gods of Old Europe 6500–3500 B.C.: Myths and Cult Images* (Berkeley: University of California Press, 1982, 2nd ed.)
— *The Language of the Goddess* (London: Harper Collins, 1987)
Glassie, Henry, *Passing the Time: History and Folklore of an Ulster Community* (Dublin: O'Brien Press, 1982)
Gregory, Augusta, *Visions and Beliefs in the West of Ireland Collected and Arranged by Lady Gregory: With Two Essays and Notes by W.B.Yeats* (Gerrard's Cross: Colin Smythe, 1920/1970, 2nd ed.)
Hannerz, Ulf, *Cultural Complexity: Studies in the Social Organisation of Meaning* (New York: Columbia University Press, 1992)
Harvey, Clodagh B., *Contemporary Irish Traditional Narratives: The English Language Tradition* (Berkeley: University of California Press 1992)
Herbert, Máire, 'Goddess and King: The Sacred Marriage in Early Ireland' in L. O. Fradenburg (ed.), *Women and Sovereignty* (Edinburgh University Press, 1992), pp. 264–75
Heuscher, J. E., *A Psychiatric Study of Myths and Fairy Tales: Their Origin, Meaning and Usefulness* (Springfield, Ill: Charles C. Thomas 1974)
Hull, Eleanor, 'Legends and Traditions of the *Cailleach Bhéarra* or Old Woman (Hag) of Beare', *Folklore*, vol. 38, 1927, pp. 225–54
Hyde, Douglas, *Saints and Sinners* (Dublin: Gresham Publishing Co., 1916)
Irigaray, Luce, *This Sex Which is Not One* (trans. Catherine Porter), (Ithaca: Cornell University Press, 1985)
Jackson, Kenneth H. (eag.), *Scéalta ón mBlascaod* (Baile Átha Cliath: An Cumann le Béaloideas Éireann, 1938)
James, E. O., *The Cult of the Mother Goddess* (London: Thames and Hudson, 1959)
Kearney, Richard, *Modern Movements in European Philosophy* (Manchester University Press, 1986)

Krappe, Alexander H., '*La Cailleach Bhéara: Notes de mythologie gaelique*', *Etudes Celtiques*, vol. 1, pp. 292–302

Kristeva, Julia, 'Outside Time' in J. Kristeva, *About Chinese Women* (London: Marion Boyars, 1986)

— 'Women's Time', in Toril Moi (ed.), *The Kristeva Reader* (Oxford: Basil Blackwell 1986), pp. 187–213

Lemonnier, P., 'Technology', in Alan Barnard and Jonathan Spenser (eds.), *Encyclopedia of Social and Cultural Anthropology* (London: Routledge, 1998), pp. 544–47

Lévi-Strauss, Claude, 'The Structural Study of Myth' in C. Levi-Strauss, *Structural Anthropology*, vol. 1 (London: Penguin Books, 1977 trans.), pp. 206–31.

Lieberman, M.R., 'Some Day my Prince Will Come: Female Acculturation Through the Fairy Tale', *College English*, vol. 34, 1972, pp. 383–95

Lodge, David (ed.), *Modern Criticism and Theory: A Reader* (London: Longman, 1988)

Lurie, Alison, 'Fairy Tale Liberation', *New York Review of Books*, 17 December 1970, pp. 420–4

Lüthi, Max, *The European Folktale: Form and Nature* (Philadelphia: Institute for the Study of Human Issues, 1982 trans.)

— *The Fairytale as Art Form and Portrait of Man* (Bloomington: Indiana University Press, 1984 trans.)

Lysaght, Patricia, *The Banshee: The Irish Supernatural Death Messenger* (Dublin: O'Brien Press, 1996 2nd ed.)

— '*Caoineadh os Cionn Coirp:* The Lament for the Dead in Ireland', *Folklore*, vol. 108, 1997, pp. 65–82

MacCana, Proinsias, *Celtic Mythology* (London: Hamyln, 1970)

— *Learned Tales of Medieval Ireland* (Dublin Institute for Advanced Studies, 1980)

— 'Placenames and Mythology in Irish Tradition: Places, Pilgrimages and Things' in G. W. MacLennan (ed.), *Proceedings of the First North American Congress in Celtic Studies* (University of Ottawa Press, 1988)

MacKay, J. G., 'The Deer Cult and the Deer Goddess Cult of the Ancient Caledonians' in J. G. Mackay, *More West Highland Tales*, 2 vols (Edinburgh: Oliver and Boyd, 1940).

MacKillop, James, *Dictionary of Celtic Mythology* (Oxford University Press, 1998)

MacNeill, Máire, *The Festival of Lughnasa* (Oxford University Press, 1962)

Maier Bernhard, *Dictionary of Celtic Religion and Culture* (Woodbridge, Suffolk/Rochester, N.Y: The Boydell Press 1997 trans.)

Malinowski, Bronislaw, 'Myth in Primitive Psychology' in B. Malinowski, *Magic Science and Religion and Other Essays* (New York: Doubleday Anchor Books, 1954)

Motz, Lotte, *The Faces of the Goddess* (Oxford University Press, 1997)

Murphy, Gerard, 'The Lament of the Old Woman of Beare', *Proceedings of the Royal Irish Academy*, vol. 55, 1953, pp. 84–109

— 'Review of J. Szöverffy, *Irisches Erzälgut in Abendland*', *Éigse*, vol. 9, pp. 133–4

Neumann, E., *The Great Mother: An Analysis of the Archetype* (Princeton University Press, 1963)

Ní Annracháin, Máire agus B. Nic Dhiarmada (eag.), *Téacs agus Comhthéacs: Gnéithe de Chritic na Gaeilge* (Cló Ollscoile Chorcaí, 1998)

Nic Dhiarmada, Bróna, '*An Bhean is an Bhaineann: Gnéithe den Chritic Fheimineach*', in M. Ní Annrachain agus B. Nic Dhiarmada (eag.) *Téacs agus Comhthéacs: Gnéithe de Chritic na Gaeilge* (Cló Ollscoile Chorcaí, 1998), pp. 152–82

Ní Dhonnchadha, Máirín,'*Caillech* and other terms for veiled women in medieval Irish texts', *Éigse* vol.28, 1994, pp. 71–96

Nic Eoin, Máirín, *B'Ait Leo Bean: Gnéithe den Idé-eolaíocht Inscne d'Traidisiún Liteartha na Gaeilge* (Baile Átha Cliath: An Clóchomhar, 1998)

Ní Sheaghdha, Nessa (eag.), *Agallamh na Seanórach,* 3 iml., (Baile Átha Cliath: Oifig an tSoláthair, 1942–5)

Ó Buachalla, Breandán, *Aisling Ghéar: Na Stíobhartaigh agus an tAos Léinn 1603–1788* (Baile Átha Cliath: An Clóchomhar, 1996)

Ó Cathasaigh, Tomás, *The Heroic Biography of Cormac Mac Airt* (Dublin Institute for Advanced Studies, 1977)

— 'The Semantics of *síd*', *Éigse*, vol. 17, 1978, pp. 137–55

— 'The Eponym of *Cnogba*', *Éigse*, vol. 23, 1989, pp. 27–38

Ó Crualaoich, Gearóid, 'Continuity and Adaptation in Legends of *Cailleach Bhéarra*', *Béaloideas,* Vol. 56, 1988, pp. 153–78.

— 'Contest in the Cosmology and the Ritual of the Irish "Merry Wake"', in A. Duff-Cooper (ed.), *Contests=Cosmos*, vol. 6 (Edinburgh University Press, 1990) pp. 145–60

— 'Non-Sovereignty Queen Aspects of the Otherworld Female in Irish Hag Legends: The Case of *Cailleach Bhéarra*', *Béaloideas*, vol. 62/3, 1995, pp. 147–62

— 'The "Merry Wake" and Popular Resistance to Domination in Early Modern and Modern Ireland' in J.S. Donnelly Jr. and K.A. Miller (eds.), *Irish Popular Culture 1650–1850* (Dublin: Irish Academic Press, 1998)

Ó Duilearga, Séamas,'Irish Tales and Story Tellers', in H. Kuhn and K. Schier (eds.), *Märchen, Mythos, Dichtung: Festschrift zum 90 Geburtstag Friedrich Von Der Leyens* (München: Verlag C.H. Beck, 1963)

O'Flaherty, Wendy D., *Other People's Myths: The Cave of Echoes* (London: Collier Macmillan, 1988)

Ó Foghludha, Risteard (eag.), *Seán Clárach* (Baile Átha Cliath: Oifig an tSoláthair, 1934)

— (eag.), *Liam Dall Ó hIfearnáin* (Baile Átha Cliath: Oifig an tSoláthair, 1939)

Ó hAodha, Donncha, 'The Lament of the Old Woman of Beare', in D. Ó Corráin, L. Breatnach and K. McCone (eds.), *Sages, Saints and Storytellers* (Maynooth: An Sagart, 1989)

Ó Héalaí, Pádraig,'Priest versus Healer: The Legend of the Priest's Stricken Horse', *Béaloideas*, vol. 62–3, 1994, pp. 171–88

Ó hÓgáin, Dáithí, *Myth, Legend and Romance: An Encyclopaedia of the Irish Folk Tradition* (London: Ryan Publishing Co., 1990)

Ó Murchú, Liam P. (eag.), *Cúirt an Mheon-Oíche* (Baile Átha Cliath: An Clóchomhar, 1982)

Ong, Walter J., *Orality and Literacy: The Technologizing of the Word* (London: Methuen, 1982)

— 'Text as Interpretation: Mark and After' in John M. Foley (ed.), *Oral Tradition in Literature: Interpretation in Context* (Columbia: University of Missouri Press, 1986)

O'Rahilly, Thomas F., *Early Irish History and Mythology* (Dublin Institute for Advanced Studies, 1946)

Ó Siochfhradha, Pádraig [An Seabhac], *An Seanchaidhe Muimhneach* (Baile Átha Cliath: Comhlucht Oideachais na hÉireann, 1932)

Puhvel, Jaan, *Comparative Mythology* (Baltimore: The Johns Hopkins University Press, 1987)

Radner, Joan N., *Feminist Messages: Coding in Women's Folk Culture* (Urbana: University of Illinois Press, 1993)
— and Susan S. Lanser, 'Strategies of Coding in Women's Cultures' in Joan N. Radner (ed.), *Feminist Messages: Coding in Women's Folk Culture* (Urbana: University of Illinois Press, 1993)
Rapport, Nigel and Joanne Overing, *Social and Cultural Anthropology: The Key Concepts* (London: Routledge, 2000)
Ross, Anne, *Pagan Celtic Britain* (London: Constable, 1967)
— 'The Divine Hag of the Pagan Celts', in Venetia Newall (ed.), *The Witch Figure* (London: Routledge and Kegan Paul, 1973)
Schmitz, Nancy, 'An Irish Wise-Woman: Fact and Legend', *Journal of the Folklore Institute*, vol. 14, 1977, pp. 169–79
Showalter, Elaine, *The New Feminist Criticism* (London: Virago Press, 1986)
Sjoestedt, Marie-Louise, *Gods and Heroes of the Celts* (Dublin: Four Courts Press, 1994 translation/reprint)
Sorlin, Évelyn, *Cris de vie, cris de mort: Les fées du destin dans les pays celtiques* (Helsinki: Folklore Fellows Communications, 1991)
Sperber, Dan, *Rethinking Symbolism* (Cambridge University Press, 1975)
Stokes, Whitley, 'The Rennes Dindshenchas: Second Supplement', *Revue Celtique*, vol. 16, 1895, pp. 279–81
— '*Aided Crimthann Maic Fidaig*', *Revue Celtique*, vol. 24, 1903, pp. 170–89
— *Echtra mac Echach Muigmedóin*, *Revue Celtiques*, vol. 24, 1903, pp. 190–203
Todd, Janet, *Feminist Literary History* (Cambridge: The Polity Press, 1988).
Turner, Victor, *The Forest of Symbols: Aspects of Ndembu Ritual* (Ithaca: Cornell University Press, 1967)
Van Gennep, Arnold, *The Rites of Passage* (London: Routledge and Kegan Paul, 1960 trans.)
Verling, Máirtín (eag.), *Gort Broc: Scéalta agus Seanchas ó Bhéarra* (Baile Átha Cliath: Coiscéim, 1996)
Von Franz, Marie-Louise, *An Introduction to the Interpretation of Fairy Tales* (New York: Analytical Psychology Club of New York, 1970)
— *Problems of the Feminine in Fairytales* (New York: Spring Publications, 1972)
Wagner, Heinrich, 'The Origins of Pagan Irish Religion', *Zeitschrift für celtische Philologie*, vol. 38, 1981, pp. 1–28
Wood, Juliette, 'The Concept of the Goddess' in Sandra Billington and Miranda Green (eds.), *The Concept of the Goddess* (London: Routledge, 1996)
Wood-Martin, W.G., *Traces of the Elder Faiths of Ireland: A Folklore Sketch*, 2 vols. (London: Longmans, Green and Co., 1902)

Manuscript Sources

Coimisiún Béaloideasa Éireann/Irish Folklore Commission
IFC, 4, 262–63
IFC, 11, 103–105
IFC, 17, 12–13
IFC, 22, 305–310
IFC, 30, 131
IFC, 49, 143–44
IFC, 54, 49–51; 72–4
IFC, 74, 14; 22–24; 261–62
IFC, 159, 473–78
IFC, 217, 453–4
IFC, 437, 392; 393
IFC, 612, 245–51; 251–57; 275–62; 262–68
IFC 623, 117–21; 122–23
IFC 788, 130–31
IFC 842, 60–63
IFC, 850, 346–50, 526–29

INDEX

abduction ('swept') by fairies, 73–4, 210–29, 286
Abhainn na Slat, 117
Abrams, Mark, 15
Acallamh na Senórach, 84, 155
acculturation, 25–6
adaptation, cultural, 3–5
Aed Ruad, 38, 39–40
affective knowledge, 7, 8
Aided (violent death), 46
Aided Chrimthainn maic Fidaig, 44–8
Ailill, 42, 44
Áine, 61, 65, 85
    name variants, 155–6
    see also Ana; *Ana ní Áine*
Áird Thoir, 144–6, 254
áirneán, 18, 23
aisling, 54–67, 68–9, 85, 156
Aisling do rinneas ar Mhóirín, An, 56–7
Aislinge Meic Conglinne, 84
Alaithe Thiar, 221
Allihies, 195
Ana, 85, 155, 161 *see also* Áine
Ana ní Áine, 172
    English translation, 150–62
    Irish version, 256–7
Ann, St, 156
anthropology, 3
Anu, 89, 155 *see also* Áine; Ana
Aoibheall, 53, 61, 67, 68, 69, 70
Aoibheall of Craig Léith, 85
Aonghus, 227
aos sí, 282
Aphrodite tradition, 87
Araoir im aisling is mé ag machnamh im intinn, 58
archetypal reality, 13
Ard Macha, 39
Ard na Caillí, 146, 147
Ardgroom, 181, 193, 210

A shaoi ghlain de phríomhscoth na sáirfhear saor, 65
ash-plant, 140–1
assemblies, sacred, 28
Athlone, 123
audience, 18–19, 23, 35
author, 18–19
Azande poison oracle, 95–6

Bà, Loch, 113–15, 116, 117, 118–19, 240–4
Badhbh, 54, 104, 150
Baile an Chaisleáin, 260–3
Baile an Chóta, 183
Baile an Rannaigh, 178, 179, 180
Baile Bhoithín, 178–81, 187–91, 265–6, 267–8
Baile na nAoraí, 210
Ballycastle, 167–73
Ballycrovane, 146
Banba, 53, 55
banshee (*bean sí*), 46, 52–4, 92, 104
Barr Iarthach, 176
Barrachan, 117
Béal Átha an Fhíona, 201, 202
Bealtaine, 100–1, 102, 103
bean chaointe, 11–12, 29, 72, 74, 75–6, 92
bean feasa, 12, 21–2, 25, 29, 71–8, 92–9
    feminist criticism, 31, 33, 34–7
    Figure, 92, 93–4
    Function, 92, 94–6
    Process, 92–3, 96–7
bean ghlúine, 29, 72, 74
bean leighis, 72, 94, 179
bean sí, 46, 52–4 *see also* banshee
Beara peninsula, 73, 76, 81, 83–4, 85–6, 89, 146–8, 175–7, 181–2, 193, 210–15
    mines, 195–9
Beare, Hag of *see* Cailleach Bhéarra
Belanagare, 125
Berrey Dhone, 89

Bettleheim, Bruno, 32
Bhean a chíodh na fairies, An, 264
Bhóinn, An, 86, 124, 207
Billington, S. and Green, M., 26
birthing, 110 *see also bean ghlúine*
Blackwater River, 205, 206-7
Blasket Islands, 84, 152
blindness, 217, 219-20, 221, 222-3
Boí *see also* Buí, 114
Book of Leinster, 38, 227
Book of the Invasions of Ireland, 90
Bourke, Angela, 15, 286
Boyne, River, 86, 89, 124, 207
Braid, Donald, 22
Bramach a goideadh agus an bhean feasa, An, 266-7
Brí Gabhann, 199, 271
Brian, 42, 44, 45, 46, 47
Bridget, St, 124
Brigit, 87, 124
Brittany, 66
Broderick, George, 89
Brú na Bóinne, 89, 227
Buachaillí Bána (Whiteboy movement), 59-65
Buí, 82, 84, 85
Bull Rock, 86
bulls, 125, 126-8, 130, 131
Butler, Isabel, 227
butter, 109

Cailín ar baineadh a hurlabhra dhi, An, 272
cailleach, 11-12, 21-2, 25, 34, 97-9
　archetypes, 81-2
　Christianity and, 145, 147-8, 150, 157-62, 165-7, 171-2, 206
　　Mass attendance, 165-6, 193
　diet, 90, 165
　feminist criticism, 31, 33, 34-7, 214
　landscape and, 28-9, 31, 82, 83, 89-90, 105-6, 119, 145
　male transmitters, 22, 33, 34-5
　modernity and, 30-1, 34
　semantics, 81-2
　sovereignty, 11, 28, 29, 39-41, 42, 45-8, 52, 55, 177, 215
Cailleach Bhéara (Ballycastle), 167-73
Cailleach Bhéara (Dún Chaoin)
　English translation, 111-13
　Irish version, 239-40
Cailleach Bhéarach and Donnchadh Mór Mac Mánais, 22, 23, 24, 132-44, 145, 149
Cailleach Bhéarra, 11, 29-30, 81, 82-91
　Lament of the Old Woman of Beare, 48-52, 82, 85-7, 114

　landscape and, 82, 83, 89-90, 105-6, 119, 145
　The mark left by Cailleach Bhéarra, 109-11
　name variants, 86-7, 88-9
　Rian na Caillí Béaraighe, 239
　sovereignty, 81, 82, 85, 87, 88, 158
Cailleach Bhéarra and Saint Caitiairn, 146-8
Cailleach Bhéarra's Shower of Stones, 104-6
Cailleach Bhéarrthach and the cold of May-day Monday, 100-4
Cailleach Bhéarthach (Carna: Áird Thoir), 144-6
Cailleach Bhéarthach (Carna: Cill Chiaráin), 163-7
Cailleach Bhéarthach and the Walker, 106-9
Cailleach Bheurr and Loch Bà-I, 113-15
Cailleach Bheurr and Loch Bà-II, 115-20
Cailleach Ghleanna-na-mBiorach, agus an tarbh dubh, 244-7
Cailleach of Gleann na mBiorach and the Black Bull, 120-32, 141
caillichín, 140-1
Cairbre, 93, 97
Cairenn, 42
Cairenn Casdub, 43, 45
Caitiairn, St (Naomh Caitiairn), 146-8, 254-5
Cam Bhaile Uí Shéaghdha, 183
Caobach, Tadhg, 216, 219
Caoilte, 155
Cape Clear, 111, 202
Carbery, 187
Carn Tighearna, 204-8, 272-3
Carna, 107-8, 144-6, 163-7, 254, 258-9
Carolus, 65
Carraig, 178, 180
Carraig Aonair, 84
Carraig Chlíodhna, 207, 224-5, 227-8
Carraig na hIngeanach, 111
Castlebar, 108
Castledonovan, 185
Cathair Caim, 175, 215-16
Celts, 25-6, 27, 84
Chailleach Bhéarach (Baile an Chaisleáin), An, 260-3
Chailleach Bhéarach agus Donnchadh Mór Mac Mánais, An, 247-53
Chailleach Bhéarra and Naomh Caitiairn, An, 254-5
Chailleach Bhéarthach, An (Carna: Áird Thoir), 254
Chailleach Bhéarthach, An (Carna: Cill Chiaráin), 258-9
Chailleach Bhéarthach agus an coisí, An, 237-9
Chailleach Bhéarthach agus fuacht luan Bhealtaine, An, 235-6

Chailleach Bheur agus Loch Bà–I, A, 240–1
Chailleach Bheurr agus Loch Bà–II, A, 241–4
'Children of Sadhbh, The', 60–2
Christianity, 30, 37, 48, 62, 87
    cailleach and, 145, 147–8, 150, 157–62, 165–7, 171–2, 206
    Mass attendance, 165–6, 193
    cosmology and, 75, 90–1, 157–8, 160, 162, 172, 182, 206
    female roles, 30, 81
    healers and, 178–82, 188–9
    misogyny, 160
Ciabhán, 227
Cill Chaitiairn, 146, 147
Cill Chiaráin, 163–7, 258–9
Cill Macallóg, 216, 220
Cill Uird, 93
Cimbaeth, 38, 40, 41
Cinderella-type tales, 32–3
Cioth cloch na Caillighe Béarra, 237
Cixous, Hélène, 36
Clann Shadhbha agus Shaidhbhín, 60–2
Cléire, 93
Clíodhna, 53, 222, 224–9
Clíodhna's Wave, 227
Clíodhna's Rock, 207
Cluain, 193
Cnoc Áine, 207
Cnoc an tSídhe, 111, 112
Cnoc Fírinne, 66
Cnoc Meadha, 143
Cnogba, 89
cognitive knowledge, 7, 8
coimcne, 3, 13
Cóir Anmann, 84
collectors *see* Irish Folklore Commission
Colm Cille, 158
Conn, Lough, 108
Connaught, 125, 131–2, 148
Conneelys, 214
consciousness and narrative, 13–14, 22
Corca Dhuibhne, 93, 97, 153
Corca Loigde, 85–6
Corcu Duibne, 51
Cork county, 93, 97, 178, 187, 201–2, 208–9, 224, 227–8 *see also* Beara peninsula
Corkery, Daniel, 69
corn harvest, 85, 139–40, 184–5
Corrigan Correll, Timothy, 92–3, 96
cortha, 186, 187
cosmology, 9–10, 11, 27, 29, 175, 185, 195
    Christianity and, 75, 90–1, 157–8, 160, 162, 172, 182, 206
    Norse, 83

cows, 114, 124
cradles, 159–60
Craig Léith, 85
Crimthann, 44, 45–6, 47–8
críona, 174, 233
Crom Dubh, 85
Cronin, Bess, 78
Cross, Tom P. and Slover, C.H., 227
Crossmolina, 108
crows, 150
Cruachain, 66
Crùlachan, 116, 119
Cuan Dor, 227
Cuan Leitid, 111
Cúchulainn, 45, 103–4
Cúirt an Mheán Oíche (The Midnight Court), 67–71, 85
culture
    as adaptation, 3–5
    as knowledge, 5–7
    material culture, 4
    personification, 10–12
    transmission, 7–10
Cum Sheola, 93
cumachta sí, 43

Dá Chích Anann, 89
Daghda, 66
death, triple-death motif, 40
deer, 91, 150
    Deer-Goddess, 124
Déidbhean, 224
Deirdre, 65
Delargy, James H. *see* Ó Duilearga, Séamas
Denvir, Gearóid, 15
Derrida, Jacques, 15
Digdi, 51
Dindshenchas, 38, 84, 155
Dingle, 112, 184–5, 189–90
Dithorba, 38, 40
dog, eight-legged, 126, 127, 130
Dóinn, 211
Domblas Mór, 122, 130, 131
Donegal, 103
Donn, 125
Donnchadh Mór Mac Mánais, 132–44, 247–53
Donn's house, 86
'Don't Believe a Woman's Words', 150
Dow, James, 76
'Dream vision I experienced of Móirín, The', 56–7
Drimoleague, 208
Droichead na mBarr, 181
Dubh, Máirín, 224, 228–9

dumbness, 201–4
Dún Chaoin, 111–13, 239–40
Dunboy, 86
Dunquin, 97, 224 see also Dún Chaoin
Dursey Island, 84, 86

Eachtraidhthe i dtaobh Mháir' Ní Mhurchú, 286
Eachtruighthe ar bhean leighis a bhí i mBaile Bhoithín–I, 265–6
Eachtruighthe ar bhean leighis a bhí i mBaile Bhoithín–II, 267
Eachtruighthe ar bhean leighis a bhí i mBaile Bhoithín–III, 268
eagles, 90, 100–1, 102–3
Eagleton, Mary, 36
Early, Biddy, 72, 75, 76, 96, 209
Earraid, 115–16, 117, 118
Eas Rua, 101, 102–3
Eas Ruad, 38, 39
Echtra mac nEchach Muigmedóin, 28, 42–4
eels, 126
Eithne, 66
Emain Macha, 28, 38–42, 46
environment see landscape
Eochaid Muigmedón, 42, 43, 44, 45
Eoganacht, 156, 159
Érainn, 85
Ériu, 53, 55
Evans-Pritchard, E.E., 95
Expulsion of the Déssi, 84
externalization, 6–7
Eyeries, 83, 175, 177, 181, 182, 193, 196, 210, 212

'Fair-day night, following on my wetting', 65
fairies, 177, 191, 200, 202, 282–3
  abduction ('swept'), 73–4, 210–29, 286
  An Bhean a chíodh na fairies, 264
  fairy lover, 189, 191
  red-haired women, 201, 203, 208–10, 217, 219–20
  superstition and social control, 194
  The Woman who used to see the Fairies, 174–5
  see also sí
famhair, 118
Fastnet, 84
feminine
  displacement of the female, 38–52
  representation, 10–12, 25–37
    goddess mythology, 25–31
    oral and literary narrative, 31–6, 98
  retention of the female, 52–78
feminist criticism, 31, 33, 34–7, 214

Fergus, 42, 44
Fermoy, 204–5
festivals, 28 see also Bealtaine; Imbolc; Lughnasa; Samhain
Fiachra, 42, 44
Filip, Jan, 84
Findbennach, 125
Fionn Mac Cumhaill, 45, 103, 155, 159
Fir Bolg, 121, 126
fir flatha, 39, 41
Fírinne, 66
Fitzgerald, John, 227
flails, 127, 128–9
flaitheas, 67 see also sovereignity
flax, 175, 176, 177
floods, 3, 90, 227
Fodla, 53, 55
Foley, John Miles, 15–16, 22–3, 24
Folklore Commission see also Irish Folklore Commission
fomór, 118
'For a time I was a placid virgin', 57–8
Friedrich, Paul, 87
fuamhairean, 118

Gaeil, 29
Gallans, 186, 187, 208, 209
Galway, 97, 106–9
Genesis, Book of, 115, 118
Girl who was struck dumb, The, 201–4
Glaise na Naíonán, 216
Glandore, 227
Glassie, Henry, 18
Gleann Fhreastail, 174–5, 202
Gleann Mór, 116
Gleann na mBiorach, 120, 121, 124–5
Glenamaddy, 132, 138, 140
Gobnait, St, 90
goddess mythology, 25–31, 185
  archetypal, 28–30
  landscape and, 28–9, 31
  literature, 30
  male hero, 85
  sovereignty, 11, 28, 29
Gormfhlaith, 87
Gort Broc, 181, 212
gospel narrative, 15–16, 23, 115, 118
Gráinne, 61
Gráinne Mhaol, 65
graveyard herbs, 216–17, 218–19, 220
Gregory, Lady Augusta, 72, 92, 96

Hag of Beare see Cailleach Bhéarra
Hail Brigit, 87
Hannerz, Ulf, 6–7

hares, 196, 198, 200
Harvey, Clodagh B., 17, 18
hazel tree, 39
healing, 8, 75, 92–3, 95, 189–91, 201, 203–4, 208–9, 210
  faith in, 191, 213
  herbalists, 73, 74, 179, 188, 190–1
  graveyard herbs, 216–17, 218–19, 220
  threat to Christianity, 178–82, 188–9
  see also bean leighis
Heaney, Séamus, 16
Herbert, Máire, 282
herons, 126, 127, 130
Heuscher, J.E., 32
hieros gamos, 39, 42, 44, 140
holy wells, 199–201
horses, 180, 182, 183–5
houses, location of, 202–7
Hull, Eleanor, 84
Hyde, Douglas, 84, 85, 123

Imbolc, 124
Inbhear Scéine, 111
Incident recounted of a healing woman from Baile Bhoithín–I, 178–81, 182
Incident recounted of a healing woman from Baile Bhoithín–II, 187–9
Incident recounted of a healing woman from Baile Bhoithín–III, 189–91
indigenous knowledge, 20
interpretative community, 19
Irigaray, Luce, 36
Irish Folklore Commission, 17–18, 71–2, 73, 93, 98, 181–2, 198, 233

Jackson, Kenneth, 152, 153
Journal of American Folklore, 22
Journal of the Folklore Institute, 72
Jung, Carl, 9, 34

keening-woman *see* bean chaointe
Kenmare, 150, 154, 156, 211
Kerry, 89, 93, 97, 112, 120, 124, 131, 189–90, 211 *see also* Kenmare
Kilcatherine, 146, 147
Kilshannig, 228
Knights of Glin, 227
Knockaney, 207
Knockmeagh, 138, 140
knowledge
  affective, 7, 8
  cognitive, 7, 8
  cultural, 5–7
  indigenous, 20
  of natural environment, 4

operant, 7, 8
personification, 10–12
prophecy and, 186, 204–6, 209
transmission, 7–10, 75
Knowth, 89–90
Krappe, Alexander Hagerty, 84
Kristeva, Julia, 27, 28, 36, 39, 43

Lacan, Jacques, 36
Lament of the Old Woman of Beare, 48–52, 82, 85–7, 114
landscape, 4, 10–11, 187, 207
  Cailleach Bhéarra, 82, 83, 89–90, 105–6, 119, 145
  dindsenchus, 155
  fairies, 282
  goddess mythology, 28–9, 31
Lanser, Susan, 33
'Last night in a dream vision while I was pondering in my mind', 58
law and justice, 21, 176, 177
leannán sí, 191
Leap, 208
Lebor Buide Lecain, 42, 44
Lebor Gabála Érenn, 90
legends, 24–5
  and belief, 154
Lévi-Strauss, Claude, 111
Liadain, 87
líos, 203
Lismore, 199
literacy, 17
literature
  goddess mythology, 30
  oral narrative and, 12–25, 35
local knowledge, 20
Loch 'á Bhonn, 176
Loch Bà, 113–15, 116, 117, 118–19, 240–4
Loch Obha, 117, 119
Lodge, David, 36
Luan Lae Bhealtaine, 100–1, 102, 103
lucht sí, 282
Lugh, 82, 85, 114
Lughnasa, 85
Lüthi, Max, 24
Lysaght, Patricia, *The Banshee*, 53–4, 92

Mac Airt, Cormac, 85
Mac an Ultaigh, 123
Mac Cana, Proinsias, 82, 87
McCarthy, Ana, 151, 155, 156, 158, 159, 161
MacCarthys, 150, 156, 227
Mac Domhnaill, Seán Clárach, 56–8, 65–6
Macha, 39, 47, 48, 54, 55
Macha Mongruad, 38, 39–41, 44

MacKay, J.G., 82
Mac Mánais, Donnchadh Mór, 132–44, 247–53
MacNeill, Máire, 28, 85
Mac Séamais, Seán, 222, 224–9, 278–80
Magh Cuilinn, 104
Magna Mater, 27, 84, 86, 88, 93, 109
Maidin lae ghil fá dhuille géag-ghlais, 62–4
Máire, Liam, 93
   St Fanahan's Well and Máire Liam, 199–201, 271–2
Máire Ní Chearbhaill and the blow from the Red-haired woman, 208–10, 273–4
Máire Ní Chearbhaill and the Heifer, 185–7, 267
Máire Ní Mhurchú, 73–4, 75, 76, 93, 96–7, 209
Máire Ní Mhurchú agus an bhean a fuadaíodh, 274–6
Máire Ní Mhurchú agus an buachaill a fuadaíodh–1, 276–7
Máire Ní Mhurchú agus an buachaill a fuadaíodh–1, 277–8
Máire Ní Mhurchú agus an Maidhnéir, 270–1
Máire Ní Mhurchú agus an sagart, 266
Máire Ní Mhurchú agus mo mháthair féin, 268–70
Máire Ní Mhurchú agus na carréaraithe, 264–5
Máire Ní Mhurchú and my own mother, 192–5
Máire Ní Mhurchú and the Carters, 175–8, 182
Máire Ní Mhurchú and the miner, 195–9
Máire Ní Mhurchú and the priest, 181–3
Máire Ní Mhurchú and the woman who was 'swept', 210–15
Máire Ní Mhurchú and the young man who was 'swept'–I, 215–20
Máire Ní Mhurchú and the young man who was 'swept'–II, 220–4
Malinowski, Bronislaw, 9
Mallow, 227, 228
Mám na Gaoithe, 189
märchen, 24, 32, 33
Marianne, 55–6, 58, 62, 66, 67
Mark left by Cailleach Bhéarra, The, 109–11
material culture, 4
Mayo, 97, 100–4, 106–10
Meadhbh, 48, 55, 59
Meadhbh of Cruachain, 56
meaning and folklore, 12–14, 99
Meelick Round Tower, 148–50, 255
Merriman, Brian, 67–71, 85
Meskel, Joan/Joanna, 59
Metrical Dindshenchas, 84
'Midnight Court, The', 67–71, 85
midwife *see bean ghlúine*

Milesians, 29
mines, 195–9
modernity, 15, 30–1, 34
Móirín, *Aisling do rinneas ar Mhóirín, An*, 56–7
Monday, 102, 158–9 *see also Luan Lae Bhealtaine*
Mongfhind, 42, 43–8, 140
Mongruad, 48
Mór Mumhan, 55
Mórrígan, 54, 103–4
Motz, Lotte, 26
Moulnagerra, 208
Mountain-of-the-Throne, 47
Muiríoch, 178
Mulberry, 199–201
Mull, 97, 113–20
Murchadh Ruadh Ó Conchubhair, 120–3, 125–32
Murphy, Gerard, 84, 86–7
myths, 8–9 *see also* goddess mythology

'*Ná creid briathra mná*', 255–6
narrative and literature, 12–25
native ear, 19
nativity, 110
natural world *see* landscape
Navan Fort, 38
Nemhain, 54
Nephin (Néifinn) Mountains, 100, 101–2, 104, 106
Neumann, Erich, 27
Newall, Venetia, 284
Newgrange, 89, 227
Niall, 42, 43–4, 45, 47
Ní Chearbhaill, Máire, 93, 96, 97
   Máire Ní Chearbhaill and the blow from the Red-haired woman, 208–10, 273–4
   Máire Ní Chearbhaill and the Heifer, 185–7, 267
Ní Chuileannáin, Móirín, 55, 58, 67
Ní Dhonnchadha, Máirín, 51, 82
Ní Ghadhra, Síle, 55, 58, 67
Ní Ghuinníola, Eibhlín, 93, 96, 97
   Incident recounted of a healing woman from Baile Bhoithíon–I, 178–81, 182
   Incident recounted of a healing woman from Baile Bhoithíon–II, 187–9
   Incident recounted of a healing woman from Baile Bhoithíon–III, 189–91
Ní L., P., 93–4, 95, 202, 233
   An Bhean a chíodh na fairies, 264
   The Woman who used to see the Fairies, 174–5
Ní Mheadhra, Siobhán, 55

Ní Mhurchú, Máire *see* Máire Ní
    Mhurchú
Ní Shléibhín, Síle Bhán, 55
Ní Shúilleabháin, Meidhbhín, 55, 67
Ní Uallacháin, Caitlín, 55, 58, 64, 67
Ní Urdail, Máire, 193
Nic Chartha, Áine, 152, 155, 156
Nic Dhiarmada, Bríona, 36
Nic Eoin, Máirín, 28, 37
Norse mythology, 88
    and placenames, 83–4
nuns, 81, 86–7

Obha, Loch, 117, 119
O'Brien dynasty, 53, 70
'O Bright, eminent one of the choicest of independent great men', 65
Ó Buachalla, Breandán, 55, 56, 58, 61, 62, 64, 66
Ó Cathasaigh, Tomás, 85, 90
Ó C'nuchúir, Friar Seán, 151, 157–9, 160–1, 162
Ó Coileáin, Seán, 62
Ó Conaill, Seán, 14, 17
Ó Conchubhair, Murchadh Ruadh, 120–3, 125–32
Ó Conchubhair, Ruairí, 125
O'Connor, 125
Ó Domhnaill, Seán Clárach, 56–8
Ó Duilearga, Séamas, 17–18, 281
    'The Gaelic Storyteller', 14–15
oenach, 28
O'Flaherty, Wendy Doniger, *Other People's Myths*, 8–9
Ó Foghludha, Risteard, 56, 64
Ó Gríofa, Muiris, 58
Ó Gúgáin, Mícheál, 215–16, 218–20, 223
Ó hAodha, Donncha, 48
Ó Héalaí, Pádraig, 94
Ó hIfearnáin, Liam Dall, 55, 64
Ó hUrdail, Roibeárd, 83
Oíche an aonaigh d'éis mo fhliuchta, 65
Oíche bhíos im luí im shuan, 66
Oileán Buí, 83–4, 86
Oileán Tiar, an t-, 94
Oisín, 155
O'Keeffes, 53, 227
Ó Mainnín, Séamas, 189
Ó measaimíd nach calm rinn den bhuairt seo i Spáinn, 64
Ó Murchadha, Pádraig, 212
Ó Murchú, Diarmuid, 216
Ó Murchú, Pádraig, 181, 182–3, 193–5, 198, 212, 214, 217, 220, 223
Ó Murchú, Seán, 196, 197–8

'On a bright morning under the green leaves', 62–4
'On a night when I lay sleeping', 66
Ong, Walter, *Orality and Literacy*, 15–17, 20, 21, 23
operant knowledge, 7, 8
O'Rahilly, Thomas F., 85
oral literature, 16–17
oral narrative as literature, 12–25, 35
Ó Rathaille, Aogán, 68–9, 156
Ó Sé, Séamas, 196, 197, 198
O'Sheas, 210, 214
Ó Súilleabháin, Eoghan Rua, 68
otters, 101, 102–3

Páidín Shéamais, 123, 129
Patrick, St, 144–6, 155
personification of cultural knowledge, 10–12
placenames, 83–4, 155
Poll, 104
Poll na Piseoige, 208, 209
port, 201, 203, 204
postmodernity, 34
post-structuralism, 19
psychotherapy, 12, 34, 75, 76–7, 223–4, 286
Puhvel, Jaan, 26
Puillín, 211

Radner, Joan, 33
ráth, 203
Rath na Dubh h-Irtich, 115
ravens, 104
red
    colour term, 39
    red-haired women, 201, 203, 208–10, 217, 219–20, 273–4
Red Jacket mine (America), 196–7, 198
Reenascreena, 208, 209
Rian na Caillí Béaraighe, 239
Ricoeur, Paul, 71, 77
ringforts, 203, 282
rites of passage, 9
Roman de la Rose tradition, 68
Rós, Chaoldubh, 224
Roscommon, 97, 125, 131
Ross, Ann, 82
Rosscarbery, 208, 227
round towers, 148–50, 255
Ruad, 39

sacred assemblies, 28
Sadhbh, 59–60
    Clann Shadhbha agus Shaidhbhín (The Children of Sadhbh), 60–2

Sadhbh Olltach, 59
St Fanahan's Well and Máire Liam, 199–201, 271–2
St Mark's Gospel, 15–16, 23
salmon, 39, 90, 101, 102–4
Samhain, 40, 44, 46–7
Sanas Chormaic, 84
saol sí, 191
Sayers, Peig, 33, 152, 153
scéalaithe, 87
Scéic, 111
Schmitz, Nancy, 72, 76, 96
scoraíocht, 209
scoraíochting, 208, 209
Scotland, 81, 82, 83, 88, 97, 113–20, 124
seagulls, 103–4
Seal do bhíos im mhaighdin shéimh, 57–8
seal-woman, 214–15
Séamas, 224, 228, 229
Seán 'ac Séamais, 222
    English translation, 224–9
    Irish version, 278–80
Seán Rua, 220–3
Seanadh, 66
seanchaithe, 87
seanchas, 21–2, 32, 185
Séarlas Óg, 59
seaweed, 90
Sentainne Bérri, 84, 86–7
Serc Caillighe Bérri do Fothad Cannaine, 86
Sgéulaidhe Gaedhealach, An, 84
shamans, 72, 93–4
Sherkin Island, 201–2
Showalter, Elaine, 36
sí, 30, 38, 186, 191, 200, 282
Sibléal, 167
'Since this sorrowful business in Spain is not splendid news', 64
sióg, 282
Sithchenn, 43, 45
Sjoestedt, Marie-Louise, 28, 47, 285
Sligo, 110
slua sí, 200, 282
social environment, 4–5
Sorlin, Évelyne, 92
sovereignty, 11, 28, 29, 39–41, 42, 45–8, 52, 55, 177, 215
    Cailleach Bhéarra, 81, 82, 85, 87, 88, 158
spéirbhean, 54–67, 156
Stokes, Whitley, 38, 42, 44, 227
Stolen colt and the wise woman, The, 183–5

storytellers, 14–15, 17–18, 33, 217
strands, 180, 221
Stuart, Prince Charles, 60, 61, 64, 65
Swinford, 148, 149

Táin Bó Cuailnge, 104, 125
Tech nDuinn, 86
technology and culture, 4
Thomond, 53, 96
tobacco, 175, 176, 178
Todd, Janet, 36
Tonn Clíodhna, 227
topography *see* landscape
Torna, 42, 43–4
Torranach, 115
towers, 148–50, 255
tradition, 8, 10, 15
Tráigh an Phéarla, 217
transfunctional goddess, 26
transmission of cultural knowledge, 7–10
triple-death motif, 40
Tuath Ó Siosta, 93–4, 95
Tuatha Dé Danann, 29, 124, 126

Ua Coíllámha, Orthanach, 87
Uí maic íair Chonchinn, 51
Uí Néill dynasty, 42
Ulaid, 42, 47
Ulster, 38–9, 42, 47, 157
unconscious reality, 13

Verling, Máirtín, 76, 96, 212, 284, 286
Von Franz, Marie-Louise, 283

Wagner, Heinrich, 82, 86
wakes, 92, 93–4, 174–5 *see also bean chaointe*
wells, holy, 199–201
Whiddy Island, 111, 146
Whiteboy movement (Buachaillí Bána), 59–65
wise-woman *see bean feasa*
witch-figures, 179, 206, 284
Woman who used to see the Fairies, The, 174–5
Wood, Juliette, 26
Wood-Martin, W.G., 3
wounding and burning, 40

Yeats, W.B., 55
Yellow Book of Lecan, 42, 44
yew trees, 90, 103
Youghal, 227